Praise for Richar

"The first time I heard him play, I couldn't believe it. He had somehow bridged the thing between classical and jazz." —Chet Baker, trumpeter

"...the few items in his discography reveal a progressive thinker of titanic proportions. His music raises obvious comparisons with Monk's, but it is also notable for its links to twentieth-century classical music and its anticipation of the later free jazz movement." —Ted Gioia, pianist and author

"Musically, he had one of the finest discriminating and imaginative minds that I have ever encountered. He progressed so easily and so intuitively and absorbed so much of the newer ideas in jazz that he was able to project many original and profound ideas of his own." —Serge Chaloff, baritone saxophonist

"He was a leading white exponent of Bud Powell, but ... his bag included Tristano and Errol Garner and some others. And when I went back [to Boston] in 1955, he had destroyed some Kenton people by playing like Bud Powell first and getting them all excited and then going into his, at that time, Schoenbergian bag while they were playing Errol Garner chords. He was like the white pianist power up there." —Cecil Taylor, pianist

"Dick Twardzik was one of those rare musicians, one with a really original concept.... The first time I heard him was late in 1954 at Storyville in Boston. His playing struck me as being fresh and very uninhibited, especially harmonically. I was so impressed that I phoned Richard Bock in Hollywood and convinced him that here was someone worth having in the Pacific Jazz catalogue." —Russ Freeman, pianist

"Richard Twardzik is one of the most astonishingly accomplished jazzmen to appear in modern jazz....His playing ... is full of all the subtlety, grace, beauty and immensity that one can ask for in a lively art. And these are projected with a pianistic facility that rivals that of the best of the modern jazzmen while quite surpassing that of the others in the group of artists to which Twardzik seems to fit." —John William Hardy, author

"After he died, there were a number of musicians I would come in contact with who had never heard of him, or had heard of him but had never heard his playing. I would play the trio recording and they would have a look of disbelief on their faces. I mean, it moves you to tears. It's art that just gets you churned up inside. You think, it's good to be alive."
—Herb Pomeroy, educator, bandleader, trumpet player

"If he had lived, he would have changed the whole course of jazz piano." —Marc Puricelli, pianist

Bouncin' With Bartók
The Incomplete Works of Richard Twardzik

BOUNCIN' WITH BARTOK

The Incomplete Works of Richard Twardzik

Jack Chambers

In memory of
Frank Brockenshire (1940-1961)
and others who died too soon

The publisher gratefully acknowledges the financial assistance of the Canada Council for the Arts, the
Ontario Arts Council, and the Ontario Book Publishing Tax Credit Program. The publisher further
acknowledges the financial support of the Government of Canada through the Department of Canadian
Heritage's Book Publishing Industry Development Program (BPIDP) for our publishing activities.

Cover: "Nice Music"
Title printed by Richard Twardzik ca. 1947-48 (page 62).
Photo image by Jack Chambers © 2004 with photographic details from Nick Dean and Herman Leonard.
Editor for the press: Beverley Daurio

Printed and bound in Canada
Printed on acid-free paper

1 2 3 4 5   12 11 10 09 08

Library and Archives Canada Cataloguing in Publication
Chambers, Jack, 1938-
Bouncin' with Bartok : the incomplete works of Richard
Twardzik / Jack Chambers.
Includes bibliographical references and index.
ISBN 978-1-55128-141-4
1. Twardzik, Dick, 1931-1955. 2. Pianists—United States—Biography.
3. Jazz musicians—United States—Biography. I. Title. II. Title: Bouncing with Bartok.
M417.T969C44 2008   786.2'165092   C2008-906295-7

Library of Congress Cataloguing Data:
Chambers, Jack.
Bouncin' with Bartók: The Incomplete Works of Richard Twardzik
Includes discography, bibliography and index
ISBN 978-1-55128-141-4
1 Twardzik, Richard (1931-1955). 2 Jazz musicians - United States - Biography

The Mercury Press
Box 672, Station P, Toronto, Ontario Canada M5S 2Y4
www.themercurypress.ca

You came to us victoriously,
To possess us and fill our lives with your wild music...

You came to us with music, poetry, and wild joy,
When we were twenty,
When we reeled home at night
Through the old moon-whitened streets of Boston
And heard our friend, our comrade, and our dead companion,
Shout through the silence of the moonwhite square:
"You are a poet and the world is yours."

...As we heard that cry,
And turned our eyes then
To the moon-drunk skies of Boston,
Knowing only that we were young,
And drunk,
And twenty,
And that the power of mighty poetry was within us,
And the glory of the great earth
Lay before us—
Because we were young and drunk and twenty,
And could never die!

Thomas Wolfe, "Immortal Drunkenness,"
A Stone, A Leaf, A Door (1945)

[Frontispiece] Richard Twardzik at the keyboard, ca. 1953. Contact prints for a publicity photo by Nick Dean. From the Twardzik-Thompson Archive, courtesy of Rosamond Thompson and Jane Sumner.

Table of Contents

Frontispiece: Richard Twardzik at the keyboard, ca. 1953 viii

Illustrations xi

Acknowledgements xvii

1   A Crutch for the Crab 1

2   Henryk and Clare 15

3   Dickie 25

4   Bouncin' with Bartok 53

5   Madame Chaloff & Son 71

6   The Happy Bird 99

7   All Stars and Lonelies 113

8   Albuquerque Social Swim 145

9   "Everyone must travel alone (most of the time)" 169

10 (World) Harmony with Hamp 175

11 The Fable of Mabel 187

12 Two Crutches? 199

13 The Girl from Greenland 211

14 Sad Walk 239

15 "Regarding Disposition Remains" 281

Afterword: "Not Too Sad an Ending" 295

Discography: Recordings and Recorded Performances 303

References 311

Index 319

Illustrations

[Frontispiece] Richard Twardzik at the keyboard, ca. 1953. Contact prints for a publicity photo by Nick Dean. From the Twardzik-Thompson Archive, courtesy of Rosamond Thompson and Jane Sumner. All rights reserved.

[1.1] *Assorted Flavors*, Pacific Jazz S-650. Packaging William Claxton/ Will McFarland. © 1956 by Pacific Jazz Records.

[1.2] *Trio* Russ Freeman/Richard Twardzik (Pacific Jazz Records 1212), © 1956. Cover design by William Claxton. Cover painting by Edmund Kohn.

[1.3] Back cover of *Trio* (Pacific Jazz Records 1212), © 1956. Cover design and photograph of Russ Freeman by William Claxton. Photograph of Richard Twardzik by Nick Dean.

[1.4] *Chet Baker in Europe* (Pacific Jazz Records 1218), © 1956. Cover photograph by William Claxton. From the Clarke Harris collection.

[2.1] Henryk Twardzik painting the clerestory windows of the Boston University Chapel at the Connick Studio in Boston, ca. 1950. Uncredited photograph with signature from *Newburyport Art Association Directory of Members and Cookbook of Their Choice Recipes*, published by the Art Association, no date. (Henryk's recipe is Greek Lamb.) From the Twardzik-Thompson Archive, courtesy of Rosamond Thompson and Jane Sumner. All rights reserved.

[2.2] Pencil sketch of "Fallen Striker," by Henryk Twardzik, date unknown. From the Twardzik-Thompson Archive, courtesy of Rosamond Thompson and Jane Sumner. All rights reserved.

[3.1] Untitled portrait of a boy with sailboat, by Henryk Twardzik, ca. 1935. From the Twardzik-Thompson Archive, courtesy of Rosamond Thompson and Jane Sumner. All rights reserved.

[3.2] Untitled seascape with woman and boy, by Henryk Twardzik, date unknown. From the Twardzik-Thompson Archive, courtesy of Rosamond Thompson and Jane Sumner. All rights reserved.

[3.3] Pencil portrait of Clare and sketch of nude figure, by Henryk Twardzik, date unknown. From the Twardzik-Thompson Archive, courtesy of Rosamond Thompson and Jane Sumner. All rights reserved.

[3.4] Pencil sketch of boy in wicker chair, by Henryk Twardzik, date unknown. From the Twardzik-Thompson Archive, courtesy of Rosamond Thompson and Jane Sumner. All rights reserved.

[3.5] Richard Twardzik, probably about 5 or 6. From the Twardzik-Thompson Archive, courtesy of Rosamond Thompson and Jane Sumner. All rights reserved.

[3.6] Richard Twardzik, about 10, with Liebestraum, the family Dachshund. From the Twardzik-Thompson Archive, courtesy of Rosamond Thompson and Jane Sumner. All rights reserved.

[3.7] Pencil sketch of mother and son in living room with piano, by Henryk Twardzik, date unknown. From the Twardzik-Thompson Archive, courtesy of Rosamond Thompson and Jane Sumner. All rights reserved.

[3.8] Young man taking piano lesson with teacher, by Henryk Twardzik, date unknown. From the Twardzik-Thompson Archive, courtesy of Rosamond Thompson and Jane Sumner. All rights reserved.

[4.1] Postcard of the Samuel Fowler House in Danvers, Masssachusetts, Richard Twardzik's family home from 1947 to 1955. From the Twardzik-Thompson Archive, courtesy of Rosamond Thompson and Jane Sumner. All rights reserved.

[4.2] Portrait of an adolescent, by Henryk Twardzik, date unknown. From the Twardzik-Thompson Archive, courtesy of Rosamond Thompson and Jane Sumner. All rights reserved.

[4.3] Richard as teenage prodigy. From the Twardzik-Thompson Archive, courtesy of Rosamond Thompson and Jane Sumner. All rights reserved.

[4.4] *Bouncin' with Bartok* by Dick Twardzik, ca. 1947–49. From the Twardzik-Thompson Archive, courtesy of Rosamond Thompson and Jane Sumner. All rights reserved.

[4.5] Pencil sketch of Sidney Bechet and his band, probably at Storyville in Boston, October 1953, by Henryk Twardzik. From the Twardzik-Thompson Archive, courtesy of Rosamond Thompson and Jane Sumner. All rights reserved.

[4.6] Richard with Clare, in the garden of Samuel Fowler House, Danvers. From the Twardzik-Thompson Archive, courtesy of Rosamond Thompson and Jane Sumner. All rights reserved.

[4.7] Mother and son reading a letter, by Henryk Twardzik. From the Twardzik-Thompson Archive, courtesy of Rosamond Thompson and Jane Sumner. All rights reserved.

[4.8] Richard at the piano with unidentified drummer and guitarist. Photograph "by Ken." From the Twardzik-Thompson Archive, courtesy of Rosamond Thompson and Jane Sumner. All rights reserved.

[5.1] Note from Richard Twardzik to Madame Chaloff, his piano teacher, probably fall 1951. From the Twardzik-Thompson Archive, courtesy of Rosamond Thompson and Jane Sumner. All rights reserved.

[5.2] Telephone message for Dick from Serge Chaloff with pencil portraits of Dick and Henryk, by Henryk Twardzik, dated 11-11-50. From the Twardzik-Thompson Archive, courtesy of Rosamond Thompson and Jane Sumner. All rights reserved.

[illustrations 5.3–6] The Serge Chaloff Trio in West Yarmouth, summer 1951. From the Twardzik-Thompson Archive, courtesy of Rosamond Thompson and Jane Sumner. All rights reserved.

[5.7] Charlie Mariano and His Groups, *The New Sounds from Boston*. Prestige 130 © 1952. Richard Twardzik plays on one track, *Mariners*, of this 10" LP.

[6.1] Charlie Parker, *The Happy "Bird."* Parker Records © 1962. Richard Twardzik plays on one track, *I'll Remember April*, of this 12" LP.

[6.2] Charlie Parker, *Boston 1952*. Uptown UPCD 27.42 © 1996. Produced by Robert E. Sunenblick and David A. Sunenblick. Design by Nicolas Moumouris.

[6.3] Charles Mingus, Charlie Parker, Symphony Sid Torin and Richard Twardzik (partially hidden by Torin's shoulder) at the Hi Hat, December 1952. Reprinted from Reisner 1962: 221. Photographer unidentified but probably Vinnie Haynes, drummer Roy Haynes's brother.

[6.4] Richard Twardzik, Joe Gordon and Charles Mingus at the Hi Hat, December 1952. Photographed by Vinnie Haynes. Robert Sunenblick collection.

[7.1] Reba Stewart in Mexico, ca. 1958. By permission of Geneviève McMillan (2002). Courtesy of Michèle Oshima.

[7.2] Richard Twardzik at The Stable. Photograph by Nick Dean. From the Twardzik-Thompson Archive, courtesy of Rosamond Thompson and Jane Sumner. All rights reserved.

[7.3] Bob Zieff in 1953. Promotional photograph by Jack Zieff, his uncle, 1953. By permission of Robert L. Zieff.

[7.4] Bob Zieff self-portrait in pencil, 1951. By permission of Robert L. Zieff.

[7.5] Charlie Mariano, *Boston All Stars*. Prestige 153 © 1953.

[7.6] The Jazz Workshop at The Stable, near Copley Square, Boston, with Jay Migliori, tenor saxophone, Jimmy Zitano, drums, Ray Santisi, piano, probably John Neves, bass, and Varty Haroutunian, tenor saxophone. From the Twardzik-Thompson Archive, courtesy of Rosamond Thompson and Jane Sumner. All rights reserved.

[7.7] Dick Wetmore, *Dick Wetmore*. Bethlehem BCP 1035. Photograph and cover design Burt Goldblatt ca. 1955.

[8.1] Richard Twardzik's bill from the American British Cowdray Hospital, Mexico, where he was treated 11–15 May 1953. From the Twardzik-Thompson Archive, courtesy of Rosamond Thompson and Jane Sumner. All rights reserved.

[8.2] envelope of Richard Twardzik's letter home from Alburquerque, New Mexico, 5 June 1953. The caricature in the upper left, under "DICKIE," appears on this envelope and the previous one. From the Twardzik-Thompson Archive, courtesy of Rosamond Thompson and Jane Sumner. All rights reserved.

[9.1] Japanese woodcut, by Reba Stewart. ca. 1958. By permission of Geneviève McMillan.

[10.1] "Lionel Hampton and His Great Band & Show." Advertisement for "Triumphant tour of Dixie," with "Dick Twardzik, Piano Star" among the featured players. Pittsburgh *Courier,* 27 February 1954.

[10.2] "Hamp's UN Combo." Lionel Hampton's band-within-a-band, from the Pittsburgh *Courier,* 27 March 1954.

[11.1] Serge Chaloff, *The Fable of Mabel.* Black Lion CD760923. Photograph by Hugh Turner, ca. 1954.

[11.2] Excerpt from the manuscript score of *The Fable of Mabel* showing the composer's annotations for the mood of the final movement. From the Twardzik-Thompson Archive, courtesy of Rosamond Thompson and Jane Sumner. All rights reserved.

[11.3] Excerpt from the manuscript score of *The Fable of Mabel* showing the composer's annotations for Serge Chaloff at the transition between movements. From the Twardzik-Thompson Archive, courtesy of Rosamond Thompson and Jane Sumner. All rights reserved.

[12.1] Dick Twardzik, *1954 Improvisations.* New Artists Records 10006CD. Recorded by Peter Morris. Drawing by Carlotta Morris. Design by Mindy Mitchell. 1990.

[12.2] Richard Twardzik and Peter Littman. Photograph probably by Nick Dean. From the Twardzik-Thompson Archive, courtesy of Rosamond Thompson and Jane Sumner. All rights reserved.

[12.3] Richard Twardzik, *The Last Set.* Pacific Jazz PJ-37. Photograph by Ron Joy. Design by Woody Woodward. © 1962 World Pacific Records.

[12.4] Waveform of opening bars of *A Crutch for the Crab* (PJ 1212) and putative alternate take (PJ 37), by James A. Harrod. Reproduced by permission.

[12.5] Matched waveforms of beginning of *A Crutch for the Crab* (PJ 1212) after introductory bars and beginning of putative alternate take (PJ 37), by James A. Harrod. Reproduced by permission.

[13.1.] Crystal Joy, ca. 1959. Photograph courtesy of Crystal-Joy Albert.

[13.2] Pay memorandum for Richard Twardzik for the week of 11 July 1955 at River Rouge, Michigan. From the Twardzik-Thompson

Archive, courtesy of Rosamond Thompson and Jane Sumner. All rights reserved.

[14.1] Chet Baker Quartet at Kurhaus, The Hague, on 18 September 1955. Photograph by Hans Buter in *Jazz Journaal* (October 1955). Netherlands Jazz Archive. All rights reserved.

[14.2] Richard Twardzik with Chet Baker at Concertgebouw, Amsterdam, on 17 September 1955. Photograph by Ed van der Elsken (1991: 28). Netherlands Jazz Archive. All rights reserved.

[14.3] Richard Twardzik at Concertgebouw, Amsterdam, on 17 September 1955. Detail from photograph by Ed van der Elsken (1991: 29). Netherlands Jazz Archive. All rights reserved.

[14.4] Cover of *Chet Baker in Europe 1955*.

[14.5] Chet Baker and Richard Twardzik backstage at Salle Pleyel, Paris, on 4 October 1955. Photograph by Jean-Pierre Leloir, *Jazzman* 89 (2003: 14). All rights reserved.

[14.6] cover of *Chet Baker Quartet* (Barclay Records, France, 1956)

[14.7] cover of *Chet in Paris*, Vol. 1

[14.8] cover of *Lars Gullin 1955/56*, Vol. 1

[15.1] Pencil sketch of gravestone and epitaph by Henryk Twardzik on MIT telephone message pad, late October-early November 1955. From the Twardzik-Thompson Archive, courtesy of Rosamond Thompson and Jane Sumner. All rights reserved.

[15.2] Pencil sketch for bust of Richard Twardzik by Henryk Twardzik. From the Twardzik-Thompson Archive, courtesy of Rosamond Thompson and Jane Sumner. All rights reserved.

[15.3] Bust of Richard Twardzik in two views, by Henryk Twardzik. From the Twardzik-Thompson Archive, courtesy of Rosamond Thompson and Jane Sumner. All rights reserved.

[15.4] Report of the Death of an American Citizen (2 pages), the last official government document on Richard Twardzik's death, February-March 1956. From the Twardzik-Thompson Archive, courtesy of Rosamond Thompson and Jane Sumner. All rights reserved.

Acknowledgements

I am most grateful to Richard Twardzik's family— to his aunts Roz Thompson and June Jones, both now deceased, his cousin Jane Sumner and his second cousin Steve Jones. Before they found me, I thought I had exhausted the subject of Richard Twardzik in an 8,000-word bio-discography. Fuller measure of what they have meant to this book comes clear, I hope, in the Afterword.

Members of the Boston jazz community flexed fading memory traces for me with great gusto. I had unforgettable conversations with Ted Casher and Bob Pilsbury. At one time or another, I talked to or exchanged e-mail with Henry Francis, Albert Krahn, Bob Nieske, Billy Novick, Reed Robins and Jim Wheaton, among others. Steve Kuhn recalled Richard Twardzik from the unique perspective of the piano prodigy who followed him in the Boston pantheon. Bob Freedman proved an invaluable witness as Richard Twardzik's earliest professional colleague, and also was a patient sounding-board on some musical mysteries.

Ron Davis, the Toronto piano player, helped me come to grips with the piece of music called *Bouncin' with Bartók* (Chapter 4). Beverley Daurio, my editor at Mercury Press, brought to it the eye of both poet and publisher. Robert Barkaloff lent his creative hand to the lay-out and design.

James Harrod solved the riddle of the takes and Dan Skea of the Rudy Van Gelder Project solved the riddle of the date (Chapter 12). Dr. Robert Sunenblick, archivist of Boston jazz, shared some of his artifacts with me. Frederick Turner, author of a profile on Richard Twardzik in *Boston Magazine*, generously left some of the documents he collected in the family archives. David Southern at Duke University Press pointed out the ironic relation between Twardzik's *Yellow Tango* and Leroy Anderson's *Blue Tango*. Walter Gross, media manager of Wind-Up Records, provided me with his superb interview with the late Herb Pomeroy. Peter Mansell, indefatigable chronicler of Chet Baker, shared numerous discoveries with me, including Twardzik's debut with Baker at Washington's Patio Lounge.

Several scholars in European jazz circles shared hard-won information with me. Lars Westin, editor of *Orkester Journalen* and director of Dragon Records, gave me resources I could not otherwise have known about and also translated them for me, including materials on the 1955 Woche der Leichten Musik and Lars Resberg's perspicacious reviews of the Baker Quartet in Stuttgart. Eric van Aro, Caterina Valente's manager, cleared up a misconception I held dearly. Olle Lind helped in reconstructing Richard Twardzik's European itinerary. Lind and Keith Knox added information on Lars Gullin, and Pär Rittsel, Gullin's discographer, provided information on and ultimately the music from the Cologne concert. From England, Anthony Barnett, champion of jazz violin, shared information he had garnered from the late Dick Wetmore when Wetmore was younger and more malleable. Geoffrey Wills, a clinical psychologist in Cheshire by vocation and an extraordinary tune detective by avocation, shed light on several borrowings in Twardzik's music and, especially, made me a believer about references to Debussy's *Fêtes* in *The Fable of Mabel* and *A Crutch for the Crab*.

Bert Vuijsje let me hear tapes of the Concertgebouw and Kurhaus concerts before they were released on CD by the Netherlands Jazz Archive. Bert also translated several Dutch reviews, and hosted an unforgettable evening in Amsterdam of cocktails and jazz talk with Jeroen de Valk and Simon Korteweg among the guests. Herman Openneer gave me artifacts of Richard Twardzik's Netherlands visit. Arie van Breda, with a little help from Jaap de Rijke, dredged up memories of a fateful evening with Twardzik in The Hague. And Frank Van Bommel, with indefatigable support from Jaap de Rijke, brought Richard Twardzik's music into the 21st century (as described in the Afterword).

The book benefited directly from critical scrutiny of several people who read it in preliminary versions. Bert Vuijsje cast his editor's eyes over my account of Twardik's European tour on Marshall Bowden's website

(Chambers 2003a), and Jeroen de Valk and Bowden also sorted out some details. Steve Spears became an advocate for the work in progress. Lars Westin edited and translated my lengthy profile of Twardzik for *Orkester Journalen* (Chambers 2003b). Stuart Broomer edited my account of Twardzik's European tour for *Coda* (Chambers 2004b). Both Jim Harrod and Krin Gabbard read the whole typescript and suggested several improvements.

For the people who knew Richard Twardzik, my queries sometimes stirred up buried sadness as well as forgotten pleasures.

Nick Dean, Twardzik's photographer and friend, told me as much as he could about a time he had truly left behind. Geneviève McMillan provided a living link to the late Reba Stewart and the people she and Richard Twardzik knew. She and Donald Kelley commissioned my profile of Reba Stewart for their retrospective at Massachusetts College of Art (Chambers 2006). Michèle Oshima of Womens Studies, MIT, was an enthusiastic intermediary. The late Robert Creeley fetched up memories of the Albuquerque social swim. Elaine Marney (nee Brehaut), who knew Dick Twardzik all his life, willingly filled in numerous blanks.

Crystal-Joy Albert was willing to try to recapture the lost world of young Crystal Joy, singer and piano player and the light of Richard Twardzik's last years.

Bob Zieff sort of belongs in all the categories above— Boston musician, teacher, friend, scholar, archivist, anecdotalist. I met him in 1985 and since then we have talked about all kinds of things, by mail at first, by e-mail later and in person at his memorable coming-out party in Vienna (Chambers 2008). I have deliberately not shown him what I have done with all our talk in this book. Some of the surprises will be mollified because my long profile of him got into print before the book did (Chambers 2004a). I expect he will grumble at some of the things I say about him, but benignly, as he did in an interview with him that was published in the Vienna program (Chambers 2007b). He is a complex man who writes complex music. I was concerned to deal with both the man and his music honestly, and I suspect deep-down he knows that. I have loved his music since the first time I heard it more than 50 years ago, long before I met him. Nothing would satisfy me more than one or two readers taking from this book the impetus to track down Bob Zieff's music.

Toronto 2008

1 A Crutch for the Crab

I first heard a recording of Richard Twardzik playing piano in 1956, when I was a high-school student. The tune was called *A Crutch for the Crab,* and it was one of the tracks on a promotional LP put out by Pacific Jazz, a sampler called *Assorted Flavors of Pacific Jazz* (HFS-1)(1.1, also page 51). It cost $1.98 brand-new, and that was the kind of bargain you couldn't pass up if you were a jazz-struck, underachieving, under-age smoker with a pompadour and black horn-rims who made five dollars on Saturdays squeegeeing the windows of Welsh's Butcher Shop and three other stores on King Street in a town called Stoney Creek on the Canadian side of the Niagara border.

Side One of *Assorted Flavors* strung together a lot of excerpts from the Pacific Jazz catalogue while a man with a radio voice told a kind of company history of West Coast jazz, starting with Gerry Mulligan's piano-less quartet at the Haig in 1952. The radio man sounded like he gargled with Coppertone. His voice-over commentary obscured the beginning of *A Crutch for the Crab,* and the ending disintegrated in a fade-out. The excerpt, counting the commentary, was less than two minutes long. It was, you would have thought, the worst way to hear any kind of music.

In fact it was sensational. Twardzik's piano playing was fluent and eccentric and painfully beautiful. His tune—a composition, really, when we finally got to hear all of it—was full of jagged turns and crisp releases. Somehow it came out sounding exactly right for its wild title, crabbily fluid with sudden lurches. It was like nothing else in the world. It was a revelation.

What the narrator said, oozing cool, was also a revelation. He said:

> When Chet Baker went to Europe in September of 1955, he took with him a startling new pianist from Boston named Richard Twardzik. Twardzik died in Paris a few months later, depriving us all of the great ability that was his. Here's the late Richard Twardzik as he sounded in 1954 playing his own composition, *A Crutch for the Crab.*

It was the only time I ever heard a news item on an LP.

I tracked down the source LP, partly fearing that I had been bamboo-zled—that Richard Twardzik would turn out to be an ordinary piano player who had been cleverly edited to make a few brilliant minutes on a promotional record. I had to wait a long time to find out. Twardzik's LP was a new release, copyright 1956, the same as the sampler. I had to order it at the record store, as an import. "It's gonna cost you, son," said the man at the record shop, "and it's gonna take six weeks at least."

The LP was called *Trio* (Pacific Jazz 1212) (1.2, also page 52). Just looking at it, holding it in my hand still swathed in its protective plastic sheath, took my breath away. The cover was the print of an oil paint-ing in shades of brown, with three solid figures, guys built like cairns, tossing boulders around as if they were helium balloons. The credit

[illustration 1.1] *Assorted Flavors*, Pacific Jazz HFS-1. Packaging by William Claxton/Will McFarland. © 1956 by Pacific Jazz Records.

line said "west coast artists series/*Edmund Kohn*," and the back cover carried a profile and a small picture of old Edmund, a round man with a handlebar mustache and a kerchief knotted around his neck, looking like the street musician with the dancing monkey you see in cartoons. It also told about Edmund's success as an illustrator and about the awards he had won at the Sacramento State Fair and other lesser places. Since then I have read testimonials by very serious people about how their lives were changed forever when they saw Picasso's *Guernica* or Botticelli's *Primavera*. For me, it will always be Edmund Kohn's unnamed cover painting for *Trio*.

[illustration 1.2] *Trio* Russ Freeman/Richard Twardzik (Pacific Jazz Records 1212), © 1956. Cover design by William Claxton. Cover painting by Edmund Kohn.

The billing on the cover indicated that Twardzik shared the LP with another piano player, Russ Freeman. In fact, it gave Twardzik second billing on the cover, but on the actual disk the six tracks by Twardzik's trio filled the first side. The second side was given over to Freeman, and I already knew something about him. He was the dean of West Coast piano players by dint of appearing on nearly every jazz record that came from California.

The back cover was packed with information (1.3): besides the box about Edmund Kohn, there were six column inches about Russ Freeman, another six column inches *by* Freeman about Richard Twardzik, and two black & white 3.5" x 4" portraits. One of the portraits was

[illustration 1.3] Back cover of *Trio* (Pacific Jazz Records 1212), © 1956. Cover design and photograph of Russ Freeman by William Claxton. Photograph of Richard Twardzik by Nick Dean.

of Freeman by the famous California photographer William Claxton showing Freeman with a pencil mustache and dark suit, looking more like a used car salesman than was surely intended. The other portrait was of "The Late Richard Twardzik" (as the caption portentously put it), and it showed Twardzik against a dark background, hollow-cheeked, staring into the distant gloom. It was (and is) brilliantly evocative, and for many years it was the only known portrait of Twardzik.

The liner credited the portrait to "Nick Dean, Boston," not a name that registered any recognition. Years later, I spoke to numerous Boston contemporaries of Richard Twardzik, and none could place Nick Dean, the photographer. But some 45 years later, I discovered more photographs by Nick Dean, as we shall see, some of them the equal of the back-cover portrait. His old business address is stamped on the back of one of the portraits: "Photograph by/ Nick Dean/41 Charles Street/Boston 14, Mass./CA 7-8440." And finally, with the help of Richard Twardzik's second cousin who was born long after Richard had died but came to maturity in the internet era, I would find Dean himself.

Freeman was credited as producer of Twardzik's recording session. In his liner notes about Twardzik's music, Freeman praises Twardzik's "really original concept," and tells how he came across him in Boston and was struck by his music, "fresh and very uninhibited, especially harmonically." Freeman said that the recordings by Twardzik came about because he phoned Richard Bock, the owner and producer of Pacific Jazz Records in Los Angeles, to tell him about this hot young player, and Bock gave him permission to record Twardzik for the label.

Freeman says the recording took place "late in 1954," but the exact date— 27 October 1954 —was only fixed 35 years later with the kind of sleuthing (as we will see later) that jazz discographers revel in. The recording was made in Rudy Van Gelder's parlor in Hackensack, New Jersey, the now-legendary recording studio that was just beginning to earn its reputation when Freeman took Twardzik and the other musicians there. Accompanying Twardzik were Carson Smith, Chet Baker's regular bassist, a Californian who was young, only 23, but already well known for playing in Mulligan's Quartet as well as Baker's, and a young, unknown Boston drummer, Peter Littman. (Complete details for these and all other recordings by Twardzik are listed in the discography at the end.)

Freeman's endorsement sounds like an understatement on the evidence of Twardzik's music. The original Pacific Jazz release included three standards, *Bess You Is My Woman Now*, *'Round About Midnight* and *I'll Remember April*, and three originals, *Albuquerque Social Swim*, *Yellow Tango* and, of course, *A Crutch for the Crab*.

The standards were fresher then than we can imagine today. Twardzik's recording of *Bess You Is My Woman Now* pre-dates by four full years the *Porgy and Bess* boom that came with its movie version in 1959 and brought with it jazz versions of its score by Miles Davis and Gil Evans, Mundell Lowe, Bill Potts, Louis Armstrong and Ella Fitzgerald, and others. Gershwin's opera had been revived in 1952 for an international tour starring soprano Leontyne Price, but that was a more operatic version than the film would be, and it hardly caught the attention of jazz musicians, except for Twardzik. Although several George Gershwin songs ranked high in the standard jazz repertoire, the ones from *Porgy and Bess* were not common among them except for *Summertime*, and that by virtue not of the opera but of a seminal 1939 jazz recording by Sidney Bechet. When Twardzik recorded *Bess You Is My Woman Now* in 1954, it was completely unknown as a jazz vehicle.

More surprisingly, so was *'Round About Midnight*. Thelonious Monk had made his original studio recording of his song in 1947 and, apart from an obscure solo recording he made of it in Paris in 1954, he did not record it again for a decade, until 1957. By then, it had been widely discovered as a jazz vehicle and Monk's interpretation of his own ballad was one of dozens, albeit *primus inter pares*. It was destined to become one of the two or three most recorded jazz compositions of all time. But Twardzik's pensive, almost introverted, take on it in 1954 caught it on its rise into the standard repertoire, and surely it was one that caught the ear of many other piano players.

Refreshing as the ballads were, Twardzik's original compositions were positively brilliant. *Yellow Tango* is a confection based on a mannerly Latin beat sustained by bass and drums while Twardzik teases the genre with high-note filigrees in the manner of then little-known Ahmad Jamal. *Albuquerque Social Swim* is tougher, its oblique melodies played staccato with sudden, unexpected stops. The improvised choruses burst into rock-steady 4/4 time, and after the stutters of the theme they come as a blessed relief. The device of inexplicable stops released into flowing melodies dominates *Albuquerque Social Swim* and animates it by creating knots of tension and unraveling them in flowing melody. In *A Crutch for the Crab* the stop-and-release is just one of several devices.

If Twardzik's side of the original LP had a flaw, it was in programming. *A Crutch for the Crab* and *Albuquerque Social Swim* were set together at the beginning, as tracks one and two, where their similarities somehow tempered their stunning differences.

A Crutch for the Crab, heard in its entirety, is a 3-minute symphony. Its structure is ambiguous: the opening exposition takes 24 bars but the final reprise takes only 20, having lost the first four bars. Those first four bars open the piece as a kind of cadence; they might be a prelude. The second four bars are syncopated, with the piano playing on one and three while the drums accent two and four. The effect is unforgettable, and sets up a repeated figure in the 17th and 23rd bars where the piano fills the second and fourth accents with its own out-of-tempo syncopations. The same figure comes back at points in the improvisation, and so do references to other melodic figures, always modulated in some way. The performance is rich with nuance. It ends too soon from one vantage point, but from another it entices you to go back to it time and again, as real art always does.

In my mind's eye, the syncopation caught the crab's motion of the title with unimaginable perfection, seemingly lurching, almost awkward, but at the same time fluid and swift. Try to catch it and it darts through your hands. It is edgy and slightly frightening, and just when you think you have it cornered, it is gone.

Twardzik offered an alternate explanation for the title in the liner notes. It came, he said, "from watching the hands of the Polish pianist, Jan Smeterlin, as they scurried crab-like into the keys." But that came too late for me. By then, I had my own objective correlative for the title embedded in the music, and it could not be shaken. Besides, there was good reason for not taking Twardzik literally. Another explanation that he put forward was obviously intended to give the finger to the unwary. *Yellow Tango*, he said, "was written as incidental music for a Shake-dance." Oh sure.

The recordings by Richard Twardzik on the *Trio* LP last 21 minutes and 44 seconds. (A mistake on the timings printed on the cover made it seem even less by more than a minute, but *Yellow Tango* is over five minutes, not 4:18.) Of the six tracks, the three ballads and three originals, all but *Yellow Tango* are around the three-minute mark, the industry standard length in the era of brittle old 78 rpm shellac records and one that was imprinted so forcibly onto the psyches of musicians and producers that it was still the industry standard length in 1954, two years after jazz recordings invariably came out on unbreakable vinyl at 33 rpm.

Twardzik's *Trio* recording was easy to miss, even for vigilant jazz fans. It was, after all, just half a record by an unknown piano player with too many consonants in his name. His music held up to repeated listenings, in fact endlessly, but there was still too little of it. You never got tired of it. You never got enough of it.

From the start I knew there was more recorded music by Richard Twardzik, because Russ Freeman, in his liner note, wrote, "He record-

[illustration 1.4] *Chet Baker in Europe* (Pacific Jazz Records 1218), © 1956. Cover photograph by William Claxton. From the Clarke Harris collection.

ed with Serge [Chaloff] and Charlie Mariano," who I knew about as two Boston jazz musicians with national reputations. Freeman added, "He also had an original, *The Fable of Mabel*, recorded by Serge for Storyville Records."

Those were tantalizing clues, and they cost me many frustrating hours. The man at the record shop could find no listings for either Chaloff or Mariano as leaders, and nobody I knew with a jazz collection had ever heard of these particular records. Even Joe Rico, the jazz jockey on Buffalo radio who seemed, in my teenage pantheon, to know everything worth knowing not only about jazz but about life, when I finally got a friend of a friend's friend to make an inquiry, just shrugged.

In 1956, channels of communication were sluggish. It was years before I realized that those other records Twardzik had played on had had mainly local distribution around Boston, and that the Mariano record was out of print even before I had started making inquiries about it. Probably the Chaloff record was too. In 1963, when I found a discography of Richard Twardzik's recordings in an English jazz magazine called *Jazz Monthly* (Morgan 1963), I finally learned more of the details—labels, titles, recording dates, personnel, instruments, compositions. It turned out there were two Mariano records with Twardzik on them, and not only did Chaloff record Twardzik's composition *The Fable of Mabel*, but Twardzik played on it too. I wrote the titles of all three records on the list of collectibles I carry in my wallet. Over the years, dozens of items on that list came and went, but those Boston LPs took on a frustrating permanence. As jazz buffs do, I watched for the records to come up in delete bins and record auctions. As my travels broadened, first in my college days when I found myself across the river from Detroit and then as my professional pursuits took me to conferences all over North America and eventually Europe, I spent hours pawing through dusty stacks of vinyl in far-flung cities on two continents.

To this day, I have never found those records, any of them, in the LP format. I finally got to hear them when the commercial boom brought on by the new CD technology at the tail-end of the 1980s led record companies to sweep out their vaults.

Freeman's liner note also offered the news that Twardzik's "professional career began at the age of fourteen," and that "he worked with Tommy Reynolds, Charlie Barnet, Lionel Hampton, Charlie Parker,

Serge Chaloff, Charlie Mariano, Sonny Stitt and Chet Baker." With
that background, somewhere there had to be live performances on
acetate or tape reels, and, sure enough, a few years later a single track
surfaced of Charlie Parker with a pick-up band in a Boston nightclub.
Twardzik's piano was largely inaudible, but he was there, and the very
existence of the performance held the promise of more, and over the
decades more performances have slowly accumulated, never out of re-
gard for Twardzik himself but usually triggered by lingering sentiments
for the leaders of the bands he happened to be playing in—Parker,
Chaloff, or Chet Baker. There is quite a bit more to come, I now know,
and come it will if the growing sentiments for Twardzik, or at least
curiosity about him, gather a little momentum.

With only the twenty-odd minutes of the trio recordings, it might
have been impossible for me and for other jazz fans to sustain interest
in the ill-fated piano player for the next half-century or so. But there
was more. Pacific Jazz Records released a new recording with Twardzik
on it the same year as the trio record, and the second recording was
a small treasure of beguiling, open-minded, cool music that provided
a whole new view of Twardzik's brilliance, and solidified his singular
ability in case there were any doubts.

The records were made in a Paris studio by the Chet Baker Quartet
in two sessions. The date of the second session was exactly one week
before Twardzik died. The LP that was issued in North America was
called *Chet Baker in Europe* (Pacific Jazz 1218), and it carried the gran-
diose subtitle *A Jazz Tour of the NATO Countries* (1.4, also page 52).
The tracks with Twardzik consisted of six pieces of extraordinary delicacy, almost like chamber music. Once again, they amounted to only
half a record. They filled the second side, all 25 minutes of it. There
were also five tracks on the first side, fillers in my mind, by Baker with
European musicians recorded after Twardzik's death.

My copy of the Pacific Jazz LP has disappeared, as things tend to do
in four decades or more. It was a rare one. It has never been reissued
in the original format and I now realize that its rarity has nothing to
do with the tastes of the company executives, about whom I harbored
resentment for years, assuming they did not know they were hiding a
masterpiece in their vaults. I now realize that the music never belonged
to the American distributor, Pacific Jazz, but had to be leased by them
from Barclay Records in Paris, the original producer and owner.

That explained why the LP came with strangely impersonal packaging, with a cover photo focusing on the tail of a Pan American airliner instead of the customary romantic pose of Chet Baker, who was not only the best-selling jazz musician of the moment but also a highly photogenic boyish hipster. I now know that Baker was still in Europe when Pacific Jazz leased this music and packaged it in an effort to keep alive the American fan interest in their hottest musician. The cover photo shows a young couple embracing in the shadow of the airliner, but it isn't even Baker, although the male figure obscured by the woman shows a Chet-like pompadour.

Baker's cover poses, except for this one, had a certain cachet. In fact, they have proven to have something close to the lasting power of art. Years later they were collected in coffee-table format in *Young Chet* (Claxton 1993). So at the time of its release, the cover of *Chet Baker in Europe* seemed a bit weird, with make-believe Chet hidden behind the young woman hugging him on his supposed return to American soil. Equally weird were all those strange foreign names of the musicians on the filler tracks. But come to think of it, they were no stranger than the names of what had been, until Twardzik's sudden death, Baker's working quartet.

Baker's young sidemen were so unknown beyond their own home-towns that advertising them by name would have stirred no expectations abroad and almost none at home.

What set *Chet Baker in Europe* apart was the music. The brilliance of the recordings Baker made in the Paris studio with Twardzik would turn out to be due in part to an invisible fifth member of the new quartet. Baker's group recorded nothing but original compositions in the Paris studio, a very unusual situation for Baker, whose reputation rested on ballads and jazz standards before this and, it would turn out, forever after. Of those original compositions, one was written by Twardzik, and the other five were written, according to the composer credit on the label, by "Bob Zieff." There were actually three more Zieff compositions recorded at these sessions but it would be several years before we knew that, except for the few fans who had access to the original French issue on Barclay Records.

Bob Zieff was another mystery man, and the mystery was hardly solved by Baker's identification of him in the liner note (1956) as "the young

Boston writer that Dick Twardzik, my pianist, brought to my attention."
His music was mysterious too. There were no funny valentines, no lilting Mulliganesque ditties, no harmon-muted bleeding sentiments—in
other words, none of the hallmarks on which Baker's popularity was
based.

Baker was well aware of the differences. His liner note added, "The
originality and freshness of Zieff's line and chordal structure is going
to please a lot of people, I think—at least musicians and other serious
listeners." That statement seemed like an attempt at preparing Baker's
regular fans for the kind of departure that Zieff's music represented. It
was, above all, cerebral music. (You can dance to it, in the bop mockery
of the hopelessly passé Swing Era, but only if you work out your steps
very very carefully.) Each composition is an intricate little gem. Each
note seems deliberately laid into its position in the composition. Each
composition sounds more difficult to play than the last one, no matter
what order you listen to them in, but the rewards of mastering their
difficulties are obvious in the subtle swing and the melodic surprises.

Playing Zieff's compositions obviously requires discipline and control,
the aspect that gives the pieces the chamber-like feel, but that should
not imply that the quartet's performances of these pieces are subdued
or in any way timid. Baker and Twardzik, the principal soloists, range
freely through key changes and tempo shifts with what seems uncanny
ease.

Baker was praised from the beginning of his career for his spontaneity.
He had a knack for inventing attractive phrases on the spot. In jazz,
spontaneous invention is essential, and most jazz musicians rely on rote
devices to relieve them of the burden of constant invention. Baker
needed fewer of them than many others. When it came to spinning
lines of disarmingly simple and lyrically attractive variations, he had
few peers. All that was widely recognized, but in his career he received
scant notice for the beauty of his tone or the fullness of his range on
the trumpet, perhaps because he displayed them so infrequently, sticking almost exclusively to the middle register. There was no way he
could do that in Zieff's music. It required him to move briskly over the
scale, especially on the tunes called *Rondette* and *Re-Search*, and to play
rapid exercise-like sequences in *Mid-Forte* and *Piece Caprice*, sometimes
requiring octave leaps. Baker carried it off with total control. He made
it sound easy. His technical skills were seldom so evident, before or

after. And through it all his lyrical bent, the heart of his talent, never flagged for a second.

Zieff's music sets Baker into brooding moods on *Sad Walk, Just Duo* and *Brash*, and winsome melodies with minor drags on *Rondette, Sad Walk* and *Pomp*. The ingenious harmonies draw out Baker's sensitivity, seeming to extract it without pretense or posing as he traces fresh melodic lines over the layered harmonies. These recordings may represent the apogee of Baker's talents as a pure musician.

The only other composition recorded by the young quartet in Paris was composed by Twardzik himself, called *The Girl from Greenland*. If I had never heard *A Crutch for the Crab* and *Albuquerque Social Swim* (and, eventually, *The Fable of Mabel*, Twardzik's other remarkable composition) it would be tempting to credit Zieff with it rather than Twardzik. The kindred feelings in the music of Twardzik and Zieff were no coincidence, I would discover 20 years later, when I accidentally sat down beside Robert L. Zieff at a conference in Oldham, Lancashire, on the music of Duke Ellington.

Twardzik's *Girl from Greenland* is a ballad (A A′B A′) built on a lilting rhythm. Baker's statement of the ascending scale of the melody is countered by Twardzik's trills at the top of the piano. When Baker and Twardzik break free of the melody in their solo choruses, they sustain the contrasting moods of their melodic motifs. Baker emphasizes the minor mood, brooding over it quietly. Twardzik mocks the mood, teasing it by spreading four bars of melody over eight and inverting phrases. Baker is involved and Twardzik is aloof. Baker is romantic and Twardzik is cynical. It is an ingenious arrangement, perfectly executed. Both musicians play their parts brilliantly, but it is the interaction of the parts that raises the music to a higher level.

And when the last note of *The Girl from Greenland* faded, there would be no more music from Richard Twardzik. Or so it seemed. As the man with the Coppertone voice on the Pacific Jazz sampler said, "Twardzik died in Paris a few months later, depriving us all of the great ability that was his." Now, to add to that, we had the eyewitness testimony of Chet Baker. In his liner notes for *Chet Baker in Europe* (1956), Baker included this diary entry in his account of his tour of the NATO countries (with the elisions in the original):

OCT. 21 — Today here in Paris, alone in his room, Dick Twardzik died suddenly at 24, cheating all of us of his very real genius.... His conception was so completely original; the way he played with meter was uncanny, turning it around and around, never goofing, always there. He leaves behind far too few examples of the genius he possessed. My association with him has enriched my life greatly and I'm thankful for that. We are all deeply saddened.... a wonderful person and a brilliant musician.

There did indeed seem to be too few examples of his genius. The Baker quartet tracks from Paris, on the Pacific Jazz release, amounted to 24 minutes and 29 seconds. Add to that the 21:44 of the piano trio recordings and you get the grand total: 46 minutes and 13 seconds. Enough to establish a reputation, but hardly enough to sustain it, by any reasonable standards. There would be, miraculously, another 15 minutes of Bob Zieff's music by Baker and Twardzik in Paris, and when it is added on it brings the grand total to 61:12, one hour and one minute and a few seconds. Eventually more music by Twardzik would be found, a fair amount really, considering the brevity of his life, some of it excellent, but the very best of it is here, in the hour from these two studio recordings.

Over the years, I have returned to this music often, and always with the fear that I would find its pleasures gone flat. As I left behind the horn-rimmed teenager I had been when I first heard Richard Twardzik playing *A Crutch for the Crab*, I feared that I might find out that my feelings for it were based on nothing more than adolescent brooding for a doomed young artist. I was afraid something inside me would say, Snap out of it, for god's sake.

It hasn't happened.

2 Henryk and Clare

When Richard Twardzik died in that Paris hotel on 21 October 1955, he was two years younger than Keats, the archetype of doomed artistic youth. Maybe, when you think of it in that light, it is no mean feat for him to have left behind a whole hour of perpetually fresh, highly individualistic, mostly unforgettable music.

It is trite to say that there would surely have been much more had he lived longer. It may also be untrue.

Twardzik died of a heroin overdose. When the band member assigned to rouse him from his hotel room for a recording session finally got the concierge upstairs with his pass-key, he rushed in and found Twardzik on the floor, in fetal position, a syringe sticking out of the crook of his left arm. He had been dead for a few hours. The blood that had trickled from the needle wound had not got far before congealing at death. According to a rumor that circulated in the jazz underworld at the time, Twardzik's corpse had turned bright blue.

There was some speculation that he committed suicide, as we will see. He did not, but the distinction has mainly forensic merit. From even the most generous of viewpoints, his death was self-inflicted, deliberate or not. So there he was at 24, his spirit snuffed like a candle. His talent squandered. Clare and Henryk Twardzik's boy genius gone before he was fully a man.

Clare and Henryk had feared something like this. Their boy had a history of drug use stretching back to his precocious entry into the jazz world six years earlier, when he was only 18. He was their only child, and the light of their lives. His drug use had not been something he felt he needed to hide from them. His parents were creative people themselves, artistic in their different ways, middle class but not bourgeois. They had fostered and encouraged Richard's creative impulses from the beginning, practically from birth.

At first when the troubles with drugs started, they accepted it with the good graces of sophisticated people who recognize the professional hazards that go with a superfluity of talent. But as time went by and Richard turned to them not only for advice but for money they could scarcely afford, Clare became critical. She complained to Henryk about the expense, and to Richard she let her silence speak. Henryk said little, as was his wont, and remained stoically supportive.

In his last years, when he was often on the road with one band or another, Richard took to sending Clare and Henryk separate letters and postcards, individually addressed. That was the only real sign that there might have been a rift between them. On a few occasions, he did not write at all, to either of them, and it turned out those were the times when *he* was most disturbed. He wrote to each of his parents, as he had written to both of them jointly all his life until then, with unforced enthusiasm about all the things he was seeing and doing, never doubting for a moment that they would be as interested as he was in the classical record he was listening to or the second-rate drummer in the band or the exhibit he saw at a famous art gallery or the state of his supposedly precarious health. As Clare's youngest sister remembered, "The Twardziks enjoyed closeness and the sheer pleasure of one another's company."

They were a family not just in the good times. As young parents, Clare and Henryk had nurtured their boy's sense of self-worth. If Richard grew up believing he was a genius, it was because they sensed it in him first. Of course, none of that brought them any solace when Richard died. It only made it harder.

Clare was born into a Boston Irish-Catholic family in the first decade of the twentieth century. Her father, Robert Charles Grant, worked as a railroad yardmaster, dispatching trains on schedule for the Boston & Maine Railroad out of North Station in Boston. Clare's mother Julie, née Maloney, devoted herself to keeping the house immaculate and to primping her young brood for parochial school and Sunday Mass. Julie carried the rock-solid convictions of the upwardly mobile second-generation Irish Bostonians. "Lace-curtain Irish," they were called, defined memorably by Eddie Condon, a Chicago jazz ruffian, as "the kind of people who have fresh fruit in the house when no one is even sick" (1947 [1992]). They put as much distance as they could between themselves and the shanty Irish, without acknowledging, or perhaps not even knowing, that the shanty was only a generation or two behind them, in their Old-Country ancestry.

Robert Grant had different roots. He descended from a long line of Nova Scotia sea captains, and he missed few opportunities, when the mood was on him, for lamenting his trading of salt spray for the sooty rail yards. He carried with him some indelible markers of his wharfside lineage, especially in his speech. The one that especially got to Julie was when he peppered his conversation with "we was," as in "We was better off *before* we got the damn radio." If he slipped one of those into the suppertime conversation, Julie was inclined to flare up and berate him for the example he was setting for the children with his bad grammar, in a diatribe that inevitably ended with the rebuke that he was the kind of man who never read anything but the *Saturday Evening Post.*

"Funny how the Irish will defend the King's English," their youngest daughter, Rosamond, said, recalling these scenes some seventy years later. But the lesson was implanted in all the children, not only that true culture was not to be found in the *Saturday Evening Post,* but, more generally, that culture counted.

There were four Grant children. The first three came in quick succession, in the Catholic family pattern of the day. The eldest, Mary Clare, known by her middle name, which had been her grandmother's name, was born in 1906. Her sister Juliette Alva, was born in 1908 and named after their mother, but was called June from birth, so as to avoid confusion. Their brother, Robert Charles, Jr., was born the next year, in 1909. Then there was a respite of seven long years before the fourth child, Rosamond Hilton, called Roz, came along in 1916. Robert, Jr., the only son, left the hearth early. All that Roz would say about him, across the gulf of years that separated them, was that "our red-headed brother ... married a girl of means whose father (it was whispered) was an old race-horse tout."

The three daughters filled the house with bright confidence. The two eldest, close in age and best of friends in childhood, emerged in adolescence with very different personalities and predilections, though their differences seemed to have little or no effect on their feelings for one another. June (1908–2001) was good in school and serious out of it. Her sisters knew they could go to her for advice on girlish problems that their mother Julie, approachable though she was, might be less receptive to. In the boom-and-bust times at the end of the 1920s, June went to work at Newton-Waltham Bank and Trust Co. in Newton Center, Massachusetts, about six miles from downtown Boston. She started as a teller, a woman's occupation at the time and normally the height of a young woman's ambitions, but she had a good head for banking, as her supervisors put it, and she was promoted to the loans department, one of the few growth areas in the Depression days. She kept working there after she married Ted Jones, and she surprised her family and friends by resuming her career even after she gave birth to their son John in 1933. Balancing career and family was uncommon for a woman of June's generation, and a sure sign not only of a lively mind but a measure of her determination to make good use of it. By the time she retired she carried the title of assistant treasurer.

Her slightly older sister, Clare (1906–1979), who would be Richard's mother, was pert and confident and flirtatious. She too would prove to be determined but as a youngster she was altogether less serious than June. All her life she took pains with her appearance, to the point where her youngest sister thought of her as a "social climber." She was artistic where June was practical, the family said, and she was rebellious.

The third sister, Roz, reaped the rewards that come to a babe with sisters eight and ten years older as well as with parents well entrenched in their middle years. "I seldom earned a living and subsisted entirely on being someone's pet," Roz told me when she was in her eighties. She too was artistic. "Her background," her daughter Jane says, "is as an artist and writer," and when she was in her seventies she was still making illustrated books, creating both pictures and text on an early-model Macintosh computer. Fifty years before, when Roz was barely twenty and a fine arts student, she married an "older man," Arthur Thompson (1907–88), an architect by training and a painter by inclination. After scrambling for ten years in Boston, they took off in 1947 with their 9-year-old daughter in search of a simpler life in the Maine countryside. There, in Wyeth country, Arthur painted to his heart's content and built a local reputation with his moody landscapes and seascapes.

Different as they were, the three Grant girls had been close while they lived at home. As adults, they showed their bonds in many ways. Each had one child and only one. Clare's Richard in 1931 was the first grandchild, and thus heir to the unspoken privileges from grandmothers and aunts that fall to the first-born in close families. June's John arrived two years later in 1933, close enough to make him and Richard allies at family gatherings in their early years. Roz's daughter Jane came later, in 1937, as Roz herself had come later in the generation before, and Jane insinuated herself into the circle of cousins by dint of personality, taunting the big boys about their pegged pants and suffering tugs on her pigtails with flattered indignation.

One of the Grant sisters' childhood traits solidified into family tradition in the next generation. The daughters called their father Dad but their mother they called by her given name Julie. So the children of Clare and Roz would come to call them by their given names. Dick's salutations beginning with his letters from camp were to Clare and Henry, or occasionally Henryk, the full and exotic-sounding middle-European form of his father's name.

Henryk Twardzik, despite the unreconstructed Slavic look of his name, was raised in Buffalo, New York. He had been born in Poland but arrived in Buffalo with his parents as a babe in arms in the wave of European immigration that peaked around 1907. At the time, all the northeastern cities of the United States were tooling up for heavy industry and their rapid growth depended on the sinews of immigrant workers. Having pretty well exhausted the supply of English-speaking immigrants from the British Isles by the end of the nineteenth century, the underpopulated New World had turned to the huddled masses of eastern Europe in order to keep the wheels of industry spinning at what had become world-leading velocity. Buffalo was a melting pot of many nationalities, mostly white and poor, but it was more hospitable to its immigrants than some other cities. For one thing, there was less old money than in cities like nearby Rochester and more distant Boston, and a less entrenched bourgeoisie, and, with it, less pressure on newcomers to "speak American" and wear J.C. Penney clothes.

Henryk's parents, Maria and Richard Henryk Twardzik, moved with their baby into a Buffalo ghetto where they were surrounded by Polish neighbors. As a result, Maria lived her life innocent of all but the most rudimentary fragments of the English language. Their son, notwithstanding the enticements everywhere but in his mother's kitchen to be American first and foremost, would grow up as fluent in the Polish language as in English. As a child, his perfect bilingualism made him a valuable go-between for the Irish-American Jesuits who found themselves running a Polish parish. One of Henryk's painful childhood memories was going door to door in his neighborhood selling the Catholic weekly, *The Pilot*, to parishioners who could hardly afford it and probably could not read it anyway.

All her long life, Maria prepared fruitcake for her son on his saint's day, "weighted down with cherries and nuts," according to Henryk's sister-in-law Roz. She also regularly sent her son long, densely handwritten letters, all in Polish. The letters rankled Clare by utterly excluding her, and it did not do much to placate her when Henryk translated his mother's greetings or her inquiries about baby Dickie. Clare's rancor sometimes erupted into rants about the clinging babushka and her not-quite-assimilated son. It certainly did not help her mood to see that Henryk saved his mother's letters, tied with string in neat bundles. They were among his effects, dozens of them, when he died in 1989.

Henryk proved to be a smart boy in his parochial school, and he was especially gifted in art, the kind of natural artist who made pencil sketches wherever he went, leaving behind a trail of caricatures, portraits and still lifes. In high school, he found teachers who started him working in oils and acrylics, and when he outgrew their teachings they saw to it that he went to study at the Albright Art School, affiliated with the Buffalo's redoubtable Albright-Knox Art Gallery. From there, a scholarship took him to the New England School of Art and Design in Boston, and when he graduated he became an apprentice at the Charles J. Connick Stained Glass Studio on Harcourt Street in Boston, the foremost stained-glass workshop in the United States at the time.

Henryk eventually became an associate at Connick's, executing stained-glass designs in the Boston studio that became part of the installations at St Patrick's Cathedral and St. John the Divine in New York, chapels at Princeton University, Boston University (2.1) and University of Pittsburgh, Denver Cathedral, the American Church of Paris, and many others.

Henryk met Clare Grant while he was apprenticing with Connick in the last years of the 1920s. By then, Clare had worked her way through Practical Arts School and become, her sister Roz says, "a meticulous, high-salaried draftsperson." Their common interest in art no doubt brought them together, though the family has no clear consensus on Clare's artistic ability. Roz considers her "modest of talent, [but] she was gifted with geometric insight." Roz's daughter Jane remembers her aunt Clare as "an artist doing fine detailed watercolors when she was younger and working on highly secretive and detailed technical drawings for MIT during the war." Before she worked at MIT, probably soon after she met Henryk, she worked at drafting in the acoustics laboratory at Harvard. She seems to have given up painting early, and nothing remains of her artwork, a stark contrast to her husband.

Roz recalls that Clare and Henryk met at what she calls "a Polish party," not directly connected to the art world, but art quickly became a factor in their courtship. Henryk asked her to model for him, and Clare was flattered. "It was Henryk who painted a winsome Clare," Roz says, "green crepe de Chine with subdued buttons from her own collection, her hair puffed at the sides in cootie garages." It was the first of dozens of paintings that Henryk would make of Clare.

Roz was a high-school student at the time, just developing her art interests, and she seized the opportunity to take some lessons from her older sister's boyfriend. "Henryk is the only one who ever taught me anything about design," she says, though a few years later she enrolled as a student at the Museum of Fine Arts.

If teenaged Roz was smitten by the dashing artist who wore Basque berets and a full mustache, she was alone, or so it seemed. Clare was decidedly cool, and their parents were ice-cold. "You Bolshevik!" Mr. Grant shouted at him from the top landing of the staircase one evening when Henryk came calling. The American Catholic church at the time had launched an offensive against Communism and Communist sympathizers. It was a sentiment that would abate for a few years in World War II when the United States found themselves in league with Russia against the Axis powers but it would then accelerate on a much broader base during the Cold War and culminate in inquisitions by a congressional committee on Un-American Activities and blacklists of known or suspected Communists. Mainstream America was not a welcoming place for Commies and pinkos and anyone who looked like one. For some of the old guard, the fact that a man had an unpronounceable name like Sacco or Vanzetti or, come to think of it, Twardzik, was enough to arouse suspicions.

Henryk's sympathies definitely leaned left, though there is no evidence either in documents or living memories that his Communist association was official in any way. His sketchpad bears one drawing, a very crude one, labeled "Fallen Striker," with a policeman poised over a picketer, ready to club him (2.2). Its technical crudity suggests that Henryk might have sketched it hurriedly on the streets. The style is agitprop, and its existence in his sketchpad would have been more than

enough evidence to brand him a Bolshevik in the eyes of the political
guardians of the day.

For the moment, the Grant family supplied Henryk with more immediate problems than uniting the workers of the world. Not deterred
by the insults raining down the wallpapered staircase, Henryk would
appear at the door bearing gifts. "Poor Henry and his roses," mother
Julie would sigh.

[illustration 2.1] Henryk Twardzik painting the clerestory windows of the Boston
University Chapel at the Connick Studio in Boston, ca. 1950. Uncredited photograph
with signature from *Newburyport Art Association Directory of Members and Cookbook
of Their Choice Recipes*, published by the Art Association, no date. (Henryk's recipe
is Greek Lamb.) From the Twardzik-Thompson Archive, courtesy of Rosamond
Thompson and Jane Sumner. All rights reserved.

At the same time, Clare was embroiled in a war of independence with her parents that accelerated, not coincidentally, with Henryk's arrival. Clare wanted to move out of the homestead and set up an apartment of her own. She was ready, she insisted, more than ready, and besides she and her father disagreed practically every time they found themselves in the same room. Tut, tut, said Julie. It was simply not done. "No mother in her right mind would allow a daughter to march out from the home where she had been reared, to set up her own apartment," Roz recalled. "The lodge ladies of the Brotherhood of Railroad Train Men might whisper and raise eyebrows."

The crisis came, as Clare surely knew it would, when she hung orange drapes in the sun parlor over the traditional Irish lace. The act precipitated what Roz called "a petty feud over bigotry," but "petty" surely underplays the feelings that the color orange could arouse at the time in Irish Catholic households. Thomas Grant laid down the law and Clare moved out in a huff. She took a studio apartment on the Fenway, which she shared with two students from the Conservatory of Music.

Young Roz, then about 13, remembers it as an adventure for her too. "How I loved boarding a train to visit the studio [apartment]," she said. "I am a movie-struck kid hyped by nouveau carrot sticks and fox-trotting with spindly Polish fellers. I am promised a trip to symphony hall but, curses, I beg over to the Bijou where they're showing Joan Crawford in *Our Dancing Daughters*." That movie was the sensation of 1928, featuring Crawford in one of her last silent roles. (Crawford made her first talkie, *Untamed*, the next year and carried on in the new era of talking pictures as the femme fatale in Metro-Goldwyn-Mayer's stock company.) In *Our Dancing Daughters*, Crawford plays a party girl with a hip flask who is forced to get serious when her lover (played by Johnny Mack Brown) finds himself attracted to a sophisticated older woman. It must have been heady stuff for a convent schoolgirl like Roz, and it might not have been much of a stretch for her to imagine her liberated older sister in the flapper role.

It was short-lived. "All this glamour ceases, the balloon bursts and comes to an end with the onset of incapacitating rheumatism in Clare's wrist," Roz remembered. She added that "it prompted [Clare] to consider 'trial marriage', a trendy solution among the not-so-sures." She moved in with Henryk, and together they began plotting their life together in art. There would be parties and hilarity and flirtations, and a hasty marriage, and then the birth of a son, and more parties with the son in a wicker basket, swaddled in wool against the Boston night air.

[illustration 2.2] Pencil sketch of "Fallen Striker," by Henryk Twardzik, date unknown. From the Twardzik-Thompson Archive, courtesy of Rosamond Thompson and Jane Sumner. All rights reserved.

3 Dickie

"Nice music."

These were Dickie Twardzik's first words — his precocious first reaction to the world around him, spoken as if moved by an impulse that he could not contain. "The child is half awakened, half aware of being bundled into his outer garments for the long winters night trip home," his mother Clare scribbled late in her life either as notes for a eulogy to her long-lost son or simply as therapy for her irrepressible grief. "A radio, or perhaps a phonograph— orthophonic it would have been in those days— is playing and the child sleepily murmurs, 'Nice music.' The family, the grandmother at whose home this was, the aunties and the parents are ecstatic. Dickie has put two words together! and for a long while it was a family anecdote to be dragged out at the holiday gatherings when they all sat around the round table after the turkey."

The incident remains locked in the Grant–Twardzik family lore, though Clare, aggrieved as she grew older, tried to appropriate it as hers alone: "As the years went on it was mentioned less frequently, and finally forgotten altogether, but the mother remembered and kept this thing in her heart." But it was never really hers alone. The incident is truly a family legend. Several years after Clare's death, before I had read her account of it, her sister Roz recounted it to me, albeit with less certain detail. "When little Dickie was able to talk," she said, "my mother Julie confided in me, her perpetual pet, that he awoke and sat up in bed listening to Nice Music. Are these his first words?"

Richard Henryk Twardzik was born on 30 April 1931. Clare was 25, Henryk a year older, and the new baby seemed like a healthy adjunct to their independence. His arrival did little to curtail their active social life. He was beautiful and adored everywhere they went and, above all, portable. Aunt Roz remembers considerable moving around by the young family in the early years, and she had a close-up view at the start. They moved into the Grant homestead immediately after Dickie was born. Roz says, "My first recollection of Dick was of a tiny head in a swinging baby tote, bobbing up to disappear again around a winding flight of stairs with Clare and Henryk descending from an evening on the town... From my overhead vantage point, I was a pimply high-schooler dangling out over a hallway banister after an evening of baby-sitting."

The irony of this domestic arrangement, so soon after Clare's heated defection, was defused, in Roz's account, by larger loyalties. "It was a time when backbiting mothers obligingly helped one another," says Roz, "moved in with one another, were loyal to one another, and with the exception of a downright slur, ours would shrug off rampant accusations that would make your ears burn. 'Our Clare wouldn't do that!' "

"Here's your baby," Clare told Henryk, thrusting the blanketed bundle at him when they arrived home from the hospital. "Don't ask for any more." They laughed at that, at Clare's audacity, and told their friends the story, counting it a sign of the free woman, pleasing her husband by producing his heir but drawing the line. It made a definite impression on their friend Kay Brehaut, and on her young daughter Elaine, who she told it to with an air of indignation mixed with admiration.

The Brehauts were the Twardziks best friends, and their house was a frequent stop, day or evening, for baby Dickie in the portable tote. Kay had got to know Henryk when she was a nursing student living on W. Cedar St. near Henryk's bachelor digs, and she took an instant interest in him as a budding artist. When she married Ellerton Brehaut, known to everyone as Bree, who would become legislative advisor for the Boston Chamber of Commerce, the friendship continued between the couples. Daughter Elaine remembers Dick as the first baby she ever saw, when she was four, and they were frequent playmates as children, with the Twardziks visiting regularly and Dick spending many of his school vacations with them while Clare worked at MIT. "I guess you could say we grew up together," Elaine told me, and she and her parents would be close by in the critical times that were to come.

As sociable as Clare was after her baby was born, she was far from casual when it came to mothering. Kay Brehaut was always quick to add, when she told the story of Clare's presentation of the new-born baby to Henryk, that Clare was totally devoted to Dick in all his boyhood traumas and triumphs. As a young mother, insecure about her maternal instincts, Clare took to reading handbooks. She looked back on her earliest experiences with her only child as a struggle to conform to the strictures of what her authorities promulgated as conventional motherhood. In her notes for a eulogy, she wrote: "The days — the weeks — the months go on in a seemingly endless procession. We learn we taste we feel we grow. The carrots no longer have to be put thru the strainer, but the endless gallons of orange juice squeezing goes on."

The pressures increased with her proximity to her mother, especially when the advice in the handbooks contradicted what Julie was telling her. "Routine is all—that's what the book says, and we are being brought up by the book. Bad cess to it would say the grandmother, but the mother was conscientious and followed the best authorities of the day on child care. She didn't know any better. He was her one and only, and she tried hard. Balanced meals, rest hour, play time, toidy—all at their appointed hour and the ticking away clock became a nightmare for the mother—she never quite caught up with it."

The Twardziks found a small apartment on Beacon Hill Place. Roz was studying at the nearby Museum of Fine Arts and a frequent visitor. She remembers Clare worrying about the dirt in the old apartment—"a dusty web, not altogether germ free, where houses jam so close together you could poke your head out through a jagged window pane and yell across to a neighbor." "I can easily recall Clare's musical vacuuming to exasperated syllables of Rich - ard Tward - zik at the peak of her lungs."

Dickie made a threesome with his parents on their social rounds by means of a baby tote. "No sitters for this family," Clare wrote with more than a little pride. "Where the parents went the child went in his own special basket — light blue it was and with two handles." Roz remembers the parents carrying the basket between them as they set out for parties, Henryk in his bohemian beret and Clare "fashionably attired." "She loved parties," Roz said, "and wasn't it awful to be left out when everyone else is dressing up to go somewhere."

In spite of the constant company of her baby, one of Clare's regrets toward the end of her life were the strictures she observed about showing her affection to the baby. "Rocking or cuddling were verboten" according to her reading of child-care authorities, "and one should never kiss the child behind the left ear. That would set up an erotic area which, for some obscure reason, was undesirable."

"Ah well, live and learn, but learn too late," she wrote. "We grow brown and strong and sturdy, despite all this nonsense."

Whatever Clare's maternal failings, real or imagined, young Dickie thrived. "We had a winsome and loving smile," she said, "and were adored as the eldest man-child in the family." Grandmother Julie they called Babus (*bab*-oosh), the Polish nursery word for granny, in a rare concession by the Irish line for the paternal side. (Dickie often called his father Tatus — *tat*-oosh — Polish for daddy.) Clare remembers her mother baking cookies, and Auntie June, now starting her career in the bank, bringing toys. Clare was especially impressed at receiving parcels from her aunt in Virginia, Julie's sister, with play suits and jerseys and other articles of clothing from a fashionable store called Best, with the slogan "Best is the best" emblazoned on the boxes. For a short period in Dickie's youth, Clare would cultivate the relationship with his relatively well-off great-aunt and great-uncle.

Dickie was undeniably cute with his bright smile and dark eyes, but in Clare's mind and Henryk's too, there was much more to their cherished son than that. Clare began her eulogy to him with an invocation to her son's special grace. She entitled her first section *In the beginning was the word*, the opening line of the Gospel of John, until 1963 recited at the end of every Roman Catholic Mass. The word that was there in the beginning, of course, was God. Clare begins, "This is not the mother's story, not that she is unimportant, being a human being, it is the story of the son—the sun—the bird—the lark the fallen lark the doomed one."

Soon after Dickie demonstrated his precocity with his "nice music" declaration, another sign followed that was similar in kind, though less portentous for the child's future. "Out into the frosty night, the blue basket carefully carried by Tatus, there is nowhere to look but up — up into the black immensity of the night," Clare wrote. "A tiny pair of eyes and one button for a nose, the apex of an ever widening triangle that extends to the far reaches of the universe itself. Barely heard under the blanket comes a phrase, 'Pretty stars,' and then sleep—oblivion—Nirvana. Another step in the long process from an embryonic sub-sub-subconsciousness to the creative man that should have been his destiny."

Henryk captured his son's special grace in his own way, by making him the subject of numerous drawings and paintings. An early painting shows young Dickie, about four, holding a toy sailboat (3.1, page 45). The yellow of his jersey and the pallor of his face stand out strikingly from the dark, textured background, where a toy rabbit and a toy dog, both on their hind legs, seem to be suspended in the murk. Although the boy is surrounded by playthings, there is no sense of play in the portrait. He holds his sailboat gingerly. The toy animals are featureless. The boy's large, dark eyes, the focal point of the portrait, stare directly at the viewer or, in the first instance, at the portrait painter, his father, but there is no feeling that the boy is looking at anything in particular. He seems to be looking beyond the viewer and beyond the painter, or perhaps through them.

It is a haunting portrait. The boy is somber, despite the toys that surround him. The nursery setting, if that is what it is, is shrouded in darkness. The boy is bemused, and no more engaged with the sailboat in his hands than with the toy animals over his shoulders.

It would surely be mistaken to imagine that Henryk Twardzik intended in this painting to portray his son Richard as a haunted, aloof, somber little boy. Although Richard was, along with his mother, Henryk's favorite model, he seems to have been essentially just that—a model. Henryk's main concern appears to be in creating a work of art, not in making a family scrapbook in oils. His paintings are representational but not realistic. They are often programmatic, conveying dramatic situations in which the models fill roles he has assigned them.

The distinction between art and the family scrapbook comes through clearly in another painting of Richard with a sailboat in his hand. In this painting, the boy stands with a woman on a rocky shoal with the sea behind (3.2, page 46). The previous portrait with the sailboat may have been a study for this dramatic painting rendered in a rather academic (or perhaps just stagey) style. This painting has the feel of a work based less on observation than on imagination. The figures are unmistakably Richard and Clare, but the portraiture is not detailed, and the seascape in the background also lacks definition.

Though this painting is technically less skillful than the portrait of the child with the sailboat, it is an admirable composition. The mother figure is delicate in her facial features but still substantial, simultaneously the adorer of the boy and his protector. The child, by comparison, is vulnerable. He is under-dressed for the elements that surround and indeed threaten them, and the way he is dressed demonstrates his need for the woman's protection. His childishness is emphasized by the toy sailboat he holds in his hand, and his dependence is also conveyed by his posture, which has him leaning back into the woman.

This painting, probably from sometime in the mid-1930s, shows Henryk's dramatic bent. The imagery is vaguely Catholic, perhaps in the obvious solicitude of the wimpled mother figure or, more generally, in the dominance of deep blue in sea and sky, symbolic color of the Blessed Virgin. The excesses of this painting verge on melodrama. In his best paintings, Henryk stops short of melodrama and creates scenes of quiet affection and simple domesticity.

As artistic values, quiet affection and simple domesticity were decidedly unfashionable in the artistic climate of Henryk's time. Scenes of any kind, for that matter, were out of fashion. Representational art had few enough advocates in the aftermath of the cubists and the early efflorescence of abstract impressionists. Those painters among Henryk's contemporaries who did choose representation, like Edward Hopper and Ben Shahn, kept their distance from their subjects, usually with ironic detachment and sometimes with stark antipathy.

If Henryk was aware of these trends in the critical climate of the art world of his day, he never bowed to them. He drew and painted all his life, moved by the inner urge to exercise his natural gift. He seldom looked beyond his immediate circumstances for his subjects. He drew and painted his wife and his son constantly. Among Henryk's works are several nude studies of Clare. His sketchbook is full of pencil drawings including candid sketches, apparently executed rapidly in the moment, and posed sittings, probably intended as studies for paintings. The pencil sketch of Clare (3.3), with only hints of her facial features, seems to be tossed off in the moment or two before she turned away, before he could get it down; the nude figure on the same page of the pad is almost generic, seemingly impersonal, and only recognizable as Clare by its resemblance to the figure in his paintings. The same sketchbook includes a study of Dick in a wicker chair (3.4), apparently in his very early teens. It has shape and shadow, and there can be little doubt that Dick sat for it. Both Clare and Dick seem to have been willing models. It was presumably something Henryk expected of them and, for Dick at least, growing up with a father who carried his sketchbook the way other men carry wallets, it must have seemed the most normal of activities.

Despite the considerable collection of his artwork that survives, Henryk Twardzik was not a professional artist in the strict sense except when he was working for Connick Associates, illustrating panels and painting stained glass. He painted portraits of his friend Kay Brehaut, whose friendship started when she admired his talent, and also of her daughter Elaine, as a coming-of-age present, when she was about 20. He exhibited his paintings when the opportunity arose, which was seldom, especially in his younger days when any kind of special notice for his art might have set his aspirations on a bolder course. The Brehauts owned some of his oils, not only the portraits but also two nude studies of Clare. Elaine remembers being shocked by them as a little girl. "I said to mother, what is going on, that woman has no clothes on. It's all right, she told me. That's his wife." In his later days, Henryk contributed paintings to exhibitions put on by the Newburyport Art Association, to which he belonged. But there are no records of sales, and no galleries, even local ones, with his paintings among their holdings. It was not his destiny to make his living as an artist, and he seems to have reconciled himself to that fate fairly early in his married life.

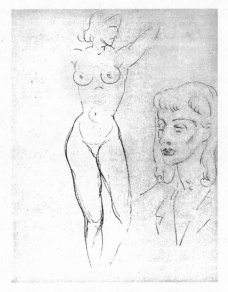

[illustration 3.3] Pencil portrait of Clare and sketch of nude figure, by Henryk Twardzik, date unknown. From the Twardzik-Thompson Archive, courtesy of Rosamond Thompson and Jane Sumner. All rights reserved.

The seascape in the background of his painting of the mother and child may be Rockport, Massachusetts. In the summer of 1933, when Dick had just turned two, the Twardziks moved to an artists' colony in Rockport, some 40 miles north of Boston on the rugged cape beyond the old whaling town of Gloucester. The move has the aura of testing a dream, attempting to leave behind the trappings of city life for the frugality of the country, living in the company of kindred spirits, where the creative juices might flow more freely.

Clare and Henryk may at first have welcomed the distance the move put between them and their domestic critics. But they seem to have been restless, and the young family moved frequently in Rockport, starting in an apartment over the First National Bank. They spent a couple of winters in Champney Place, according to a chronology Clare made of these Rockport years in her memoir, but the summers were spent with a family named Thibault, in their summer home or perhaps in a place rented from them, since the Thibaults were involved in real estate. Clare soon found fresh outlets for her busy social life and carried

[illustration 3.4] Pencil sketch of boy in wicker chair, by Henryk Twardzik, date unknown. From the Twardzik Thompson Archive, courtesy of Rosamond Thompson and Jane Sumner. All rights reserved.

on much as she had in the city, but Henryk seems to have struggled to find his métier in the new setting.

They were living in Rockport when the greatest family trauma struck. Dickie contracted rheumatic fever in late November 1934, on Thanksgiving Day. He was three and a half years old. He woke up complaining about pains in his legs, and when the complaints persisted and the pains intensified the next day, he was rushed to Boston children's hospital. The medical staff diagnosed rheumatic fever and determined Dick's case to be critical. He was placed in an isolation ward.

Rheumatic fever is bacterial, and in the Western world it has been largely controlled since the latter half of the twentieth century by antibiotics, but when Dick contracted it and for centuries before that it was one of the most fearful of all children's diseases. It affects soft tissue. Its onset is signaled by intense arthritic pain in the joints, either in the legs, as for Dickie, or other extremities. If the sufferer's immune system cannot check it at this stage, the disease spreads and often leads to inflammation of the heart tissues. This could cause heart failure and be fatal, and those who survived suffered from chronic weakness of the heart, spoken of in hushed tones as "rheumatic heart." At its most severe, rheumatic heart led to symptoms known as St. Vitus Dance, a condition that caused jerky, uncontrollable movements of the head and arms. Parents everywhere were well aware of the grim prognosis for rheumatic fever and dreaded it.

When young Dickie fell into a coma in the isolation ward, everyone feared the worst. Henryk and Clare called their friend Kay Brehaut, a trained nurse, to join the rest of the family in the hospital vigil. The doctors opened Dick's joints to relieve the swelling. As a last resort, they suggested a blood transfusion in hopes of shoring up the antibodies to fight off the disease. Robert Grant, progeny of sea captains and now dispatcher of trains, matched his first grandson's blood type. "Penicillin had not been invented," Roz points out, "but there's hope for a transfusion from a maternal grandfather who had cured himself of blood poisoning by soaking his wounded leg each night in a tote-pail of sea-water, whether or not it contained a prankster's crab." He volunteered to provide the blood for a transfusion that might dilute the germs coursing through the boy's veins.

There was no apparent improvement in the boy's condition. The doctor took Henryk just outside the room, Kay Brehaut remembered, and said, "Mr. Twardzik, we have done everything we can at this point." A weak little voice called out from inside the room, "Mr. Twardzik?" Dickie emerged from his coma and began the long recuperation.

Clare's memoir never got as far as Dickie's illness, but she left rough notes to guide her if and when she got back to it. The notes give a telegraphic hint of a mother's anxiety: "That first night. —Childrens hospital, relief, bottle of wine — danger list next day — despair, waiting for phone, watching operation, grandfather transfusion." She was well aware that Dickie was not alone in his agony, but was part of an epidemic. She could not have found any consolation in the grim consequences she saw around him. Her notes include this ominous entry: "Death of Polis child from st[reet]."

Clare's notes include the cryptic entry "(I'm hungry)," presumably Dick's words on regaining consciousness. And then these notes, with a characteristic rebuke of her own maternal impulses: "Pink ice cream in a purple bowl — 'Drink it' — stern mother." And finally: "Isolation (Thanksgiving to Easter) End of danger list, Easter Sunday — Convalescence — Home in casts —Beach every day. Sean teaches to walk."

Dickie's illness and his recuperation lasted four full months, from Thanksgiving to Easter. He probably spent his fourth birthday, 30 April 1935, on the Rockport beach. Visiting there with her parents, Elaine Brehaut says, "I can remember Dick having to learn to walk again." He would walk with a slight limp ever after. Auntie and Uncle Bill Longwell, the Virginia relatives who had sent generous gifts to their newborn great-nephew, must have visited Dickie during his recuperation and brought along their Irish setter named Sean. Dickie's affection for the dog, the beginning of a lifelong love of dogs, may have spurred him into playful activity and, in so doing, into exercising his weakened legs.

Roz remembers visiting the Twardziks in Rockport in "a two-story white clapboard house on High Street." This would have been 1936, probably in the fall, going by Clare's chronology, and Roz was likely accompanied by her husband Arthur Thompson, whom she had married the previous year. Five-year-old Dickie had by then fully recovered, but a family fetish had taken root. Dickie's health would be a constant concern for him and for his parents for the rest of his life.

On her Rockport visit, Roz found Henryk in a dark mood, deeply disturbed. It was the first time she would see him like this, but not the last. Similar depressions would come upon him for the rest of his life when he felt pressured by circumstances. In Rockport, he complained of dizzy spells and other ailments.

"When I raise this arm, it hurts."

"Don't raise this arm," said his doctor.

Henryk was a robust man, not given to hypochondria. His hurts were real, though apparently not physical. "We recall his blank face drifting in a small boat, as if worries would disappear with the shoreline," Roz said. "Sorting stamps and rare coins, his sole concentration."

Soon after, the Twardziks moved back to Boston—Roz says, without further explanation, "to be rid of the burden of extramarital affairs of an artist's colony in a small town."

They moved to Commonwealth Avenue, where Dick attended Prince School—"unwillingly," in Roz's recollection, for "he is no scholar." A photograph taken in his first school years shows him in robust health and high spirits (3.5).

Richard's constant companion when the family moved back to Boston, for all his childhood and much of his adolescence, was Liebestraum, a Dachshund (3.6). The Twardziks bought Liebie, as she was called, almost immediately after they re-settled in Boston, as a puppy. Dick would keep close company with dogs all his life, starting with his great-uncle's setter. When he started playing piano professionally, he sometimes took his dog with him to gigs, even on the road. Of them all, Liebie was the longest lived and her closeness to Dick became another piece of the family legend. Roz says, "I truly believe that aging Liebie (Lullaby) was a secular dachshund in league with the devil because in later years, during one of Dick's frequent absences when I couldn't help thinking of him, she got down from her couch and waddled across the room to let me know. That's funny, said Henryk, she never does that, she never gets up for anyone."

Clare's fragmented notes for her eulogy about Dick's school years, though impossible for even her sister Roz to fill out, evoke a busy, active time. "Now we are tenish," Clare wrote, and then she listed several points, most of them about the onset of a musical bias: "School piccolo. drummer with kettle lids—Piano in kitchen—Mozart—Count Basie & cowboy hat. Chinese & Colored schoolmates with soft musical voices. Liebe & the fire escape. Stravinsky forced on schoolmates. Boys downstairs—first lessons. Boogie-woogie"

Dick began taking piano lessons at first at his mother's insistence. "All we need to know about the mother," Clare wrote about herself, "is that she would rather have played piano than anything in this world. Alas—she could read the notes and strike them properly—but no music, no singing came out. Just notes hit properly." After Dick's first few lessons, buoyed no doubt by his mother's praise, he took to the piano with considerable zeal. Roz remembers Clare's coaching: "You have to say something, she counseled the young virtuoso." Clare never seems to have doubted that Dick would make up for her own lack of pianistic

[illustration 3.5] Richard Twardzik, probably about 5 or 6. From the Twardzik-Thompson Archive, courtesy of Rosamond Thompson and Jane Sumner. All rights reserved.

flair. From that day forward, the piano occupied part of all Dick 's days. Elaine Brehaut remembers him wearing out their old piano whenever he stayed at her parents' house on school vacations and other visits, and Clare's push for self-expression had obviously taken hold. "I think he was taking lessons," she says, "but he played *his* way and what *he* wanted."

Naturally, as the piano came to occupy a central place in Dick's days, it also became part of the domestic imagery in Henryk's art. It shows up in the background of a pencil sketch of Clare on a sofa, legs crossed, apparently knitting, and young Richard, in his early teens, sitting backwards on a chair, facing the artist, his back to the piano (3.7). The sketch is meticulously composed but cursorily drawn, lacking all but the most rudimentary physical detail. It is too rough for Henryk to have intended it as an end in itself, and was probably intended as a study for a painting.

[illustration 3.6] Richard Twardzik, about 10, with Liebestraum, the family Dachshund. From the Twardzik-Thompson Archive, courtesy of Rosamond Thompson and Jane Sumner. All rights reserved.

Another painting by Henryk, evidently from a few years later, shows a young man at an upright piano with his teacher (3.8, page 47). The piano is awkwardly placed in the room, presumably to serve the artist's view of the scene, which is through an open doorway from some distance down a hall. The perspective, though it seems unnatural and somewhat forced, conveys the idea of the privacy of the act under observation, the communion between teacher and pupil. That idea is also conveyed by the closeness of the two figures at the piano, and their rapt attention to the lesson, which allows the painter to eavesdrop unnoticed. Though the piano-playing figure is not detailed enough for a portrait, Richard was undoubtedly Henryk's prototype.

By 1941, when the United States joined the Allies in the war in Europe, Clare took up her position as a draft technician at the acoustics lab at Harvard. The family now moved to Foster Place, Cambridge, to what Roz calls "an affordable apartment in the Italian district on the outskirts of Harvard Square." The Twardziks rented the downstairs

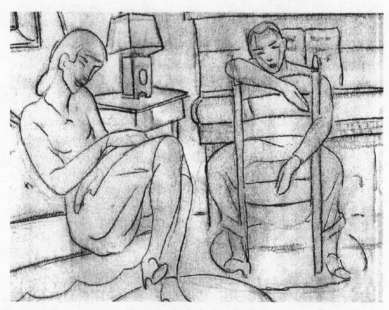

[illustration 3.7] Pencil sketch of mother and son in living room with piano, by Henryk Twardzik, date unknown. From the Twardzik-Thompson Archive, courtesy of Rosamond Thompson and Jane Sumner. All rights reserved.

to Roz and Arthur Thompson and their three-year-old daughter Jane. They chose the Thompsons as renters, according to Roz, because no one but a blood relative would have put up with Richard's incessant stomping on the floor while he played boogie-woogie above them.

Roz remembers those days mainly for their privations. "It is wartime," she wrote, "and pocketbooks are shrinking almost to the lining as supplies are being saved to feed the troops." Arthur, educated as an architect, took menial work converting Commonwealth Avenue mansions into apartment blocks. Roz too tried menial work in what she called "a sweat shop," stuffing envelopes with greeting cards, but she quit after three weeks when the supervisor asked her to scrub walls.

She remembers Clare fretting about standing in a line half a block long for her ration of cigarettes. Roz's personal peeve about the rationing, as "the younger sister (the profound pet)," was the lack of anything sweet, because sugar, chocolate, cocoa, and candy of all kinds had been cut off. Together, she and Clare conspired to stash canned goods behind Clare's sofa as a secret hoard against the day (which never came) when food supplies would be cut off.

It was in these years that Clare grew serious about cultivating familial ties with her childless aunt, whose smart gifts for Dickie from Best's Department Store had made such an impression. Hannah Marie Longwell (née Maloney) was grandmother Julie's sister. She was known simply as "Auntie" to Clare and her sisters, and later to Dickie as well. Auntie and her husband, Uncle Bill, lived in Blacksburg, Virginia, where Uncle Bill cut an imposing figure as Major W. F. M. Longwell, United States Army Corps. The Longwell's trip to Rockport to console the recuperating little boy further cemented their special relationship. Now plans were underway for Dickie to spend a few weeks of his summer vacation with his aunt and uncle in 1941, the year he turned 10.

A letter to Master Richard Twardzik from Uncle Bill and Auntie on 10 May 1941, a couple of weeks after his birthday, begins: "Hello Dear Lamb! We hope you are better…" These few opening words evoke a couple of themes that would be constants in Dick's relations with those closest to him. The first was his health, a constant concern after his brush with death. The second was the lamb image, which was probably picked up by Uncle Bill and Auntie, as devout Catholics, from the conventional image of innocence: Christ as *agnus Dei*, the lamb of God. It would resound in Clare's mind after Dick's death, when he became to her the sacrificial lamb, symbol of spoiled innocence. The second heading in her memoir about Dickie's infancy is "Little Lamb," and the section ends with a recollection that simultaneously captures Dickie's precocity and links him to the lamb image. Clare wrote: "As the mother read, she would share selected bits from here and there and share with the ever growing child mind. 'Little lamb who made thee dost thou know who made thee' sang Blake so long ago little dreaming that the child would sit in the sunlight and hear the song and draw the little lamb with a little bell around its neck."

Dick spent the last weeks of his summer holidays with the Longwells in Blacksburg. Auntie doted on him. He loved licorice, and his cousin Jane remembers that soon after he arrived he suffered from "an overdose of licorice." Uncle Bill was mainly concerned about involving him in manly outdoor activities. A letter home from Richard on 31 August begins:"Dear Clare & Henry/I went to Narrows yesterday and we went on a ferry…"

Dick's relations with the Longwells brought him momentarily into contact with his Roman-Catholic roots. Clare and Henryk had both been raised as Catholics, but neither of them practised their religion as adults. Their defection seems to have been the result of benign neglect rather than any atheistic convictions. In the Grant family, Catholicism simply lapsed after Julie's generation. For the younger generation, it lives in family memorabilia solely because of a dramatic turn it took when the parish priest came calling at Foster Place. Roz's daughter Jane, about nine years old at the time, answered the door and explained that her parents were not home. She did not realize that Henryk Twardzik was in the upstairs apartment, and listening. The priest then lingered a while in the foyer and questioned Jane about the religious practices of her parents and the other occupants of the house. As Henryk listened in silence at the top of the stairs, Jane answered the priest's questions, and proudly informed him that she was the only one in either family who ever went to church.

The Longwells not only attended church regularly, they also took a militant interest in propagating the faith. (Family gossip maintains that Major Longwell was eventually discharged from the Army for his zealous Catholic stance on all matters.) A letter to Dick from Uncle Bill on 29 December 1941, the Christmas season following Dick's visit, says, "Dear Dick/ We were delighted at your Christmas card. It showed the truly Catholic spirit. Keep it up. Hope you can come to Mountain Lake with us again next summer." The letter ends: "Well, God Bless you, old fellow, let me know about serving mass, catechism class and Confirmation, when they happen." He closes the letter with "xxx (count 'em)/Bill," evidently intending his three Xs as symbols the Holy Trinity.

One of the prime attractions for Dick in visiting his great-aunt and uncle was their Irish setter, Sean, the latest in the line of Uncle Bill's purebred Irish setters, one of which had played a role five years earlier in getting Dick back on his feet after his bout with rheumatic fever. Dick's love for dogs was unconditional, and he may have failed to notice that his great-uncle's setters, all of them named Sean, were cowed animals. "Every dog was thin thin thin," Dick's younger cousin Jane remembered, "and severely trained to know their place (low low low), thanks to Uncle Bill. They were beautiful purebreds who did not lead happy lives, I'm afraid." For Sean, and perhaps for Auntie as well, the boy's company in the summer of 1941 must have been a blessed relief.

Besides Sean, one of the highlights of Dick's summer visit to Blacksburg was the BB gun Uncle Bill gave him. He took to it instantly, and the next year, around the time of his eleventh birthday, he began agitating for a .22 caliber rifle. The request caused his parents some consternation, and Clare ultimately appealed to Auntie to put it to rest. "Dear Dick," Auntie wrote in a letter addressed to Master Richard Twardzik on 20 July 1942, "That was a nice letter. Such a lot of news. I do not like the idea of your touching a 22. Your brand new B.B gun is here waiting until your Mother says you can have it and we will mail it to you. I think you ought to stick with the B.B gun until you are older." She closes with a peace offering: "Here is a dollar for spending money."

The visit to Blacksburg nurtured in Dick an interest in the outdoors that lasted for a few more years. Back home in Cambridge, he joined the Boy Scouts, and went camping with his troop. He spent at least one summer and probably more at a camp on Contoocook Lake near West Ringe, New Hampshire, across the Massachusetts border. In 1947, when he was 16, he worked as a counselor there, supervising waterfront activities with the campers.

"Dear Parents," he wrote in a letter postmarked 19 August 1947, "I take my pen in hand to write (?) you of my health and my sincere love of my beloved parents." Most of the spacey handwriting is taken up with a familiar theme: "MY HEALTH on the whole has been pretty good, a cold which kept me in hospital for 2 days, 9 blisters, 4 real bad, and a toe which may be broken at the least badly sprained."

His growing taste in music is also indicated: "Henry: Would you please send me a copy of LOP-POW by 3 Bips and a Bop (on Blue Note)."

Aunt Roz recalled, some 55 years later, her nephew's growing pains from her vantage point in the downstairs apartment:

> "It was in this upstairs-downstairs apartment in Cambridge that I became acquainted with Dick Twardzik, the tease. Fresh from high school, unfailingly, each afternoon he would swing open the front door, rush upstairs, straddle a piano stool and boogie woogie with relentless thumping on our passive ceiling...
>
> "Dick's music is an open door to a stairway, a note struck, and we're off to everywhere.
>
> "One evening he sneaked into my gourmet spice shelf and transferred culinary aromatiques into abstract containers of misnomer. Only now do I understand how a delicious debut of tomato-garlicky chicken with a dismal follow-up of Fanny Farmer 's pasty Fort Lincoln might have hastened his decision to quit eating with us weekly. Was there a family row over having to prepare and fix his meal before going out for the evening? Dick's favorite food: picky-picky fruit cocktail, remnant from a guarded childhood. His least favorite: Clare's peanut butter cookies made from heart-healthy-oleo. His most gleeful accusation: so-and-so is a hood (the forties version of a nerd) followed by a broad grin."

The families separated soon after the War ended, in 1947. Roz and her family moved to Maine, and Clare and her family moved to Danvers, northeast of Boston. It was a kind of dispersal ritual, a grab at personal liberties after the restrictions of the War years. With June and her family standing pat in Newton Center, at the Boston city limits, the Grant girls found themselves separated by several miles and increasingly preoccupied by their own affairs. For the extended Grant clan, the parents and the three daughters, it signaled the effective end of the proximity they had known since childhood.

Thereafter, because of the distance between them and also because of the natural aging of the grandparents and the unnaturally premature death of Richard, there would be few occasions when they would get together in significant numbers, and only one true reunion. That took place at Thanksgiving, probably in 1948 or 1949. The clan gathered at the Grant homestead, in the "avian wallpapered dining-room with an Edwardian bay window," Roz recalled. The three daughters were there with their husbands, Clare with Henryk, June with Ted, Rosamond with Arthur, seated around the dining-room table, extended to its full length by the addition of two leaves. The children, Dick and John and Jane, sat at a card table "where they can yell and throw things in peace," according to Roz. Grandfather Grant is at the head of the table, grumbling because Julie has not yet emerged from the kitchen with the turkey. He is "the yardmaster, responsible for trains leaving on time," Roz said, and "Julie is never on time." When at last she appears bearing the perfect turkey, "beautifully trussed, crisp," on a platter, she has obviously been weeping. She looks around the table at the assembled family and bursts into tears, almost as if she knew, Roz later thinks, it would be the last Thanksgiving for them as a family.

Earlier that afternoon, as the members of the family were arriving, Dick surprised Aunt Roz, whom he had not seen for over a year, with his grown-up ways. He put his hands on her shoulders and kissed her on the cheek. "You look so young!" he said.

Roz would see him only one more time, a few years later. "He was in a white hospital bed with a light white blanket draped over both knees, a frail body unable to withstand the prevailing drug culture. His face was flushed almost red," Roz said, and then she remembered the better part. "He was wiry and filled with fun and ready to go. How Arthur and I and Dick blasted a whole afternoon away."

4 Bouncin' with Bartok

"I'm excited as H— about the new house and can hardly wait to get home," Dick wrote from summer camp at Contoocook Lake on 27 August 1947. The new house excited Clare and Henryk too. It was in Danvers, Mass., 17 miles northeast of Boston, and in that region it was a landmark. It was known as the Samuel Fowler House, named for its original owner, the mill and tannery owner who had the mansion built there, at 166 High Street, in 1809. It was filled with period furniture, and surrounded by rolling lawns. Clare and Henryk moved in as resident custodians of the house and grounds, and they basked in the patrician aura of their surroundings. They lived in part of the house as if to the manor born and kept the rest of it dusted for occasional tours.

It was a Danvers showplace. Tourists could buy postcards of the place. Clare and Henryk would collect their nickels and send three cents to the supplier, the American Art Post Card Co. in nearby Brookline (4.1). Not that the house was architecturally interesting. It was a two-story brick cube with an observation deck on the roof where the peak should be. The walls were mostly ivy-covered except for the large rectangular window-frames that broke the monotony of the stolid architecture and at the same time established their own monotony by their uniformity of design and regularity of placement on both levels.

Grand is the word that sprang to the lips of most tourists. My, what a grand house, they would say, and Clare would accept the compliment demurely. Grand it is, and it is set in a region of considerable historical grandeur. Danvers was founded in 1638 as Salem Village, a name that marked it as an adjunct of neighboring Salem, one of the first colonial settlements in North America. Salem proper became notorious as the site of the witchcraft persecutions of 1689–93, when several women were convicted of sorcery and executed. Salem Village was the actual site of some of the trials, imprisonments and hangings. In 1992, the tercentenary of the trials, Danvers erected the Salem Village Witchcraft Victims' Memorial. By naming the victims, the city government intended it as a monument for expiating the collective guilt of the persecutors, but everyone knows it is there mainly to draw attention to the old witchcraft connection, which has always been the main tourist attraction in the region. Plaques mark the victims' homes, the old stocks are kept on view, and other reconstructions keep the witchcraft era alive in Danvers.

The town's exploitation of its most notorious historical moment for the tourist trade belies the shame originally felt by the Salem Village elders. They petitioned to re-name the village Danvers in hopes that the new name would dissociate it from the Salem scandals, and finally succeeded in 1752. As Danvers, the town played a distinguished role in opposing the British governors in events leading up to the American Revolution. All able-bodied men in the town fought in the Revolutionary armies, and in 1775 seven militiamen from Danvers lost their lives in one of the first battles of the War of Independence.

American independence evokes intensely personal feelings in Danvers to this day, as it does in most of New England, and Samuel Fowler is one of its symbols. He saw his mansion on High Street as a bastion of American spirit. Here he was, the local miller, putting up a homestead as grand as any British duke, right in the heart of Danvers. There are numerous other patriotic links to the new republic on all sides, all of

[illustration 4.1] Postcard of the Samuel Fowler House in Danvers, Massachusetts, Richard Twardzik's family home from 1947 to 1955. From the Twardzik-Thompson Archive, courtesy of Rosamond Thompson and Jane Sumner. All rights reserved.

Folio

Illustration 3.1—Untitled portrait of a boy with sailboat, by Henryk Twardzik, ca. 1935. From the Twardzik-Thompson Archive, courtesy of Rosamond Thompson and Jane Sumner.

[illustration 3.2] Untitled seascape with woman and boy, by Henryk Twardzik, date unknown. From the Twardzik-Thompson Archive, courtesy of Rosamond Thompson and Jane Sumner. All rights reserved.

[illustration 3.8] Young man taking piano lesson with teacher, by Henryk Twardzik, date unknown. From the Twardzik-Thompson Archive, courtesy of Rosamond Thompson and Jane Sumner.

[illustration 4.2] Portrait of an adolescent, by Henryk Twardzik, date unknown. From the Twardzik-Thompson Archive, courtesy of Rosamond Thompson and Jane Sumner.

[illustration 4.7] Mother and son reading a letter, by Henryk Twardzik. Oil painting, undated. From the Twardzik-Thompson Archive, courtesy of Rosamond Thompson and Jane Sumner.

[illustration 9.1] Japanese woodcut, by Reba Stewart. ca. 1958. By permission of
Geneviève McMillan.

1.1. Pacific Jazz S-650
Packaging by William Claxton/Will
McFarland [USA 1956]

5.7. Prestige LP 130 (10")
Designer unknown. [USA 1952]

6.1. Parker Records PLP 404
Produced by Aubrey Mayhew [USA 1962]

7.5. Prestige LP 153 (10")
Photograph and design by Harold
Crowley [USA 1954]

11.1. Storyville EP 426
Design by Burt Goldblatt. James Harrod
collection. [USA 1955]

7.7. Bethlehem BCP 1035 (10")
Photograph and design by Burt Goldblatt.
[USA 1955]

1.2. Pacific Jazz LP 1212
Design by William Claxton. Painting by
Edmund Kohn. [USA 1956]

14.4. Philology W 42-2
Painting by Mary Jo Schwalbach Gitler
[Italy 1991]

14.6. Barclay Disques. Photograph by
Jean-Pierre Leloir [France 1956]

1.4. World–Pacific 1218. Photograph by
William Claxton. Clarke Harris collection
[USA 1956]

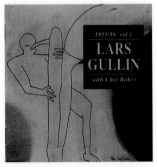

14.8. Dragon DRCD 224. Painting by
Hans Viksten. Design by Willa Westin
[Sweden 1992]

12.3. Pacific Jazz PJ-37. Photograph by
Ron Joy. Design by Woody Woodward
[USA 1962]

them preserved faithfully, in the best New England tradition. Fowler House is listed to this day among the "Places of Interest," and is still open to the public.

The Twardziks knew about Fowler House because their friends, the Brehauts, had moved to Danvers some years earlier, in 1934, as its custodians. Though the Brehauts soon moved into their own house, a 1650 colonial relic they bought from the Fowler estate, the Twardziks had been frequent visitors at both places. Richard had often stayed there with the Brehauts on school vacations.

When Bree Brehaut told Henryk that the custodian position at Fowler House was coming vacant, he lost no time applying. The Twardziks took advantage of the spacious grounds at Fowler House by partitioning a large piece of them for purebred kennels. Clare and Henryk had begun raising German Shepherds as show dogs while they were still apartment-dwellers in Cambridge. Roz remembers Clare making an incongruous entrance at a personnel office to apply for a "crummy position" stuffing envelopes that Roz had recently quit. Clare arrived for the job interview "flanked by two leather leashes of thoroughbred shepherds." She was turned down.

The company of large purebred Shepherds obviously suited Clare, and on the capacious grounds of Fowler House she and Henryk became the proprietors of Harbor Kennels, a name chosen because, Henryk said, "harbor" is the English translation of his Polish surname.

They were benevolent masters. The dogs seemed to spend more time in the house than in their kennels. Visitors to the house were likely to come away more impressed by the noble animals than the antique trappings of the house itself. A letter sent to Henryk near the end of his life from a young neighbor captures something of the atmosphere of the household. The neighbor, Helen Peters, wrote:

> I have such fond memories of the many weekends I spent as a young girl with you and Clare going to dog shows and just visiting your lovely home, enjoying the antiques, the art work and the stained glass. I expect to see dogs, though, every time I turn a corner in the house. I especially expect to see Asia [one of the Shepherds] under the table in the dining room.

In the years to come, when Dick was on the road, his letters to Clare and Henryk seldom failed to inquire about one or another of the dogs. The star of the kennel was a rare black Shepherd named Black Erich. The Brehauts owned one of his offspring, a dog they named Raven. Dick would pay homage to him a few years later by entitling one of his compositions *Black Erich*, an ambitious big band chart that he scored for Herb Pomeroy's rehearsal orchestra.

For a 16-year-old lad with a vivid imagination, Fowler House was a world unto itself. Here he was, the new boy in town, ensconced in American Gothic, with servant stairways leading to hidden rooms in the back of the house, and the front of the house out of bounds for family use. The whiff of colonial dust rose from horsehair chesterfields and yellowing antimacassars. There were hiding places galore for boys and dogs, though the creaking hardwood could give you away if you weren't cunning. Sometimes the hardwood creaked even when no one was there, and the wind rustled the ivy on the windows. When storm clouds rolled in from the sea, the lightning projected strange shadows off antique commodes and ornate chandeliers.

As soon as Dick got to his new home after summer camp, he enrolled at Holten High School in Danvers. The transfer credits that followed him from Cambridge High and Latin School show indifferent results. He had failed Latin in his first year at Cambridge High, replaced it with Geometry in second year and failed it too. His best grades in his first high-school year in Cambridge were in English (79) and Ancient History (82), but in second year his marks dipped perilously close to the 60 percent pass-fail line in all his academic subjects (English 60, German 61, Spanish 63, along with 46 in Geometry).

Only Physical Education, at 78, held much promise, but this provided cold comfort because Dick's interest in athletics and physical activities was waning fast. At Holten High in Danvers, he would manage a pass in Gym in his first year, but the next year, his fourth and final high-school year, he got himself excused from Gym class for two straight terms, probably on health grounds, took a failing grade one term when he couldn't get excused, and withdrew from Gym class altogether in the last term.

The change in attitude toward athletics and outdoor activities stands as a kind of milepost marking the crystallization of young Richard's resolution that he would henceforth seek his fortune in music. He arrived in Danvers completely unknown, of course, though he knew something of the place from his visits to the Brehauts, and he appears to have taken advantage of his anonymity to re-invent himself as an esthete. Doing so led him to reconstruct his identity not qualitatively but quantitatively, beefing up his image as the piano-playing son of the stained-glass master and underplaying the side of him that had been the badge-collecting would-be lifeguard—underplaying him, in a matter of months, to the point of extinction. To his Danvers friends, as to the people in the jazz community who would get to know him in the years to come, the idea that he had once toted a BB gun, gone on Boy Scout hikes, or counseled little kids at summer camp would have seemed simply absurd. "He spent very little time with anything else outside of the arts," his jazz mentor Serge Chaloff would say of him a few years later, by way of explaining why Twardzik showed up for a Boston Red Sox game with a beret on his head and a book sticking out of his pocket.

As Richard matured physically, it had to be admitted that his physique was better suited to the piano bench than the diving board. Henryk was barrel-chested and short-legged, but Richard was narrow across the shoulders and slender, like his mother. His nose took prominence on his face not so much because it was disproportionate but because it had no rival. His forehead was high and sloping, and his chin receded slightly, perhaps not weakly but certainly unassertively.

Henryk Twardzik's artist's eye, attentive as always, caught his son in the transition. An oil portrait captures Richard in the full flush of adolescent ambiguity between the outdoor boy and the deep thinker (4.2, page 48). As Henryk portrays him, it is possible to imagine Richard, with his brush cut and open collar, guarding the dock at Contoocook Lake, but at the same time there can be no doubt that his mind is not on his work. His eyes show a brooding presence, self-involved, bemused, averting his gaze from the anxieties of adulthood but knowing, deep down, that they are coming. It is the face of the alienated adolescent, who was, at the very moment Henryk expressed it so eloquently in his portrait, about to capture the world's imagination in various guises—as James Dean, Holden Caulfield, Nature Boy, Montgomery Clift, Dean Moriarty, Chet Baker, Jean-Paul Belmondo, and many other rebels without causes. When Henryk painted this portrait, around 1947-48, the family's first year in Danvers, soon after Richard turned 17, these iconic figures had not yet surfaced.

Henryk's prescience may indicate that he was in possession of keen artistic antennae, but it may equally indicate that his subject, young Richard, had his own keen antennae. He was sharply attuned to the cultural currents that were about to come into play as he moved toward adulthood.

The year before Richard moved to Danvers, 1946-47, his Cambridge high school transcript includes credits for "Outside Music," thus marking for the first time his progress in private piano lessons. In his two years at Holten High, he would continue to receive credits for "outside music," and he also earned academic credits for participating in Glee Club both years. Those credits bolstered his average, but in fact all his grades would rise fairly dramatically. In both his years at Holten, he studied English (82, 80), history (89, 72) and a modern language—Spanish the first year, French the second—earning a mark of 80 in both of them. (Six years later, Chet Baker would marvel that Twardzik "had begun to speak French after only about a month in France" [1997: 70].)

As his interests in sports and other physical activities shut down, Richard kept up an active social life that centered on music. Clare's cryptic note in her eulogy about "Stravinsky forced on schoolmates" probably refers to events from this period, although they may have begun in Cambridge and carried over to Danvers. One of his classmates in Danvers, Bill Lee, recalled going to the High Street house with a few other friends for music-listening sessions (Turner 1999: 172). Richard would dim the lights in the room and put a classical record on the turntable for his school friends. Afterward, he would probe them for their reactions to the music, and then go to the piano and play classical and jazz pieces for them. "For unsophisticated kids this was quite an experience," Lee told Frederick Turner fifty years later.

Richard settled comfortably into the role of young prodigy that his parents had conferred on him from birth. He posed for a photograph in the manner of a publicity still wearing an ascot and checked sport coat, with the Victorian scrollwork of an upright piano visible over his shoulder (4.2). He cultivated his knowledge of painting and architecture as well as music. After he began traveling as a musician, his letters home often talked about the buildings he had seen and the galleries he had visited. Serge Chaloff wrote in a eulogy for *Metronome* (Chaloff 1956):

> Dick had an unquenchable desire for learning. He was never without books covering all forms of art and Philosophy and spent every available moment at Symphony concerts, Art museums and of course his practising. Even after some very late gigs, he would still be at his piano the next morning at nine o'clock practising so that his afternoon would be free to study the other forms of art that he loved.

He came by his predilections honestly, of course, surrounded by antiques in households where one corner was set aside as his father's art studio. It was not only his parents who nurtured his esthetic interests. In Cambridge, his Uncle Arthur had also hived off a corner of the downstairs apartment for his studio. To young Dick, it must have seemed perfectly normal for the man of the family to dabble in art.

Aunt Roz remembers Dick discussing "the onset of abstractionism and stream of consciousness writing coming out of Europe and Canada" with the adults in the household. One of the forms his teenage rebellion took was an aggressively modernist stance in music and art. He espoused Bartók over Beethoven, and Schoenberg over Schumann. He championed abstract art, and he was beginning to cast a critical eye over his Uncle Arthur's impressionist landscapes and his father's conservatory tableaux. The new rage was action painting, which was transmuting bebop spontaneities onto canvases laid out on garret floors. Next to Jackson Pollock and his friends, Arthur's and Henryk's canvases seemed Jurassic. Uncle Arthur made a spirited response to his nephew in the ongoing debate. Roz says Arthur painted "four large acrylic non-objectives whose graduating musical circles frightened anyone prone to hysteria."

In Danvers, Richard was naturally stirred to make his own personal proclamations about the main currents of the day. Dazzling his school chums with boogie-woogie soon grew stale, and eventually even the uncanny ambidexterities of Béla Bartók's piano solos in book IV of *Mikrokosmos* came to seem like hollow victories, gratifying in the praise they evoked but somehow impersonal. Richard began searching for his own musical microcosm. Eventually, of course, he would map it out

in *A Crutch for the Crab* and *The Girl from Greenland*. The first steps in
the search came, as far as we will ever know, with a composition called
Bouncin' with Bartok (4.3).

When I came upon the manuscript of *Bouncin' with Bartok* in Twardzik's
effects, there was a kind of archeologist's thrill. Here was an original
piece of music, unknown to the world. There would surely be more, I
thought at the time. But there was no more. It is the only music found
among Twardzik's effects except for a performance score of *The Fable
of Mabel*. So the romantic dream of unearthing a cache of unknown
compositions was met by the reality of one piece of juvenilia that
Richard composed, almost certainly, sometime in 1947–49, his Danvers
high school years.

The words "*Bouncin' with Bartok* by Dick Twardzik" are neatly printed
across the top of the staff paper, in black, indelible India ink, and the
piece is transcribed in the same ink and with the same fastidious hand.

[illustration 4.3] Richard as teenage prodigy. From the Twardzik-Thompson Archive,
courtesy of Rosamond Thompson and Jane Sumner. All rights reserved.

It is a transcription style that is far removed from the process of composition. It is clearly intended to give the final draft the permanence of printed sheet music, and it is easy to imagine its 18-year-old composer bent over the pages and setting down the notes just so for posterity.

Juvenilia it may be, but *Bouncin' with Bartok* is sophisticated enough to be daunting for amateurs. In its density of tied notes and especially in its independence of left and right hands, it superficially resembles the pieces in *Mikrokosmos*, but it does not seem to be beholden to any particular piece by Bartók. The reference to him in the title is apparently to his spirit. As the only original music in Twardzik's effects, it takes on iconic significance. I was dying to hear it performed, but incapable of playing it myself and at the same time reluctant to surrender completely the thrill of coming to grips with it in rehearsal. So I found a compromise. I persuaded the Toronto jazz piano player, Ron Davis, to rehearse the piece while I sat beside him, talking about it with him and taping the whole process.

Ron did not require much persuasion. Although he was born a couple of years after Twardzik died, Ron owned the *Trio* CD and admired it. If that wasn't enough, when he heard the title he was sold; as a student, he had cut his teeth on *Mikrokosmos*. Not only that, Ron has a history of sticking his neck out. After struggling to make it as a jazz piano player when he finished high school, he made a detour into law school. After practising law for a few years and playing occasional gigs, he grew restless again and returned to university to take a Ph.D. in French linguistics. He worked in academe for a few years, and then went back to full-time piano playing with a little backroom legal work to supplement his income. With a background like that, a cold rehearsal in the presence of a tape-recorder was hardly intimidating.

Bouncin' with Bartok is a 74-bar piece in 2/4 time. It is by no means jazz, though it has blue notes and, in a few places, an insistent beat, which is what gives it its "bounce." But each rhythmic pattern is set up in order to be upset. "He keeps throwing these twists and turns in," Ron said on running afoul of the reversible shift from double notes to single notes in the bass clef at bar 52.

The piece does not have a key, or a chordal pattern. It is organized in thematic segments with two- or three-bar transitions. The longest segment takes in the first 18 bars, in which the opening eight-bar melody

[illustration 4.4] Bouncin' with Bartok by Dick Twardzik, ca. 1947–49. From the Twardzik-Thompson Archive, courtesy of Rosamond Thompson and Jane Sumner. All rights reserved.

is repeated an octave lower in bars 11–18. A twelve-bar sequence (33–44) with thick, rhapsodic, two-fisted chords gives way to bright, sixteenth-note repetitions for ten bars (45–54). A three-bar transition (at 29–32) reminded me of the transition to the main melody at the end of *A Crutch for the Crab*. When we took a break after a couple of hours and listened to Twardzik's records, Ron agreed. When *Albuquerque Social Swim* came on, he said *Bouncin' with Bartok* "is from the same essential soundscape." And it certainly is, however indefinable that might be.

Clearly, *Bouncin' with Bartok* was intended by Twardzik as his party piece, an extravaganza for him to show off in company, especially, perhaps, when the girls were watching. It was his own *Soda Fountain Rag*, another piece of juvenilia written 30 years earlier by another 18-year-old, Duke Ellington, for the sole purpose of turning heads.

Seeing *Bouncin' with Bartok* as a party piece clears up one of its anomalies. Its first eight bars are written with exactly the same notes in the
treble clef for both hands. Taken literally, the notation would require
the pianist to place the right hand on top of the left and depress each
key with two fingers. The musical result, of course, would be exactly
the same as if the pianist used *either* the right hand *or* the left to play
those notes. So, literally, Twardzik has two hands doing the work of one.
When Ron Davis played these bars, he gave both hands different work
by transposing the right hand up an octave and playing unison lines
in the treble clef. It sounded fine, but I suspect Twardzik intended his
notation to be taken literally, with those eight bars played by the two
hands laid one on top of the other on the same keys. It does nothing
for the sound of the piece, but it certainly makes a great visual impression, like legerdemain. There is more than a little legerdemain in
Bouncin' with Bartok, as there also is, come to think of it, in Twardzik's
later compositions.

It is easy to imagine Twardzik dazzling his high-school friends with
a bit of boogie, throwing in a bit of Debussy, maybe *Fêtes* from *Deux
Nocturnes,* and then capping it off with 74 well-rehearsed bars of flying fingers. What the heck was that? his friends would say. It's a little
something I'm working on, says Richard, with a shrug. Wow! they say.
I call it *Bouncin' with Bartok,* he says. Cool!

Although Twardzik's piano studies exposed him mainly to the classical repertoire, his interests in jazz were also developing. He joined
something called the Interracial Jazz Society, writing away to their
headquarters at 1406 Madison Avenue in Baltimore, Maryland, and
receiving an "Honorary Member" card duly signed by its president,
one Jerry Blumberg.

Henryk had an interest in jazz that undoubtedly stimulated Richard's
interests in the first place. Henryk's sketchbook, which served him as
a kind of diary, includes a rapid pencil sketch of a jazz band in action
(4.5). A scribbled note in the margin indicates that the bandleader is
Sidney Bechet, the New Orleans jazz pioneer (1897–1959), and it is
likely that Henryk sketched him onstage in 1953 at Storyville, the
Boston jazz club named after the district in New Orleans where jazz
originated and where, incidentally, Bechet grew up. A couple of years
before Bechet played in Boston, he had moved as an expatriate to
France, where he became a national celebrity. He seldom returned to

the United States after that, but Storyville's enterprising young owner, George Wein, scored a coup by persuading Bechet to play an engagement at his club. Wein knew Bechet from having played piano in his band as an emergency fill-in when Wein was still in college, and he would play piano for Bechet again for the engagement at his club (as heard on *Sidney Bechet at Storyville* [1201 Music CD]).

When Sidney Bechet played in Boston, Twardzik had been playing professionally for three years and his jazz bearings were well established. By then, he must have found his father's affection for an old-timer like Bechet laughable, and maybe even embarrassing. The prevailing mood in the jazz world at that moment was split sharply between traditionalists and modernists. The warring camps were labeled in the rhetoric of the day as "moldy figs" on one side (or "Mouldy Fygges," to the advanced wits) and "cats" on the other. The cats originally called themselves "hepcats," but that word quickly developed its own stigma. ("When it was hip to be hep, I was hep," Dave Frishberg wrote in a song called *I'm Hip*.)

The split between the two camps was tense, with much name-calling on both sides and utter contempt for those who lined up on the other side. But then, at the time, the whole world was tense, with the threat of instant atomic destruction looming over the suburbs and Commie sympathizers supposedly conspiring to overthrow democracy in every office block. It should have been the best of times, after the privations of the war years, now that the world was at peace and industries were throbbing to turn out cars with fins and television sets with rabbit ears. But people seemed reluctant to relax. The world of jazz was hardly exempt, even with its newfound cultural resonance as concert music and its upwardly mobile audience. The atmosphere, in fact, was frigid. "During these Cold War years, fans split into factions, and factions subdivided faster than suburban real estate," Ted Gioia (1997: 278) says in his history of the music. "Of course jazz had always been a source of controversy, since at least the time of Buddy Bolden. Only now the disputes were mostly fratricidal, with few besides jazz fans paying attention."

Bechet was decidedly a moldy fig, and among the cats his broad vibrato and raw emotions made him Public Enemy No. 1. Vibrato and emotion were both anathema to the bebop esthetic, which promulgated straight tones and cool detachment. "Play without any vibrato," Miles

Davis's first trumpet teacher told him, in an anecdote known to every hipster. "You're gonna get old anyway and start shaking" (Davis 1957).

So intense was the rancor between the two sides that most adherents were blinded to any notion that there might be common ground. In fact, both sides denied that the other side played jazz at all. Some of the heat generated in the controversy comes through in letters to the editor from the time (quoted by Feather 1987: 87, 88–89). From a moldy fig:

> Every single year there's a new crop of phoneys—black and white—trying to pervert or suppress or emasculate jazz. This year it's Diz Gillespie... The professional vipers—the real mad cats— headed by Diz Gillespie...try to cut the heart out of the real main line jazz...because they want to be frantic.

From a hepcat:

> Just as the fascists tend to divide group against group..., so do the moldy figs try to categorize New Orleans, Chicago, swing music and 'the real jazz'... The moldy figs are frustrated by their musical illiteracy, just as they are frustrated by their inability to foist their idiotic views on the public, and frustrated by the ever-increasing public acceptance of the critics and musicians they hate.

The jazz world into which Twardzik was insinuating himself in his Danvers years was, for better or worse, a world of passion and hotly held convictions.

To high-school kids initiated into modern jazz in the late 1940s and 1950s, myself among them, Sidney Bechet seemed hopelessly out-dated. (It is sobering to realize that he was only in his fifties.) For me, it took some fifteen years before I could bring myself to listen to Bechet's recordings, sometime in the late 1960s, after he was dead and gone, and then only because I chanced upon Duke Ellington's state-ment that Bechet was "the very epitome of jazz" (Ellington 1965: 14). In the hipster *Weltansicht* that formed my first tastes and those of my contemporaries in the first world-wide, socially mixed audience for concert jazz, Bechet was corny, Louis Armstrong was exhausted after recording the Hot Fives in his long-vanished youth, and Eddie Con-don, court jester of the moldy figs, self-confessed inept rhythm-guitar player and mock leader of Chicago-style free-for-alls, was prized for his wit—"The boppers flat their fifths. We consume ours," he said (in 1947)—but pitied for the pseudo-music he represented.

Beyond any doubt, Twardzik inherited these hepcat prejudices, probably all the stronger for the virulence with which they were held by Serge Chaloff, Charlie Mariano, and the other leaders of the Boston jazz scene when he arrived to take his place in it.

Twardzik's early exposure to jazz was filled with more than the moldy figs his father listened to. Boston, in his formative years, was as good a place as any to hear the real cats as well. Roz remembers "on warm evenings, Dick and Uncle Arthur pal-up and hang out for a concert of Dizzy Gillespie or whoever is hot."

As his high-school years neared completion, Twardzik was eager to test his performing skills in professional company. Bob Zieff, who would

[illustration 4.5] Pencil sketch of Sidney Bechet and his band, probably at Storyville in Boston in October 1953, by Henryk Twardzik. From the Twardzik-Thompson Archive, courtesy of Rosamond Thompson and Jane Sumner.

later become Twardzik's teacher, came across him for the first time at a Sunday afternoon jam session at the Melody Lounge in Lynn, ten miles north of Boston and only three miles south of Danvers on route 107, the main highway. The brief encounter probably took place in 1948 (not 1946 as sometimes reported). Zieff remembers that a friend of his, Bob Kendall, a New York bassist, was one of the players on the stand when the 17-year-old strode in with his father a few paces behind him. "The kid was wearing the jazzman's obligatory dark glasses," Zieff told Frederick Turner (1999: 170), "but there was no pretence when he sat in on piano. All the other pianists were still caught up with swing star Teddy Wilson, but when the young Twardzik kid put his hands on the keys, out came the avant-garde styles of Art Tatum, Bud Powell, and Tadd Dameron." Two years later, Twardzik would importune Serge Chaloff at another Lynn jazz club to let him sit in.

His reputation spread locally. Herb Pomeroy, a high-school trumpet player from nearby Gloucester who was about to enter Schillinger House, heard about him. "A mutual friend of ours took me to his house and I never heard anything like it in my life," Pomeroy said (Gross 1998: 10). The impression the 17-year-old made on the jazz-crazy 18-year-old could trigger his boyish enthusiasm years afterward. "He had magnificent technique," Pomeroy said. "He understood classical literature and he could swing so hard. He understood Bud Powell and Thelonious Monk. Harmonically he was a combination of the most advanced bebop of the day and 20th-century classical music."

Twardzik's Danvers years appear to be an interlude for marshalling his resources to face the larger world. His sense of style in both his personal image and his music crystallized there. His improved high-school record suggests that Dick was happy with the school and with the company he was keeping.

As he lost the adolescent gawkiness, it became obvious that his features, like his physique, came mostly from Clare (4.6). Richard was fine-boned, with none of Henryk's solidity. The point was not lost on Henryk. In his paintings, he exaggerated, or perhaps idealized, the resemblance of mother and son. One oil painting shows mother and son perusing a letter, their heads together (4.7, page 49). The mood of the characters is somber, and the painting was perhaps intended as a dramatization of a family receiving news of wartime casualties, a familiar situation at the time, and one that would have been readily recognized

[illustration 4.6] Richard with Clare, in the garden of Samuel Fowler House, Danvers. From the Twardzik-Thompson Archive, courtesy of Rosamond Thompson and Jane Sumner. All rights reserved.

by contemporary viewers of the painting. The painting gains its drama from the closeness of mother and son, the feeling of shared intimacy, reflected in both their posture and their appearance.

Richard organized his first piano trio as a teenager in Danvers. He was photographed at the piano with an unidentified guitarist and drummer in Samuel Fowler House (4.8). The colonial trappings are incongruous, and the sheet music spread out in front of Richard looks like a hipster put-on. It is *Jesu Joy of Man's Desiring*, though the demeanor of the musicians hardly suggests that they are playing Bach.

The photograph catches Richard in high spirits, without shades or sham. The sense of well-being in his Danvers years envelops him. His high-school transcript shows that he missed 19 school days in his third year and 25 in his senior year, but it is impossible to guess if the absences should be attributed to ill health or to other diversions, like rehearsals and occasional gigs. The last lines of the transcript record that Richard Twardzik earned 75.5 credits, and that he graduated on 9 June 1949.

With high school behind him and seemingly unbounded talent pushing him to explore new worlds, Twardzik seemed eminently equipped for the decade that was about to dawn. The 1930s of his infant years had imposed the privations of economic depression and the 1940s of his youth had carried the rationings of war. The 1950s, when he would come to manhood, held the promise of peace and plenty. It was a time when music and the other arts could take their rightful places. Nothing in the world was more serious.

For Henryk and Clare Twardzik, the possibilities for their young prodigy must have seemed endless. Genius will out. "They raised their son, and then, you know, they let him go his own way," Crystal Joy, a singer and piano player who was Twardzik's girlfriend in the last two years of his life, told me many years later. "And I think they were disappointed, really." Certainly they were if it was personal peace and material plenty they hoped for in their only child. He would find neither. But it appears that he wanted neither. He wanted something else entirely, and it is not at all clear whether or not he found it.

[illustration 4.8] Richard at the piano with unidentified drummer and guitarist. Photograph "by Ken" (written in pencil verso). From the Twardzik-Thompson Archive, courtesy of Rosamond Thompson and Jane Sumner. All rights reserved.

5 Madame Chaloff & Son

It is not certain when Richard began studying with Madame Chaloff of the New England Conservatory of Music. He seems to have taken lessons from her intermittently for a number of years, perhaps as his schedule permitted after he began playing professionally and traveling. This protracted schedule indicates that she taught him privately rather than as a student at the Conservatory or the Berklee School of Music or Boston University, where Madame Chaloff was an adjunct faculty member.

Margaret Stedman Chaloff (1896–1977) was a legendary teacher. Although she taught the classical regimen, she was especially prized by jazz pianists because she understood their special interests and loved the music they were striving to make. She was proud to let people know that Charlie Parker referred to her as "Mama" (Williams 1970: 237). Leonard Bernstein was one of her most celebrated students. Jazz pianists who studied with her include George Shearing, Ralph Burns, George Wein, Toshiko Akiyoshi, Steve Kuhn, Herbie Hancock, Chick Corea, Keith Jarrett, and Mulgrew Miller, as well as Twardzik.

Madame Chaloff was English by birth. Her Russian surname came from her husband, Julius L. Chaloff (1892–1979), himself a graduate of the New England Conservatory of Music in 1910. Julius would become the pianist for the Boston Symphony and proprietor of the Chaloff School of Music on Newbury Street in Boston, but in his early days he taught at the New England Conservatory, and one of his students there was Margaret Stedman, who had emigrated to America to pursue her studies and seek playing opportunities.

Margaret and Julius Chaloff married in 1919 and raised two sons, Richard (b. 1920), an engineer, and Serge (1923–57), a renowned jazz musician who would return to Boston, fatefully, at the very moment that 18-year-old Dick Twardzik was setting out from Danvers to seek his fortune in the jazz world.

Twardzik, according to Serge Chaloff, "was studying classical piano technique and interpretation with my mother" at the time of his death in 1955 (Chaloff 1956). He first came to Madame Chaloff some years before that, perhaps the year after his graduation from Holten High, and she must have been impressed with the performance skills he brought

in the classical repertoire and his abiding interest in modern composers as well as his predilection for jazz. She had a reputation for instill-
ing keyboard discipline and thoughtfulness in her students. She could
also, according to her son Richard, play pyrotechnical swing "like Art
Tatum" (Simosko 1998: 15).

Madame Chaloff's teaching methods came to be celebrated under the
rubric of "the Russian technique." Exactly how the technique might
have been enacted on Twardzik is impossible to guess. The descriptions
from Chaloff's alumni indicate a highly individualized, even idiosyn-
cratic, kind of pedagogy. Sumi Tonooka, an American who studied with
Chaloff in the 1970s, describes her lessons as if they were some kind
of digital aerobics. "She had me pretend that I had holes on the tips
of my fingers and that I was *blowing* on the keys," Tonooka said. "She
was trying to impress upon me the importance of thinking in breath-
length phrases, which horn players do automatically" (Davis 1986: 92).
Toshiko Akiyoshi, who took private lessons with Chaloff around the
same time as Twardzik, when she was a Japanese visa student at Berklee,
seems to have been subjected to a kind of brainwave inversion. "Before, my method was to move the fingers and let the brain remember
the movements by repetitive playing," Akiyoshi said (Lyons 1983: 253).
"She taught me to reverse that process. Am I making this clear? She
had me learn music so that I could tell her the order of the notes backwards." Steve Kuhn got elements of both these methods, along with
some spiritual calisthenics (Lyons 1983: 233):

> You breathe as if you were playing a horn, from the diaphragm. You
> think of your fingertips as a reed and the keys as a mouthpiece. The
> sound comes out of you; it travels to the soundboard and out of
> the piano… If you want an incredible sforzando, the sound should
> come from the bottom of the feet, and you should push off the
> floor so that the sound travels up through the feet, the knees, the
> hips, the torso, through your shoulder and elbow, and out through
> the fingertips.

(Kuhn's interviewer, Len Lyons, responds to this statement by saying,
"It sounds like a fairly traditional method of tone production." Really.)
All Mulgrew Miller would say was, "It was a unique experience. She
was a very spiritual and mystical woman and she had this very involved
technique" (Simosko 1998: 5). Amen to that.

The only concrete evidence that remains of Twardzik's relation with Madame Chaloff is a note he wrote to her in pencil on staff paper from the Berklee School. It says on one side: "TO MRS. CHALOFF" (5.1). On the other side is "1 BAR OF THE FABLE OF MABLE," referring to Twardzik's composition (with *Mabel* misspelled *Mable* in Twardzik's characteristic way). Twardzik wrote *The Fable of Mabel* in the fall of 1951, when he began working with Serge Chaloff. It was not recorded for three more years, until September 1954 (and is the subject of a later chapter). The note to Madame Chaloff could date from the time of either performance, but it seems likely to be from its first performances. It is tempting to think that the bar that Twardzik transcribed for her might have originated in an exercise she devised for him or directed him to.

"She was a beautiful person," said Crystal Joy about Madame Chaloff. Crystal Joy had taken up the piano as a youngster mainly so she could accompany herself as a singer, and Madame Chaloff worked with her on exercises but appears not to have unloaded the full weight of the Russian technique on her. "She told me, 'Do your own thing'," Crystal Joy said. "Obviously I wasn't going to be a classical pianist." She also contacted a vocal coach for her. Crystal Joy started taking lessons with her in 1956, after Twardzik died, when she found herself visiting Madame Chaloff's Back Bay apartment to keep company with her son Serge, who had been Twardzik's mentor and who became in the last years of his own life, in Crystal Joy's words, "my good buddy."

Madame Chaloff's younger son returned home to Boston in 1950. He was famous by then in the jazz world because he had been a star in Woody Herman's Second Herd, a jazz orchestra that had rivaled Duke Ellington's and Count Basie's in inventiveness and Stan Kenton's in derring-do. When Herman disbanded the Second Herd in November 1949, Serge Chaloff was immediately picked up by Count Basie, who had also disbanded his big band and was trying his luck with an octet. With Basie, Chaloff joined a stellar group of young boppers including trumpeter Clark Terry, clarinetist Buddy de Franco and tenor saxophonist Wardell Gray in what was, for Basie, a desperate attempt at finding an audience by abandoning Kansas City swing for the new sounds. Chaloff made the first tour with the Basie Octet and cut a few records with them, and then he quit to return home to Boston, eleven years after leaving as a seventeen-year-old to travel with the Tommy Reynolds orchestra.

By breaking up their big bands in 1949, Herman and Basie added their names to a growing list of ex-bandleaders. At the end of the 1940s, the swing era was finished, and the big bands faced bankruptcy. Popular music had become the domain of singers—crooners and thrushes for the moment, but there was a grass-roots movement that favored punchy rhythms and more primitive lyrics, audible as long ago as the young camper's request for *Lop Pow* by Three Bips and a Bop. In a few years it would rise to the surface under the name rock 'n' roll.

Changing tastes in popular music were dictated partly by new-style domestic arrangements that were taking hold at the time. Suburban living brought with it nightly exoduses from the inner cities, where the jazz clubs were located, and daily commuting for work took the joy out of driving to exurban dance pavilions on the weekend. Hi-fi systems brought music into rec rooms, and the promotional patter claimed that if you got the right tweeters and woofers it sounded just like the band was right there in the room. Television arrived with the force of a modern miracle. Night clubs and dance halls were not the only victims. Movie theaters closed, band shells fell into disrepair, piano teachers scuffled, sheet music disappeared, touring stage companies became relics. Ellington kept his band together through it all, and Herman re-formed his new band, the Third Herd, in 1951, as did Basie, but they would be among the few to claim a share of what had suddenly become a niche market.

The long-term consequences were barely visible in 1950. Serge Chaloff returned to Boston in triumph. In the Second Herd, he had been one of the Four Brothers, the vaunted saxophone section with Stan Getz, Zoot Sims and Herbie Steward on tenor saxophones and Chaloff on baritone. They were largely responsible for the distinctive sound of the band, celebrated in their namesake recording, *Four Brothers*, composed by Jimmy Giuffre (recorded December 1947). Giuffre's voicing gave Getz the lead with Chaloff playing in unison an octave below him and the other two tenors harmonizing in between. Their sound had a rich resonance in the absence of higher-pitched reeds, alto saxophones or clarinets, part of the conventional blend, but it also managed to be surprisingly supple. The "Four-Brothers sound" became a catchword. Musicians imitated it, and fans latched onto it as the latest thing.

Even before his term with Herman in 1947–49, Chaloff was well known. He started playing with Boston-area bands at 16, in 1939, and hit the road with name bands at 20. From 1943 until he joined Herman, he traveled the country with the bands of Shep Fields, Ina Ray Hutton, Boyd Raeburn, Georgie Auld and Jimmy Dorsey. In his years with Herman and immediately after, he won polls in both *Down Beat* (1949–51) and *Metronome* (1949–53) as the leading baritone saxophone player.

Chaloff's reputation in jazz circles was based in the first place on his astonishing dexterity. Baritone saxophones stand about three and a half feet tall, with over two feet of tubing doubled up along the shaft at the bottom to form the bell, and nearly another foot coiled at the top of the shaft to form the mouthpiece. They are attractive to look at in the way steam locomotives are attractive, for the feeling of force and power.

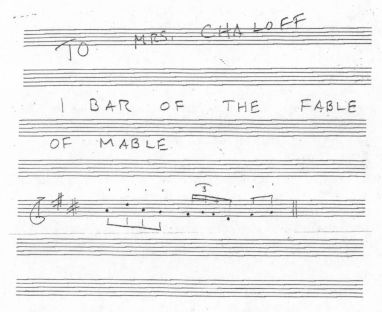

Berklee School of Music — formerly Schillinger House — Boston, Mass.

Burrows Music Co., Inc.

[illustration 5.1] Note from Richard Twardzik to Madame Chaloff, his piano teacher, probably Fall 1951. From the Twardzik-Thompson Archive, courtesy of Rosamond Thompson and Jane Sumner.

They are also ungainly and heavy, and playing them requires moving a formidable column of air. In Chaloff's formative years, the prevailing bebop esthetic demanded technical fluency. Dizzy Gillespie and Charlie Parker set the standards, and their standards included unbounded range from the top to the bottom of their instruments and eighth or sixteenth note runs at allegro tempos. That came much easier on their instruments, trumpet and alto saxophone, than on many others, but the boppers made no allowances for that. Trombonists struggled at first, hampered by the imprecision of the slide, but eventually players like J.J. Johnson and Kai Winding emerged with precise and rapid intonation that made their bebop lines almost indistinguishable from a valved instrument.

Baritone saxophone posed obvious hazards, requiring coordination of the air column with manipulation of intricate, spaced-out keys. Yet Chaloff played his baritone as facilely as his brothers in the Herman band played their tenors, and he did so without sacrificing any of its fullness. Parker was his inspiration. "At first I listened to Harry Carney and Jack Washington, the baritone men with Duke and Count. That's how I formed my first style," he said in the liner note to *Boston Blow-Up* (1955). "But it was an alto man, the great Charlie Parker, whose work made me change my style." Chaloff was the first baritone saxophone player to succeed at playing bebop, and, thanks to a few small-band recordings he made after his Herman days, including *The Fable of Mabel* with Richard Twardzik, he remains the paragon of bop baritone to this day.

Besides being a great saxophone player, Serge Chaloff was also a heroin addict, and had been for years. Some accounts say that his return to Boston was motivated by his desire to clean himself up. His brother Richard said he talked obsessively about the time his closest friend in the Herman band, trumpeter Sonny Berman, "had died literally right in his arms from an overdose" when they were shooting up together (Simosko 1998: 30). But that had happened in January 1947, almost three years before, and there is no evidence that Chaloff seriously tried to cure his addiction then or any time in his first four years back in Boston. The idea that he went home to clean up has no more credence than the wry claim that Woody Herman broke up the Second Herd to rid himself of Serge Chaloff, which is not literally true but makes a point.

Chaloff was notoriously self-indulgent, a mama's boy who did whatever he felt like doing and scoffed at the consequences. Ralph Burns, Madame Chaloff's student who went on to become the chief arranger for Herman's First Herd, attended high school with Serge in Newton, Massachusetts, but they were never friends in spite of their common interests. "I never used to pay any attention to him then because he was kind of like a nutty kid," Burns said (Lees 1995: 90). The die was cast. Saxophonist Al Cohn, who knew him briefly when their tenures with Herman overlapped, said, "Serge would always be drunk. He was quite a drinker. Whatever he did, he did too much" (Gitler 1985: 238–39).

Stories about his escapades are plentiful. One of his Herman bandmates, vibraphonist Terry Gibbs, used to figure out his hotel accommodations based on where Chaloff was staying (Gitler 1985: 237–38):

> When we checked into a hotel…if he was on the [tenth floor], I'd go to the ninth because [then I knew] I could get out of the hotel. Serge Chaloff had a way, 'cause we all know that Serge was sick those days. He'd fall asleep with a cigarette all the time and always burn a hole in the mattress. Always! In about twelve hotels. When we'd go to check out, the hotel owner—Serge always had his hair slicked down, even though he hadn't taken a bath in three years. He had his hair slicked down and when we'd check out the manager would say, 'Mr. Chaloff, you burnt a hole in your mattress and—' 'How *dare* you, I'm the winner of the *Down Beat* and *Metronome* polls. How dare you?' After the conversation, the manager would always say, 'I'm sorry, Mr. Chaloff,' and apologize to him.

Johnny Mandel, one of Herman's arrangers, remembered an occasion in San Diego when "Serge, with his big mouth, succeeded in infuriating some sailors. They were going to take him apart," until some other band members rescued him (Lees 1995: 173).

Chaloff was not the kind of addict who aroused pity. He was arrogant and acid-tongued. He ridiculed anyone whose values were different from his own, especially musically. His old boss Woody Herman (1913–87) was one of the people who bore the brunt of it. Twenty years older than Chaloff and most of the other musicians in his Second Herd, Herman played swing-style clarinet and alto saxophone and sang in a plain-spoken, unschooled style. Chaloff and some of his confreres, especially Stan Getz and Zoot Sims, mocked Herman nightly on the bandstand, making gagging motions and holding their noses when he soloed or sang.

Chaloff had a satanic reputation as (in Whitney Balliett's words) "a drug addict whose proselytizing ways with drugs reportedly damaged more people than just himself" (1972: 382). One of Herman's biographers says, bluntly, about Chaloff, "Hiring him must be accounted one of Woody's worst errors. Serge was a serious heroin addict and, like so many of his kind, a dedicated proselytizer for the drug. He would hook a number of Second Herd bandsmen" (Lees 1995: 153). But blame is hard to fix. Chaloff could be charming and witty, and if some of his bandmates were naïve enough to think he was that way because he was a junkie, it was hardly his fault if they fell in with him. Most of them had tried heroin before they met him, and some of them were already into it as deeply as he was.

On his return to Boston, Chaloff moved into his mother's apartment in the Back Bay area. Madame Chaloff nagged him privately about getting medical help for his addiction and protected him publicly. Her loyalty to her younger son was sorely tested but it never wavered. One of her young students, Steve Kuhn, said, "He was very abusive to Margaret in many ways. He would be taking appliances from her house and pawning them and being physically abusive to her and she just had the patience of a saint" (Simosko 1998: 78). Steve Adamson, one of Chaloff's saxophone students, recounted this tale (Simosko 1998: 78–79):

> I had two horns, a tenor sax…and an alto… Serge would borrow the horns, as he told me for gigs, and I wouldn't see the horn. I would lose track of the horn, Serge, everything, and I would call his mother, and she was just in resignation, saying, 'Oh, that again!' He hocked them, and she knew where to go. She would fetch the horns, or horn. I would go to her house, get the horn. I would pick up the horn just from Margaret. Serge wouldn't be around. I was on friendly terms with her. Serge would come and give me the lesson, and somewhere along the line borrow a horn or two and we would go through this. I think we went through this two or three times.

Adamson's patience seems as surprising as Madame Chaloff's, but Serge Chaloff had a way with people. Even Steve Kuhn, despite his reverence for Madame Chaloff, prefaced his memories of Chaloff's mistreatment of her by saying, "Serge was like a big brother to me."

Whatever his personal baggage, Serge Chaloff's return to Boston added spice to bubbling jazz culture. The 1950s were, as almost every Boston musician told me, a golden period for Boston jazz. The expansion of Berklee School from the former Schillinger House made it the first jazz conservatory of international stature anywhere, and it attracted scholarship students from all over the United States and the world. Several clubs in Boston and the surrounding towns booked jazz regularly, and there was a strong pool of local musicians, several of them destined to make their names nationally as the decade went on. Though it would take a few years to crystallize, the Boston musicians came to realize that they were a good as anyone, maybe better. "All the musicians in New York knew about the musicians in Boston and vice versa," said Sam Rivers, who would make his reputation as a tenor saxophonist after moving to New York from Boston in the 1960s. "Boston musicians, I mean, had a better musical education than New York musicians. We sort of looked down on the reputation of the New York musicians because they were all there before they were ready. We knew that. They got the on-the-job training. We waited and got ourselves together first and then we went to New York" (Cohen and Fitzgerald 2002: 60).

Serge Chaloff's homecoming took place near the beginning of the Boston jazz naissance, and was one of its seminal events. He swaggered back into Boston and quickly established himself as a regular at the Hi Hat, one of the two preeminent jazz clubs, and also at a seedier place across town called the Petty Lounge. At the Hi Hat, he found work fronting the local band that alternated with the featured attraction. The Hi Hat had a radio hook-up, and Chaloff's appearances there got radio exposure on remote broadcasts and helped keep his national reputation alive. (Two broadcasts are preserved on *Boston 1950* [Sunenblick 1994].) "Chaloff could fill a club," said Gus Dixon, a professional musician before settling down as a club owner. "In 1950, he played my club, the Red Fox Café in Lynn, on a Monday night. I had placed an ad in the *Boston Daily Record*, and the place was jammed. He was phenomenal" (Sunenblick 1994: 2).

It was in Dixon's club that Chaloff first ran into Richard Twardzik. Chaloff recalled the occasion a few years later (Chaloff 1956):

My first meeting with Dick Twardzik occurred one night in early September, 1950, a night I shall always remember… I had just left the Woody Herman Band and was in Boston doing a few singles

at the various Jazz Clubs around town. This particular night I was
playing at a club called the "Red Fox," owned by a fellow that once
played trombone for the Georgie Auld band in 1945, his name Gus
Dixon. During the evening a very young, studious, good looking
boy came over to me and asked if he could sit in for a couple of
numbers. I hated to comply with him, as he was so young-looking.
It didn't seem possible that a fellow his age could be playing some
of the music that was being played. He sat in with us for a set and
amazed everyone at the session with his fluent and original ideas.
He had a completely new approach to his piano playing and in the
way he voiced his chords. Dick was about eighteen years old at the
time.

For Twardzik, the chance encounter was a perfectly timed. Chaloff had
been using Nat Pierce on piano when he first returned to Boston, but
Pierce was a leader in his own right, who devoted most of his energy
to leading his own big band, a rehearsal orchestra featuring the best
Boston jazz musicians that was the focal point of the jazz community.
Early in 1951, a few months after Twardzik took his place for one set
at the Red Fox, Pierce would leave town to join Woody Herman as
pianist and arranger in Herman's Third Herd, the successor to the Four
Brothers band, in what would turn into a long association.

Even before Pierce left Boston, Twardzik became Chaloff's piano player whenever he needed to put together a band. They shared more
than musical ideals. "Dick and Serge were very close," Herb Pomeroy
recalled (Gross 1998: 9). "Unfortunately part of their closeness was due
to narcotics. But they were also very close musically. Two very strong
personalities." In spite of Chaloff's seniority, he accepted Twardzik as
his peer almost from the start. "We were to spend many enjoyable
years together along with a few not so enjoyable ones," Chaloff said.
"Though we both had our rough days we remained very close friends,
probably Dick being my closest friend in many years."

By November, they were playing together often enough that they
could get their dates mixed up. A telephone message for Richard from
Henryk, dated 11 November 1950, says, "Dick—Shaloff [sic] called—
you were supposed to work tonite. He will call you tomorrow. H.T."
The message, scribbled on a scrap of yellow paper, is decorated with
two striking pencil portraits, one of care-worn Dick with sunken eyes
and hollow cheeks, and the other a self-portrait of Henryk (5.2).

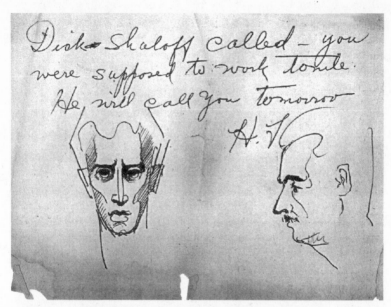

[illustration 5.2] Telephone message for Dick from Serge Chaloff with pencil portraits of Dick and Henryk, by Henryk Twardzik, dated 11-11-50. From the Twardzik-Thompson Archive, courtesy of Rosamond Thompson and Jane Sumner. All rights reserved.

Henryk's odd spelling in the telephone message—"Shaloff" for Chaloff—was intentional. Henryk was being derisive, punning on "shallow." Henryk always referred to Chaloff that way. Richard played on it himself in a letter home in August 1951 when he gave his road address "c/o Serge Shaloff Band" (with a C carefully superimposed on the S). Henryk's pun shows that he regarded Chaloff as a man of little substance. Chaloff's reputation as an addict was no secret, and Henryk must have feared that his high-flying son might be drawn into Chaloff's vortex. Or maybe he knew that he already was drawn in.

At the end of the year, Twardzik got his first road experience as a member of Chaloff's band for a string of short-term gigs in Ohio, Pennsylvania and West Virginia. An undated letter from Dick to his mother from the Youngstown Hotel in Youngstown, Ohio, which may have served as the band's home base, was probably written in late December (based on Dick's witticism that "we won't get paid until next year"). The band member Twardzik mentions as his roommate, Roy Shayne, was a bassist from Boston who did not play in Chaloff's later bands. (It is hard to predict what might stick in the mind. When I asked one old musician if he remembered Shayne, he thought hard for a while and then told me, "Oh, yeah. Roy's ex-girlfriend became Nat Pierce's first wife, Sylvia.")

Twardzik's remarks to his mother in his letter, scrawled in ballpoint pen on both sides of hotel stationery, resounds with boyish pride about facing the manly rigors of the road for the first time:

Dear Clare

Well, this is no life for a growing boy. We just got back to Youngstown were [*sic*] we're staying from a long trip over to West Va. and then over to Pittsburgh!

I've been getting loads of sleep and I feel pretty good. I've finally mastered the technique of sleeping in the car thus arriving at the hotel tired but not exausted [*sic*]. We've found several places in town where there is good music especially the Cotton Club a pretty foreboding [*sic*] place on the outside but lovely inside (ya' know the kind of a place you can take your mother) hmmmm! Roy Shayne and I are rooming together and we have a nice room with a shower. The only trouble is the lunatic heating system which doesn't allow for our irregular sleeping habits. We're working Sat. Sun. & Monday here in Youngstown and a couple of one nighters over in Akron (45 mi) which should give us a chance to rest up (comparitively [*sic*] speaking). The weather here has been pretty cold with a couple of nice days so far no snow. There is a laundry service here in the hotel which is one less problem. As expected the money I took with me didn't go far at tall [*sic*] and while I eat here at the hotel on a tab, We're all dependent on allowences [*sic*] on next weeks salary. Just think we won't get paid untill [*sic*] next year! There is some talk of our going directly to New York but nothing definite as yet.

Hope to see you soon

Send my love to Julie and Dad

Hi Henry. Let me hear from you.   bye for now

XX Love Dick

Dick's closing, "Hope to see you soon," suggests that the tour was nearing its end. Certainly Chaloff had good reason to be back in Boston. A month later, in January 1951, he would marry nineteen-year-old Joann Mary Black, known to everyone as Linda, a model who had won a beauty contest to become Miss Port of Boston 1949 (Simosko 1998: 63). She would give birth to their daughter Linda Jeanne the following October.

For the next six months, Twardzik's playing engagements are unknown. In addition to his work with Chaloff, he probably started getting work as an intermission pianist in the Boston clubs, keeping the audience warm between sets by the big-name musicians who were the main attraction. Though he would only turn 20 in April, his reputation began spreading as a kind of eccentric genius in the Boston-area jazz community. The image started with his music—that "completely new approach to his piano playing…in the way he voiced his chords" that Chaloff talked about—but it did not end there. He took to wearing a sleeveless black overcoat, a kind of cape. He sat around reading in dark corners of the clubs, and reading what the other musicians considered heavy stuff, like *The Psychology of Music* by Mursell. His constant companion was his dog, Stinky, a lapdog, curled up under his table or following him on a leash with quick little steps.

Not that he was stand-offish. In fact, he could be downright garrulous. He loved to talk. Nick Dean, a young photographer trying to make a living on jazz, interrupted him one night to tell him how much he liked his playing and thereafter he often found himself debating the hot topics of the day whenever they met—the pros and cons of chlorinating the water supply or building backyard bomb shelters or banning the bomb. "He was an inveterate arguer," Dean said (1956).

Legends began sticking to him. Dick Creeden, a musician who booked bands around the north shore, including Danvers, appreciated Twardzik's talent and tried to help him out by giving him work whenever possible. One version of a story passed along by Bob Nieske, a composer and piano player who was too young to know Twardzik, says that Creeden, "an old cornet player from the north shore, used to book weddings and events and he told me he would always try to get Dick work because he liked him. He said one day there was a wedding and Dick showed up two hours late wearing Bermuda shorts instead of a tux and he had a Chiwowa [*sic*] on a long length of rope. The dog was running around the tables getting the rope caught everywhere." Bob Pilsbury, a piano player who played with Creeden in a Dixieland band at a place called the Village Green in Danvers, told me a similar story about his relations with Twardzik. Pilsbury says Creeden was a bass player—"not a good bass player but he knew he wasn't a good bass player." (In fact, he may have set aside his cornet to fill in on bass for this gig.) According to Pilsbury, "Creeden hired Twardzik for an Elks Club or Knights of Columbus gig, and Twardzik showed up with two poodles, a fur coat and a beret. Creeden said to him, 'I hate to say this, but not here, man.' "

After his late-night stints as intermission piano player, it was too late to go back to Danvers. "Dickie would sleep over at my house after playing at the Storyville," his aunt June told me years later (though on cross-examination she was not absolutely certain if it was "the Storyville" or some other club). She owned a big house on Channing St. in Newton. She would set up the divan for Dickie, she said, and he would take the trolley to the end of the line, a stop called Newton Corner, and walk the rest of the way. "I had a piano that also attracted him," she said. By the late afternoon when Dick's cousin John got home from high school, where he was a senior, Dick would be awake and sitting at the piano, working on the tunes he might play that night at the club.

Twardzik was on the road in May 1951 when he received a Selective Services envelope containing a four-page Order to Report for Armed Forces Physical Examination. In the aftermath of World War II, the American military held the power to draft the male youth of the nation for two years at age 18 or after they finished their educations. Twardzik's draft notice arrived at an awkward time in terms of his career, which was just starting to take shape. Besides that, the rising conflict in Korea and the growing determination of the United States to keep the communist North out of the republican South meant that draftees had a fair chance of facing unfriendly fire in southeast Asia. None of this appears to have fazed Twardzik. On receiving his notice, he scribbled a postcard full of sophomoric enthusiasm to a friend named Norman Gross in Brookline:

Dear Norman.

A few lines to say Hello and to wish you well. I just received the stunning news that the Army wants me—and soon. So I'll be home soon to tell about life in these here United States.

Deutchland [*sic*] über alles!

XX DICK X

(The postcard is German but its stamp is American; it is undated and was apparently never sent.) In the end, nothing came of the draft notice. Twardzik reported for his physical examination, as required, and a year later, in May 1952, he received his Notice of Classification informing him he was 4-F, which meant that he was deemed physically unfit for military service. No explanation was given.

In the summer 1951, Twardzik turned up with Serge Chaloff in a resort area on the south shore of Cape Cod that must have been a prized summer gig. The venue was a club in West Yarmouth, just a mile or two from Hyannis, the commercial center for wealthy seaside communities like Hyannisport.

Chaloff's band was a trio with Twardzik on piano and a drummer, at first Larry Carreno and later Gene Glennon. The combination of baritone saxophone, piano and drums was an odd one. The choice of drums to fill out the trio instead of more melodic percussion instruments like bass or guitar was probably dictated by the fact that the band was hired mainly to play for dancing in a large hall, where the rhythm had to carry to the furthest reaches of the room. The trio played for dancing every night of the week and put on a jazz concert on Sundays.

For a few weeks in the early part of the summer, the trio unexpectedly expanded. Trombonist Mert Goodspeed and trumpeter Don Stratton, who had played in Nat Pierce's Boston bands, found work for a few nights in a place called Harwichport, about nine miles from West Yarmouth. They knew that Chaloff was playing down the highway. Goodspeed recalled, "So one night I said, 'Why don't we bust in on Serge?' So, Don and I got our horns, put them in the car, and went blowing marching right into the club. The owner loved it! It created a little atmosphere. So we played for the rest of the evening. Then the guy hired me. We played for a couple of weeks. Not long. So the trio turned into a quintet, or something like that" (Simosko 1998: 68).

The atmosphere of the West Yarmouth hall is captured in a set of grainy black and white snapshots that were found among Twardzik's effects (5.3–6). The high ceiling gives some idea of the size of the room. The bandstand appears to be pushed up against a booth, and similar vinyl-covered booths may have ringed the room. The tables had Formica tops, like common kitchen tables of the day. The main feature of its decor appears to be indestructibility. But the bandstand offers some re-lief. There is ample room for the musicians, even allowing for Carreno's maximalist drum set, very much the fashion of the day. There is also ample space to accommodate Goodspeed and his friends, or any other musicians who might have dropped in. Best of all, the piano is a grand, which might have pleased Twardzik, depending upon its tuning, and he did not complain about that.

It might have been an idyllic summer gig, except that Chaloff and Twardzik couldn't stand working with Carreno as their drummer. That problem was solved fairly quickly. By the time Twardzik wrote home to his parents, he could tell them about the new drummer along with the usual topics of his personal health and his cultural pursuits.

Twardzik's letter to Henryk and Clare, from Silver Sea House in Hyan-nis on 14 August 1951, is written in pencil on three crowded pages of flimsy, and it presents the Twardziks with a romantic view of their son and the Chaloff family taking their ease in a kind of artist's commune by the sea. Its cheerful intelligence is a poignant reminder of Chaloff's comment that he and Twardzik "were to spend many enjoyable years together along with a few not so enjoyable ones." This one clearly be-longs to the good times:

Dear Parents:

It's 2:30, the Bloch Suite for Viola is playing, Serge is reading Kafka, Linda is sitting on the porch, Gene [Glennon] the new drummer is swatting the few mosquitoes remaining Stinky is in on my bed, a wide double bed, with Jackie Linda's little brother. I am well and happy and despite the cloudy and foggy weather for the last week or so I have an excellent tan. Every good day we go to the beach, fresh and salt water. It has taken weeks of effort but now Stinky goes in the water of her own volition. She went in and pulled a log raft in by herself. We are living in a cottage one of a group under the name Strom Villa, a stone's throw from the club. Business has tripled and we work a seven day week with Sunday Jazz Concert night.

Life is pleasant here. Recently we were guests up at Oyster Harbor a terrifically expensive resort and took a trip on a yacht owned by two sons of the DuPont family. Watta Boat! Even Linda went for the weather wasn't too bad. She has entered her ninth month of pregnancy and is a pretty damn active girl fooling around and today shocked the pants off Serge by riding a bicycle a few feet! The dog and the Chaloffs have become very attached. I mix vegetables and greens with Stinky's food to ensure her health. She's in wonderful shape.

I was happy to receive your letter, disappointed to hear about Salsedo's poor performance [at a dog show], and I do hope everything [is] all right. Your head, Clare, and your teeth, Henryk.

Gene the new drummer is wonderful. and we are now 3 working as 1.

The 19th chorus close.

Let me know your plans and I'll be happy to arrange accomations [*sic*] for you.

Good Luck at the show!

I just put on Wozzech [*sic*] and I feel it deeply

We have a phonograph and the cottage echoes to Bartòk Bird and drums from the Belgian Congo. I sent the money to Gates. The next union fee and our agent takes a considerable slice of my salary but I'm managing.

Once again, I hope all is well. I'll close as I'm very tired. I work very hard.

See you soon

Love

your son

Richard

xxxx

5.3 The trio with Serge Chaloff, baritone saxophone, Richard Twardzik, piano, and Larry Carreno, drums, in West Yarmouth, summer 1951. From the Twardzik-Thompson Archive, courtesy of Rosamund Thompson and Jane Sumner. All rights reserved.

5.4 Richard Twardzik, 20, relaxing between sets

5.5 Chaloff soloing with Twardzik comping

5.6 Twardzik soloing while Chaloff waits his turn

The musical ambience in the cottage was obviously Twardzik's doing. *Suite for Viola* by Ernest Bloch (1880–1959), the Swiss composer, and *Wozzeck*, the opera by Alban Berg (1885–1935), belong to the modernist repertoire Twardzik favored and that he might have tried out on his high-schoolmates a year or two earlier. Bird, the bebop guru Charlie Parker, would soon become a personal presence in Twardzik's life and career, though Twardzik could hardly have guessed that. He does not say what he was listening to by Bèla Bartòk (1881–1945), the Hungarian composer who was exiled to the United States in wartime, but the only record found among Twardzik's effects was Bartòk's *Suite for the Miraculous Mandarin*, conducted by Tibor Serly, on an obscure specialty label (Bartòk Records PB 107). The disk is clear red vinyl, considered a mark of prestige at the time, and it has the owner's signature, "Dick Twardzik," in the upper left corner of the sleeve. The drums that Twardzik refers to in his letter probably came from a record that Twardzik bought through a mail-order catalogue from General Records, New York, which offered, among other exotica, a selection from a company called Belgian Congo Records.

Twardzik's pleasant summer on Cape Cod seguéd into a busy fall, as Serge Chaloff continued making headway establishing himself on the New England circuit. In October and November, he led a quartet in a club called Primo's in Lynn. Along with Twardzik, Chaloff hired Jimmy Weiner on drums and Bob Maisel on bass. Weiner was from Boston but Maisel was from East St. Louis, Illinois, and may have come to the Boston area intending to further his studies at Berklee. Chaloff's daughter was born during this long homestand.

In December, Twardzik made his recording debut in a band led by Charlie Mariano. The LP was called *The New Sounds from Boston* (5.7, also page 51). Ira Gitler, then working as producer for Prestige Records in New York, chose Boston as the first venue for a record series on jazz in various American cities. He picked Mariano to head the group because, as he said in the liner notes, he is "easily the best known modern musician from the Boston area, excepting Serge Chaloff and Roy Haynes who gained their recognition away from the Hub" (Gitler 1952). Mariano chose an octet for all but two tracks of the 10" LP (24 minutes), and his piano player on all but one track is a man named Roy Frazee. Twardzik plays on the other track, which might have seemed like a slight except that his appearance is clearly calculated as a virtuoso turn.

Frazee, a workmanlike player in the ensembles, steps aside in favor of Twardzik on a Mariano composition called *Mariners*. The piece is scored for a sextet rather than the larger band on most of the tracks. Mariano uses it to showcase his dense chordal writing for the horns (trombone, alto saxophone and tenor saxophone) at beginning and end, but the thick textures of the horns are relieved in the middle by two solo choruses, one by Twardzik and the other by Mariano. Twardzik thus inaugurates his recorded legacy in a context carefully laid out to showcase him, and his performance bristles with a rather formal, self-conscious chorus that nevertheless suits the mood adroitly. His exposure was minimal, but it was impressive, and, at 20, it was a milestone.

[illustration 5.7] Charlie Mariano and His Groups, *The New Sounds from Boston*. Prestige 130 © 1952. Richard Twardzik plays on one track, *Mariners*, of this 10" LP.

Another milestone passed at almost the same time when Twardzik received his first mention in the national press. Nat Hentoff, who ran a jazz radio show on WMEX in Boston and worked as a stringer for *Down Beat*, heard Chaloff's quartet in Lynn and filed a news item about Chaloff in *Down Beat* (14 December 1951) under the heading "Serge seeks action again after two years in Boston." Hentoff quoted Chaloff on the topic of his new ambitions: "So now I'd like to get a quintet going, hit Birdland, and then maybe move over the country. Three rhythm, myself, and a trombone. I already have a fine book for that instrumentation. Shorty Rogers wrote it for me when I left Woody." The trombonist he had in mind was probably Sonny Truitt, a New Yorker who was in Boston studying at Schillinger House, and is one of the players on Mariano's *The New Sounds from Boston*. Chaloff added, "And I'd like to bring with me an amazingly mature young pianist from here. His name is Dick Twardzik. He's only 21, and he's been working with me at Primo's in Lynn." Twardzik was, in fact, only 20.

Chaloff was thwarted in his ambition to form the quintet with trombone, with one momentary exception a few months later. He was also thwarted in his ambition to "hit Birdland," the famous New York club. But he did get to move around the country. Early in 1952, he led a quartet for three and a half months in the American Midwest in Illinois, Michigan, back to Illinois, and then a month in two Wisconsin cities. For Twardzik, young and ambitious, it would prove a rough baptism, with grueling miles and rough clubs along the way.

Chaloff undertook the tour partly out of necessity. He was pressed to get out of Boston, according to Sunenblick (1994: 2–3), when "a politically motivated North Shore judge started probing drug use in the Boston area." Chaloff was targeted, and he roused the band for a hasty escape. Weiner told Sunenblick, "We left in a snowstorm and drove all night to Detroit."

The bookings gave them a chance to establish themselves in clubs for extended runs (Simosko 1998: 69): in Chicago at the Preview from January 20 to February 17; in Detroit at the Crest Lounge February 19 to March 3; in East St. Louis, Maisel's home town, at the Terrace from March 11 to 24; in Green Bay at the Picadilly from late March to mid-April; in Appleton at the Log Cabin Inn until end of April 1952. The clubs were mainly joints in working-class neighborhoods. The Crest Lounge, Weiner said, was "a combination bowling alley and club," and the other places were no better. The musicians lived out of their suitcases. Twardzik's address for the whole tour, he told Clare and Henryk, would be via the booking agents: McKonky Artists Corp., 127 No. Dearborn, Chicago.

When the tour ended, Chaloff got his mother to send him plane fare and flew back to Boston from Chicago. "He flew home and abandoned us," Weiner said (Sunenblick 1994: 3). Chaloff convinced the others that it was important for him to get home to see his six-month-old daughter. Maisel went home to East St. Louis, and Twardzik and Weiner were left to nurse Chaloff's beat-up car across half the continent.

They had barely reached home after three and a half months when Chaloff decided they had better leave town again. Twardzik and Weiner had no compunction about rejoining him. With Jack Lawlor added on bass, Chaloff took his quartet on the road again for a hastily assembled tour that would take them to Schenectady NY, Bethlehem PA, Hagerstown MD, and other cities south of Boston.

One of the stops was Albany, New York, where the band played a remote broadcast hosted by a disk jockey named Les Deuel on radio station WOKO. Their performance included two tunes with a trombone added to the ensemble, the quintet instrumentation Chaloff had told Hentoff about. Two quartet numbers feature Twardzik prominently. The broadcast was recorded mainly because Deuel commissioned an original by Chaloff, called *Listen to Les*, for his radio theme. (A tape recording survived but has not yet been issued; see the discography.)

On this tour, Twardzik apparently caught a performance by the Philadelphia Orchestra, and he wrote home to let his parents know about it. Only a fragment of the letter survives, and the legible scrap of writing paper conveys Twardzik's impressions of Eugene Ormandy (1899–1985), the Hungarian-born conductor who led the Philadelphia Orchestra from 1936 to 1980:

> Ormandy is not at tall [*sic*] like I pictured him instead he's a balding foppish little squirt who holds onto the bottom of his vest and takes tremendous bows a crowd pleaser who conducts with the vim and gusto that Red Skelton would use if conducting a band on T.V. and who insists on the band taking innumerable bows

The image of Twardzik looking down on Ormandy from the balcony conjures up a moment of calm in what appears to have been a depressing tour. The band members had arrived in Bethlehem, a steel town where the band played week-long gigs in two different clubs, in the middle of a Steelworkers strike, and played to mainly empty rooms.

Jimmy Weiner recalled an incident in Schenectady when a man kept shouting requests to the musicians and calling Chaloff "Buster" (Sunenblick 1994: 3):

> Serge put down his saxophone and got off the bandstand and went up to the guy and said, 'My name's not Buster.' Serge was a flamboyant guy who always took people up on their threats. Next thing, Serge is lying on the floor yelling. The trio finished the set without him. He had the imprint of the guy's ring on his forehead for a week.

It is hard to guess how the pacifistic Twardzik — "without a mean bone in his body," as Nick Dean said—might have felt about this incident and others like it, but nothing could dim his admiration for Chaloff.

In the end, the tour did nothing to solve Chaloff's problems. The narcotics officers were waiting when they returned to Boston and Chaloff was arrested for heroin possession. His car was impounded, but he skipped bail and hid out. Jimmy Weiner remembers catching a glimpse of him one night as he peered in the window of the Melody Lounge in Lynn (Sunenblick 1994: 3) but he did not dare to go in. For more than a year, his life in music was on hold.

So Richard Twardzik's partnership with Serge Chaloff came to a sudden stop. It would resume, but not for a long time. While it had lasted, it provided him with an invaluable apprenticeship. From the fall of 1950 to late spring 1952, a year and a half, Twardzik picked up invaluable playing time, in West Yarmouth and Lynn and numerous cities in middle America. If the settings were often squalid and the bandleader had crazy spells, well, those were occupational hazards that jazz musicians of the day had to learn to cope with. The places became a blur anyway, nondescript and interchangeable. What counted most were the moments when Serge would look over his shoulder at the young piano player and say, Yeah, baby, or when the bass player would say, as they were leaving the stand, I don't know where you came up with that lick, man. The joint where you chanced to be playing when those moments happened—what city, what club, what night, what set—didn't really matter. The important things stuck with you. You remembered what tune you were playing at the moment, and how the chord inversion worked, and how to do it again, and maybe how to take it out further. Make their eyes bug out again.

Playing in public with good musicians has always been the best education for a jazz musician, maybe the only real education. If the audiences are tough and the guys on the stand expect a lot from you, so much the better. Twardzik's special gifts for finding unexpected harmonies and turning the time around got sharper, edgier, from doing those things while the music was in motion, as it unfolded in real time. He learned the essential jazz skill of finding the good notes faster than the brain could work them out. At 21, Richard Twardzik now had hours of performing to augment all those years of practice.

Not only that, but he had made his first professional recording, and he had been mentioned in flattering terms in *Down Beat*. People were starting to notice. Chaloff would not return to music until 1954, and when he did he and Twardzik would resume their partnership as if he had never gone away, but in the meantime Twardzik would forge ahead, without Chaloff, in more auspicious settings. He still had some dues to pay, lots of them, but he was on his way.

Not all the lessons he had learned in his time with Chaloff took place on the bandstand. Far from it. They were lessons in life, and they left tell-tale marks on him, but at this point they were mild ones, barely noticeable except to those who knew him best. Clare and Henryk could see them, for sure. The signs showed in a kind of carelessness that was out of character. On the Chicago trip, he had forgotten some of his clothes, or abandoned them. They ended up in the possession of Bob Maisel, the bass player. Eventually Clare received a letter from Maisel's mother in East St. Louis, explaining that she had tried to get Dick's address through the Union and failed. Finally she decided to try sending a letter to "Mrs. Twardsik [*sic*], c/o M. I. T., Boston, Mass." "My son played with him in Chicago and has neglected trying to get his address," Mrs. Maisel wrote. "Surely hope I have your name spelled correctly and that Dick can have his clothes."

Richard Twardzik still had the air of the dandy about him, with books under his arm and his dog on his lap, but now there might be ashes on his overcoat sleeve or a collar-tip curling over the lapel. For the moment, it hardly seemed to matter. He was, in the jargon of the day, chippying, scoring a taste of heroin in the alley between sets, seeing how it might affect the music when it was time to go back on the stand. Or getting high and sitting around all night long talking about composing and improvising and other important things, and seeing what revolutionary ideas might come up.

Crystal Joy maintains that even by the time she got involved with Twardzik, late in 1953, Richard and his friends were not "wake-up-in-the-morning-and-score kind of addicts." But as much as she tried to put the best face on it, she had to admit that she didn't really know the full story because she kept her distance from him when he was using heavily. "I was really shocked when I saw him taking drugs," she said. "I found it disgusting.'How can you?' And I'd run away. And after that he'd clean up for a couple of days so I would come back."

From the start, she saw that drugs took a toll on him. "His whole face would change," she said, "and he had no tolerance for it. He'd take the drug and he'd throw up immediately." Then he would make a joke about it, praising the rush that could bring him so quickly to his knees. If he passed out and later saw real alarm in the faces of the people around him, he would brush it off as the after-effects of the childhood rheumatic fever that nearly killed him. "He always used that a lot," Crystal Joy said. "He worked it. He let people know about it." It was a bonus, he said, having a low threshold. That way, you got where you wanted to go in a hurry.

6 The Happy Bird

Jazz history has kaleidoscopic motion, with the greatest players converging in brilliant, intense musical encounters and then splaying outward and converging again with more intensity in new hues. Its thrust has been directed by face-to-face encounters between individuals: Louis Armstrong rising out of King Oliver's band, Coleman Hawkins out of Fletcher Henderson's orchestra after Armstrong transformed it, Dizzy Gillespie and Charlie Parker conspiring as bandmates in Billy Eckstine's orchestra, Miles Davis emerging out of Parker's quintet, John Coltrane out of Davis's, and so on. These partnerships took place at the cutting edge of the music, but the history is also full of minor meetings that carry no small weight.

The imprimatur of Serge Chaloff helped to establish Twardzik in Boston's vigorous jazz culture. Herb Pomeroy, one year older than Twardzik, would take a few more years to establish his rank, but when he did it would have staying power. For decades, Pomeroy would be the local leader in Boston jazz circles, as bandleader, teacher, television host and ambassador as well as first-call trumpeter. Years later, he acknowledged that his association with Chaloff, and incidentally with Twardzik, was instrumental at the start. "I remember going over to Serge's apartment on Newbury Street with Dick Twardzik," he said:

> I'd known Serge since about early 1950. I was a freshman at Harvard and would go to the jazz clubs, and Serge was just back in Boston from being on the road with Woody... I don't remember a concrete moment when I met Serge, but we were playing together by 1951. I'd left Harvard by then and was studying at the Schillinger School of Music, which later became Berklee. I was a kid hanging out with the big star, and hanging out with Dick Twardzik. Dick and I were very close, and Dick and Serge were *very* close musically, and of course in other ways also, the drugs and everything. Serge didn't let many people close to him personally, but I was as close as any of the Boston musicians with Serge musically, once I proved myself with Serge, and after that we were together a lot (Simosko 1998: 85).

In 1952, Serge Chaloff was a local hero, but Charlie Parker was the jazz guru. Everywhere he went, there was an aura of excitement. There had

never been a player like him. He was endlessly inventive and technically flawless. His sixteenth-note runs at breakneck tempos seemed
simply impossible, but he not only carried them off, he gave each of
those notes its fullest value. "Ravel wrote to him, and Prokofiev wrote
to him," said his manager Teddy Blume (Reisner 1962: 62), himself a
classically trained violinist. "They wanted to get some idea of how the
hell he did it." And whether that is literally true or not, the idea of the
greatest European composers seeking Parker's advice had credence in
the jazz world. Once his admirers got past his amazing technical skill,
they could then notice that his solos were full of feeling and swing.
He played the blues as naturally as any of the Kansas City masters who
were his models when he was growing up, different though his syntax
and his lexicon were. Like them, he always placed each note perfectly
in the musical pulse. Even his elders learned from him, and the younger
players worshipped him.

In the early fifties, Parker traveled the jazz club circuit with his own
band. It was impossible to know at the time, without the perspective
of his whole career, that his greatest music, the culmination of what
he had to give, was already behind him, and that he was destined, as an
intuitive genius, to repeat himself as long as his skills were intact, which
would be, tragically, only a few years more.

In 1952, the year he turned 32, Parker played in Boston twice at the
Hi Hat, in March and December. It was probably on the first of those
visits, 3–9 March 1952, that he heard Richard Twardzik playing intermission piano. Parker instantly took a liking to the young pianist, and
the two men started a friendship and an occasional musical partnership
that would be renewed whenever their paths crossed for the three remaining years of their lives.

It was Twardzik's piano playing, surely, that caught Parker's attention.
Once that brought them together, they would have discovered that
they shared certain tastes. One of their common tastes, surprising as
it might seem, was Béla Bartók. It was surprising because Parker was
educated on the streets and he was street-smart like no one else. His
musical genius, according to the legend, came to him without tutoring,
from some mysterious inner source. His appetites for food, sex, alcohol
and drugs were legendary; his nickname, Bird, was said to have been
conferred on him because of the pounds of fried chicken he bought
from sidewalk vendors as a teenager.

All that seemed to leave precious little space for intellect in any guise, but in fact he had another voracious appetite that few people got to see. He was endlessly curious about politics, literature, painting and especially music. In his last years, he took to dropping in on the modernist composer Edgar Varèse. "He'd come in and exclaim, 'Take me as a baby and teach me music. I only write in one voice. I want to have structure. I want to write orchestral scores,' Varèse said. "He was so dramatic it was funny, but he was sincere."

During his Hi Hat gig in March, Parker was interviewed on local radio and the host, John McLellan, played him an excerpt from *Music for Stringed Instruments, Percussion and Celeste* without identifying it. "It's one of Bartók's works, I forget the name," said Parker, "but Bartók is my favorite, you know" (Vail 1996: 130).

None of the jazz musicians Parker met on his travels knew more about Bartók and the other modern composers than Richard Twardzik. It was the basis of their friendship, and the common ground between the guru and the kid.

Parker and Twardzik also shared the taste for heroin, and because buying and using heroin are criminal acts there is a kind of gravitational pull that brings junkies together. Parker had been addicted since he was fifteen, before he left Kansas City, and he had to scuffle to make connections wherever his travels took him. "That preoccupied a lot of his time off the bandstand," said Ray Brown, the bass player. "It took up most of his social life; it dictated the type of friends that he was to have. Unfortunately, he was relegated to just dealing and running in certain areas to get what he wanted to get, to keep up with his needs" (Gillespie 1971: 250). While Parker's intellectual bent was little known to his fans and admirers, his narcotics bent was notorious, a key element in his legend, and his example was the catalyst for a heroin epidemic in jazz, wittingly or not, as we will see.

One of the anomalies in Parker's recorded works and the most mysterious in Twardzik's is a home-made recording at a jam session from which only one title, *I'll Remember April*, survives. The only positively identified musicians on it are Parker and Twardzik. The track has circulated since 1962, when it appeared on an LP called *The Happy "Bird"* with a bright red cover on a label called Parker Records (6.1, also page 51), dedicated to preserving air checks and home recordings of Parker, for which there has always been an insatiable demand regardless of the quality of the recording or the performance. *I'll Remember April* is by no means the worst example of the genre, but there is no doubt that the original tape or acetate would never have survived, let alone been transferred to vinyl and ultimately to compact disc, were it not for the presence of Parker.

The setting and most of the players are unknown, but Robert Sunenblick has put forward his best guess that it took place at a restaurant called Christy's in Framingham, a few miles south of Boston, where the owner, an avid jazz fan, attracted musicians to late-night jam sessions by providing free food and drink. It possibly happened at the time of Parker's second 1952 visit to Boston in December (Sunenblick 1996: 24–25; see the discography at the end). With so many unknowns, it is also possible that the session took place some months earlier, on Parker's March visit, soon after Parker and Twardzik met for the first time, when they became aware of the kindred feelings that would lead Parker to hire Twardzik on his later visit that year.

Twardzik was a regular participant at Christy's. According to Dick Wetmore, who played alongside Twardzik numerous times as either a trumpeter or violinist, Twardzik was the piano player in the house band led by Boots Mussulli, who had earned an international reputation as Stan Kenton's alto saxophone soloist. The versatile Wetmore played bass in the band with an instrument he borrowed from the bartender, and Roy Haynes was the drummer, with Howard McGhee on trumpet during a brief residency in Boston. "They were really good musicians," Wetmore said (Barnett 1998: 19). "Night after night we would have all the best musicians in Boston out there playing." Wetmore remembers Sarah Vaughan, Bobby Hackett, Dizzy Gillespie, Miles Davis, Bill Harris, Bob Brookmeyer, Bob Wilbur, and, one night, the entire Kenton orchestra. "Everybody just sort of went up and played for a while, sat down, and other people got up. Bass players would change, drummers would change in the middle of a tune," Wetmore says. "It was an amazing place, and this went on for about two years." Rumors persist about a cache of homemade tapes from Christy's, presumably many with Twardzik, but so far only the Charlie Parker performances have come to light.

Listeners have to bring a measure of devotion in order to find the merits in the homemade recording of *I'll Remember April* with Parker and Twardzik at Christy's. The sound is awful (and, significantly, much worse than other tracks on *The Happy Bird*, also with Parker but not Twardzik, which are known to have been made at Christy's on an earlier occasion). The ensemble playing is slap-dash, and the audience is noisy. The first chorus of Parker's solo is partly obscured by a loud woman insisting that someone, perhaps one of the musicians, should leave "Right now!" Finally, mercifully, a man shouts, "Shut up!" and the nagging subsides. The shouting match is off-mike, but so is Twardzik's piano solo.

The ensemble on *I'll Remember April* includes a trumpet and a tenor saxophone as well as Parker's alto, but neither of those players is allotted a solo. Parker's solo is a generous four choruses, and his remarkable fluency shines through, easily vindicating the preservation of the performance. Twardzik follows him with two choruses, but he is so under-recorded behind the walking bass as to be barely audible. The bassist, almost certainly Charles Mingus, then takes three choruses of his own, and the imbalance of the sound rights itself by default. The sound imbalance may be deliberate, as if the jazz fan operating the recording device placed his microphone so that it gave the bias to the visiting heroes rather than the local boy.

Behind the bass solo, Twardzik can be heard comping very actively, playing ambitious little figures intended, in the stylistic conventions of bebop, to invite the soloist to embellish his line contrapuntally by referencing the background figures. But that does not happen here. Mingus pointedly ignores Twardzik's prompts, and the two players work out their parts autonomously, as if they are playing in different rooms. Parker then returns for the closing ensemble and enlivens it by inventing a counter-melody around the trumpet lead, again blessing attentive listeners, notwithstanding the murky sound, with a glimpse of his genius for invention.

Musically, this ten-minute track is second-rate. From the beginning, it seemed more important for its relative weight in the sparse works of Richard Twardzik than for any contribution it might make to Parker's oeuvre. It now takes on added significance as a musical fossil of the bond between the 32-year-old virtuoso and the 21-year-old novice.

In the last four years of his life, from 1951 on, Parker traveled widely. The first two years he was on the road because his access to New York clubs was restricted when police suspended his cabaret card (Vail 1996: 122), a licence issued by the State Liquor Authority that gave musicians and others the right to be booked in New York clubs. In his last years, after his card was reinstated, Parker had to travel frequently in order to find work, because his erratic behavior led many club owners to ban him from his old haunts, including Birdland, the Broadway club named for him.

Boston was on his circuit. Sunenblick documents nine visits by Parker from 1951 to 1954 and several others to neighboring areas (1996: 21–32). Twardzik's relationship with Parker was cemented on his visit in December 1952 when Parker hired him as the regular piano player in his quintet for the week-long gig at the Hi Hat. In these years, Parker usually brought his own band with him. Parker's regular piano player was Walter Bishop, Jr., who had been in the band he brought to the Hi Hat in March, and had also played in Parker's orchestra with strings at Carnegie Hall in November, three weeks before Parker's second visit to

[illustration 6.1] Charlie Parker, *The Happy "Bird."* Parker Records © 1962. Richard Twardzik plays on one track, *I'll Remember April,* of this 12" LP.

Boston. Parker may have left Bishop behind this time because he knew Twardzik would be available in Boston after their meeting in March.

Young Twardzik was in heady company with Parker at the Hi Hat. The band was a mix of local players and imported ones. The trumpet player and the drummer both hailed from Boston but their local roots had grown tentative. Joe Gordon had been heard to good advantage on *The New Sounds from Boston* and had subsequently gone off in search of a wider reputation with the Lionel Hampton orchestra. In the next few years his aggressive style would prove highly compatible with the hard-bop style of Art Blakey and Horace Silver. When he joined Parker's band at the Hi Hat, Gordon had only been traveling with Hampton for a few months, and he was closer to his Boston roots than the other Bostonian in the band, drummer Roy Haynes, who had moved to New York a few years earlier and rapidly earned a national reputation, often with Parker, including his recent Carnegie Hall concert.

Charles Mingus, the bassist, had only settled in New York in 1951, after several years as a young lion in the Los Angeles jazz community, where he grew up. In New York he found himself starting over in faster company. He was still being tested by the New York musicians, and he had the kind of temperament that aroused competitive instincts. He was an imposing figure, proud and bombastic. Those traits would seem more becoming a few years later when it became clear that he was indeed one of the great composers and bandleaders in jazz. Immediately before coming to Boston with Parker, he had been out of music altogether. In Mingus's reconstruction, Parker called him and said, "Mingus, what are you doing working in the post office? A man of your artistic stature? Come with me" (quoted by Reisner 1962: 151). Mingus says he took the post-office job because he was not getting the recognition he deserved in music; the less romantic version is that he was waiting out the probationary period for his New York union card. Parker offered him $150 a week, and the exposure beside Parker gave him the kind of leverage he was looking for in the eastern jazz community.

Twardzik was the least experienced member of the band and the youngest. His tenure as Parker's piano player is commemorated by a radio broadcast on Sunday afternoon, 14 December, at the end of the Hi Hat week (6.2). The live broadcasts from the Hi Hat were the brainchild of another legendary figure in modern jazz, Symphony Sid Torin. One of the first-ever disc jockeys, Torin began by hosting an

all-night record show on Fridays on a small station in the Bronx starting in 1937. He soon graduated to the national network, with remote
broadcasts of live music from clubs as well as recorded music. Lester
Young composed Torin's theme song, "Jumpin' with Symphony Sid,"
which quickly became a jazz standard and, like Torin himself, survived
the transition from swing to bop. In 1945, when the jazz press raised
a clamor about the "chaotic" new sounds emanating from the likes of
Dizzy Gillespie and Charlie Parker, Torin embraced their music pas-
sionately, playing their records repeatedly on his program, denouncing
the moldy figs, and, through it all, educating the first wave of hepcats.
He was the chief propagandist of the bebop revolution.

Torin's fame grew with the music, and he went on to become a concert promoter as well as a network broadcaster. Highly visible in his
illuminated radio booth in the Roost on Broadway and later in Birdland, he became a hipster celebrity in his own right. Then, in 1952, his
career appeared to be finished when he swore volubly in range of an
open microphone. His radio station, WJZ, fired him.

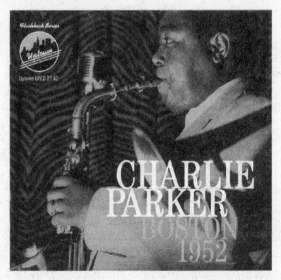

[illustration 6.2] Charlie Parker, *Boston 1952*. Uptown UPCD 27.42 © 1996. Produced
by Robert E. Sunenblick and David A. Sunenblick. Design by Nicolas Moumouris.

Torin packed up and moved to Boston, where he stayed for five years, until he was reinstated in New York. He carried the torch for bebop with him. He was mainly responsible for getting Charlie Parker as a regular visitor. "I just feel he is the whole jazz story of today," he said (Reisner 1962: 219). "Every musician I speak to, the young ones coming up today, they all say that Parker was the inspiration to the whole jazz scene." At a time when Parker was often put down by club owners and others as unreliable, Torin stood up for him. "When I was up at Boston he worked the Hi Hat and Storyville," he said, "and he always did good business for everyone."

A garrulous, ultra-hip wise guy, Torin aroused mixed feelings. Herb Pomeroy said, "He knew the music, and he knew the players, and even though he was full of shit, he enhanced the Boston jazz scene" (Sunenblick 1996: 19). Exactly how well he knew the players is debatable. On the Sunday afternoon broadcast, he forgets Twardzik's name when he is introducing the band members and offers a lame apology: "All week long I remembered and now I forgot. Oh well, what can you do? It's early in the morning." (It was 2 p.m.)

The Hi Hat broadcast catches Parker in high spirits playing his standard night-club repertoire. The 40 minutes of the radio show make a respectable minor addition to Parker's discography, and for Twardzik they provide unexpected evidence of his ability to adapt to the strict bebop conventions. Twardzik suffers from a couple of mechanical glitches. The piano was under-recorded on the original tape and the technician for the CD release had to mix the piano solos high in order to bring them into the foreground, which inevitably also brings the background noise up. And there is an audible splice in Twardzik's solo on *Cool Blues*. But Twardzik solos on every title. The immediacy of the live recording gives his playing a kind of refreshing candor. He fumbles through one of his choruses on *Scrapple from the Apple*, apparently searching for ideas. He distinguishes himself on *Cool Blues* with a series of cascading runs uniquely his own, and especially on *Don't Blame Me*, the only ballad, he creates a stunning effect by doubling the time while the bass and drums hold the original tempo.

Again, as on the *Happy Bird* performance, Twardzik's comping behind Mingus's bass solos is notably active, and, again, it sounds to me as if Mingus pointedly ignores Twardzik rather than reacting to him (6.4). Their independence is especially noticeable on *Cheryl*, where Mingus

walks through his solo while Twardzik embroiders the background—
or what is supposed to be background—with lacy filigrees.

Soon after listening to these performances for the first time, I remarked
to Bob Zieff that they showed Twardzik and Mingus at odds. Zieff
doubted my interpretation, not based on the music but on an encounter he had with Mingus some years later. "Charlie said to me that
when he was in Boston and played with Dick Twardzik, it was instant
music—instant musical rapport," Zieff said. But that seems to be revi-
sionist history on Mingus's part, and there are other indications besides
the music they made together that Mingus bickered with Twardzik all
week long.

Their differences apparently flared up first over Mingus's nightly showcase, *Body and Soul*, played only by the rhythm section. According to
Sunenblick (1996: 9), "Twardzik took his solo way out harmonically
and apparently angered Mingus." On another occasion, according to
Jimmy Weiner, Parker paid his respects to Twardzik's mother by an-
nouncing Clare's presence in the audience one night, and Mingus

[illustration 6.3] Charles Mingus, Charlie Parker, Symphony Sid Torin and Richard
Twardzik (partially hidden by Torin's shoulder) at the Hi Hat, December 1952.
Reprinted from Reisner 1962: 221. Photographer unidentified but probably Vinnie
Haynes, drummer Roy Haynes's brother.

leaned over to Twardzik and said, "If I was your mother, I'd take you across my knee." To Twardzik, it was not funny. Weiner told Sunenblick, "His face was ashen. He couldn't speak. He was so sensitive and Mingus had really upset him."

Twardzik's work as an accompanist, for Mingus and everyone else he played with, was certainly ambitious. To musicians who favored self-effacing, impersonal background support from the rhythm section, it seemed pushy. John Williams, a pianist with Stan Getz when he played in Boston in 1953 and 1954, remembers sharing the piano with Twardzik at jam sessions on two occasions. "While everyone was 'impressed' by his inventiveness, his pianistic skills, and his dissonant reaching-out, etc., as far as most horn players were concerned he was a pain in the ass," Williams told Steve Voce (2002: 9). "Dick didn't have a *clue* as to how to work in a rhythm section and make it swing."

Twardzik's comping style would become more acceptable a few years later with the autonomy of free-form players and would eventually become accepted in the jazz mainstream with McCoy Tyner and Herbie Hancock in the 1960s bands of John Coltrane and Miles Davis. Even in Twardzik's day, more open-minded musicians were beginning to recognize that what he was doing was intended as a spur for the soloist rather than a challenge.

Bob Pilsbury, a Boston piano player a few years older than Twardzik, said, "Twardzik started out playing those fancy chords, and Bird turned to him and said, 'Man, don't play those chords. If you play that way, I gotta go where you wanna go. Just play triads, okay?' " On the surface, the anecdote might seem to blame the young piano player for over-reaching himself, but Pilsbury's delight in passing the story along to me made it clear that he did not see it that way at all. To him, the anecdote glorifies Twardzik's harmonic sense, showing the local prodigy taxing the old vet with his new concepts.

The same spirit clings to memories of Twardzik's clash with Mingus. He comes off as the clever hometown kid whose conception pushed the imported star harder than he liked. With Mingus, there seems to have been real conflict, not the first and far from the last that Mingus would have with other musicians. With Parker, there was none at all.

"This week has been genuinely a pleasure," Parker tells Symphony Sid at the start of the Sunday broadcast. For Twardzik, it must have been a week of self-fulfillment, in spite of his tensions with Mingus. Parker praised Twardzik every night from the bandstand. They hung out together after hours at Christy's and other late-night haunts. Maybe they listened to Twardzik's Bartók records and talked about what they were hearing, mindful of the expanded vocabulary that Parker secretly and Twardzik openly craved.

After their week together at the Hi Hat, Twardzik and Parker would occasionally find themselves in the same place at the same time. When they did, they hung out together.

On Parker's return to the Hi Hat in January 1954, thirteen months later, he discovered that Twardzik was playing at the Jazz Workshop.

[illustration 6.4] Richard Twardzik, Joe Gordon and Charles Mingus at the Hi Hat, December 1952. Photographed by Vinnie Haynes. Robert Sunenblick collection.

Parker took his horn to the Workshop on Friday afternoon and, unannounced, played duets with him (Sunenblick 1996: 9).

A few months after that, in July 1954, with Parker's health deteriorating both physically and mentally, his partner Chan Richardson Parker saw the need for a respite from the big-city demons that were afflicting him. She arranged a few weeks at a summer house in East Brewster on Cape Cod (Vail 1996: 161), in hopes that spending some time in the sand dunes with their two-year-old son Baird might restore his spirits.

It was an uncommon setting for Parker in more ways than one. "Brewster is one of the most exclusive places—not only is it restricted but the poor are prohibited," Symphony Sid Torin said:

I don't know who Charlie Parker knew there. Somebody must have dug him very much to allow him and his wife to have a cottage on their property. Bird did a gig out there at a place called the Red Barn. It was a dance and there was Chan with the baby sitting on the bandstand, and that was the last time I saw Bird. He looked beautiful and healthy, and he said, 'Say, Sid man, we're having a ball, the baby's having a ball. I don't care if I work.' He was having a wonderful time (Reisner 1962: 219–20).

Parker did take a paid gig in Boston at least once during that summer, and he hired Twardzik as the piano player in his impromptu band. Chan Parker recalled that they played "a hot, crowded, tacky dance." After the gig, Twardzik drove Parker and Chan to the club where Crystal Joy was singing that night. When she finished, the four of them went to Crystal Joy's parents' house for breakfast. They then spent the rest of the day in East Brewster.

For Chan, it remained a happy memory, if only momentarily. "Dick Twardzick [*sic*] drove us back to the Cape that morning," she wrote in her memoirs (1993: 48). "We spent the day on the beach with him and his old lady," meaning Crystal Joy, in the hip slang of the day for 'girlfriend'. (Crystal Joy was all of 20 years old at the time.) And then, thinking of Twardzik, Chan Parker added, "He died shortly after. He was a gentle soul."

The grim reaper hovered over both men as they watched the sun rise over the sea from the sand dunes on the Cape that morning. Parker would die before Twardzik. His death would come eight months after their day on the beach, in March 1955, when he was 34. Twardzik, more than ten years Parker's junior, would die six months after him.

7 All Stars and Lonelies

"I wasn't a bone-fried bopster, and Dick had outgrown it," Bob Zieff told me. "He even listened to Brubeck before Miles Davis kosher-ized him. So there were very few of us lonelies." But if Zieff counted Twardzik among the outsiders, there were many others in the Boston arts community, including the bona fide bopsters, who counted him among the all stars, and both sides had a good case.

Twardzik began attracting attention wherever he went. Bob Pilsbury remembered him showing up one night at a club called Izzy Ort's Golden Nugget—"a sailor pick-up bar," according to Pilsbury. Pils-bury was playing there with a trio called Trenton Hall and the Melody Ramblers, made up of clarinet and drums and Pilsbury's piano, and the bandstand was huddled in one corner of the room. The crowd was inat-tentive, occupied with other things, except for Twardzik, who came in off the street in a long, dark overcoat and stood in a corner listening.

At the end of the set, Pilsbury watched Twardzik pick his way toward him. He sidled up to him and said, quietly, "Man, you play too fuckin' loud." "Which I did!" Pilsbury told me, with a great guffaw. He remem-bered that Twardzik sat down and played a couple of chords, and then wandered out of the club.

By the end of 1952, after his week at the Hi Hat with Charlie Parker, Twardzik was actively working at composing, and it was probably at this time that he wrote *A Crutch for the Crab*. Pilsbury, still an active player with a long-standing New England trad group called the Black Eagle Jazz Band, also had joyous memories of *A Crutch for the Crab*. When I spoke to him he had not heard it for quite a while because his ex-wife sold his LP, he told me, "not out of spite but because I couldn't get it together." Still, it sticks in his mind. He loves the tune, he said, "not only for the title—but of course that'll grab you—but because it's not bebop, it's not Tristano, it's different from anything you've heard."

This relatively stable time in Twardzik's life would not last long, but in it he forged three important friendships. The first was with a painter named Reba Stewart, with whom he shared several professional predi-lections and would come to share more. The second was with the pho-tographer Nick Dean. The third was with his sometime music teacher Bob Zieff.

Reba Stewart, one year older than Twardzik, came to Boston from Miami as a scholarship student at the Museum of Fine Arts School, where
Twardzik's Aunt Roz had been a student many years earlier. Stewart
was born on a farm in Michigan, into a poor family. She was raped by
her father at 10 or 11, and made a ward of the state. She was taken in
by a foster family and moved with them to Florida. She served them as
a kind of au pair, her patron and friend Geneviève McMillan told me,
looking after the children and doing other household chores.

Like Twardzik, Stewart was precocious (7.1). She had just turned 18
when she arrived in Boston in the fall of 1948. She had discovered
African art as a high-school student and found it a source of inspiration for her own painting. Through it she became curious about jazz
and African-American culture. Bob Zieff remembers that she had a
"show/display" at the Storyville club, with her artworks on the walls
surrounding the jazz audience. Before that, she may have supplemented
her scholarship money by working part-time as a server at Storyville
or the other jazz clubs.

She probably met Twardzik in 1951. Their tastes intersected in all
kinds of ways, and for almost two years, into 1953, they made a striking young couple in Boston's art community. Nick Dean remembers
Stewart as "one of the up-and-coming young Boston painters, a little
on the wild side or maybe just a bit bohemian, but as I recall a thoroughly nice person." Though Geneviève McMillan met her a few years
after her affair with Twardzik, she was aware of her reputation. "When
she came to Boston, she was well known for lots of parties, for giving
parties," McMillan says.

When I told McMillan that she was probably using heroin with
Twardzik, she said, "I wouldn't be surprised. She was very adventurous." McMillan remembered Reba earning money by participating
in a drug experiment with a clinical psychologist at Harvard, a Japanese gentleman, who wanted to test her reactions. "She withstood the
drugs," McMillan said. "The Japanese psychiatrist later told me that
Reba was very strong-willed, very strong. She was a person of great
strength and self-confidence, though not consciously of course."

When I told McMillan that one of Reba's photos made her look like a
pin-up girl, she laughed and said, "I have many poses of her as a pin-up
girl, and as a doll, and as a nun. She enjoyed the fantasy. She was very

interested in it." Zieff remembered her, in her youth, as a "chubby, short blond," but he also recalled a very different impression when he met her in New York a few years after Twardzik's death. She had recently returned from Japan on a study grant and, Zieff says, "she was slim and quite stunning—and living in a converted storefront." Certainly his later impression is the dominant one. "She had greenish eyes, greenish-grey eyes," McMillan says, "and when they set on you, well, I saw this many times, all the men succumbed."

Reba was much tougher-minded and more resilient than Richard, as might be expected from the way she had prevailed over her upbringing. Their intense affair would end, as we will see, after Twardzik skidded back into heroin use after a cure that taxed the energies of both of them.

One of the denizens of the jazz clubs where Twardzik played was a well-dressed young man with curly red hair who could sit attentively

[illustration 7.1] Reba Stewart in Mexico, ca. 1958. By permission of Geneviève McMillan (2002). Courtesy of Michèle Oshima.

with a beer on his table for the whole night. He was Nick Dean, a photographer, and he sometimes brought his camera to the clubs and got permission from the musicians to photograph them in action. In this way, he came to the attention of George Wein, the owner of Storyville, and Dean was thrilled when Wein offered him a bit of extra work. "I did George's darkroom work in return for one night 'on the house' at Storyville per gig," he said. "It was a pretty good deal, nursing a beer while listening to some of the greats of the fifties." Nick's wife Zibette often accompanied him. On those nights when he crouched around the bandstand snapping action shots of the musicians, he made sure he was efficient and unobtrusive. Dean tried to make himself invisible, and to his surprise the musicians took notice. They gave him a nod from the bandstand when they saw him sitting in the corner, and eventually he counted some of the regulars—Errol Garner, Count Basie, the members of the Modern Jazz Quartet—as friends.

Dean cannot recall how he came to meet Twardzik. All he remembers is that "both my wife and I liked him very much almost immediately, his musical talent aside." Dean's jazz sideline meant that he was often in the same room as Twardzik. He thinks he might have simply congratulated Twardzik on his playing one night and found himself engaged in a conversation. It is also possible that their first meeting involved photography. Perhaps Wein sent Dean to photograph Twardzik for a display portrait that he could use when he was playing intermissions at Storyville, or perhaps Twardzik needed a portrait for publicity purposes and approached Dean about it. In any case, the only two photographs of Twardzik that were published in his lifetime were taken by Dean—the full-face portrait on the back cover of *Trio* and a profile that accompanied Serge Chaloff's eulogy (1956) in *Metronome*. There were several other photographs by Dean among Twardzik's effects, including sheets of contact prints (Frontispiece) and a few performance shots taken at the Stable (7.2; also 12.2).

To Dean, the events surrounding all these photos now seem like ancient history. He gave up freelance jazz photography a few years after he took them, when his first child was born, and went to work in the Polaroid Research Laboratories. He never looked back. "I think of Dick occasionally, but have pretty much lost touch with Boston jazz people," he says now. So completely did Dean make his break that the only person I spoke to who could place him was Crystal Joy. "Oh yeah, he loved Dick," she said. "He used to go to the Stable, and he would photograph Dick there. I used to have a picture on my wall, a photograph of Dick in ecstasy, with his head thrown back. I don't know where it went. I moved so much." (The photograph is illustration 12.2 below.)

Dean appears to have been Twardzik's link with the day world, a decent hard-working family man who loved jazz music and whose profession gave him one foot in the art world. Soon after they met, Twardzik confided that he was looking for a place to live, as he often was, and Dean invited him to bunk with him and Zibette in their apartment on Charles Street at the foot of Beacon Hill. When I asked him if bringing home a jazz musician was unusual, Dean said simply, "Over the years we had quite a collection of strays whom we'd met here and there."

[illustration 7.2] Richard Twardzik at The Stable. Photograph by Nick Dean. From the Twardzik-Thompson Archive, courtesy of Rosamond Thompson and Jane Sumner. All rights reserved.

Twardzik would move in with them again, a few years later, as we will see, when he needed a sanctuary where he could kick his drug habit.

After Twardzik's death, Bill Coss of *Metronome* asked Dean for a photograph that he could publish with Serge Chaloff's eulogy. Dean sent the portrait and enclosed a note about his friend. To his surprise, Coss printed excerpts from his note as a kind of preamble to the eulogy. In it, Dean (1956) said, "Dick…liked Scotch, Bach, single-breasted, blue serge suits. He was an inveterate arguer, always reading and with an encyclopedic memory. He wanted to do some things on the harpsichord; if you listen to his style you'll see how thoroughly grounded he was in the baroque era. He was one of the finest people I'll ever hope to meet, without a mean bone in his body."

Years later, long after most of his memories of those times had vanished, Dean held one vivid recollection. "We urged him *not* to fetch up with Chet Baker," he said.

Around the time Twardzik's ashes were air-freighted back to Boston, Dean's professional interest in jazz ended, coincidentally or not. The job at Polaroid was the first of several salaried jobs he took to provide for his growing family. In the mid-1960s, his work took him away from Boston for good. He moved to Maine, but he did not bother taking his Boston jazz negatives with him. When I located him in 2002, he said, "To dredge my name up you must have a memory like an elephant." But his name was there all along, in the fine print on the back cover of *Trio*.

Robert L. Zieff, an aspiring composer, chanced upon Twardzik when the teenage piano player sat in at a jam session at the Melody Lounge in Lynn, Zieff's home town. At the time, Zieff was a Boston University student just out of military service. He was studying trumpet and composition, but he was mainly interested in exploring advanced harmonic ideas. Of his professors at Boston University, he says, matter-of-factly, "very few were good." His predilections naturally drew him to the jazz community, but he aspired to be a composer rather than an instrumentalist, an uncommon choice in the jazz world. He started taking students privately to make ends meet while he composed for woodwind choirs and brass combinations.

Born in 1927, he was only 21 when he met Twardzik, but he already held the musical convictions that would guide him for his entire career. He is an exacting man, and he believed, then as now, that the composer's duty was to examine mainstream musical conventions critically, digging under the surface of what was commonly accepted and extending the logical bounds. Zieff recognized something of that spirit in the kid from Danvers the very first time he saw him. "He sat in playing much Bud [Powell] with Tadd [Dameron] voicings thrown in," Zieff recalled. "At the time very few pianists had much idea what was happening with such musicians."

A few years after catching Twardzik's debut at the jam session in Lynn, Zieff was introduced to Twardzik through a mutual friend, a bass player named Eddie Mazman. Twardzik started studying with Zieff soon after, and it did not take long for them to recognize that their musical kinship had deeper roots. To Twardzik, Zieff appeared to hold the kind of convictions essential for someone who was determined to make uncompromising art. As different as Zieff's music was from the conventional, he could rationalize every nuance. He had it figured out, and not only the music. Behind the clean-cut façade, so much the style of the day, Zieff looked at everything in his own way (7.3). He seemed to conform to no model. Apparently he never had.

He was born in Lynn, and his parents were Lithuanian refugees. According to Zieff they were no ordinary immigrants. His father was orphaned as a child and became a circus acrobat, and then a barber in Russian army camps. His mother was a circus fortune-teller and a hotel chef, "between psychotic episodes," he says. Psychosis ran in the family. One of his brothers was confined to the state mental hospital, and when Zieff met Twardzik he was immediately struck by "something very similar in their appearance, their mien." When Zieff told Twardzik that he and his brother shared that mad look, Twardzik was flattered. It was one more thing they had in common. In the recesses of bohemia, where a few kindred spirits labored against the gray-flannel mainstream to create new beauty and liberating art, everyone knew that a touch of madness was essential. It was part of the bohemian creed and, if it was something of a guilty secret at that moment, in a few years it would be shouted from the rooftops. "The only people for me are the mad ones, the ones who are mad to live, mad to talk, mad to be saved," Jack Kerouac would proclaim, "the ones who never yawn and say a commonplace thing, but burn, burn, burn, like fabulous yellow roman candles exploding like spiders across the stars." It was a virtue,

this madness, and Twardzik found Zieff's parallel to his mad brother so
intriguing that he persuaded one of his Danvers neighbors, a man who
worked at the mental hospital, to get him a pass so that they could go
and visit Zieff's brother after hours.

Zieff was a composer first, but he also did some pencil sketching (7.4),
and Twardzik found that appealing too, yet another point of contact.
Zieff's music lessons were most important, and with both young men
moving around unpredictably, they fit the lessons in where they could.
Zieff's Lynn apartment was best, but they discovered that they could
concentrate wherever they happened to be. One lesson, Zieff remembers, took place in a car while Twardzik was on his way to a gig some-

[illustration 7.3] Bob Zieff in 1953. Promotional photograph by Jack Zieff, his uncle,
1953. By permission of Robert L. Zieff.

where. One of the other musicians, Dick Wetmore, broke it up when he shouted from the back seat, "Hey, I'm with you guys too."

The first motif of *A Crutch for the Crab* originated as an exercise Zieff concocted for Twardzik. Zieff describes it as "the slightly opulent opening march-like theme," and recalls how Twardzik altered it. "My version of it had a more clipped character," Zieff says, "with some more staccato notes and a bit faster in concept." In his recollection, Twardzik's first version of *A Crutch for the Crab* used that motif in the bridge rather than at the start.

[illustration 7.4] Bob Zieff self-portrait in pencil, 1951. By permission of Robert L. Zieff.

Twardzik loved Zieff's musical concepts, and it was through him that Zieff's music came to occupy its niche in Chet Baker's repertoire. Twardzik also praised Zieff's music to Serge Chaloff when Chaloff returned to active playing, and urged him to bring some of Zieff's compositions into the repertoire. "Serge said I must be good because Dick didn't seem to like anything," Zieff told me years later. "This surprised me because I found Dick much more open to things than I was!"

Chaloff never got around to using Zieff's music, and so it is Zieff's association with Baker that stands as the most conspicuous of his composer credits. Not that Zieff ever tried particularly to impose himself on a larger public. He is self-reliant and self-contained, a latter-day Emersonian Yankee though he put New England behind him by the time he was 30, moving to New York, Los Angeles, Mexico City and New York again before finally settling in Pennsylvania.

Zieff calls himself an "underground jazz composer." He has never fit into any more conventional category. In 1959, Leonard Feather alloted Zieff one column-inch in the *New Yearbook of Jazz* (Feather 1959: 153), the forerunner of Feather's encyclopedias. Almost half of that stingy space was used up by this cryptic comment: "He has written for Chet Baker, Bill Harris and others, but favors the Viennese school of composers."

As an instrumentalist, Zieff's most conspicuous performances took place at Randall's Island Jazz Festival, New York City's annual festival before the Newport Festival moved there. In 1958, Zieff sat in on piano with Chet Baker when Baker's regular piano player, Bobby Timmons, fell ill. The quartet played two of Zieff's compositions, *Slightly Above Moderate* and *Medium Rock*. "This made quite a stir," Zieff said. "Mingus and Mulligan came up at the end and were congratulating Chet—on the adventuresomeness among other things." The next year, 1959, Zieff was given his own spot at the Randall's Island Festival. He conducted a band made up of woodwinds, brass and string bass in several of his compositions. Band members included Phil Sunkel, co-leader and trumpet, Tom Stewart, trumpet, Steve Lacy, soprano saxophone, Harvey Phillips, reeds, Dick Meldonian, alto and tenor saxophones, Gene Allen, bass clarinet, and Bill Takas, bass. The "unusual instrumentation" was mentioned the next year in the first comprehensive edition of the *Encyclopedia of Jazz* (Feather 1960) where Zieff's biography was allotted two column inches. (The entry for Zieff was dropped from all subsequent supplements and editions.) Since then, Zieff's performances have been sporadic, and mainly local events, but he has never stopped performing altogether, even as teaching duties took more of his time. He continues to favor instrumentation with several wind instruments and a bass, which to him does not seem "unusual" at all.

In 1983, before I met Zieff, I asked Chet Baker about him between sets at a Toronto jazz club called Bourbon Street. One of my questions was why Zieff was not better known when he was so obviously talented, and Baker, behind hooded eyes, opined, "Some people don't much want to give real talent a break." I am not certain whether Zieff shares that sentiment but I suspect he does. If so, that would make it the one thing Baker told me that night that was almost true. Among other things, Baker told me that he met Zieff when Zieff was working at a Los Angeles radio station. I later found out from Zieff that he never met Baker when he lived in Los Angeles although one of the things he did there in the late 1960s had a radio connection, compiling educational programs for a company called Pacifica in Los Angeles. In fact, they first met face-to-face in a New York studio two years after Twardzik died, when Baker's label agreed to record Baker with a chamber ensemble conducted by Zieff. (On another topic, Baker told me at the same interview that he could not have met Miles Davis at the Lighthouse in Hermosa Beach, California, in 1953 because the first time he met him was in 1954 in New York. Are you sure? I asked. "I wouldn't forget something like that," Baker said. Soon after I published that as a fact [Chambers 1983: 174], Prestige released the LP *Miles Davis at the Lighthouse* with a cover photograph of Davis and Baker together at the Lighthouse in 1953 [*pace* Gioia 1992: 202].)

In spite of his problems with facts, Baker's feeling for Zieff's music lasted long after Twardzik was no longer around to intercede on behalf of his one-time teacher. Baker, in his memoir, wrote, "I found Bob Zieff's music a delight. Every line and harmony was different from the next, never going the way you thought it would, but somehow complete, logical, and unique" (1997: 71).

Besides the seven Zieff compositions recorded with Twardzik in Paris, Baker recorded two more (*Slightly Above Moderate, Medium Rock*) in Los Angeles in 1956 (on *Chet Baker and Crew*, Pacific Jazz) and another record-ful in New York in 1957 with Zieff conducting a chamber ensemble. The 1957 recordings went unreleased until 1994 when four titles (*Twenties Late, A Minor Benign, Ponder, X*) were finally issued on an anthology (Chet Baker, *The Pacific Jazz Years*, CD 4). The 1957 chamber ensemble is made up of Zieff's winds-and-bass combination, specifically trumpet, French horn, bass clarinet, bassoon, cello and bass. The instrumentation and the genre scared the Pacific Jazz managers, even though Baker's name alone would have guaranteed reasonable sales at that time. Baker said, "The album was never released... because the record company decided that it just wasn't commercial enough" (1997: 79). Their failure to release the music effectively kept Baker on a musical diet of ballads for the rest of his days. And, of course, it helped to keep Zieff underground.

Baker carried Zieff's compositions with him whenever he could, but as his life became more peripatetic and zany, he had perpetual problems keeping track of his book of arrangements. I asked Zieff what happened to his charts for the chamber ensemble, and he said, with an audible shrug, "Chet left the music in a taxi and could never track them."

When I drew Zieff's attention to a 1985 performance of *Sad Walk* by Baker in Münster, Germany, with Philip Catherine on guitar and Jean-Louis Rassinfosse on bass (on *Strollin'*, Enja Records), 30 eventful years after the original recording with Twardzik in Paris, Zieff lamented the new rendition somewhat. "The other two players do not have the harmonic idea of the piece," he said. "Also, the tempo is awfully slow compared to the recorded version, which was more like what I had in mind." But he understood perfectly why it went wrong. "Chet lost the music way back to my things and that's why he didn't play them," he said. "That is, he played them till he lost the music. Many of them are unorthodox enough so that they can't be too easily picked up off records even."

I asked Zieff why Baker would try to resuscitate *Sad Walk*, one of the more complex pieces, after so many years. Zieff replied, "Maybe Chet especially liked *Sad Walk*—or, as Phil Urso [Baker's tenor saxophone player in his 1956 band] mentioned to me, when they played the Streets of Paris [a Los Angeles club] opposite Art Blakey's band [the Jazz Messengers], Blakey's players went for that piece."

Because the charts had a way of slipping through Baker's fingers, Zieff's music got little play from Baker, in spite of Baker's good intentions.

"At one time there were a number of my pieces that he did that were never recorded," Zieff says. "I would guess they were lost. In fact, a well-known West Coast bassist whose name escapes me kept Chet's library because he didn't get paid." Later, Zieff remembered that the bassist was Monty Budwig. "I remember Monty telling me that Chet didn't pay him for working so he kept the library," Zieff said. "But this might have been a much different library than in the mid-'50s. This was in the '60s or '70s."

Baker made a few attempts to work with Zieff after the chamber ensemble recordings, but nothing came to fruition. It was not always Baker who was the sticking point. "There was a film score in the works for me to write and for Chet to be on the soundtrack," Zieff says. Baker's manager, Joe Napoli, approached Zieff about composing the soundtrack for the film *Compulsion*, based on Meyer Levin's best-selling novelization of a thrill-killing by two college students (Leopold and Loeb) with Übermensch delusions. The film adaptation was a great success in 1959, with Dean Stockwell and Bradford Dillman as the murderers and Orson Welles as the legendary attorney Clarence Darrow, who saves them from hanging. It is not hard to imagine Baker's moody trumpet accompanying the action, or Zieff's orchestrations providing subtle dramatic contexts for it, but it was not to be. "Joe Napoli had no idea of my thinking of course," Zieff says. "I don't know that I would have done it if it had come through."

Another opportunity came up more than a decade later. "Chet wrote me about recording some of the things of mine with strings in Italy— in the 1970s I think," Zieff said. "But he was going to have an arranger over there do it. So I nixed it."

Around the same time that Twardzik was introducing Baker to Zieff's work, a few other musicians were picking up on it as well. They had to do so on Zieff's terms. Zieff takes some satisfaction in knowing that his compositions have been recorded by the likes of Kenny Burrell, Art Farmer, Bill Harris, Jack Nimitz, Tony Ortega and Oscar Pettiford, but he seems never to have wished for greater exposure if it meant compromises of any kind, and by his standards compromises would have been almost inevitable. As a result, he is less well known than he deserves to be except among Chet Baker devotees and Boston jazzers of a certain age. (A Dutch band recently released a CD with a track called *Who the Hell is Bob Zieff?* "If you go to my name on Google or some such search engines you will see it," Zieff told me.)

As he reaches his late seventies, Zieff's recorded legacy, though relatively small and spread around unevenly, has an unmistakable integrity. The compositions carry his fingerprints whether they were recorded by Chet Baker or Tony Ortega (*Jazz for Young Moderns*, Bethlehem BCP-72 [1959]) or Dick Wetmore (*Dick Wetmore*, Bethlehem BCP-1035 [1955]), although Baker, Ortega and Wetmore have almost nothing in common apart from their obvious delight in playing Zieff's music. That integrity exists because Zieff protected it, and presumably that is what he prizes most of all.

Zieff has stood outside the mainstream, and seems to have no regrets. He has been, as he said, one of the "lonelies." He was gratified, for the few years it lasted, that his one-time student Richard Twardzik was willing to keep him company out there.

Twardzik had to be more flexible than Zieff about crossing ideological lines. He needed to play in good company in order to hone his performing skills. Chaloff gave him his basic training, and his stint with Parker had been his grad-school seminar. There was more to come. From the end of 1952, when he played with Parker, through the spring of 1953, he was the piano player in the house trio at the Hi Hat, usually with Bernie Griggs on bass and Gene Glennon on drums. Glennon was the drummer whose work had pleased Twardzik so much on the Hyannis gig the summer before. Bernie Griggs was a veteran player, now settled in the city after traveling with Dizzy Gillespie's band the year before.

As the house band, the trio got to play occasional features as interludes, but their main work was accompanying the horn players who were brought in as headliners for two-week stints. Not the least of its rewards was exposure on Symphony Sid's Sunday night broadcasts. For itinerant jazz musicians, playing with local rhythm sections in places like Peoria and Pensacola brought weighty uncertainties, but in many cities the house bands were competent, and in a few they brought their own panache. The house trio at the Hi Hat was one of them.

The list of leaders Twardzik got to accompany at the Hi Hat included Lee Konitz, Zoot Sims, Gene Ammons, Gene Quill, J.J. Johnson, Sonny Stitt and Allen Eager. Eager's stint at the end of January 1953 appears to be the only one of the Symphony Sid broadcasts from the Hi Hat that has been preserved with Twardzik in the band. The leader is a tenor saxophone player who had served his apprenticeship with big bands as a teenager, like Serge Chaloff, and then broke into the front ranks of bebop for a few years, including his weeks at the Hi Hat. He dropped out of music soon after and went into various pursuits including ski instruction, horseback riding and racecar driving. The 20-minute broadcast, released as part of Allen Eager *In the Land of Oo-Bla-Dee* (Uptown UPCD 27.49 [2003]), shows the band in easy rapport and grants Twardzik almost equal time with the guest star.

His status in the front ranks of Boston piano players in his 22nd year was flagged by an event with the symbolic significance of a coming-of-age ritual. Thirteen months after Charlie Mariano had given him a one-track guest shot on *The New Sounds from Boston*, Twardzik found himself hoisted to full-fledged membership in Mariano's *Boston All-Stars* for the sequel (7.5, also page 51). In January 1953, Prestige's producer Ira Gitler was again dispatched to Boston to record a band of local musicians under Mariano's direction. In his liner notes, Gitler said, "The response to [the first] album was very warm from critics and fans alike and in answer to this enthusiasm PRESTIGE is presenting Charlie Mariano once again" (Gitler 1953).

The warm reception and commercial success Gitler talks about presumably took place largely in the Boston marketplace. Though by this time Prestige had national distribution, I know from the experience of trying to find these recordings a few years after they were issued that they did not travel far or have long shelf life. After the first pressing, they went out of print and they were not reissued for 37 years. Finally, in 1990, in the first peak of the digital boom, OJC (Original Jazz Classics) reissued both *The New Sounds from Boston* and *Boston All-Stars* on one CD. (Even then it would have been hard to find it in your corner record store; OJC issued it in their Limited Edition series.)

The reissue of *Boston All-Stars* beefs up Twardzik's legacy with another twenty minutes of studio-quality recordings, and it is notable especially for illustrating his stylistic roots. The session is dominated by Charlie Mariano, as was the first one. This one provides even greater exposure for Mariano's facile, Bird-driven alto saxophone. This time out, he is not at all interested in showing off his arranging talents. On the earlier record, he framed solo choruses in lush textures provided by as many as five wind instruments, but here the arrangements are rudimentary when they exist at all.

The band is a quintet with the conventional small-band configuration of trumpet and saxophone fronting a rhythm trio. Each track follows the formula of an opening melody statement followed by a parade of solos and a repeat of the melody. Ensemble playing is minimal. Mariano either states the melody alone (*I'm Old-Fashioned, Bess You Is My Woman Now,* and his tasteful original *Erosong* [Eros + song 'love song']) or states it with a trumpet obbligato (*Stella By Starlight*). He then leads the players into the sequence of solos. *Barsac,* one of two Mariano originals, takes a fling at ensemble playing over a pseudo-rumba beat, but it starts out confused and ends messily. Of this track, Gitler says, perhaps by way of apology, "Pianist Dick Twardzik discovered a tom-tom in a corner

[illustration 7.5] Charlie Mariano, *Boston All Stars.* Prestige 153 © 1953.

of the studio and incorporated it into the ensemble by placing it at the end of the piano bench and propping it against the piano itself. While he comped with his left hand he brought the tom-tom into play with his right." Gitler joins the confusion by playing bells. (For details, see the discography.)

The old Dixie chestnut *Bye Bye Blues* offers some relief from the formula by requiring each member of the quintet to construct a stop-time chorus before deconstructing it as bebop. It is the most ambitious track on the record until it degenerates into a klutzy drum break near the end.

Though little more than a year had lapsed between the two Prestige recordings, Mariano has chosen a brand-new roster for his all stars. Twardzik is the only holdover, but this time as a full-timer; he plays on all six tracks. The other players are new. Bassist Bernie Griggs is from the Hi Hat house band. The other new recruits, Herb Pomeroy on trumpet and Jimmy Weiner on drums, were closer to Twardzik's age (22) than Mariano's (29).

Since the album is mainly a blowing session, with the musicians relying on spontaneous resolutions rather than charted figures, Twardzik has to rely on his native resources. As Gitler notes, "There are many different moods represented and Dick helps to make them convincing both by his backgrounds and the ways in which he infects [*sic*] his solo material." Twardzik's accompaniment is the band's main reference point on all the tracks, and he improvises witty rubato introductions to *Bye Bye Blues* and *Stella By Starlight.* He contributes a quirky, stop-and-go solo on *Bye Bye Blues.* Best of all, on *Erosong,* an effusive Bird call obviously intended by Mariano as his personal tour de force, Twardzik shines with sensitive, subtle comping and a rhapsodic half-chorus.

Throughout the record, Twardzik echoes some other piano players, making his performance a kind of rite of passage through his stylistic forebears. On *Stella By Starlight,* his solo draws slavishly on Bud Powell. Virtually all comments on Twardzik's style, beginning with Russ Freeman's liner notes, cite Powell as Twardzik's prime influence. On the recorded evidence, this always seemed to me far from obvious until I heard *Stella By Starlight.* To some extent, every post-bop piano player leans on Powell. But Twardzik is no more beholden to him than most of his contemporaries, and much less than the West Coast piano players, including Freeman. The pervasive Powell feeling on *Stella By Starlight* seems slightly out of character in light of his later style but may be the best recorded evidence of his starting point.

Twardzik's more characteristic turns always seem to me to have much more of Thelonious Monk in them than Powell, although Twardzik is more pianistic than Monk and not nearly as percussive. Historically, Twardzik belongs to a small coterie of piano players who absorbed some elements of Monk's style before it became fashionable. Twardzik and a few others were attracted to Monk, in historian Ted Gioia's words (1997: 247–48), "as a patron saint for those who saw jazz as an underground movement resisting assimilation." Twardzik notably shared Monk's "vertical conception" as "a robust alternative to the essentially linear approach of most postwar pianists," including Powell. On *Stella By Starlight*, it is Twardzik's dogged linearity that evokes Powell.

Elsewhere on these recordings (but less so than on his trio recordings a year and a half later), Twardzik chips away at Monk much the way that Herbie Nichols does. Of all the piano players in jazz history, Nichols (1919–63) seems to me closest to Twardzik in terms of shared sensibility, starting with their link to Monk's vertical conception. Although Twardzik never mentioned Monk, Nichols did. Monk and Nichols were contemporaries (Monk was born in 1917), more than a decade older than Twardzik, a stylistic generation in jazz terms. But Monk was in the vanguard, and Nichols may have retarded his own acceptance by following Monk's lead in his formative years, when no one else was tagging along. Nichols stood up for Monk from the beginning, long before most piano players or jazz critics. "I was honest," Nichols said. "I knew people hadn't caught on to him, but I raved about him anyway. Leonard Feather and those other people [i.e., critics] didn't even know what he was doing; they hated him" (Spellman 1966: 162). Though the attitude toward Monk's music was softening by the early fifties, when Twardzik was picking up on him, it would still take a few more years before Monk would be acknowledged as a seminal figure in the music.

Beyond their general conception, Twardzik and Nichols share a feeling for artful dissonance more subtle than Monk's. Both cultivate their touch on the keyboard with finesse that is found nowhere in Monk. They also have more in common harmonically with one another than either does with Monk, probably because they paid more attention to modern classical composers. Nichols even wrote a piece called *Bartok*; it was finally recorded some 36 years after his death and influenced no one, but it was one more free-floating bond he had with the Boston soul-mate he never knew. Any suggestion that Nichols might have had a direct influence on Twardzik is out of the question. Nichols's opportunities to record his own music came belatedly, in the mid-1950s, when he was in his late thirties. That was too late for Twardzik to hear him—and almost too late for Nichols to find an audience.

Another echo in Twardzik's playing on the *Boston All Stars*, much more obvious, comes in the first eight bars of his solo on *Stella by Starlight*, where he unleashes a string of block chords that jazz listeners, even casual ones, will identify instantly with Dave Brubeck. In January 1953, when Twardzik improvised these Brubeckian bars, Brubeck himself was just emerging from what had been, until then, the jazz boondocks of San Francisco. In 1950–52, though he was already in his thirties, all he had recorded were a few trio tracks, some quartets with the totally unknown alto saxophonist Paul Desmond (the base group for his international prominence starting in 1954 on Columbia Records), and some short pieces with a forward-looking octet, all for Fantasy Records, then a fairly obscure California label. An important step in Brubeck's recognition was an engagement at Storyville in October 1952, where Boston musicians, including Twardzik, got a preview of the style that would soon turn heads everywhere.

Brubeck's records were hard to find outside of California, but they had an underground reputation among musicians searching for broader concepts, especially the experimental octet. Brubeck himself always maintained that his octet recordings were not actually unknown but simply unacknowledged. "Within the past ten years," Brubeck wrote in 1956 when his opinion suddenly counted among fans as well as musicians, "I can think of very few released recordings with more musical importance than the work of the Octet," and he offered these reasons:

I have seen within the time lapse of a decade the growth of so-called West Coast jazz. I have heard more and more of the Octet innovations being used and accepted in the 'mainstream' of jazz. I have seen the individuals of the Octet, once removed from the geographic isolation of their San Francisco home, rise in esteem and prominence in the eyes of fellow musicians, critics, and the public. But, as a *group* these contributors to jazz were unacknowledged,

except by flattery of imitation, primarily because the jazz-con-
scious public, the agents, the recording companies, the jazz journals,
the reporters, all had their eyes and ears focused on the East Coast
(Brubeck 1956).

Miles Davis and a few other east coast musicians began playing Brubeck tunes (*The Duke, In Your Own Sweet Way*), and Columbia Records
gave his music international distribution. Twardzik never mentioned
Brubeck, but we have Bob Zieff's statement that Twardzik "listened
to Brubeck before Miles Davis kosherized him." Twardzik had the
musical temperament that would have led him to seek out Brubeck's
experiments. With his interest in contemporary classicism, he would
certainly have been fascinated by Brubeck's association with Darius
Milhaud, the expatriate French composer who was Brubeck's teacher
at Mills College in Oakland. The most obvious connection to Brubeck
is Twardzik's tacit homage to him in those eight bars Twardzik played
in *Stella by Starlight*, but there was, in the early 1950s, a lot that was
worth learning from Brubeck. Twardzik was not the only one listening.
Brubeck's role in expanding the harmonic foundations of jazz in the
early 1950s has been unjustly overshadowed by the 50 years of commercial and, in jazz terms, popular celebrity that followed (Chambers
1999), and it is salutary to glimpse it, momentarily unassimilated, in the
playing of young Twardzik.

A particularly noteworthy sign of Twardzik's development in these
early recordings comes on *Bess You Is My Woman Now*. Twardzik would
later record this ballad with his trio, as we have already noted, in a
delicate, pensive version. His affection for the song might have started
with his exposure to it in the studio with Mariano. It is impossible
to know whether Twardzik suggested it to Mariano for this session
or vice-versa. Whatever the circumstances, the two recorded versions
by Twardzik could hardly be more different. On the *All Stars* version,
Mariano trowels out Gershwin's melody with heavy vibrato, turgidly
or perhaps just melodramatically. On my first listening, I expected him
to collapse in a Carmen Lombardo satire, but he keeps a straight face.
In fact, he seems dead serious. Twardzik responds with stunning originality. He plays a sparkling, chiming accompaniment in the upper register that sets off Mariano's quavering lead like lace trimming on black
velvet.

These recordings served their professional purpose for the leader. Charlie Mariano left Boston soon after with the Chubby Jackson–Bill Harris band, a splinter group from Woody Herman's First Herd, and from there he went on to the California-based Stan Kenton orchestra (1953–55, 1958–59) and the high-profile small band known as Shelley Manne and His Men (1955–58). Then, for the next four and a half decades, he pursued an international career on a scale unprecedented in jazz or any of the other arts, taking up residencies in Japan, Malaysia, Belgium, India (where he learned to play the nagasuram, a classical Indian flute), Switzerland, the Netherlands, and several other countries.

Mariano's departure hardly made a dent in the Boston jazz community, which was thriving, as the Prestige managers had rightly surmised. After Symphony Sid's success with his remote broadcasts from the Hi Hat on WCOP, a second station, WHDH, began broadcasting from Storyville with announcer John McLellan. Star players came to town regularly. There were talented young musicians everywhere, thanks to the Berklee School and the New England Conservatory, and there were a growing number of places for them to play. Besides Storyville and the Hi Hat, there was the Jazz Workshop at a club called The Stable, where the local talent could play (7.6).

There were also informal settings where the musicians got a chance to work out ideas and gain experience. One hotbed was the top floor of a rooming house at 905 Boylston Street. It was around the corner from Berklee, and for a couple of years it was a musicians' hangout, rehearsal space, dormitory and playground. Some musicians paid rent, but it was never entirely clear who was living there and who was just visiting. Ted Casher, a reed player in Boston trad and swing bands, told me that Bob Zieff had been a roommate of Dick Twardzik's there, but actually Zieff was the regular resident and Twardzik an occasional one. Twardzik went there for his lessons with Zieff, or for jam sessions and rehearsals, and to score drugs. He lived there for some months around the beginning of 1954, when Crystal Joy's parents, in whose house he had been living in Jamaica Plain, asked him to leave because they found out about his drug use. He moved in to 905 Boylston, and for a while Crystal Joy defied her parents by staying there with him.

The folklore surrounding 905 Boylston included a tale that someone donated Easter chicks to the house and, according to Casher, "they grew up into chickens on the top floor." Zieff couldn't place it. "The closest to raising chickens," in his recollection, "was that a Rosicrucian contingent including bassist Ray Olivieri had a tree growing upside down out of a box hanging from the ceiling." The room with the suspended tree also had the best piano, and Zieff used it for his lessons.

The top floor had private rooms on both sides of the hallway and opened out into a common living room and kitchen at one end and a common bathroom at the other. Some of the musicians—"a couple of drummers at least"— spilled down onto the second floor, according to Zieff. The second-floor drummers were probably Jimmy Weiner and Peter Littman. "They were always on the scene together in their teens," Zieff said.

Littman started showing up in the jazz musicians' haunts when he was 16, in 1951, looking for any chance he could get to sit in on drums. He

[illustration 7.6] The Jazz Workshop at The Stable, near Copley Square, Boston, with Jay Migliori, tenor saxophone, Jimmy Zitano, drums, Ray Santisi, piano, probably John Neves, bass, and Varty Haroutunian, tenor saxophone. From the Twardzik-Thompson Archive, courtesy of Rosamond Thompson and Jane Sumner. All rights reserved.

was from nearby Medford, where his mother directed choral groups in a synagogue. She had started him on piano at an early age, but he could not sit still long enough to hone his keyboard skills. Drums suited him better, with his restless hands and bobbing head. On drums, for better or worse, he felt no need to bother with lessons. He was persistent, and eventually he got some chances to play, and the word spread that he kept reasonable time and threw in accents in a kind of uninhibited way that kept the music loose. "He played passable drums," Crystal Joy said. "He wasn't a virtuoso or anything." That was about as positive a review as his drumming ever got from anyone.

Twardzik took to him immediately, and they came to share a taste for heroin, among other things. Though Crystal Joy told me that "Peter was chippying—he wasn't that badly strung out," people like Russ Freeman thought of him as a serious addict from a very young age. The conflicting views may have come from knowing Littman at different points in his brief career. "Peter just wanted company to go and score," Crystal Joy said, probably remembering him as the high-school truant at 905 Boylston, "so he would go and get Dick, and get him to go with them while they scored." For Twardzik, it would turn out to be a fatal friendship.

The Boston jazz musicians had a saying, Casher told me: "When you get up to the top floor at 905 Boylston, you know you're gettin' high." Crystal Joy remembered an occasion when the police raided the top floor. "They found works in the bathroom, but they couldn't blame it on anybody because everybody used the same bathroom," she said. "So they got away with one that time."

I suggested to Zieff that 905 Boylston might have been Boston's counterpart to Gil Evans's basement apartment on 55th Street in New York, where in 1947–49 young musicians like Miles Davis, John Lewis, Gerry Mulligan and George Russell brought about "the birth of the cool" (Chambers 1983: 90–133). Zieff would have none of it. "Comparing it to Gil's is rather far-fetched in that the locals were largely fledglings—very few creative original thinkers," by his standards. "It was Art-Is-Imitation country."

Yet the rooming house undeniably served as a jazz think tank, and the creative output it nurtured, or at least played a role in, was original and sometimes daring, encompassing Charlie Mariano's Prestige recordings and, more auspiciously, works by Zieff himself, by Dick Wetmore, Serge Chaloff and, of course, Richard Twardzik. Zieff is right, of course, in saying they cannot be compared to Miles Davis's nonet recordings in terms of impact and influence— should not, perhaps, be mentioned in the same breath. The Boston recordings are obscure. But they deserved to be heard further afield, and they would have been if they had originated in New York.

For Zieff, the jazz community that congregated around 905 Boylston gave him a chance to hear his arrangements brought to life. He was aided and abetted in this by Dick Wetmore, a musician who was willing to take on the responsibility of organizing bands for rehearsing Zieff's music and other purposes. Wetmore was a kind of musical polymath, with professional skills on both violin and trumpet, and stylistic facility in everything from Dixieland to bebop and beyond—all the way to Zieff's chamber jazz. For these few years, he seemed to be involved in everything that was happening. Almost every Boston musician I spoke to 50 years or so after these events brought up Wetmore in some connection or other.

Zieff first met Wetmore at the Melody Lounge in Lynn when Wetmore was working with Charlie Mariano and various pianists, sometimes Dick Twardzik and other times Al Wolcott or Jaki Byard. The combinations at the Melody Lounge were remarkably fluid. Twardzik played there with Wetmore on trumpet in October 1953 in a quintet led by Sam Margolis, a Boston tenor saxophone player who favored Lester Young's swing style. The repertoire that night, heard on Symphony Sid's radio broadcast (and recorded privately, as listed in the discography), included the riff tunes *One O'Clock Jump*, *Stompin' at the Savoy* and *Jumpin' at the Woodside*, considerable departures from Twardzik's usual fare, but hardly a stretch for Wetmore, the stylistic chameleon.

Not long after the Melody Lounge gigs, Wetmore played with Bob Pilsbury in the Excalibur Jazz Band on Cape Cod in a real throwback style. "Tommy Benford was in that band," Pilsbury told me. "He played with Jelly Roll Morton, for Chrissake." Several veteran musicians recounted a story about Pilsbury giving Wetmore a handsome old cornet he had inherited. "I didn't need it," Pilsbury said. "I couldn't play it." Jim Wheaton volunteered the information that Wetmore had been a "hanger-on" in a band Wheaton played in at the Southward Inn in

Orleans, Cape Cod, in 1954. "He plays nice cornet as well as violin," he said.

Wetmore's versatility and skills made a lasting impression on everyone who came across him, both the figs and the cats, a rare achievement in his generation. It was destined to be a strictly local reputation, the way it played out. Looking back on his career at 70, Wetmore said, "Most of my life, to be honest, I've just played and gone wherever I was going to play... I've just sort of accepted what was offered me and played on it" (Barnett 1998: 10). So, nearing the end of a long career, Wetmore's discography is sparse, to say the least, most conspicuous, perhaps, for a few dates with the Vinnie Burke String Jazz Quartet, including four tracks backing Gerry Mulligan that went unreleased for 40 years.

Wetmore's obscurity hardly seemed likely in his early years in Boston. In 1953 and '54, the 27-year-old Wetmore assembled at least two pick-up bands with different instrumentation in hopes of landing a record deal. One band had Wetmore on trumpet with Dick Johnson on alto, Bill Nordstrom on bass and Jimmy Weiner on drums. They used different piano players, though apparently never Twardzik, and for at least one rehearsal Bill Wellington came in on tenor ("a fine jazz tenor player," Zieff recalled, "who was shy about reading"). Wetmore was quick to recognize the special quality of Bob Zieff's writing, and brought him in as composer/arranger. The instrumentation, conventional by Zieff's lights, was mainly in aid of enticing record producers. At one point Wetmore and Zieff thought they had an agreement with Bethlehem Records, a small independent company in New York, but in the end it did not work out. After Zieff moved to New York in 1954, this project petered out.

More successful in every way was the second rehearsal band with Wetmore on violin and a rhythm trio. Ironically, this band set out purposely to be experimental, starting with the violin as centerpiece, a peripheral jazz instrument at the best of times and one that had no standing at all in bebop and its fallout. Twardzik was the piano player, and in this context he was expected to give free rein to his harmonic imagination. The original bassist in the group was Jimmy Woode, and Woode and the trombonist Sonny Truitt also contributed some arrangements. But at some point Wetmore decided that their charts didn't fit with Zieff's—"or vice-versa," Zieff says—and the group started rehearsing Zieff's charts exclusively.

The music they worked on and eventually recorded has an eerie familiarity in hindsight. The compositions, all Zieff's, are *Rondette, Sad Walk, Re-Search, Piece Caprice, Just Duo, Pomp* and *Brash*—seven of the eight pieces later recorded by the Chet Baker Quartet in Paris. There is another one, *Shiftful*, that Baker did not record. (And Baker did record one, *Mid-Forte*, that Wetmore did not.)

Wetmore's rehearsals were not public, but they were open. Zieff's music was recognized as "advanced," and word spread among musicians when Wetmore was rehearsing. Zieff remembers Percy Heath, about to become the lifelong bassist in the Modern Jazz Quartet, showing up to listen, probably while he was touring with Dizzy Gillespie's band. The rehearsals became communal events. "When we rehearsed at 905 [Boylston]," Zieff said, "Rudy Vanelli appeared listening; then when we took a break he would play finger-style classic guitar."

They sometimes rehearsed at the Stable in the afternoons when Twardzik was working there in the evenings as intermission pianist. And as the musicians mastered the intricacies of the arrangements, brought them up to standards that Wetmore and even Zieff found acceptable, they started looking for a place to make a set of acetates for demonstration purposes. Recording studios were impossibly expensive, with sound booths full of new-fangled reel-to-reel tape machines and highly trained technicians who had to be paid professional fees for running them. Acetates were record-like disks cut with a stylus, and though they were much cheaper than the magnetic tape machines coming onto the market at the time they were also much less flexible. For one thing, they imposed strict time limits on the performances to be recorded, just like 78 rpm records, and they also required an experienced eye on the decibel meter to make certain the stylus stayed on track.

Wetmore needed a place where the acoustics were good and the neighbors were tolerant. It was Twardzik who came up with the solution. Reba Stewart lived in a building on St. Botolph St. with studio apartments—artists' lofts with high ceilings and lots of light coming through high windows. In the basement apartment there were, in Zieff's words, "three guys who let two or three other people stay there." The ceilings were lower in the basement than upstairs, which meant that it was at least theoretically possible to control the echo. The immediate neighbor was a hypnotist, so presumably he would be no problem.

Best of all, one of the three tenants was an electrical engineer, George Murdoch, who, according to Zieff, "recorded organs all over for Aeolian-Skinner."

By a quirk of fate, neither Twardzik nor Woode was around for either the demo session or the actual recording. "What happened was that Jimmy got an offer to go with Duke Ellington, and so he left town to do that, and Dick Twardzik got busted for heroin, and was put away for a while at that time," Wetmore told Anthony Barnett (1998: 18). Wetmore's recollection of Twardzik being jailed is not exactly right, but he was on the lam because of narcotics offenses, as we shall see. The absence of Twardzik and Woode pained Wetmore for the lost opportunity. "The quartet we put together was a fabulous group," he said with a sigh. "It really was an excellent group, but those things change as people move around."

For years, rumors persisted that the demo recordings had Twardzik and Woode on them, but Wetmore scotched them. "Those acetates, they got lost, which is a shame because I believe that some of those were actually better than the performance we did in the studio," Wetmore said (Barnett 1998: 21). But it was not because they had Twardzik and Woode on them. Wetmore believes that the rhythm trio on the demos was the one that later made the studio recording with him: Ray Santisi on piano, Bill Nordstrom on bass and Jimmy Zitano on drums.

With the acetates in hand, Wetmore and Zieff made an appointment with Tom Stewart at Bethlehem Records at 1650 Broadway in New York. Stewart was a friend, a New Englander from Connecticut who had led local bands, and would later join Zieff's woodwind and brass band as a trumpeter at Randall's Island. Nevertheless, Stewart found the music on the demo records a hard sell. Eventually a 10" LP would materialize, simply titled *Dick Wetmore* (Bethlehem BCP-1035, recorded in September or October 1953 at Coastal Studios in New York, and not released until August or November 1955; Wetmore says August and Zieff says November). The record had a momentary shelf life, and then it was out of print until 2000, when it reappeared in a limited-edition virgin vinyl 10" facsimile LP from Toshiba-EMI [TOJJ-1035] in Japan (7.7, also page 51).

In the liner notes, Stewart (1955) displayed uncommon candor. Most liner notes are promotional, but Stewart's notes offered little incentive for anyone to buy the record. Instead, he devoted the limited space on the back of the 10" sleeve to providing what he considered fair warning about Zieff's non-conformist music, much of it via self-denigrating quotations from Zieff himself. Stewart begins:

> One morning a few weeks ago, Dick Wetmore and Bob Zieff came up to the offices of Bethlehem with some demonstration records they had cut in someone's basement back in Boston. Bob told me that "a group of musicians (who weren't working together) started rehearsing for a record date. I was asked by Dick to write some music for the rehearsing group. A mixture of passivity, antagonism and enthusiasm (among other things) helped and hindered this venture."

[illustration 7.7] Dick Wetmore, *Dick Wetmore*. Bethlehem BCP 1035. Photograph and cover design Burt Goldblatt ca. 1955.

Stewart then picks up Zieff's tone for his own comments on the music. He seems overly cautious about the putative irregularities in the music, especially for someone who was a technically adroit trumpeter in his own right. He warns potential listeners about irregular forms ("the compositions do not fall into the familiar four, eight, twelve and sixteen-bar patterns") and harmonics ("none, with the possible exception of *Rondette*, adhere to any commonly used harmonic structure"). Even his apparent endorsements of the music are couched in negatives ("deeper understanding was not prerequisite to the enjoyment of the music," "there is none of the uncomfortableness here that accompanies most 'experiments' of this kind"). Stewart's notes seem to warn potential listeners to steel their nerves before taking a chance on this music.

None of that was really necessary. The music has obvious charms, and if it had been listened to in a receptive critical climate it might have given Wetmore and Zieff the boost commensurate with their talents. But Bethlehem was small-time and conservative. It was not a label listeners turned to for adventurous or experimental music. Tom Stewart got the music into print, but almost no one was listening. The producer of the *Dick Wetmore* LP was identified on the liner as Creed Taylor. He was unknown at the time, but would go on to earn a reputation in the 1960s by introducing pop elements into jazz recordings at Verve Records, after its founder and chief producer, Norman Granz, sold the label. After that, in the 1970s, Taylor guided his own label, CTI (Creed Taylor Inc.), to considerable prosperity with even more blatant pop compromises. His successes, though profitable, proved ephemeral, and all of the jazz labels he out-sold in his heyday (Blue Note, Riverside, Prestige, and the jazz divisions of Capitol, Victor and Columbia) produced some lasting jazz classics while many of his hybrids have ended up on the rubble heap with zebra-stripe pedal-pushers and tie-dye underpants. In a lifetime of searching for soft markets, Taylor was not likely to find much to his liking in *Dick Wetmore*.

Zieff remembers the recording session with a sour taste. "We drove all night and had about two hours sleep," he says. "And the bassist played blind drunk." Zieff got in an argument with the producer. "Creed Taylor didn't want to pay me anything in front," he says, possibly because he was the composer/arranger rather than a player, but in Zieff's recollection it was because, according to Taylor, "if I was to get anything the cover would [have to] say: DW plays BZ." The credits on the back cover listed "Bob Zieff—compositions and arrangements" among the musicians. Wetmore alone gets leadership billing.

To make matters worse, the Bethlehem LP was released into a highly volatile marketplace. Ten-inch vinyl records at 33 rpm had supplanted 10" 78 rpm records, but these in turn were almost immediately supplanted by 12" ones. The three-minute limit on tracks was freed up to four or five minutes, and, though most musicians and listeners found it hard to imagine, habituated as they were to brevity, in theory they could go as long as 15 minutes (and soon 20). Monaural sound had been superseded by high-fidelity (microphone separation and mixing), and it was eclipsed almost immediately by stereo. Technically, Bethlehem's hi-fi 10" LP *Dick Wetmore* with its three-minute tracks would have been old-fashioned if it had been released in late 1953, when it was recorded, but two years later, when it was actually released, it looked positively quaint.

There was no market for the LP except for a few musicians. It remains one of the most obscure great records in modern jazz history.

As if his apologetic liner notes were not enough, Tom Stewart then had the temerity to give Bob Zieff the last word. "As an additional aid to the listener," Stewart wrote, with no apparent irony, "I will include below a technological [*sic*] description of each piece, written by Bob at my request."

Zieff's annotations (1955) are hardly designed to draw listeners in. Zieff is not like that, as Stewart must have known. As a marketing device for a general audience, his annotations have about as much appeal as scratch-and-smell musk oil in a Chanel ad. Though they are informed and serious, they are vague at the core and more than a bit arcane, with no superlatives. That is to say, they are perfectly in character. They supply approximate guidelines to the composer's intentions on each piece (and in that respect they double in value because they serve listeners to the Chet Baker versions exactly as well as the Dick Wetmore versions). Here are Zieff's annotations (except for *Shiftful*, which was not included in Baker's repertoire). They appear here in the order Zieff "suggests they be listened to … since they form a unit: the suite" (though they have never been ordered this way on any release of this music by either Wetmore or Baker):

1. Piece Caprice: A A' B A form. The A' section develops the A section. The top and bottom parts are built around typical jazz-styled inner-voice parts.

2. Just Duo: a broken form consisting of the measure-grouping: 2 + 1 + (2 + 2) + 2.

3. Pomp: of blues orientation. Its first four-measure phrase lacks the usual fourth measure; i.e., a measure order resulting: 1 + 2 + 3 + 5 + 6, etc. Its overall phrase grouping is: 3 + 2 + (2 + 2).

4. Sad Walk: A A' B A form as in Piece Caprice. Now the B section is "free" for the performer to improvise upon.

5. Brash: A A' B A form again. Here used are less familiar harmonic progressions and melodic movement.

6. Re-Search: A A B A form. The title alludes to its feeling of jazz in the '30s.

8. Rondette: a twice-repeated twelve-measure section. This alternates with different B material. B appears in the following order: original; inversion; original played simultaneously with the inversion (mirrored) and original followed by inversion forming one continuous phrase.

The annotations, removed from the recordings, belie the straightforward charm that is at the heart of the appeal of the music itself. To musicians, the main appeal undoubtedly comes from the melodic interplay at the foundation and from the harmonic inversions, what Zieff later called (in a 1987 letter to me) "parenthetic key regions." To ordinary listeners, the appeal lies in the stately movement of the music that sometimes takes surprising directions but never loses its grace. Like a swan on a pond, Zieff's music is serene on the surface and busy underneath.

Richard Twardzik grasped the music in all its profundity at Wetmore's rehearsals at 905 Boylston and the Stable. He was mightily impressed. Two years later, when Chet Baker told him to bring some new music for the quartet, Twardzik phoned Zieff in New York and asked him to send all the music he had. "I adapted what I wrote for Wetmore for Chet," Zieff said. "Seven of the eight pieces. One didn't seem especially adaptable at the time [*Shiftful*]. I sent one different piece [*Mid-Forte*].

Dick asked me for as much music as I had and they would record it. I gave him eight and said telegraph me if you need more."

In the late summer of 1955, when Twardzik was in New York getting ready to embark on the Ile de France for Paris, he visited Zieff in his room in the Alvin Hotel, the old musicians hangout. It was the first time the two "lonelies" had met in over a year. "Dick Twardzik went over all the music with me before they left for Europe—as to tempo, phrasing, etc.," Zieff said.

The Wetmore recordings and the Baker recordings of those seven Zieff compositions are soulmates, even though, as Zieff rightly says, "the soloing was world's apart on those two dates," with Baker's quartet far superior. Twardzik would never hear Wetmore's record, but on both recordings, the compositions are the same in texture, feeling, mood and nuance. The common bond, of course, is Bob Zieff.

Twardzik would carry Zieff's instructions with him to Paris where he would pass them along to his band-mates. The integrity of Zieff's compositions is impeccably preserved in spite of the time and distance between the two recordings. But Zieff expected no less from the young man who had been his student. That afternoon at the Alvin Hotel, they went over Zieff's charts so intensely that Twardzik was afraid he would miss his boarding call. As he stuffed his suitcase into the trunk of the cab, he gave an absent-minded wave toward Zieff, and Zieff watched for a minute as the cab scurried off in the direction of the docks. They would never meet again.

8 Albuquerque Social Swim

A couple of months after cutting what should have been his break-through record with Charlie Mariano's Boston All Stars, Twardzik hit the road for points unknown in the back seat of a Cadillac, ditching the Hi Hat job and the camaraderie of the Boston community, the only place he had a reputation as a piano player. Exactly why he left is not known. He was strung out, and he would eventually try to sort himself out on the trip, but that does not seem to have been the purpose. Maybe he was dodging the same narcotics officers who were making Serge Chaloff lie low.

From the beginning of April to the end of June 1953, Twardzik would drift around Mexico and the American Southwest. Reba Stewart was with him for the first six weeks, and they traveled with a Boston couple, Charlie Vachsteen and his wife, Gene. (Richard was never certain about the spelling of their surname, usually attaching a question mark to it in his letters home.) Gene may have been studying art with Reba, or at least they met through painting. "She tried to be a painter," Reba's patron, Geneviève McMillan, remembered. "Reba did not believe in her as a painter, I think. She was more interested perhaps in matadors." McMillan's remark is especially prescient considering she did not know they traveled in Mexico together until I told her. McMillan remembered Charles, from her brief acquaintance a year or two after these events, as "erratic, brusque, very nervous, always trying to make an impression." "He didn't have much self-confidence," she said. Gene, on the other hand, was "very very cool—she was the opposite of him."

The Vachsteens owned the car, and Twardzik paid them for gas and maybe more. They bopped around several towns and cities, but their home base at first was Mexico City, for April and most of May, and then when Twardzik was left on his own he went to Albuquerque, New Mexico, until the end of June.

Henryk and Clare agreed to pay Richard's way. It must have seemed a good idea at first. Maybe they thought they were helping him break away from the company he was keeping in the jazz underground, or perhaps were saving him from rough treatment at the hands of the narcs and the tarnish on the family reputation that went with it. Richard chronicled his trip in a steady flow of letters home, but he says nothing about why he left or why he chose the Southwest. His time in Mexico City would culminate in a five-day hospital stay for an ailment defined by various symptoms (dysentery, respiratory problems, infection, constipation) but presumably resulting inadvertently in a cure of his heroin addiction. If so, he did not stay clean for more than a few days.

The southwesterly direction was probably Reba Stewart's idea. She had a professional interest in pueblo art and would later receive scholarships to work and study in Mexico several times in her career. This was her first trip.

Twardzik's first postcard home, from Acapulco on 2 April 1953, thanks his parents for subsidizing the trip. His high spirits recall the enthusiasm he showed as a kid writing home from camp:

> Saludos Amigos! I am very happy, and I hope that everything is fine. This is the most informative trip of my life. Thank you again. I spent a day in Mexico City. Some of the most beautiful modern buildings. My greatest regret is that you both are not here with me. Look up Acapulco on the map. WOW! these roads are terrible! This is not the tourist season thank God.
>
> una carta mañana. XX DICK XX

The euphoria did not last (and the next day's postcard, the promised *carta mañana*, never materialized). Almost three weeks went by before he wrote again, on 29 April. This time it was a letter, and it started out sunny but quickly shifted to recount a string of mishaps that would strain the credulity of anyone except, perhaps, indulgent parents:

> Dear Folks —
>
> Love and Kisses, I'm back in Mexico City.
>
> This has been an unfortunate trip in terms of accidents. After two days in Mexico City, we drove to Acapulco, a 10 hr. trip. Charlie drove the entire distance and when we arrived at Acapulco, he fainted and fell down on some rocks cutting himself badly in many places and hurting his nose and closing one eye. Four days later he became sick, so sick that he spent a week in bed in Acapulco and we have to spend another week in Mexico City. The doctor's verdict: Malaria, so we are just waiting hopefully.

Charlie Vachsteen's brush with malaria carries an ominous overtone, like one of those uncanny coincidences in a Thomas Hardy novel that foreshadows someone's doom hundreds of pages later: in 1971, eighteen eventful years after the Mexico trip, Reba Stewart would come down with malaria on a painting excursion to Africa, and the disease would kill her at the age of 41.

Charlie's malaria seems important to Twardzik mainly for its economic repercussions. He says:

> I had hoped that we would be spending our time in the rural areas living like the natives. But because of Charlie's sickness, a week in Acapulco (a rich tourist town) and a week in Mexico has damaged my bank account severely despite my best efforts, and it is absolutely necessary that you please send me $50 if I am to have enough money to live. (Clare: if you can make it $60 I'll be able to pick up the most marvelous pair of shoes)!

He takes a few lines to justify his penury and urge his parents to action:

> Prices so far have been uncomfortably close to U.S. standards in some things. Oh, about the money, my piano upstairs will serve as collateral. I never play it any more and you surely will be able to get $100 for it, but please send the money now so that it gets here before Sunday, on which day Charlie's health permitting we set out for parts unknown.

It seems that Clare, for one, was not impressed. This plea for money was the last one that would involve her. Hereafter, Henryk alone would hear from Richard on money matters. "I think you had better wire it so it gets here on time," he says, and he gives his address as HOTEL CASABLANCA, CALLEJON GARCIA LORCA (OFF AVENIDA JUAREZ) MEXICO D.F.

His troubles do not end here, however. It turns out that he and Reba had been victims as well as Charlie:

> I have other bad news. I smashed my heel on a rock, nothing serious; and a harpoon gun went off sending a long iron harpoon 3 inches into Reba's shoulder! Not knowing it had barbs the fools tried to pull it out, causing internal bleeding. Very messy! But she's up and around now.

Lest anyone begin to suspect stupor and recklessness behind all these mishaps, Richard closes on a spunky final note:

> DON'T get me wrong! I'm having a wonderful time learning the language, meeting many wonderful people and getting a whole new perspective, musical and psychological.
>
> I really wish you were here. Henry: YOU'LL LOVE MEXICO CITY
>
> Love to all
>
> Happily DICK XX

The letter was postmarked on the eve of his 22nd birthday, but he does not mention it.

The bad luck kept coming. His next letter begins by thanking his parents for sending the money, and congratulates them on the birth of a litter of puppies. "I bet you've really got your hands full, and all black at that!" he says, sharing their delight at breeding Black Erich. Then the woes begin:

> This trip is proving far less interesting than expected. Instead of going around the country visiting ruins, pyramids etc., the Vachsteens (sp?) are spending all their time in Mexico City. One reason for this is that they've some friends who aspire to be matadors, and these guys seem to have become the focal point of their existence in Mexico. All well and good, but to me, Mexico City is just like countless cities I've stayed in while I was on the road, and the country has so much to offer…

Gene Vachsteen, according to Geneviève McMillan, would move to Mexico and marry a matador a few years later. For Richard, the split with the Vachsteens naturally exacerbated his financial difficulties:

> So — Reba and I have been taking little field trips by ourselves to outlying cities; Puebla, Touscon, Toluca (where I am now), Villa de Bravo etc. This means taking the bus and riding for hours and hours and paying the fare besides. Money is the one big thorn in my side. Ouch! Ouch!

Richard then turns to the subject of his health:

I haven't been feeling too well for the past three or four days, and this morning I woke up with a raging cold, the climate in Toluca here is undoubtedly largely responsible.

But through it all, he manages a tourist observation:

You see, from time to time incredible poverty and signs of suffering, but one of the most amazing things is the cheerfulness of the people. Some of the poor Indians really seem to have a ball out of life —

Music comes to his mind, and his comments make it clear that he has not been much involved with it on the trip:

I haven't been able to locate Bob Allen but the other night I walked into a club in Mexico City and nearly fell out! There sitting at the piano was a guy that I used to be quite chummy with in Boston. The guy plays terrible but seems to be doing O.K.

I've been writing for reviews of my record [*Boston All Stars*]; no luck so far, altho' I have an idea that it's out in New York. I've got many new ideas and I'm getting anxious to get back to work.

He closes with a list of valedictions, and he reverts to his childhood name in the signature, as he would in all his pleading letters from here on (illustration 8.2 below):

I hope all is well and that nobody is sick —

I'll be seeing you in about two weeks with luck.

Lotsa love to all

Dogs, dogs, dogs, dogs, dogs !!!

XX Dickie XX

If luck was really involved with getting him back home in two weeks, then once again his luck did not hold. The Vachsteens left then, but Twardzik did not go with them. Instead, he found himself in the American British Cowdray Hospital, in Mexico City.

His letter about his change of plans about returning home is written to Henryk alone, and Richard opens it calling him by his nursery name "Tatush." He has been in touch with Elaine Brehaut, the daughter of Bree and Kay who had been his friend since childhood. Elaine had

finished her nurses' training in Boston, following in her mother's foot-
steps, gone to Dallas for specialist training, and taken a job in hospital
in San Angelo, Texas (misidentified as San Angeles by Richard). "He
needed money and he wanted to stop by," Elaine told me years later,
and so she wired him funds for his trip to Albuquerque. San Angelo is
about 450 miles east-southeast of Albuquerque.

Richard's letter was written on 12 May, a Tuesday, the day after Henryk
sent $64.58 to his son via Western Union telegram, which apparently
arrived as Richard was writing, and is acknowledged at the end of the
letter:

Tuesday —

Henry Ole 'Tatush'!

Everything seems to happen at once — First the good. I've got a
job in Albuquerque N.M. with Buddy Berlin, a wonderful guy who
has been living the past year in Spain. Six nights a week and the
money's good.

I was supposed to leave Mexico on Monday but this is my second
day in the hospital and I may be here for at least 3 more days at
which time I'm going to Albuquerque, stopping on the way to see
Elaine and rest up for a few days.

I got Dysentery, a pretty bad case but I'm feeling much better and
the doctor (a woman from N.Y. She's been down here for 17 years)
says my recovery will be rapid. They're doing all sorts of tests on
me here at the hospital and I'm taking penicillin inhalation with
oxygen tanks which is running into money. My room costs 45 pesos
a day & I owe the doctor 25. I paid her 75 already.

Elaine sent me some money for transportation but it's all going for
the hospital. I have enough for two more days so please send some
money right away. I realize that my trip has been a terrible drain
on you but as soon as I'm situated in Albuquerque I'll live frugally
and I'll pay back every red cent! Oh, incidentally we heard on the
radio last night that a tornado went right through the center of San
Angeles, the town where Elaine is! I hope she's all right.

Please don't worry about me. I'm feeling much better. I have a lot of confidence in the doctor and all this medicine they're shoving into me really seems to be doing some good.

He closes with a report on his final indignity at the hands of the Vachsteens:

After agreeing in Boston to refund half my transportation money if I didn't return with them, the Vachsteens wouldn't come up with a penny. Those sons of bitches! Here am I flat on my back and I don't know when I've ever needed money more. How low can people sink? She spends that much every day on those F—— bullfighters she adores so much —

But enough — I just received your telegram!! I'll sleep easier tonight!!

Love to ALL 15 OF YOU !!

XX DICKIE

Two or three days later he wrote again to Henryk. The financial stakes had gone up considerably:

Hello Henry —

Listen, I think this Doctor's really going to fix me up. Right now I'm preparing for a nasal irrigation so that the penicillin inhalations will be more successful. Today I had my first bowel movement — eminently satisfactory!

I just finished a long talk with the doctor and she feels that this may clear up my nose and throat problems.

About finances — my previous estimate was way out the window. My bill for the first two days was 300 pesos! And the doctor gets 50 pesos a visit, so there's 250 more.

The exchange rate is roughly 85 pesos for $10, so figure it out. She realizes my financial condition and is trying to keep things down. My total resources now are 700 pesos which is probably what my bill is now —

However the doctor says that Blue Cross is in effect here so if I am covered send down the stuff immediately. If not I'll surely need at least $100 more to get me out of here and up to Elaine's.

The sums he was asking for were far from trivial at the time, and Twardzik's unblinking requests bespeak volumes about his bond with his father. But in case his physical problems were not incentive enough, he devotes the last half of the letter to his spiritual ones:

> It's very lonely here, there's only one person that I've met so far that speaks English and my struggles in Spanish with the nurses sometimes get terribly involved.

> The day I really got sick my "friends" lit out on a trip to South Mexico. Not that I want to see those idiots bastards any way, but it does leave me completely alone with no one to come and see me.

> I think my new L.P. with Charlie Mariano is out, tell me what you think —

> I hope everything's O.K. at home and as I said in my last letter DON'T WORRY everything's all right. I don't know if I'll be here two or three days more so, as soon as you receive this letter act immediately with the Blue Cross or the money as the case may be. Even with the Blue Cross I'll need $35 more for transportation.

> Keep the faith!!!

> Regards to Queenie

> Love to Clare

> XX DICKIE

Henryk responded dutifully by wiring $125 via Western Union on 15 May, the day Richard was discharged. The hospital bill (8.1), in American dollars, totes up $180 for room, $115 for laboratory analysis, and $98.89 for medicines, for the total $393.89.

Twardzik's stay at the American British Cowdray Hospital, if it was an attempt at curing his addiction, joins a long list of confinements by jazz musicians for that purpose. Dozens of them went through drying-out programs, not always voluntarily. Charlie Parker was confined in Camarillo State Hospital in California, and later in Bellvue Sanitarium in New York. Charles Mingus and Thelonious Monk also spent time in Bellvue. Sonny Rollins took three 'sabbaticals' from music in unnamed clinics. Art Pepper went to Synanon in Santa Monica, California, after long stays in Sing Sing and other prisons. Serge Chaloff would spend three and a half months in Bridgewater State Hospital in Massachusetts. Best known of all the treatment centers was the Federal Hospital in Lexington, Kentucky, a place where convicted addicts could be sent for medical help. So many jazz musicians were housed there that the hipsters claimed the best jazz band was in Lexington. Chet Baker was happily surprised when he got there to find the legendary Tadd Dameron leading the prison orchestra (Baker 1997: 79).

The heroin epidemic that Twardzik was caught up in raged among jazz musicians for more than a decade, from 1947 to 1959. It was not solely a jazz problem, but it was probably most conspicuous there. Besides Twardzik, some of the musicians who died drug-related deaths in those twelve years included Freddie Webster (1917–47), Sonny Ber-

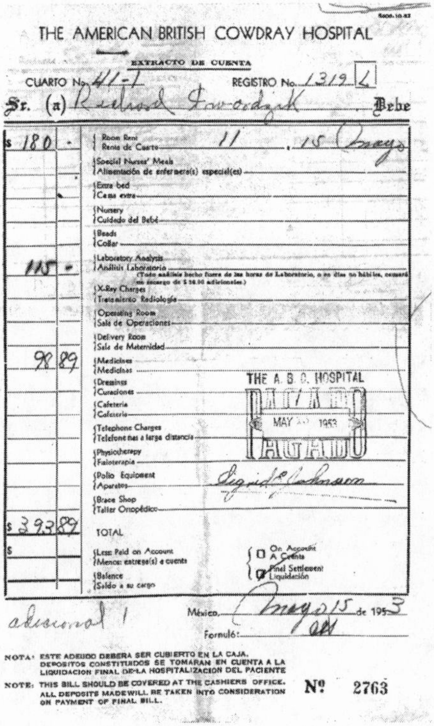

THE AMERICAN BRITISH COWDRAY HOSPITAL

EXTRACTO DE CUENTA

CUARTO No. 41-1 REGISTRO No. 1319

Sr. (a) [illegible] Bebe

$ 180	-	Room Rent / Renta de Cuarto 11 . 15 mayo
		Special Nurses' Meals / Alimentación de enfermera(s) especial(es)
		Extra bed / Cama extra
		Nursery / Cuidado del Bebé
		Beads / Collar
115	-	Laboratory Analysis / Análisis Laboratorio (Todo análisis hecho fuera de las horas de Laboratorio, o en días no hábiles, causará un recargo de $ 10.00 adicionales.)
		X-Ray Charges / Tratamiento Radiología
		Operating Room / Sala de Operaciones
		Delivery Room / Sala de Maternidad
98	89	Medicines / Medicinas
		Dressings / Curaciones
		Cafeteria / Cafetería
		Telephone Charges / Telefonemas a larga distancia
		Physiotherapy / Fisioterapia
		Polio Equipment / Aparatos
		Brace Shop / Taller Ortopédico
$ 393	89	TOTAL
$		Less: Paid on Account / Menos: entrega(s) a cuenta
		Balance / Saldo a su cargo

THE A. B. C. HOSPITAL PAGADO MAY 1953 PAGADO

On Account / A Cuenta — Final Settlement / Liquidación

México, mayo 15 de 1953

Formuló:

NOTA: ESTE ADEUDO DEBERA SER CUBIERTO EN LA CAJA. DEPOSITOS CONSTITUIDOS SE TOMARAN EN CUENTA A LA LIQUIDACION FINAL DE LA HOSPITALIZACION DEL PACIENTE

NOTE: THIS BILL SHOULD BE COVERED AT THE CASHIERS OFFICE. ALL DEPOSITS MADE WILL BE TAKEN INTO CONSIDERATION ON PAYMENT OF FINAL BILL.

Nº 2763

[illustration 8.1] Richard Twardzik's bill from the American British Cowdray Hospital, Mexico, where he was treated 11–15 May 1953. From the Twardzik-Thompson Archive, courtesy of Rosamond Thompson and Jane Sumner.

man (1925–47), Fats Navarro (1923–50), Tiny Kahn (1924–53), Charlie
Parker (1920–1955), Wardell Gray (1921–55), Serge Chaloff (1923–57),
Bob Graettinger (1923–57), Ernie Henry (1926–57) and Billie Holiday
(1915–59). Many more spent periods in what should have been their
peak years in prisons, including Joe Gordon, Parker's fill-in trumpeter
the week Twardzik was in his band, and many of the most talented
players—Bud Powell, Dexter Gordon, Gerry Mulligan, Red Rodney,
J.J. Johnson, Zoot Sims, Stan Getz, Gene Ammons, Sonny Stitt, Art
Blakey, Jackie McLean, Hampton Hawes, Monk, Pepper, Baker.

Drug use was bound up with creative frenzy in the post-War esthetic,
and it found its sublimation in the famous opening lines of Allen Ginsberg's *Howl* (1956):

> I saw the best minds of my generation destroyed by madness, starv-
> ing hysterical naked,

> dragging themselves through the negro streets at dawn looking for
> an angry fix,

> angelheaded hipsters burning for the ancient heavenly connection
> to the starry dynamo in the machinery of night.

> who poverty and tatters and hollow-eyed and high sat up smoking
> in the supernatural darkness of cold-water flats floating across the
> tops of cities contemplating jazz…

Howl gave first voice to what came to be known as the Beat Generation, a name that came into common parlance only in 1957, with the
publication of Jack Kerouac's novel, *On the Road*. Jazz musicians were
charter members of the Beat Generation, years before it had a name.
The literary coterie took a while to catch up to the jazz people, but
when they did they gave it a verbal style as distinctive as bebop had
been after swing.

On the Road sounded the clarion call for the Beats. It took six years
for it to get published, but by then the world was prepped for it. It
immediately imprinted the figure of the beatnik on the popular consciousness, either as an anti-bourgeois hero or as a bourgeois antihero,
depending on the eye of the beholder. Kerouac became the figurehead,
and he took it as his mission to spread the word. He spent a lot of creative energy defining the Beat ethos, starting with an essay in *Esquire*
magazine (1958):

The Beat Generation, that was a vision that we had...in the late Forties, of a generation of crazy, illuminated hipsters suddenly rising and roaming America, serious, curious, bumming and hitchhiking everywhere, ragged, beatific, beautiful in an ugly graceful new way...—the subterranean heroes who'd finally turned from the "freedom" machine of the West and were taking drugs, digging bop, having flashes of insight, experiencing the "derangement of the senses," talking strange, being poor and glad, prophesying a new style for American culture, a new style (we thought) completely free from European influences....

By the time the notion of the Beat Generation reached the wider public, Richard Twardzik had been dead for almost two years, but it was clearly *his* generation. *A Crutch for the Crab*, as much as any single work of art of the day, fulfils Kerouac's definition of something "beautiful in an ugly graceful new way." Twardzik's crab-like motion across the Mexican landscape, four years before the publication of *On the Road* but almost simultaneous with its real-life plot-line, shared the Beat spirit as proclaimed by hyperactive Dean Moriarty to the novel's narrator Sal Paradise in what became a kind of Zen *koan* (Kerouac 1957: 240):

"Whee. Sal, we gotta go and never stop going till we get there."

"Where we going, man?"

"I don't know, but we gotta go."

Twardzik was a prime carrier of the Beat esthetic though he did not live to know its name.

In the quest for kicks, soft drugs like marijuana were common among the literary Beats. Hard drugs were less common, and mostly associated with the jazz community. There, heroin use took root suddenly and, as in any epidemic, spread rapidly and apparently uncontrollably. New York was the epicenter. One of the witnesses was Frankie Socolow, a tenor saxophone player who left New York for California with the Boyd Raeburn orchestra in 1945. "When I came home I was shocked by the whole thing, 'cause I had only been gone for a year or two," he said. "When I came back, everybody—*everybody*—was a junkie" (Gitler 1985: 275).

Growing up in Harlem, Sonny Rollins, seventeen years old in 1947 and about to graduate from high school, said, "Heroin just flooded the community" (Chambers 1983: 139). How did it get there? One of the more persistent urban myths claims that the Mafia moved into the hard drug business around this time, at the end of the War, reluctantly but out of the need to protect their monopoly in gambling, bootlegging and prostitution. The Mafia dons purportedly feared that if they let the Harlem upstarts get a toehold in drug trafficking, they would eventually lose control of their other rackets. So they moved in but, according to the myth, restricted their drug initiatives to black neighborhoods and entertainment districts, where their own children, they felt, would not be exposed to temptation. Whether or not this is how it happened, the chronology and demography both align perfectly with the heroin epidemic.

There were addicts long before the epidemic, of course. Charlie Parker, for one, began using heroin in 1935 in Kansas City when he was fifteen. As Parker's jazz genius set the world on fire, his heroin addiction got mixed inextricably with it. The illusion of a cause-and-effect link between the two provided a powerful role model for young boppers. "If he jumped out of a window, twenty kids would jump out too," Mingus said (Reisner 1962: 152). Parker became a hero well beyond jazz. "Jack Kerouac likes to write about Charlie Parker as god and himself as the prophet," according to one critic (Gold 1960: 156). There were other idols besides Parker, like poet Dylan Thomas (1914–53) and movie star James Dean (1931–55, an exact contemporary of Richard Twardzik), and older icons like painters Van Gogh (1853–90) and Modigliani (1884–1920), poet and playwright Federico Garcia Lorca (1889–1936), and poet Hart Crane (1899–1932). All lived short, luminous, hell-bent lives. Parker was the living luminary, the messiah.

The epidemic was so virulent that jazz eventually caught the attention of a few social scientists, mainly in psychoanalysis and sociology, the softest of the soft sciences. Professional articles from the time carried portentous titles like "Jazz: resistance to the diffusion of a culture pattern" (Berger 1947), "Jazz—a study in cultural conflict" (Esman 1951), "A theory on the psychology of jazz" (Margolis 1954), "Sociological notes on the jam session" (Cameron 1954), "Understanding the jazz musician: the artist and his problems" (Anonymous 1956-57), and "The use of drugs by jazz musicians" (Winick 1959-60).

Some of the commentary lays an academic veneer over a racist subtext, as in this purported explanation of the psychological sources of jazz (Esman 1951: 222):

Produced by a "primitive" group in an area where a less repressive morality flourished, jazz was by its very nature associated with vital libidinous impulses —sex, drink, sensual dancing— precisely the id drives that the superego of the bourgeois cultural sought to repress.

"The psychology of adolescence is central to the understanding of jazz," according to a psychoanalyst (Margolis 1954: 276), a claim that should have sounded alarm bells in a society where many people still addressed African-American men as "boy." Cameron (1954: 180), with a flair for a turn of phrase that was uncommon among his peers, put it more eloquently:

... adolescence in America is typically a period for critical appraisal of the cultural values and a time to experiment with sacred trusts and forbidden fruits.... Jazz is at once radical and idealistic and suffused with the glamour of Promethean artistry and the raw vulgarity of the brothel. And, like athletics, it is one of the few fields in which the young actually can achieve a leading role as the quick reward for hard work and personal ability. To become a great jazz artist when one is sixteen is a wonderful way of running away from the triple tyranny of home discipline, school discipline, and financial dependence. It is revolt as a hero, or at least as a martyr, and not as a runaway child.

The theory gains some credibility from watching Twardzik pouting and preening to keep the parental support coming in Mexico. It would be no great stretch to claim that Twardzik never outgrew his adolescence. He went off to seek his fortune at 18, but in a sense he never left home. He stayed in his old room in Danvers or, when he was working too late to get home, he bunked at Aunt June's house or with the Deans or Crystal Joy's parents or in Peter Van Cortland Morris's apartment or with one of the guys at 905 Boylston. He never had a place of his own, and apparently never cooked for himself, filed a tax return or had a bank account. He was, in effect, a dependent his whole life. His mother nurtured his genius and protected him from mundane concerns in his early years, as did, in radically different social circumstances, the mothers of Charlie Parker, Ben Webster and Chet Baker.

But the range of possibilities is almost limitless. Other jazz musicians carried adult responsibilities almost from birth. Some were breadwinners for their families at an early age (Louis Armstrong), many came from father-dominant families (Bix Beiderbecke, Lester Young, Art Pepper), a few had no families at all (Jabbo Smith, Helen Jones), and a few raised their younger siblings on their own (Bessie Smith).

Jazz musicians are probably harder to categorize psychologically or socially or developmentally than most other occupational groups. Their talents require uniqueness, at least for the greatest players. Standards are not there to measure up to, but to be reinterpreted. Charlie Parker reconfigured the music, and only then could other people hear it his way. Richard Twardzik wrote *A Crutch for the Crab*, and everyone who heard it knew it was beautiful even though they had never heard anything like it before.

For all the self-destruction, only the most tight-assed puritan would maintain that there was no upside to the use of drugs. Musicians believed their music got an edge from the freeing up of feeling, and many of the so-called solid citizens—record producers, promoters, talent agents, bandleaders—obviously agreed with them. Not that they could say so out loud. Mercer Ellington, years later, admitted it for the greatest of all bandleaders, his father. "He felt, I think, personally, that a person under the influence of narcotics was more creative than if they were plain sober—or whatever," Mercer said (Nicholson 2000: 328). "If ever Ellington was prone to the admiration of anything, it was creativity. So he had no qualms about hiring or watching a man—although he never advocated it—but knowing a man was under the influence of narcotics being relative to his music. He felt he was getting a more creative feeling as a result of this."

Paul Bley, the avant-garde piano player, tells a tale that resonates deep into the jazz ethos. "When I recorded *Footloose*," Bley told Francis Davis (2001: 115), "the choice before me was to repeat the stuff I had played in the '50s or to push forward. I was nervous at the recording date and I remember asking [drummer] Pete LaRoca what he thought I should do—stick with what I knew or take a blind leap into something I might mess up. He handed me a fat joint and said, 'Smoke this, and the answer will reveal itself.'" It was as if jazz musicians, in the bebop revolution and its progressive aftermath, sought direct access to feeling, bypassing ratiocination and all semblances of petal-pulling. The ideal, as composer George Russell put it with epigrammatic eloquence (Ullmann 1980), was "an intellect of the heart."

Whatever the psychedelic advantages of drugs, it soon became evident that they were only leased, not given. Casual drug use was a possibility only for the steeliest of psyches, one in a thousand. The others soon found themselves mired in a social cesspool with single-minded cravings far removed from making a brand-new resolution on the changes of *I Got Rhythm* or any other esthetic puzzle.

An article by Charles Winick on "The use of drugs by jazz musicians" (1959–60) is one of the few that provides real data on the milieu Twardzik and the others were living in. In 1954–55, Winick went out and asked jazz musicians about drug use in the bands they had most recently played in. He approached 690 musicians for interviews, was rejected by 281 of them and accepted by 409, of whom 357 provided usable results. His interviews put him face-to-face with his sources, and, although he followed a standard interview protocol, he encouraged the musicians to comment freely as they answered his questions (241). He used their comments to flesh out the analysis. One of his subjects, identified as a "very successful musician," offered this rationalization for using heroin (245): "It lets you concentrate and takes you away from everything. Heroin is a working drug, like the doctor who took it because he had a full schedule so he could concentrate better. It lets me concentrate on my sound."

Winick's goal was to get an objective measure of the extent of drug use in the jazz community. He asked musicians to describe drug use of all kinds by the members of their bands. They were told they could exclude themselves, but two-thirds elected to describe their own use anyway. In this way, each interview provided details on the behavior of five or six jazz musicians on average. Taking their information at face value, Winick tabulated the core results as follows: on heroin use, 53 percent used it at least once, 24 percent were occasional users, and 16 percent were regular users (242). (Years later, Wills [2003], reviewing the clinical histories of a sample of jazz musicians with mental health problems, a subset of Winick's sample but much larger than the national average, found that 52.5 percent of them suffered from heroin addiction.) Winick's figures for marijuana use were 82 percent for once-at-least, 54 percent occasional users, and 23 percent regular users.

The results are useful, but there are two sources of error. First, the musicians who refused to be interviewed make a large proportion, almost 41 percent. Winick concedes that "it is possible that those who refused were concerned about being identified with drug use and thus may have been more familiar with it than were the musicians who were interviewed" (241). The same might be said for the one-third who excluded themselves from their reports and the ones who gave him useless results. Second, Winick's method was based on self-reports of behavior rather than observations, and is thus subject to mistakes on the part of the musicians interviewed, either from self-deception or outright falsities. Both sources of error bias the results in the same direction, tending to "improve" the real situation, that is, to bring the reported behavior more closely into line with socially accepted, conventional mores.

While there is no foolproof way of correcting the results, the marijuana figures might give an insight into the size of the error, at least roughly. Since the percentage of jazz musicians who try marijuana "at least once" realistically approaches unanimity, it looks as if the reported number, 82 percent, could be augmented by about 12–15 percentage points, bringing it up to 94–97 percent. No musician I know would consider that number far-fetched. Taking the 12–15 percent 'correction' as a rule-of-thumb and projecting it onto the heroin figures would bring the percentage of occasional users to almost 40 percent and hard-core users to about 30 percent. That amounts to some 70 percent of jazz musicians involved with heroin regularly. Again, those numbers do not seem out of line for the time, based on eyewitness accounts by musicians looking back on the epidemic a few years after it had passed its peak.

What changed in the years following the most destructive period was the jazz esthetic. By 1960, Merriam and Mack noticed that the jazz community was changing so fast as to be practically redefining itself (1960: 221):

> The tremendous increase in acceptance of jazz as a musical form in the past eight to ten years has surely affected the jazz community, as has the increasing emphasis upon social responsibility, the founding of Schools of Jazz with jazzmen acting as faculty, and the emphasis upon jazz as a scholarly subject in schools across the country.

The "intellect of the heart" was gradually superseded by musicians and teachers working out its theoretical base. Attitudes toward drug use changed too. Winick, noting that the jazz community had established a psychiatric clinic in New York in 1957 to treat addicted musicians, says, "Its very existence may have helped to make drug-taking less of a socially approved phenomenon" (1959–60: 252). But it is impossible to guess which came first, the decline in drug use or the displacement of the bebop esthetic.

While it lasted, it wrought alarming suffering and unsurpassed creativity. The survivors themselves make better sources than the psychologists—more reliable for having been there, straighter in saying what they mean, and more articulate. Red Rodney had been a junkie, and he came to understand why with perfect clarity. "That was our badge," he said (Gitler 1985: 282). "It was the thing that made us different from the rest of the world. It was the thing that said, 'We know, you don't know.' It was the thing that gave us membership in a unique club, and for this membership, we gave up everything else in the world. Every ambition. Every desire. Everything."

Richard Twardzik never saw it with such clarity, but of course he was not lucky enough to look back on it from a safe distance. After his stay in the Mexican hospital, he thought he was winning back everything. His first letter home afterwards, addressed to Clare as well as Henryk, on 25 May, ten days after leaving the hospital, promises a new start in a new setting:

Dear Parents

I'm fully recovered, still a little shaky but really feeling fine. I'm in Albuquerque N.M., my address is 1403 Barcelona Rd SW. I'm renting a house here right next to Buddy Berlin, a friend from Boston who has been living in Spain the past year.

I'm joining the union here but I'll need my Lynn card so if you have a minute send a card to Chester S. Young, 70 Fairoaks Ave, Lynn, and get my card. I'm behind since December so it'll cost about $6.

I worked 2 nights last week and have 3 this week. My steady gig starts next week with a three month contract so I certainly should straighten you on the money issue. I stopped in [on] Elaine on my way up. She's fine, looks great, has Suki with her, and fed me a gigantic steak —WOW! —

There's not too much happening here musically but the house I'm renting has a wonderful piano so I'm getting a lot of work done.

Please forward my mail [to] 1403 Barcelona Road S.W. Albuquerque N.M.

I'm going to study Spanish at the University, Organ & Tenor Sax.

XX DICK—

In the upper left corner of the envelope, where the return address normally goes, Twardzik has scrawled "DICKIE" with a caricature underneath. It would re-appear on the next envelope as well (8.2) and later on the manuscript score of *The Fable of Mabel*, as Twardzik's personal happy-face.

His sense of well-being got a boost en route to Albuquerque with his visit to Elaine Brehaut in San Angelo, sponsor of his trip and provider of, as he tells his parents, a "gigantic steak." Her dog Suki was a Dachshund, like Twardzik's own Liebie. He arrived on her doorstep, Elaine

[illustration 8.2] Richard Twardzik's letter home fromAlburquerque, New Mexico, on 5 June 1953. The caricature in the upper left, under "DICKIE," appears on this envelope and the previous one. From the Twardzik-Thompson Archive, courtesy of Rosamond Thompson and Jane Sumner. All rights reserved.

remembers, with marijuana in his suitcase. "I didn't give you money for that," she told him, but he laughed and told her it was an occupational necessity. "I can feel the music," he said. "I can live it."

She took him to a club with a live band. "Don't you know he ended up on the stage playing with them, and I ended up sitting on my own most of the night," she told me, still mildly annoyed 50 years later. "I think he went up and talked to them, and next thing I knew he was on the stage, waving to me from the piano."

He stayed with Elaine a couple of days, and then moved on to Albuquerque, where he was well provided for by an old Boston friend, Buddy Berlin, who had hired him for his band. His living arrangements, as he described them in a later letter (17 June), were congenial. "I have a whole house to myself, a cute place with a bed and a piano," he said. The house belonged to Buddy Berlin, and was next door to a larger house where Berlin and his wife Mary Ann, known to everyone as Wuzza, lived. "I pay the Berlins 15 a week for food plus more for extras like gas, electricity," Twardzik said.

Twardzik's benefactor is a shadowy figure in the jazz world. The poet Robert Creeley met Buddy Berlin when they were at Harvard, and, he says, "it was he who really gave me active connection to Dizzy Gillespie, Charlie Parker and all the rest of the mid-forties action." Berlin seems to have been constantly on the move, family and all, from Boston to Spain and New Mexico and several other stops before his death in the 1990s in Berkeley, California. In Albuquerque he and Wuzza presided genially over a kind of Beat commune in the two adjoining houses in South Valley, the old Chicano section of the city. People came and went freely. Creeley remembers that the house Twardzik lived in was later rented by Race Newton, another pianist and old friend of Berlin.

Twardzik's next letter home, 11 days later, concedes that Berlin is a "good" alto saxophonist. Otherwise, Twardzik had his usual reservations about the level of the musical company he was keeping, especially the drummer, who, as luck would have it, seems to have been the bandleader:

> The job started last night. Buddy the alto player is good the trumpet is quite good, (potentially) Bass—fair but the drummer! My God! It's his job tho' what can I do? I am writing all the music

Everything from the Grande Overture to a watered-down version
of an American in Paris.

Playing under such conditions makes it doubly hard to retain your
musical integrity. It [is] sink or swim.

Elaine spent a weekend with Richard in Albuquerque, bunking with
the Berlins. "I stayed with some of the band members and watched
while they got high," she said. The first morning, at the breakfast table,
Berlin went to a drawer and reached for the marijuana bag, and then
he stopped. Twardzik said, "She's okay, Buddy. She won't say anything."
At the club, Friday and Saturday nights, Elaine watched Richard inject
heroin, along with the others. "I can get into my own little world," he
told her. Remembering their discussions years later, she shrugged and
said, "You couldn't tell him otherwise."

The life Richard was leading, he grudgingly admitted in a letter home,
was pleasant:

> After the fast? life of the past I'm becoming gradually conditioned
> to living out in the country with many hrs. of each day to myself,
> practising, reading a good deal and riding a Czech motorcycle on
> which I'm becoming fairly proficient. My hair is growing quite
> long and I look like a veritable Hermes zooming down the high-
> way. Some Fun!

On one occasion, he mingled with the local intelligentsia at a cocktail
party, and it left him ruffled. He lets slip a hint about his own insecuri-
ties in educated company ("perhaps my personality *is* inadequate to
enter the ring with these people"), odd for a young man who impressed his friends by walking around with books under his arm:

> I've met the inner circle of the Albuquerque intellectuals and altho'
> I was forewarned went to a party held at the mildly esoteric home
> of Kenneth [illegible ?Nash] who edits the New Mexico Quarterly
> a "little" magazine which is truly little. A beautiful place adobe—up
> in the mountains. With very few exceptions I didn't like most of
> the people there. I found them (it seemed to me) runner ways [*sic*]
> from the outside world, personality-conscious, slightly Bohemian
> who don't seem to know much about what they're talking about.
> Strange people—I watch from a distance. Perhaps my personality is

inadequate to enter the ring with these people but I prefer to keep
walking foreward [*sic*].

Twardzik was always an indifferent speller, and here he slips in what
looks like a gem: "runner ways" for *runaways*. Like every Bostonian
of his generation, Twardzik pronounced "runner" as *runna* (and "park"
as *paak*, "Harvard" as *haavad*, and so on), up to and including "runner
ways" as *runaways*.

Twardzik eventually turned his encounter into artistic fodder. It became the source for *Albuquerque Social Swim*, the witty, oblique composition he would record with the trio on Pacific Jazz the next year. In
the original liner notes for his LP, Twardzik wrote, "*Albuquerque Social
Swim* was inspired by some young intellectuals in Albuquerque with
their pompous pronouncements to awkward pauses. But they like jazz-
music."

Twardzik interrupted his letter about the social swim because, he says,
"Groucho Marx just came on the radio. I'll finish when I get home
from work." When he resumes, he invokes his standard themes to finish
the letter:

The next day 〜〜〜〜〜

Bela Bartok's music for stringed instrument celesta & percussion is
on (the one classical record here). It's a beautiful day (the're [*sic*] all
beautiful.

To keep from getting too lonely I try to keep busy. How are things?
please write and let me know. Henry, if you see Reba please make
sure that she sends out a copy of my new record with Charlie
Mariano which hasn't been reviewed yet in the trade newspapers.

Buddy Berlin and his wife Wuzzer [*sic*] are real nice people and I
am feeling well and all's quiet on the Western Front.

                                        XX XX Dickie

Twardzik's comment suggests that Reba Stewart, having returned to
Boston with the Vachsteens, may have taken to dropping in on Henryk
at Connick Associates, his Boston workplace.

Twardzik's next letter home apparently answers a reply he had from
Henryk. "It sure did me good to hear what you had to say about in-

tegrity, musical and otherwise," he said. But if Henryk's letter was an attempt to temper his son's criticism of the other musicians and work to his own standards, it made no difference. Less than two weeks later, on 17 June, Twardzik announced that his comfortable set-up had come apart:

Last night the bubble burst. We came to work and there were no drums. The substitute drummer apparently in close touch with the idiots who run the club didn't show up. Thanks to his stab in the back, the conniving of a female agent who wants her band in, and the regular leader's disappearance to Conn. leaving a string of bad checks, we were fired no warning, no two weeks union notice, because they claim default by virtue of the leader's disappearance and his failure to register the contract at the union office. The union won't stand behind us so there is nothing that can be done about the situation.

It came as a complete surprise. Everyone loved the band. (One night some guy gave me $5 to play "anything at all. It all sounds wonderful!")

The owner's stupidity is colossal. They are just poor stupid bigoted people who have a big elephant on their hands: They're probably 5 or 10 thousand behind now and no[t] realizing that our band is the only thing that will save them (plus good shows, of course). They listen to all the voices around them, people who [have] something to gain by changing the band, particularly one real evil bitch, a big fat Agent named Marty Gonzales, a real slob who runs stag shows for the soldiers and who has a boy friend who plays drums. This whole thing Stinks!

The band did eventually make a claim for two weeks pay with the support of the Union, according to a later telegram, but they were told it would take months before there would be a ruling about it. The rest of Twardzik's letter outlined an escape plan:

There are very few jobs here so the situation is critical. Peter Littman wrote me of a wonderful job in Everett (I can live at home) with Herb Pomeroy and Jack Carter. If I only can get home I can start work immediately. I just learned that had I been in Boston last week I could have been back to work with Charlie Parker ($135).

It's quite a disappointment—what a difference between Parker and this band.

Parker had played at the Hi Hat two weeks before, from 8–14 June 1953, and he used a piano player named Dean Earl, the leader of the house trio. Twardzik's year might have been very different had he been available to work for Parker. Now, he told Henryk, he was looking to Herb Pomeroy to rescue him:

> At the same time that I'm sending this off I'm also sending a letter to Herb Pomeroy, 115 Hemenway St. Boston asking him to verify the job and to wire some money so that I can get home. I've got my fingers crossed that he'll come through. I hope so, but there's always a chance that he won't. My financial situation is desperate. I have had two paydays and all that has gone for board and room. Thinking that I'd be here for a little while at least, I paid my rent for a month, which was necessary...
>
> If no money comes from Herb and the fellows the only course is to get a day job in order to get enough money to get home. And I do want to get home before the summer season starts so that I don't spend another summer in the city—Albuquerque is hot but it's a dry heat and a lot of asthmatics come here to live.
>
> The reason I speak of a day job is that the jobs are as scarce as hen's teeth here and it sure is walking backwards for me to stay here.
>
> Goodby for a while.
>
> Please write!!
>
> XX Dickie XX

Mention of a day job, with its connotations of failed artistic aspirations, got a rise out of Henryk. When no money came from Pomeroy, Twardzik sent Henryk a telegram, very much on the defensive: "THIS FIASCO DEFINITELY ISNT MY FAULT I WORKED HARD ALL AROUND AND LIVE CHEAPLY...PLEASE SEND $75.00 IMMEDIATELY AND GOD WILLING ILL BE HOME BY WEDNESDAY LOVE TO ALL."

"I think...that you could tell from my phone call that I [am] very unhappy here and that I long to be home," he wrote to Henryk. So with Henryk's money, he boarded a Greyhound and headed north. The sojourn in Mexico and Albuquerque reached its anticlimax. Presumably he carried with him in his battered suitcase the draft manuscript of *Albuquerque Social Swim*. Maybe that alone was enough to vindicate the twelve-week adventure.

Not notably chastened or, as we shall see, much wiser, Twardzik made his way back home, where he could count on affection in many forms. As soon as he got to Boston, he ran into Bob Zieff. Twardzik was on his way to Reba Stewart's. Reba had been looking after Stinky while he was away. "Dick returned from the road and we went over to Reba's," Zieff said, "and when she answered the door, [she had] the dog with her—and when he saw Dick he pissed on the spot!"

9 "Everyone must travel alone (most of the time)"

Richard did not stay long in Boston—or anywhere else. The "summer season" that he had wanted to get home for came and went without any great advances in his career, at least none that made the public record. He was using drugs again, more than ever.

He had returned home to find his father suffering from various ailments. Henryk had something like phlebitis in his leg, which made walking difficult. Richard was prepared for that; he had ended his telegram from Albuquerque with the words, "STAY OFF THAT LEG." But Henryk was also suffering from dizzy spells, as he had in Rockport, when the stress and anxiety of Richard's rheumatic fever had sent him into a spin. He had had mild attacks through the years in times of stress, but now they were back again, and strong.

Clare's stresses smoldered inside her. After Richard's first weeks in Mexico, she had grown taciturn. Now that he was back, they sometimes flared into the open in unguarded moments. Naturally, Clare blamed Richard for Henryk's anxiety attacks. That was one more thing added onto her exasperation with Henryk for being too easy on Richard, and onto her own anxieties about the boy himself.

By the fall of 1953, Richard had taken off on another Beat excursion. He got into shouting matches with Clare and Henryk. The night it all came to a head, he slammed the door behind him and screamed something about stowing away on a cargo ship to Haiti.

He got as far as Miami Beach. After a long silence that pained Clare and Henryk in its own dark way, he wrote home on 6 November, from an address he gave as 2335 Pinetree Drive. He was deeply troubled. There is an apologetic air to the letter, and a measure of self-hatred. Neither of those feelings had surfaced on his Mexican jaunt.

The letter is addressed to both parents, and it begins like several other letters, by blaming the city he finds himself in for his mood:

Dear Henry and Clare

This town stinks! It's the absolute lowest! There's no beauty here. It's all cheap gaudiness and the gleaming white hotels look like crazily

cut pieces of cheap poisonous cake. Everything is in the service of
the great God money: it's a miserable rathole and I'm trapped here
like a rat—

He tells them he has finally found the heart to break his silence:

This is not the first letter I've written. As you know I find it ex-
tremely difficult to write or talk to people if things are amiss. I just
can't paint a glowing cheerful picture if things are not that way at
all.

My cheerfully nebulous plans for Cuba and Haiti have, of course,
gone right down the drain.

An early success with a Miami Beach band soured quickly, and his hard
luck again raises the specter of a day job:

From the start, things looked good. I landed a wonderful job right
off the bat at the best place in town with a colored band. I was
happy, making good money, but not for long

this is the SOUTH and white and negro just don't mix down here.

I'm going to work in a department store in Miami (I'm living in
Miami Beach now) to get some money to get out of here. Unfortunately the employment agency gets 1/2 of your 1st month's earn-
ings and so it may be quite a while.

He glosses over the darkest aspect of the incident with the African-
American band. He told Elaine Brehaut that when he left the club
one night he was surrounded by a gang. "White men don't play with
niggers," they said. They roughed him up and told him they would kill
him if he went back on the bandstand.

In his letter, he claims that he has confronted his demons, and he lets
his parents know that he does not particularly like what he sees:

But —it does seem that the more trouble and worry I go through,
the clearer I can see other things, namely you both whom I love
very much and am sorry to have treated so badly, and the direction
in which I am to go in music and in life. The way ahead seems bale-
fully dim and as usual considering the people who seem to be all
around me, there is no one to talk to, no one to help, which isn't a

tottaly [sic] bad thing because (as you know) everyone must travel alone (most of the time)

Please don't be angry with me because it was an impulse and for better or worse I felt that it was an improvement over the hole (of my own making of course) into which I felt myself sinking.

I've got to find the answers myself.

He closes on more mundane matters, plainly heartfelt:

My technique is going to hell, largely psychosomatic, but I['m] doing a lot of reading and thinking.

I hope you both and Reba have come to be friends. She's a fine girl and she needs you altho' she might not admit it. She's alone too —

Love to all. A kiss for you, Clare, and Henryk: "I'm in your corner. Daddy"!

XXXX   DICK

Rough and unproofed as the letter is, it is eloquent. It is not hard to imagine a doting mother's remorse as she reads it. On one reading or another, long after her boy was lost to her forever, Clare fastened on Richard's misspelling of "tottaly" and neatly printed in pencil above it, "one T."

For Richard, these were the darkest days. He would survive, and come back stronger, at least momentarily. For the two years that remained of his life, although there would be other dark nights, his dedication to his music would be unwavering, and his art would attain its razor edge. Meteorically. Momentarily.

Reba Stewart would not be there to share his successes. His assumption that she was biding her time while he was finding himself—"she's alone too"—was merely naïve. Reba had her own ambitions, and her own dark nights to get through in order to attain them. She came to realize that Richard was turning out to be a high-maintenance companion, very different from the chattering young dilettante she had first met in the jazz clubs. Geneviève McMillan, who would enter her life a few years after Twardzik, saw the same attitude in later affairs. "Reba was disciplined, clean and organized," she says. "She sometimes lost patience with people who were not. Of course she tried to do it with humor, but it was not easy for her. She was strikingly ambitious. She did not spend time with anyone who might be a waste of her time or perhaps too needy." Reba's ambitions carried her into different spheres.

Reba Stewart would be as restless in her pursuit of her art as Twardzik was in his, and she would go on to carve out a bright career as teacher and painter. She and Richard shared one artistic triumph, but it was purely accidental. Reba was a featured young artist in the exhibit at the Boston Arts Festival in 1955, and that same year Richard also made a great impression playing there in Serge Chaloff's band. If they were aware of one another on that occasion, when they both found the spotlight as rising stars, there is no hint of it.

Coincidentally or not, Reba Stewart's talents flowered immediately after Twardzik's sudden death. In 1958, she received a scholarship to Japan and studied woodblock printmaking (9.1, page 50). It was a seminal experience for her. "I learned more there [in Japan] in one year than in Boston in ten years, and if I go someplace to live again, it will be Japan," she said in 1960 (McMillan 2002). But it was not to be. New ambitions got in the way. In 1961, she earned her M.A. from Yale, and after that she went where her teaching positions took her, first to Monticello College in Alton, Illinois (1961–63) and then to the College of Art at Maryland College (1963–71).

Geneviève McMillan, called Ginou by her friends, discovered Stewart's art soon after Stewart returned from Japan. McMillan is French, and she had arrived in Boston as a war bride in 1946. As a university student in Paris during the German occupation, Ginou and her classmates did what they could to keep their heads above the military morass that surrounded them. They smoked cigarettes and read Malraux, the novelist (according to whispers) now fighting for the Résistance, and they mocked their bull-necked, hobnailed oppressors behind their backs. It was a time when the only safe liberties were intellectual ones. One of the young men in Ginou's circle introduced her to African art and she was smitten. When she arrived in Boston with her dashing Army officer husband, an architect by profession, she told me, "I came already with a small collection of African art."

Some of those works of art were put on display at McMillan's chic restaurant Henri Quatre (affectionately mispronounced "hungry cat" by the American help), on Winthrop Street in Cambridge. Eventually, Reba Stewart's woodcuts and paintings were displayed there too, along with other works by promising young American artists.

McMillan's patronage bolstered Stewart's confidence and her career. She believed in her talent, and she generously provided Stewart with opportunities for painting. "I had a small house in Puerto Rico which Reba loved," McMillan says. She spent her summers there painting acrylics and making mobiles from driftwood.

In her lifetime, Stewart's works were exhibited in Boston, Tokyo, Kyoto, and Tours, and they are part of permanent collections of the Maryland Institute of Art, Fogg Museum at Harvard, the Boston Museum of Fine Arts, and other public galleries, and in private collections including Reginald Isaacs, the New York architect, as well as McMillan's.

In 1970–71, on her first sabbatical, Reba Stewart went on painting excursions in Liberia and Ghana, at McMillan's urging. There she contracted malaria, the virulent falaparum strain that infects the brain and liver. McMillan had her moved by air ambulance to her home in Puerto Rico. "She received expert medical treatment," McMillan says, "but she could not be saved." She died in 1971, at 41. In 1997, McMillan instituted a memorial by funding the Geneviève McMillan–Reba Stewart Lectureship at the three Cambridge universities, Radcliffe, MIT and Harvard, to bring filmmakers and other artists from francophone Africa and elsewhere as visiting faculty and guest lecturers.

10 (World) Harmony with Hamp

In 1954, Walter White, leader of the National Association for the Advancement of Colored People (NAACP), proclaimed, "The Lionel Hampton United Nations band is producing more harmony in the world than any other agency in the world." The piano player in that United Nations of bebop, representing Poland, was Richard Twardzik.

When Twardzik joined his pal Herb Pomeroy in the Lionel Hampton orchestra, he hoped he was settling into a steady gig with a high-profile band that would bring him a measure of stability after his eight months of pointless wandering. After a week or two with Hampton, he felt as if he had sold his soul to a creature from one of those UFOs that everyone was talking about. In truth, Lionel Hampton was not a creature from outer space but a creature from the Swing Era, and one who had a generous dose of vaudeville in his DNA. The fact that he was now fronting a bebop band, far removed from the music that made him famous with Benny Goodman, only meant that he knew what it took to attract an audience. Audiences were what he lived for. He exulted in their hand-clapping, their shrieks and whistles, their loving touch as he brushed by them in the conga-line finale of his nightly shows. If it took a bebop band to get them into the auditorium, then he would give them bebop (as he did from 1948–56), just as he had once given them jitterbug swing (starting in 1940, when he left Goodman, and including his 1942 hit *Flying Home*), boogie woogie (starting in 1941), jump blues (starting in 1944 with young Dinah Washington in the band), and would end up, when there was no longer an identifiable contemporary big-band style, giving them Swing-Era nostalgia (for more than four decades until his death in 2002, at 94). Whatever it took.

Audiences filing out of the auditorium at the end of his shows in any of these transmutations, flushed and a bit giddy, often failed to notice that behind Hampton's sweaty bonhomie lurked one of the masters of jazz improvisation. Hampton used his music as a prop for comedy, and most nights it was the comedy that left the biggest impression. Even Gunther Schuller, one of the rare critics to give Hampton his musical due, could not praise him without first pointing out that he was well aware of Hampton's downside. "When he assaults his drums, brutalizes the piano keyboard in his hammered two-finger style, pounds the vibraphone into submission," Schuller wrote (1989: 393), "the perspiration quotient is high indeed, its *in*spiration equivalent often considerably lower."

Hampton started off as a drummer and then he taught himself vibraphone in the 1920s, and made it his main instrument, but he also played piano in a dazzling finger-mallet style, and if all that was not enough, he would grab the microphone and intone a few choruses of his *Vibraphone Blues*, with a pearly smile to make sure you knew he did not mean what he was saying for a second:

If the blues was whisky, I would stay drunk all the time.
If the blues was whisky, I would stay drunk all the time.
Now if I get drunk, babe, I would leave you behind.

Hampton also, perhaps needless to say, danced, sliding into a slow shuffle on a ballad number or, on jump tunes, leaping up, legs akimbo, "and coming down right in the center of the beat" (as one newspaper reviewer described it). Maybe it was because the music came to him so easily that he needed the rush of high-energy clowning to feel he had put in a night's work.

To a young hotshot like Twardzik, at first it was enough to know that Hampton worked steadily and paid well. After wandering around the country and frittering away his parents' life savings, those things had to look good. Sure, he had a few doubts at the end of the audition, when Hampton's wife and manager, Gladys, came up to him and said, "Twahtsik? What kind of a name is that?" I'm from Boston, he told her, and she said, "But your name—," and when he told her it was Polish, she said, "Puhfect," and walked away. He was happy to get the gig but, unenlightened by the historical perspective of someone like Gunther Schuller, he would not stay happy for long.

Very early in his career, Hampton had played with Louis Armstrong, his comedy idol as well as his musical master. He recorded the first-ever jazz vibraphone solo with Armstrong's band as a 22-year-old in October 1930. "That first experience with the vibraharp didn't excite me enough to switch instruments," he said later (1989: 38), and although his fame as a musician rested solely on his vibraphone playing he never gave up doubling and trebling as part of his show-biz routine.

Hampton made his most abiding impression on the music when he was fairly young, as do most great jazz musicians. In 1936, when he was

28, Benny Goodman conscripted him for his Quartet, which served as a kind of straight-jazz entr'acte for his swing orchestra, the greatest musical attraction in the world at the time. Hampton's vibes melded magically with Goodman's clarinet, Teddy Wilson's piano and Gene Krupa's drums. The combination was so scintillating that audiences were willing to overlook the racial mixing on stage, in an era when the military service, professional baseball, dance halls, jazz clubs and all but two or three colleges were segregated. For four years, Hampton played bright, unfettered, sparkling music with the Goodman Quartet. (Their recordings have never gone out of print.) Hampton, the ebullient African-American in the quartet with the debonair Wilson, basked in the adulation of bobby-soxers crowding the bandstand no less than Goodman and Krupa. By the time Hampton left Goodman, he was almost as big a star as Goodman himself.

By the time Twardzik joined the Hampton organization, fourteen years later, it had become a traveling vaudeville show with a jazz core. "That is one of Hampton's secrets of success," according to a reporter in the Pittsburgh *Courier* (Brown 1954), an African-American daily. "He knows how to sell to an audience and he gives them real modern jazz."

With the post-war decline of the dance bands, selling the audience was at least as important as playing jazz. A double-page ad in the *Courier* trumpeted "LIONEL HAMPTON and his Great Band & Show." The company Twardzik joined included tap dancer Curley Hamner, comedy duo Cook and Brown, crooner Al Taylor, blues singer Sonny Parker, and ballad singer Pearl Thuston (10.1). For at least part of the time, it also included "Hamp, Jr.," Hampton's ultimate gimmick. "He was a four-year-old drummer from Nashville," Hampton wrote in his autobiography (1989: 102). The boy would toddle onto the stage dressed in a double-breasted suit like Hampton's and take him on in a drum battle. It stopped the show night after night. That was the only impression it made on Hampton himself, at least in the long run. When he got around to writing his memoirs, Hampton said about Hamp, Jr., "I'm sorry to say I don't remember his real name. He was a big hit with audiences."

Twardzik actually joined the orchestra shortly before all these show-biz elements were in place. It is tempting to think he might have had second thoughts if he had known the full extent of Hampton's extramusical ambitions. A newspaper review of one of the first concerts, early in January 1954, probably sent to Clare by Auntie Hannah Longwell, specifically decries the absence of "a girl vocalist" and makes no mention of the crooner, the comedy team or Hamp, Jr. The headline shouts "Hampton Band Gives Exciting Concert Here," in a city where "the cold and snow kept at home many who had purchased tickets, but those who came found the concert exciting, and the human dynamo bandleader had to be relentless in order to shut the proceedings down at 11 o'clock" (Kyes 1954). The review preserves a detailed account of the performance, giving full value to the Hamptonian shtick:

> Curly [sic] Hamner started to sing, shifted to much better dancing, and wound up as a veritable whizz [sic] on the drums. Then Maestro Hampton said he would give him a lesson, and he did. Finally, the two joined forces with the full band, and operated on four snare drums and both sides of a bass drum, with cymbals, etc., thrown in. The result was terrific—you might call it super-rhythm.

[illustration 10.1] "Lionel Hampton and His Great Band & Show." Advertisement for "Triumphant Tour of Dixie," with "Dick Twardzik, Piano Star" among the featured players. Pittsburgh *Courier*, 27 February 1954.

...His program is top-heavy with boogie-woogie, but that's what the customers want. It has a generous dash of bebop also. Some of the boogie-woogie is mild and almost "sweet," and some of it builds up with tantalizing slowness to almost deafening noise and fierceness of pulsation.

...the evening kept this critic wide awake and feeling as if he had enjoyed a neat little musical spree.

The reviewer takes care to itemize the program and identify soloists. That was useful for contemporary readers (and, incidentally, for archivists) because Hampton's orchestra was almost entirely new. He had fired his previous orchestra en masse, urged on, according to the musicians, by Gladys, who ran his affairs autocratically. That band had included an extraordinary aggregation of youngbloods, including Clifford Brown, Art Farmer and Quincy Jones in the trumpet section, Jimmy Cleveland and Buster Cooper among the trombones, Gigi Gryce and Tony Ortega in the saxophone section, George Wallington on piano, Monk Montgomery on bass, Alan Dawson on drums, and Annie Ross on vocals.

In the fall of 1953, that band had played 87 concerts in seven European countries in fifteen weeks (Hampton 1989: 101). Dissension reared its head when they reached Paris. There the jazz cognoscenti were much less interested in them collectively, as the Hampton orchestra, than individually, as young jazz stars in their own right. Offers came in for them to record and perform on their own. Gladys Hampton flatly denied permission on the grounds that she was paying their travel, accommodations and wages. When the musicians defied her, she issued the edict to fire them. (Hampton skips past the unhappy incident quickly in his autobiography, conceding only that he might have been annoyed at the time and that his late wife "must have been" annoyed, and then brushing it aside by saying, "I don't harbor any grudges about it" [1989: 100].)

Gladys's stranglehold on her husband's affairs comes abundantly clear in the two-page ad in the *Courier*. A soft-lens portrait of her dominates the spread although she worked strictly behind the scenes. Even Hampton himself gets less space than Gladys, effectively giving the "business manager and coordinator" top billing.

Twardzik joined Hampton's replacement band along with Pomeroy and another Bostonian, Jackie Crown, a trombonist. In the end, the three Bostonians stayed a little more than four months, from December 1953 to mid-April 1954. The brevity of their stay seems to have bugged Hampton. "Twardzick [*sic*] and Pomeroy and Crown—they didn't stay around long," Hampton wrote, years later (1989: 103), as if it still stung him.

Even so, they covered, as we shall see, several thousand miles with Hampton. Mysteriously, only newspaper clippings survive from Twardzik's months with Hampton. There is no correspondence from Twardzik to his parents. That almost certainly means there was none—that he never wrote home in the four months. So the serious rift over his Mexican adventure and its Miami aftermath evidently persisted.

There are also no recordings. Hampton recorded prolifically throughout his career, but he never recorded with the band that had Twardzik in it. It was an unlucky break for Twardzik and for the other young musicians who, like him, joined the band for the exposure it would gain them. The personnel, reconstructed from press clippings, had Wallace Davenport, Eddie Mullens, Herb Pomeroy and Walter Williams on trumpets; Buster Cooper, Dave Ecker, Al Hayse and Jackie Crown, trombones; Bobby Plater, clarinet and alto saxophone; Jerome (Jay) Dennis and later James Araki, alto saxophone; Jay Peters and Ricky Brauer, tenor saxophones; Oscar Estell, baritone saxophone; Richard Twardzik, piano; Billy Mackel, guitar; Curtis Ross and later Arnold Greenstein, bass; Floyd Williams, drums. These names included five holdovers from the European tour band—Williams, Cooper, Hayse, Estell and Mackel— but none of the stars. It was not, in hindsight, made up of potential stars. Davenport and Plater would go on to spend long careers as section men with Count Basie, as would Cooper with Duke Ellington. None of the band members except Pomeroy and Twardzik would ever record as leaders on major labels, and none would lead their own touring bands or establish international reputations.

In the *Courier* review of a performance by the band at the Apollo in Harlem, the vocalist is Betty Carter, and she is lauded as "one of the most talented singers on the stage today with a wonderful sense of phrasing and a selling voice" (Brown 1954). (Pearl Thuston, listed as a featured player in the ad for the band and described by the inscrutable epithet "Song Lovely," has disappeared from the historical record.)

In performances, Hampton introduced Carter as "Betty Bebop" and brought her on to sing scat syllables to tunes like *The Hucklebuck*. "Betty did not like it when I called her Betty Bebop," Hampton admitted (1989: 94), "but Gladys told her just to go along with it, and when Betty had the experience she needed she could leave the band and call herself anything she wanted." (Her real name, which she discarded while still an amateur, was Lillie Mae Jones.) According to Hampton, Carter left his band because she wanted to sing lyrics. She would do that as leader of her own trio for more than four decades until she died in 1998.

Twardzik must have seen his stint with Hampton as his launching pad. In all the publicity about the new band, he is singled out as a rising star. Hampton said, "I wanted to have some modern jazz musicians in my [new] orchestra," and he makes it clear that in his eyes the Boston contingent was the pick of the bunch (1989: 102): "I got three guys who had been making names for themselves in modern jazz in Boston—Herb Pomeroy on trumpet, Dick Twardzick [*sic*] on piano, and Jackie Crown on trombone." In the *Courier* ad (10.1) Twardzik is billed as "Piano Star" and listed among the featured attractions. The review of the Apollo concert in the same paper says, "Among his new stars [is] Dick Twardzik, a young piano star from Boston who actually teaches music" (Brown 1954), somehow managing to get the word "star" into the sentence twice. Hampton also gave Twardzik a featured turn with the maestro himself. At the early concert in cold-weather conditions, the reviewer noted that "Lionel's famous vibraharp and Dick Twardzik's piano did some of their best co-operating in *Stardust*" (Kyes 1954).

"It was the most integrated band I'd ever had," Hampton said (1989: 102), and its racial and ethnic integration was entirely intentional. Among the many paradoxes of Hampton was a serious and unflinching commitment to social justice when he was off the stage. In the 1970s, he would found the Community Development Corporation for inner-city low-income housing (sponsoring buildings known as "Lionel Hampton Houses") and other initiatives for disadvantaged people.

In 1954, at the moment when Hampton was forming his new band with Twardzik in it, American apartheid policies had been cracked, and Hampton was one of the activists willing and ready to drive a wedge into the crack. In an act of enormous symbolic significance, major-league baseball had been integrated in 1947, but now there were bigger stakes. The Supreme Court under Chief Justice Earl Warren ruled in favor of school desegregation in a case prepared by the NAACP, the lobby group led by Hampton's close friend Walter White. Resistance to the landmark decision in the American South was expected to be bitter and violent.

"It was Walter White who suggested I take an integrated band down south," Hampton said (1989: 98). "This was earlier—about 1951. He thought it would be a good thing to show whites—because I was do-ing a lot of concerts at white halls and clubs—that black and white can get along together." At the time of the Supreme Court decision in favor of school desegregation, Hampton was in Europe with the band with Clifford Brown and Quincy Jones. His first opportunity to act on Walter White's suggestion came with the re-formed band on his return to the States.

Hampton set about publicizing the band's national (and, by inference, racial) mix by forming a splinter band that he called the United Na-tions Combo (or, earlier, in the *Courier* advertisement, the UN Sextet, but in the end it had eight members). A grainy photo from the Pitts-burgh *Courier* on 27 March 1954, one month after the double-page ad, shows the odd spectacle of three African-Americans and five Euro-pean-Americans identified by their immigrant origins (10.2). Wallace Davenport of New Orleans becomes French Moroccan, Herb Pome-roy of Gloucester, Mass., becomes English, and the two Bostonians become Norwegian (Crown) and Polish (Twardzik). Hampton, shown in the photo sharing the piano bench with his arm draped around Twardzik's shoulders, is identified, uniquely, as "a native of the U.S." The UN Combo is, the caption says, "a group that places democracy in action above bigotry and hypocrisy."

After getting the band up and running with northern tryouts, Hamp-ton would fulfill the NAACP mandate by swinging through the south-ern states in a series of one-nighters. The "Dixie Tour," as it was called in the advertisements, would provide a showcase for racial cooperation in a dazzling run starting on 26 February in Norfolk, Virginia, and ending six weeks later, on 5 April, in Pittsburgh, Pennsylvania. Those two cities are only about 500 miles apart (as the crow flies) but in the six-week interval between them the band would play 31 concerts in 39 days in 30 cities and towns, moving in a kind of geographical crazy quilt that took in Virginia (Norfolk), West Virginia (Charleston), Virginia again (Richmond, Roanoke), North Carolina (Raleigh), South Carolina (Columbia, Spartanburg), North Carolina again (Charlotte, Fayetteville), Florida (Bradenton, Orlando, Jacksonville, West Palm Beach, Miami, Fort Lauderdale, Tampa, Pensacola), Mississippi (Biloxi), Louisiana (New Orleans), Mississippi again (Jackson), Texas (Houston, Austin), Oklahoma (Oklahoma City, Tulsa), Texas again (Fort Worth, Dallas), Mississippi again (Oxford), Tennessee (Nashville), Ohio (Cincinnati) and Pennsylvania (Pittsburgh).

The Oxford, Mississippi, date near the end of the tour set the miscegenated band in the heart of Ku Klux Klan territory, where crosses burned on the lawns of the uppity and black corpses had recently

Hamp's UN Combo—"The Lionel Hampton United Nations group is producing more harmony in the world than any other agency in the world," said Walter White recently in his NAACP offices. And Hampton likes it that way. He poses here with his UN aggregation of the famous Lionel Hampton orchestra, rated one of the greatest today, and a group that places democracy in action above bigotry and hyprocrisy. Left to right, standing: Bassman A. Greenstein, of the New State of Israel; trumpeteer Wallace Davenport-T, of French Morocco; drummer Flugie Williams, from Jamaica, British West Indies; rear conter, tenor saxophonist Rucknie Bauer, of Germany; trombonist Jackie Crown of Norway, and trumpeteer Herb Pomeroy of England. Center left, leaning over the piano, is Hamp in the flesh, the ace of the vibraharp, and right front is pianist Dick Twardzik, of Poland. Of course, Hamp is a native of the U. S.

[illustration 10.2] "Hamp's UN Combo." Lionel Hampton's band-within-a-band, from the Pittsburgh *Courier*, 27 March 1954.

swung from poplar trees. In the ten years *after* Hampton's show there, Mississippi would be the scene of some of the most violent acts in the civil rights movement. Hampton approached the concert with trepidation but he was delighted by the reception (1989: 103):

> I especially remember Mississippi because we played at the University of Mississippi in Oxford, and at the time I had a white piano player, Twardzick [*sic*], and a Japanese guy named James Araki on alto saxophone. But we didn't have any trouble at all-white Ole Miss. In fact, it was one of the high spots of our season. The audience was jammed to the rafters, and when we finished, we got twelve standing ovations. After the concert, the students crowded around the bandstand and shared their liquor with us, and we all drank from the same bottles and danced for about an hour.

Hampton seems to have had more success with world harmony than internal harmony in this band. Much of the short space he devotes to it in his autobiography is fixated on trying to figure out exactly why the three Bostonians left so precipitously. "At the time, I thought I had the best band ever," he says (1989: 102), "but none of those guys lasted very long." By the time he gets through mulling it over, he comes up with three different reasons that might explain their defections. Any one of them might have sufficed.

First, he says, "maybe they couldn't take the string of one-nighters" (1989: 102). Amen to that.

Second, he says, "Maybe they didn't like it that the first recordings I did after they joined up weren't with the band but with a 'Lionel Hampton Quartet' that included Oscar Peterson on piano, Ray Brown on bass, and Buddy Rich on drums, and a 'Lionel Hampton Quintet' that added Buddy De Franco on clarinet" (1989: 103). These recordings marked the beginning of Hampton's association with Norman Granz, the impresario who mounted concerts known as Jazz at the Philharmonic in the late 1940s and required local promoters to integrate audiences, which must have been a point of contact between the two men. Hampton's recordings with the likes of Peterson, Stan Getz and piano virtuoso Art Tatum on Granz's Clef, Norgran and Verve labels would prove to be the most challenging and musically fulfilling works of his career after Benny Goodman.

True enough, the young band members must have expected to get some record credits, and Hampton might be right in thinking they felt slighted at not getting them. Why Hampton did not record with this band is inexplicable. He had perfect hooks for a record album in the racial harmony theme and the imprimatur of the NAACP, which should have made the record album newsworthy beyond the jazz audience. A further irony with all the one-nighters this band performed, no audience recordings or air checks have shown up anywhere.

Hampton made his first recording for Granz on 12 April 1953, exactly one week after the last of the one-nighters on the Dixie tour. "Whatever the reason or reasons," he writes, with an audible shrug, "around the time I did those recordings in New York, Herb Pomeroy had gone back to Boston. I'm not sure if Jackie Crown and Dick Twardzick [*sic*] stayed that long."

The third possible reason he offers for their departures may come closest to the heart of the matter. He says, "I don't think they could relate to my style of showmanship, which was always to give the audience what it wanted to hear, not what the musicians wanted to hear" (1989: 102).

Twardzik, predictably, hated Hampton's pandering. Twardzik's only surviving comment about his time with Hampton is an anecdote he told about gulling the old leader, much the way that Serge Chaloff had once gulled Woody Herman. Except that Herman felt it where Hampton, according to Twardzik, was oblivious. Two years after leaving Hampton, when Twardzik was on his fateful European tour with Chet Baker, a Swedish music critic, Lars Resberg, asked him about his Hampton days. Twardzik's most memorable moment—the only one Resberg set down for his readers—took place nightly at the grand finale, while the band was roaring toward the climax on Hampton's signature tune, *Flying Home*. Beneath the din, Twardzik would pound out scales on the piano in completely alien keys. It was most gratifying, he said, when Hamp, hearing a particularly sour chord in the mix, would flash him an enthusiastic thumbs-up.

11 The Fable of Mabel

While Richard Twardzik was flitting around the southeastern United States with the Lionel Hampton road show, Serge Chaloff came out of hiding. He had lost none of the old swagger, and he still held the amoral high ground that was his perch for spitting on the squares. But there was something different about him. He complained about the monkey on his back. He kept saying he was going to kick the old habit. People who knew him best thought it was just a ruse to get some sympathy, because he had used up all his favors before he disappeared. Bookers, agents, club owners and musicians had given up on him after too many short sets and no-shows and fuck-yous.

Maybe there was more to it this time. Chaloff was meeting with a counselor, and he talked about that all the time too. Maybe it had dawned on him that he was caught in a loser's game as he huddled for days on end in his bedroom with the sounds of his young wife and his baby daughter filtering through the gloom from the bright reaches of the apartment. Or maybe it had only dawned on him after they moved out and the sounds of their voices were stilled. At some point in his lying-low period, he looked up and they were gone.

"Serge came back to Boston with no horn," Jay Migliori remembered (Sunenblick 1994: 3), but he started a band and he recruited Migliori, a 23-year-old tenor player in his first year at Berklee, who happened to know how to get him a baritone saxophone.

It did not take long for Chaloff to get himself back in circulation. His first break came from Bob Martin, a disc jockey who hosted record shows and live broadcasts from Storyville, the competition to Symphony Sid at the Hi Hat. "I'd always been a fan of his," Martin told Robert Sunenblick (1994: 3–4), and that provided the only opening Chaloff needed. Martin interviewed him on the air, and Chaloff was articulate, wry and full of anecdotes about the glory days of the Second Herd. Somehow, Martin ended up as Chaloff's agent. "I was trying to help the guy," Martin said. "Help him book and keep his records straight and keep things together, which was the most difficult part of it."

Amazingly, Chaloff had won the *Metronome* magazine poll as best baritone saxophone player in 1953 (as he had since 1949), getting votes from distant fans even while he was in hiding. That gave him some public-relations capital, and Martin set about building on it. He started by getting him a booking as the back-up band at Storyville, persuading his boss, George Wein, of Chaloff's good intentions.

Chaloff led a band at Storyville for two weeks in March 1954, opposite the Chet Baker Quartet. He soon showed that he had not lost his old flamboyance. "Serge was a wild character," Migliori told Sunenblick. "We were working at Storyville and, if he was feeling good, he used to let his trousers gradually fall down during the cadenza of his feature, *Body and Soul*. At the end of the cadenza, his trousers would hit the ground."

George Wein would give Chaloff several breaks in his comeback year, but he kept a watchful eye. One of Chaloff's students, Steve Adamson, said, "I remember Wein being there, and his disposition. He was kinda cranky" (Simosko 1998: 76–78). But Wein never let his personal tastes get in the way of his entrepreneurial instincts. His first ambition had been to become a Dixieland piano player, and while he was a student at Boston University he got the best private tuition available, studying with Madame Chaloff and his idol Teddy Wilson. When he opened the Storyville club in 1950, at 25, some of the musicians joked that it was the only way he could get to play piano with the likes of Sidney Bechet, Vic Dickenson, Bobby Hackett, Pee Wee Russell, and his other heroes. But it soon looked like a lame joke. Wein brought in modernists too, like Parker, Baker, Errol Garner, George Shearing, Stan Getz and Dave Brubeck. Live recordings from the club by Brubeck on Fantasy Records and by Bechet, Getz and others on Wein's own Storyville label helped spread the club's name.

That was just the beginning of Wein's ambitions. In 1954, at the very moment when Baker and Chaloff were alternating on the Storyville stage, Wein was busy planning a summertime trial run of continuous, outdoor jazz concerts for two days in Newport, Rhode Island, a small New England city that John Hammond, himself a Vanderbilt, called "stuffy old Newport, that bastion of entrenched wealth" (1977: 335). It was a completely novel idea, and the success of Wein's dress rehearsal in 1954 would lead to the first Newport Jazz Festival the summer after that, a week-long extravaganza that established the format for all jazz festivals to come, in what has been a jazz growth area for over fifty years.

When Wein heard Chaloff on his Storyville stage, he recognized that he was playing better than ever and, at least as important, was making a strong impression on audiences that had come, in the first place, to hear Chet Baker. Wein extended his good graces by offering Chaloff a record date on his Storyville label.

No one recalls who Chaloff's piano player was at the Storyville gig, but Richard Twardzik was still away when the record date came around in March and so Chaloff conscripted Russ Freeman from the Chet Baker Quartet. The recording group Chaloff led in the studio had unconventional instrumentation (two reeds and rhythm, no brass) and musicians with stylistic differences. In this precarious context, Chaloff seemed to be the only one perfectly at ease. The recording that resulted was quite ordinary, especially compared to a later Storyville recording with Twardzik in the band. One of the oddities is a tune called *Zdot*, written by Chaloff and co-arranged by Madame Chaloff, in what appears to be her only jazz credit. The one exceptional track is *Easy Street*, an obscure ballad that supplied the best evidence of Chaloff's newfound mastery as a jazz soloist in a small-band context. Chaloff made *Easy Street* memorable with a gliding, highly mannered interpretation, "at a tempo that would be dangerously slow for many players," the English writer Max Harrison wrote (1963: 163), in a survey of Chaloff's recordings a few years after his death. "This solo, like his *Body and Soul* of the following year, is very moving for its suggestion of a dreamlike inner landscape of haunting loneliness," Harrison wrote, and he proposed that "the desolation of this music, partly foreshadowed by his 1946 *Nocturne* with Sonny Berman," was some kind of esthetic symptom of heroin addiction.

Twardzik returned to Boston in April, missing out on Chaloff's record session by only a few weeks, and he took over immediately as Chaloff's regular piano player. He would work with him for the next year and a half, whenever opportunities arose. Work was still not plentiful for Chaloff, far from it. "He didn't work a lot because the word was out," Bob Martin said (Sunenblick 1994: 4). "You had to talk to somebody to give him a chance to play. When you got him a gig in a club or a hotel, he would usually mess it up. But when he did show, and got playing, it was 'Stand back, baby!'"

Herb Pomeroy came back with Twardzik. Steve Adamson recalled the bustle of jazz activities at the time: "I was once at The Stable for a rehearsal, and I met, a couple of times, Peter Littman, a wonderful drummer that's passed away. Dick Twardzik, I met him a couple of times. There was a nice bass player that I met, Jimmy Woode. There was a circle. Herb Pomeroy, he was flitting in and out, he still does" (Simosko 1998: 78).

Part of the activity involved preparations for the Boston Arts Festival, which would take place on Boston Commons on 9 June. The Festival was an annual celebration of the arts sponsored by the city. In 1954, the featured performers would include Martha Graham's dance troupe and an exhibition of abstract expressionist paintings. For the first time, jazz would be included, and Serge Chaloff, capping his triumphant return, was invited to lead the modern band, which would alternate with a traditional band led by George Wein.

Wein recorded the traditional group at the Boston Arts Festival but not the modern one. Besides Twardzik, Chaloff's band included Charlie Mariano. One of the tunes they played was *The Goof and I*, Al Cohn's now-venerable feature for Chaloff from their days in Woody Herman's Four Brothers, and a constant in Chaloff's small-band repertoire since Twardzik's first days with him in 1951.

After Chaloff's band played their set, they were replaced on stage by Wein's traditional band, and then at the end both bands crowded the stage for a jam session on *How High the Moon* (Simosko 1998: 80). Twardzik did not re-appear for the final jam. Instead, he told Steve Kuhn, the 17-year-old student and protégé of Madame Chaloff, to take his place, and the boy leapt at the chance. Twardziik was one of Kuhn's heroes. "I admired Twardzik very much, particularly harmonically," he said in an interview years later (Williams 1970: 238). "He listened to all the European composers and was quite advanced. He once paid me a compliment on my playing—I was still very young then—and of course I've never forgotten it."

Wein was impressed again by Chaloff's playing and the audience's response to it. After passing up the chance to record the modern band at the Arts Festival, even with remote recording facilities already in place for the trad band, he invited Chaloff to make a another recording for Storyville, this time with a bigger group and more elaborate arrangements.

Chaloff's reputation as a baritone saxophonist was originally based on powerhouse ensemble work and nimble solos in front of a roaring band, realized prototypically in his features with Herman, and it was those performances that won him the magazine polls for so many years. Now he was commanding respect, at least among musicians, in quieter contexts as well, as previewed on *Easy Street*. Chaloff would put his new mastery on abundant display in three studio recordings that stand as his best recordings, though ironically they belong to the last three years of his life, when his reputation was fading. The first of those recordings would be his second Storyville recording in September 1954, and Twardzik would play a central role in it.

In the writing and the playing for the LP, called *The Fable of Mabel*, there is a workshop feeling, a sense of adventure and experiment, the product almost certainly of the general enthusiasm that was part of the Boston jazz community at the time.

The recording session almost did not happen. The musicians began assembling in the studio when someone came up with the idea that they should see about getting some drugs to see them through it. Chaloff headed out into the streets, with Twardzik, possibly Mariano and a few others. They were gone for hours. "The other guys, the straight ones, Herbie Pomeroy and them, they got fed up," Crystal Joy recalled. Not that they didn't expect it. It was an occupational hazard. "It was hard on them," she says. "Sometimes those other guys didn't show up [at all]. They'd forget gigs, stuff like that. It was awful for the other guys."

Like the Mariano recordings for Prestige, these recordings for Wein's Boston-based label proved almost impossible to track down until the CD boom, when Alan Bates brought them out in Europe in 1990 on the Black Lion label in all their glory—five unissued takes and very good sound from a recording session that is a revelation (11.1, original on page 51). In the accompanying liner note, British critic Alun Morgan says, "Of the handful of recordings under [Chaloff's] own name, this collection surely ranks as his greatest ever." While most listeners would raise their voices in favor of Chaloff's highly praised 1956 LP called *Blue Serge* (Capitol CDP 7243 [1998]) and some others might plump for the 1955 *Boston Blow-Up!* (Capitol TOCJ-9354 [Toshiba Japan 2001]), this little-known earlier recording with Twardzik in the band at least merits mention in the same category.

Chaloff's brilliance that day is a testament to his junkie resilience in more ways than one. "Serge was not in the best of shape and his horn was in the pawn shop," Pomeroy remembered (Gross 1998: 9). "On a borrowed horn you can hear things that he is trying to do that do not happen instrumentally. But his heart and soul went into it. He was a glorious player."

The obscurity of *The Fable of Mabel* for some 35 years did a disservice to Twardzik even more than to Chaloff, because the focal point of the recording—what Simosko (1998: 81) calls "the masterpiece of this date"—is Twardzik's composition and arrangement of the suite-like composition that gives the album its title, *The Fable of Mabel*.

The Storyville LP featured adventurous writing for a mid-size band. There are passages of conventional big-band swing by the brass section (especially *Let's Jump* and *A Salute to Tiny*) sometimes contrasted with dissonances from the soloists and counter-melodies (*Eenie Meenie Minor Mode* and *The Fable of Mabel*). Twardzik is forced to play a badly-tuned instrument but almost always makes an impression, often by halving the tempo in the right hand and improvising spare, upper-register melodies. His playing is individualistic and confident, and clearly

[illustration 11.1] Serge Chaloff, *The Fable of Mabel*. Black Lion CD760923. Photograph by Hugh Turner, ca. 1954.

presages the maturity of his trio recordings that would be made only six weeks later.

Twardzik's *The Fable of Mabel* (or *Mable*, as he invariably spelled her name) is stunningly complex, so much so that it required three complete takes before the musicians were satisfied. Chaloff and Twardzik had been playing the piece together in a quartet version since 1951 but it had obviously evolved in the ensuing three years, and in its recorded version it has been re-made for a nine-piece orchestra. In the album notes, Twardzik says that "audiences found this satirical jazz legend a welcome respite from standard night club fare," another indication of Twardzik's belief that jazz audiences deserved more than blues and ballads.

Its complexity comes from its shifting themes, accompanied by tempo changes and exclamatory transitions. In an attempt to "explain" the musical structure, Twardzik supplied this elaborate program note:

> In the legend, Mabel is depicted as a woman who loves men, music and her silver saxophone that played counterpoint (her own invention which proved impractical). The work is divided into three movements, first, *New Orleans*; second, *Classical*; and third, *Not Too Sad an Ending*. The soulful baritone solo by Serge Chaloff traces Mabel's humble beginnings working railroad cars in New Orleans to her emergence as a practising crusader for the cause of jazz. During her Paris days on the Jazz Houseboat, her struggle for self-expression is symbolised by an unusual saxophone duet by Charlie Mariano and Varty Haroutunian. Mabel always said she wanted to go out blowing. She did.

The description is facetious but not irrelevant to the music. One reviewer missed the point by taking Twardzik's narrative too literally. "The story did not seem to fit the character of the music," Simosko (1998: 81) says, "although as program music 'describing' Mabel's adventures it would be easy to visualize a modern dancer performing the role." Twardzik may have hoped the music would some day be interpreted in dance, as Simosko suggests. He loved Bartók's *Miraculous Mandarin*, which also had a phantasmagoric narrative that was sometimes pantomimed by actors over Bartók's score.

The *Fable* is clearly organized in the three movements Twardzik describes in his narrative. The *New Orleans* movement (to 1:30) is based on a vamp in 2/4 time, the traditional two beats to the bar of New Orleans jazz. Chaloff states this theme in an extravagant style, venturing outside the changes for two bars and ending his phrases with a broad Bechet-like vibrato. His statement leaves the impression of an avant-garde moldy fig, richly oxymoronic. The second movement (to 3:30), which Twardzik calls *Classical*, literally bursts into bebop, doubling the tempo over some thunderous drumming. Herb Pomeroy imitates Dizzy Gillespie with bright, rapid quarter-notes (played *too* fast on take 2), and he is followed by one chorus of an improvised alto saxophone duet by Charlie Mariano and Varty Haroutunian, and then by an ingenious chorus by Twardzik in which he halves the time and seems to ride above the propulsive rhythm, and finally by one chorus in tempo by Chaloff. The short final movement, *Not Too Sad an Ending*, reprises the opening melody as a ballad in 4/4, closing with Chaloff's melancholy statement in the lowest reaches of his baritone.

Twardzik's score anticipates several features that lay ahead in jazz history, notably simultaneous improvisation by the two saxophone players,

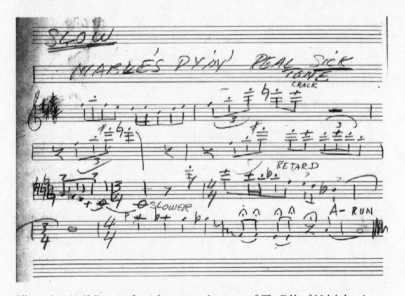

[illustration 11.2] Excerpt from the manuscript score of *The Fable of Mabel* showing the composer's annotations for the mood of the final movement. From the Twardzik-Thompson Archive, courtesy of Rosamond Thompson and Jane Sumner. All rights reserved.

the lack of chordal movement (a modal approach) in the last movement, and Chaloff's free-form statement, venturing outside the chord
changes, in the opening section.

The handwritten score of *The Fable of Mabel* is the only one of Twardzik's
scores that has come to light so far except for the juvenile *Bouncin' with
Bartok*. It is almost certainly the score that the musicians played from
the next year at the 1955 Boston Arts Festival, but it may be the one
used for this 1954 record session as well. Twardzik's annotations include
the scrawled instructions "SLOW   MABLE'S DYIN'   REAL SICK
TONE" on Chaloff's part (11.2). His annotations are mainly metro-
nomic, spelling out the shifting tempos for the players ("TWICE AS
FAST," "CRES. —— DECRES." and so on), but a couple of them
underscore the light-hearted satire that was the composer's main intention. A note on Chaloff's score marks the transition between movements. "TAKE A REST AND TURN THE PAGE," Twardzik writes,
and under that he places his "Dickie" caricature (11.3).

[illustration 11.3] Excerpt from the manuscript score of *The Fable of Mabel* showing
the composer's annotations for Serge Chaloff at the transition between movements.
From the Twardzik-Thompson Archive, courtesy of Rosamond Thompson and Jane
Sumner. All rights reserved.

Twardzik's arrangement is sophisticated, complex and brilliantly original. He embeds the solo sequences in some striking ensemble writing, especially for the brass. The transitions between movements are signaled by bebop fanfares and the solos are punctuated by big-band riffs. It is an arrangement loaded with devices, and replete with special effects. Unfortunately, it all takes place in only four minutes and twenty seconds.

The arrangement is so highly concentrated that it goes by almost too quickly to be absorbed, and on the first few listenings its main impression is manic intensity. After several listenings, it becomes possible to pick out details such as an oddly familiar syncopated sequence that lasts exactly ten seconds (1:26 to 1:36) and marks the transition from the New Orleans movement to the Classical movement. It is familiar because it recurs in *A Crutch for the Crab*, where it is slowed down and repeated (0:27 to 0:47) and altogether more integral. That momentary figure, it turns out, is borrowed quite directly from Debussy's *Fêtes* (as pointed out to me by Geoffrey Wills), an impressionist work that obviously seared itself into the psyche of the Danvers high-school student. "He was getting familiar with things like Debussy and Ravel pieces that involved harp," Bob Zieff said (Sunenblick 2003). "These things were in his ears, a resource sort of thing."

If *The Fable of Mabel* had been recorded a couple of years later, when the long-play format was firmly established as the industry standard, it would surely have been decompressed to twice its length or more. Its greatest flaw is its brevity.

This Storyville recording session of *The Fable of Mabel* turned out to be something of a convocation exercise for a couple of members of the thriving Boston jazz scene. Visiting musicians like Charlie Parker, Russ Freeman and Chet Baker were not the only front-rank players taking notice of the talent there. Stan Kenton's orchestra had come through earlier in 1954 and taken Mariano away with them when they departed. Mariano's appearance at the Boston Arts Festival in June and on Chaloff's recording in September must have come about on brief homecomings. Mariano rejoined Kenton after the session, and Herb Pomeroy went with him for six months. So Pomeroy, recently back from the Dixie tour with Lionel Hampton, began a new road excursion.

When Pomeroy returned to Boston after touring with Kenton, he would assume a leader's role that would last more than four decades. The groundwork for that role, he realized later, had already been laid before his experience with Kenton. "I know that some of my rehearsal techniques as a band leader stem from playing on that *The Fable of Mabel* session," he said (Gross 1998: 9). "At that point I felt very undeveloped as a player. Serge, Charlie Mariano and Dick Twardzik were much more developed. Charlie and Serge were a bit older, and Dick was a year younger than me but he was already a brilliant talent in his late teens. The tune Dick wrote, *The Fable of Mabel*, was so unlike what people were hearing at the time."

Twardzik stayed home, and his playing and writing gathered strength. *The Fable of Mabel* was a culmination of sorts, as Pomeroy said, a shining moment for Twardzik both as player and composer, but it would not stand alone for long. Twardzik would match it and surpass it in the months ahead.

12 Two Crutches?

"The first time I heard him play, I couldn't believe it," Chet Baker said about Richard Twardzik. "He had somehow bridged the thing between classical and jazz" (Weber 1988).

It was at Storyville where Baker heard him. Twardzik was playing there in Chaloff's band for a week in October, one month after recording *The Fable of Mabel*. Baker's Quartet was the featured attraction that week, back for the second engagement at the club that year. Twardzik had missed their first engagement, on the road with Lionel Hampton, but this time he was very much in the show. Baker was not the only one singing his praises. Russ Freeman got on the phone to Richard Bock, the record producer for Pacific Jazz in Hollywood. "There's a young guy here who plays piano like you wouldn't believe," Freeman told him (de Valk 2000: 60). "You have to record him." Freeman's sense of urgency was probably heightened because he knew about Twardzik's recent recording with Chaloff. If that record was destined to be too local to establish Twardzik's reputation outside of his home town, Freeman must have surmised that word of mouth would do it, and soon. Bock heard the urgency in Freeman's voice. He told Freeman to take Twardzik into a studio as soon as he could set it up.

"Twardzik was happy to have this first opportunity to record with his own group," Freeman said in his notes (1956), and he added that the trio format for the recording was Twardzik's choice. So, three days after they closed at Storyville, Freeman and his bass colleague in Baker's band, Carson Smith, met Twardzik and Peter Littman at the studio of recording engineer Rudy Van Gelder in Hackensack, New Jersey, to make the recordings that would be the crowning achievement of Twardzik's short career.

The occasion was not, at the time it happened, an auspicious one. Little more than a year later, when Freeman sat down to write his notes for the release of this music, the closest he could come to dating it was "late in 1954." Rudy Van Gelder was destined to become the most celebrated sound engineer in jazz history, but when he recorded Twardzik he was just beginning to earn that reputation. So far the only people who had noticed him were a few New York musicians and a couple of independent producers. Freeman identified him in his notes as "Rudy Gelder," which seems like an embarrassing gaffe now but was close enough at the time. In fact, by day, Van Gelder worked as an optometrist. Making jazz recordings started as an avocation, because he liked messing with sound equipment and microphone placement and other minutiae of the rapidly evolving reel-to-reel technology.

Van Gelder's legacy would eventually come to include the magnificent Blue Note catalogue from 1953 to 1971, and much more. But when Richard Twardzik and the others pulled up outside his modest house in Hackensack on a Wednesday in 1954, they were met by an unprepossessing young man with thick glasses who—incredible as it now seems—made records mainly on Wednesdays and Sundays, because those were his days off from the eyeglass store. Not only that, but he made the records in a sound booth he had built into his parents' living room. It would take until 1959, five more years, before Van Gelder would have his own purpose-built sound studio, which he put up in Englewood Cliffs, about six miles closer to Manhattan than Hackensack, though still in New Jersey.

The date of Twardzik's recording session was settled by Dan Skea, a musician and researcher who runs the Rudy Van Gelder Project. One of Skea's aims is to fix the dates when Van Gelder worked, and I got to know him by e-mail after he found my 1998 discography on the internet with its gross approximation of the recording date as October–December 1954. My confusion about the recording date came about because Michael Cuscuna, in his notes accompanying the first CD issue of this music (1989), wrote, "While Russ [Freeman] and Chet Baker were at Birdland that December, Freeman produced Twardzik with his own Boston drummer Peter Littman and Baker's bassist Carson Smith at Rudy Van Gelder's studio in Englewood Cliffs, New Jersey." Ignoring Cuscuna's mistake on the location of the Van Gelder studio at the time, I had to think that he had some inside information about the date. I had previously listed it as 27 October, the date from Alun Morgan's original discography of Twardzik (Morgan 1963: 27). Cuscuna was not only the liner-note writer for the CD but also its producer, presumably with access to the original files. He was also the star producer of the CD boom, responsible for releasing more jazz music from studio vaults, including alternate takes and unissued sessions, than any fan could hope for. So I hedged on the date.

Dan Skea phoned Russ Freeman in June 1999 to see if he could get a closer approximation, and Freeman told him, "It might have been late '54 but I'm not sure it was as late as December." A few days later, Skea phoned him again and they had this conversation:

DS: You said you remembered coming down [to Hackensack] with Twardzik and Carson [Smith], from Boston.

RF: Yes, yes.

DS: And did you drive in one car?

RF: Oh, boy. Well, my guess would be yes. But I'm not absolutely certain. But now I think Peter Littman was also on that date.

DS: That's right—Peter Littman—that's right.

RF: So it would have had to have been drums and bass…

DS: Probably a couple of cars, maybe.

RF: Might have been a couple of cars.

DS: And were you, at that time, were you and Chet still doing an engagement in Boston?

RF: Yes.

DS: Did you go back to Boston then, and play some more. In other words, at Storyville, I believe, at the time?

RF: To the best of my recollection, that's right.

DS: So it might have been, like, on your day off from Storyville.

RF: Right.

It should be easier than this, I said aloud after I read the transcript of their conversation. "You're right," Dan Skea said, "it should be easier than this."

Two months later, Skea knew that none of the details he got from Freeman held. Skea found the date 27 October 1954 beside a Japanese Toshiba entry for Twardzik's *Round Midnight,* which had been issued in Japan on a fifteen-volume compilation, and even though the recording site was listed incorrectly as Boston, Skea thought the date had to be right. "This has got to be the correct date for the Hackensack session," he said. "October 27 was a Wednesday, a day that Rudy said was his day off, when he did a lot of recordings. It is also an empty date on his log to this point." Skea's date, obviously, corroborates Alun Morgan's original date for the session. It also makes sense from everything else we know about the chronology. It was in fact the first Wednesday after the Sunday closing for the bands that Freeman and Twardzik were playing in at Storyville in Boston, and thus the first available date that they could take advantage of Van Gelder's services.

So Freeman and Carson Smith probably drove to Hackensack from their New York base on their off-day, and met Twardzik and Littman there as they came down from Boston. Freeman thought that Chet Baker might also have been there. "We were hanging out together," he said (Gioia 1992: 184). "Chet might even have driven up with us to Rudy Van Gelder's studio for the session." Whether he was there or not, Baker got to know Littman well enough to call him when he found himself suddenly in need of a drummer a couple of months later, and a few months after that he would call Twardzik when he had to replace Freeman.

Plans for the trio recording were laid in Boston, and one of the spin-offs is one of the most curious documents in the history of jazz recording—a tape of Twardzik rehearsing that was released 36 years later on CD. There seem to be three separate rehearsal sessions on the tape, judging by the aural evidence (as indicated in the discography). While the extraordinary polish of Twardzik's Pacific Jazz recording left no doubt that he had prepared himself fastidiously for it, it is amazing to find that we can sit in on his preparations. It is very rare, almost unheard of, to find a permanent record of the preliminary musings for any musician. Perhaps for good reason. Twardzik's rehearsals are rough and impulsive, unpolished and occasionally crude. He seems completely self-absorbed. On the assumption that he knew he was being recorded, his lack of self-consciousness is a striking index of his legendary powers of concentration at the keyboard.

If Twardzik had gone on to a 30-year career, these souvenirs could have been charitably forgotten. Under the circumstances, they add weight to the discography. The rehearsals surfaced in 1990 as a compact disc called *1954 Improvisations*, with a decidedly homemade look and sound, on a label called New Artists (12.1). It is, for all its shortcomings, an astounding find.

The recording is credited to one Peter Morris, and when I asked Bob Zieff if he could place the name, he said, "Peter Morris? Please—Peter *Van Cortland* Morris. Son of Newbold Morris." That places him in the direct line of descent from Dutch-American *patroons* and makes him the grandson of an Astor, at the fag-end of the American aristocracy that drew its wealth from entailed estates. "I think I remember him," Crystal Joy told me. "He had a lot of money, and he had a piano." Zieff also remembered Morris as a tenor saxophone player, sometime student of Lennie Tristano and Tristano's disciple, Warne Marsh. "He had an apartment in Boston with a grand piano in it, which was where some fledgling jazz players bunked in, a hangout of sorts," Zieff says. The piano, at least the one Twardzik played, was actually an upright, not a grand.

Morris's apartment was on Huntington Avenue, and Twardzik was living there at the time with some other musicians, probably including Peter Littman. Morris was not in the habit of recording his guests as

[illustration 12.1] Dick Twardzik, *1954 Improvisations*. New Artists Records 10006CD. Recorded by Peter Morris. Drawing by Carlotta Morris. Design by Mindy Mitchell. 1990.

they went about their business, but he admired Twardzik particularly and got his consent to capture on tape some forty minutes of his practice sessions. Morris's brief explanatory note in the liner, the only text apart from titles and times, serves simultaneously as a *credo* and a *caveat emptor*:

> I am putting out this CD because after 36 years I have come to think of it as one of the handful of great recordings of music of all time. I think admirers of Charlie Parker, Bud Powell and Lennie Tristano will find this so. The listener must be patient with an amateur tape recording, sections of practice and an upright piano untuned till the Yesterdays track.

The first six rehearsal tracks find Twardzik alone at an untuned piano, working on *'Round Midnight* and trying out four other standards that he would discard before the studio session (*Nice Work If You Can Get It, Get Happy, It Could Happen to You, All the Things You Are*). The piano, as one reviewer noted, "is more out-of-tune than anything you've heard on disc before" (Priestly 1990). Twardzik appears to be worrying over the harmonies, looking for tonic resolutions he might have missed before, and searching for novel paths. There is a candor in the performances that is usually well hidden by the time the performer actually performs. At best, the tracks reveal Twardzik's creative restlessness. Nick Dean (1956) said, "I'll always remember how dissatisfied he always was with everything he did—and his impatience with anyone else who wasn't a perfectionist. ...Not impatience so much as an inability to understand *why* anyone else didn't want to be perfect." Some of that impatience is evident in the mood of these crude etudes.

At the second rehearsal, the piano is tuned, and Twardzik is accompanied by Peter Littman and momentarily by bassist Jack Lawlor. *Bess You Is My Woman Now* takes pretty much the form it will take on the Pacific Jazz recording. The other four titles failed to make it as far the studio recording, but one of these, an untitled original that Bob Zieff identifies as a tune based on the chord changes of *I Got Rhythm* with substitute chords at the end of the A sections, provides a glimpse of Twardzik applying his crab-like pauses to a simple, post-bop line in what is a well-coordinated performance with the drummer. This performance provides a genuine addition to what we otherwise know about Twardzik's talent.

At this second rehearsal session, Jack Lawlor, the bassist who played on Mariano's *New Sounds from Boston,* lasts less than two minutes. He sets down a straightahead walking line on *I Get a Kick Out of You,* but for some reason his playing seems to disturb Littman, who responds by placing odd drum accents that disrupt the melodic line. After about a minute, Lawlor calls out in exasperation, "Ah, come on, Peter!" and a few choruses later, the piece stops abruptly. Lawlor is not heard from again. His defection, or dismissal, is presumably the reason that Carson Smith had to be imported for the recording session. Presumably Smith rehearsed for the recording with Twardzik and Littman after hours at Storyville in the week leading up to the studio date.

The third rehearsal session on Morris's CD is made up entirely of variations on *I'll Remember April,* a valuable eight-minute addition to Twardzik's legacy. Twardzik prefaces the tune with an unaccompanied meditation before erupting into the bright, uptempo swinger similar

[illustration 12.2] Richard Twardzik and Peter Littman. Photograph probably by Nick Dean. From the Twardzik-Thompson Archive, courtesy of Rosamond Thompson and Jane Sumner. All rights reserved.

in style to the version that ultimately appears on the trio recording. On the swinging section, Twardzik is accompanied by Littman playing either a drum pad or a table top, and playing with great panache, even trading fours with the piano player (12.2).

Thus prepared, Twardzik made his remarkable debut as a leader in the Van Gelder studios. It would take about a year and a half to get the recording pressed and into the stores. It caused a ripple of interest, small but persistent. (Morris's *1954 Improvisations* rides on that ripple decades later as, of course, does this book.) The ripple swelled somewhat when Twardzik's recordings with Chet Baker from Paris were heard, and those recordings have come back into print more often due to the drawing power of Baker's name and the happy accident of their being produced in Europe, where commercial considerations play a smaller role in determining what gets issued. Later generations have had few opportunities to discover the brilliance of Twardzik's trio sides.

The second opportunity came in 1962, when Pacific Jazz issued a compilation LP titled *The Last Set* (Pacific Jazz PJ-37), with the six known tracks from *Trio*, plus a previously unissued ballad, *Just One of Those Things* (12.3, also page 52). To fill out the LP, or at least bring it up to minimum length (the total time is only 31 minutes), Twardzik's *The Girl from Greenland* from the Chet Baker Paris session, is added to the trio tracks.

The liner note for *The Last Set*, by John William Hardy (1962), offered no new information, but did point out the abiding interest in Twardzik seven years after his death:

> The [trio] recording, for some time now unavailable, has become a modern collector's item. For a while, hardly a month went by that an inquiry as to its availability did not come to the World Pacific offices. For that reason, and because we feel strongly that Richard Twardzik is one of the most astonishingly accomplished jazzmen to appear in modern jazz, all of the trio recordings plus the impressive quartet recording have been gathered together to superbly showcase the talent of Richard Twardzik.

Hardy's main contribution in his notes was to offer a kind of apologia for uninitiated listeners about what they were going to hear on the LP: "It will be said that Richard Twardzik…is somewhat difficult to understand (requires attentive listening) and is not lyrical (does not speak in the trite songs of the day). But I recommend you give his playing an extended opportunity, for it is full of all the subtlety, grace, beauty and immensity that one can ask for in a lively art." Hardy's assessment ends with this encomium: "these performances will wear and are timeless. For their substance is not device, chicanery, or cliché, but rather they are composed of thoughts, imagery, and emotion of a most gifted and sensitive human being, as purely and clearly transported to and from the piano as these ever were."

For the initiated, *The Last Set* seemed to offer an unexpected bonus. As we spun the new LP in 1962, the familiar strains of *A Crutch for the Crab* seemed somehow reshaped. Suspicions that we were actually hearing something we had not heard before seemed to be confirmed by the evidence from a stopwatch. The take issued in 1956 ran 3:25, but the 1962 take ran only 3:14. (The "official" times listed on the liners were 3:22 and 3:19, respectively; small discrepancies are inevitable when timings are made on different playback equipment, but the eleven-second difference on the stopwatch between the original 1956 version and the new 1962 one ensures that something is different.) Rumors quickly circulated that Pacific Jazz had put out a previously

[illustration 12.3] Richard Twardzik, *The Last Set*. Pacific Jazz PJ-37. Photograph by Ron Joy. Design by Woody Woodward. © 1962 World Pacific Records.

unissued take of *A Crutch for the Crab*, apparently mistakenly, in place of the original. So instead of one *Crutch*, it seemed that we now, hal-leluia!, had two.

With such a happy accident, it seemed churlish, perhaps, to observe that the two *Crutches* were so similar to one another that the new take hardly revealed anything further about Twardzik's talent. That they were indeed different takes seemed to be confirmed when the CD version of *Trio* arrived in 1989 (Pacific Jazz CDP 7 46861), fairly early in the CD revolution, with all Twardzik's trio pieces including two ver-sions of *A Crutch for the Crab*, one of which was labeled "alternate take." The CD presented the alternate take side by side with the original for the first time, so you would hear them in succession by default. The experience was, frankly, anticlimactic. Of the alternate take, I wrote (in my 1997 website bio-discography), "It sounds mightily like the origi-nal, with all the elements, written or improvised, in the same order." Anticlimactic it might be, but there was no way I was going to take a negative tack on three additional studio minutes of Twardzik playing his finest composition.

With hindsight, it looks as if all of us who celebrated the discovery of the second take of *A Crutch for the Crab* from 1962 onward were suf-fering from emperor's-new-clothes syndrome. Above all, you *want* to believe it. No matter what your senses tell you.

The "alternate take" is a delusion. James A. Harrod finally put the claim to rest conclusively in November 2000. Harrod has been research-ing the Pacific Jazz catalogue since 1994, sorting out discographical puzzles and compiling a history of the label. (Among the first fruits of his research are three CDs of *Chet Baker Quartet Live* [2000-2001] with Harrod's annotations.) One of Harrod's discographical puzzles was the putative alternate take of *A Crutch for the Crab*. He compared the two takes acoustically, making visual waveforms with SoundEdit 16 software using a finely detailed sampling procedure. The takes look different at the start (12.4), but on closer inspection that is illusory. The master take (PJ 1212) includes opening bars that are simply miss-ing from the putative alternate take (PJ 37). When the waveforms of the two takes are aligned *after* the missing opening bars, they match perfectly (12.5). The match-up remains perfect note for note, nuance for nuance, Hz for Hz, for the entire three minutes and eighteen seconds, in a waveform display that takes up about 19 feet in a hard-copy print-out.

So the performances are identical. Or, rather, there is only one performance. It would be totally impossible for different performances to attain perfect homogeneity, even in classical performances, where homogeneity between performances is an ideal, and no chance at all in jazz, where it is eschewed. The illusion of difference came about because the version of *A Crutch for the Crab* released in 1962 was truncated.

One additional oddity is that on the CD, where the two takes are presented side by side, the timing difference that originally led listeners to suspect two different takes has vanished. The official times of the two tracks are listed as 3:18 and 3:19. The explanation appears in very fine print on the liner: "Discographical note: On the original tape of Pacific Jazz 1212 [*Trio*], the introduction to the original take of *A Crutch for the Crab* has been destroyed by severe tape stretch, therefore it has been edited off of the CD version." Presumably the tape-stretching was discovered (or perhaps it happened) when the sound engineer was mastering *The Last Set* in 1962, and resulted in the truncated version that was released on that LP. The CD issue compounds the defect by releasing *A Crutch for the Crab* twice with its opening bars cut off, one presumably from the master tape and the other from a pristine copy of *The Last Set*.

"The missing opening bars are inexcusable," Harrod says, "but I should not get started on the lack of attention to detail or lack of proofreading" at Capitol-EMI, the multinational corporation that controls Pacific Jazz and numerous other labels. Where once we imagined that we had two takes of *A Crutch for the Crab*, we find instead that there is only

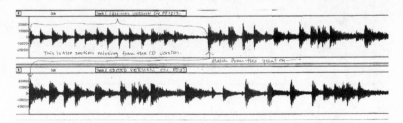

[illustration 12.4] Waveform of opening bars of *A Crutch for the Crab* (PJ 1212) and putative alternate take (PJ 37), by James A. Harrod. Reproduced by permission.

one. The first release of Twardzik's trio music in 27 years presented listeners with the defective version, played twice. The only intact version of *A Crutch for the Crab* is the one on the original 1956 LP, but knowing that means that it can be remedied. In the summer of 2001, Harrod took a pristine copy of the original *Trio* LP (Pacific Jazz PJ-1212) to the Capitol Tower in Hollywood where the mastering engineer for a Japanese Limited Edition CD reissue, Ron McMaster, made a tape transfer of the opening bars of *A Crutch for the Crab*, thus restoring it to its original 3:25 playing time. The limited edition (Toshiba TOCJ-9347 [2002]) may not be widely heard, but Capitol-EMI now holds a restored master for future issues.

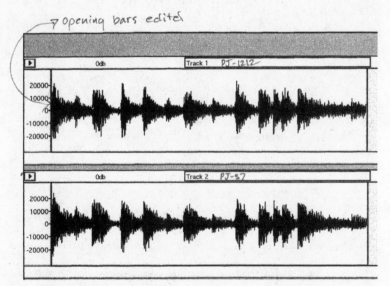

[illustration 12.5] Matched waveforms of beginning of *A Crutch for the Crab* (PJ 1212) after introductory bars and beginning of putative alternate take (PJ 37), by James A. Harrod. Reproduced by permission.

13 The Girl from Greenland

Early in 1955, Richard Twardzik was back at the Stable as intermission pianist. Herb Pomeroy had left Stan Kenton and was again back in Boston. But this time Pomeroy felt exhausted and frustrated by his experiences as a road musician, and he came back determined to create a setting in Boston that would provide musical rewards for talented musicians who chose to stay at home. He took charge of the house band at the Stable, and began taking on the responsibilities that would soon lead to his recognition in *Down Beat* (Cerulli 1958) as "a strong leader whose life is jazz."

Twice nightly at the Stable, after Pomeroy's band members left the stand at the end of their sets, Twardzik would mosey up to the piano vacated by Ray Santisi, Pomeroy's regular piano player, adjust the stool with great care, wipe down the keyboard, and flex his long fingers. Then, leaning close to the keyboard, he would sound a chord and add a few notes in the treble clef. After some exploratory notes, he would sidle into a melody—*'Round Midnight* or *I'll Remember April* or *Yesterdays* or something no one would be able to put a title to, at least not for another year and a half, when Pacific Jazz would finally release his trio recordings. He would ruminate on the tune, working out substitute chords, neighboring harmonics and passing tones. Often he would worry the same tune for the whole intermission.

At the same time he was playing with tempos, moving out of straight 4/4 and experimenting with Latin counter-rhythms. One of his new friends was a piano player from Latin America who was studying at the New England Conservatory. Bob Zieff met him with Twardzik, and he remembers that, through this friendship, Twardzik had acquired a cardboard box full of Latin American piano music. "When Dick left for Europe he left the box of Latin American piano music with me," Zieff told me, "but when I moved once it disappeared completely!" Twardik's composition *Yellow Tango* in his trio recordings is the palpable result.

The jaunty mood of *Yellow Tango* matched Twardzik's mood perfectly in the months leading up to his Pacific Jazz date and for several months afterward. Even its title, at the time, evoked smiles from the jazz crowd. Everyone knew a tune called *Blue Tango* by Leroy Anderson, purveyor of pop instrumentals (*Syncopated Clock*, *Sleigh Ride*). *Blue Tango* topped the

Hit Parade for weeks, wafted to those heights in the American suburbs on fantasies of chattering castanets and swishing crinolines. Twardzik's *Yellow Tango*, with its plaintive musing and understated rhythm, could hardly be more different, an irony that was not lost on any hipster who heard its title.

Yellow Tango is Twardzik at his sunniest. It adroitly caught the playfulness he liked to show in public. "He wasn't the usual addict," said Jay Migliori of Twardzik. "He was always on time. Always well dressed. Always upbeat. He was into the arty element—he liked hanging around with artists and poets" (Sunenblick 1996: 7).

Twardzik's buoyant mood was definitely helped along by his girlfriend, the singer and piano player Crystal Joy, whose outgoing personality and good cheer not only rubbed off on Twardzik but also warmed up audiences in night clubs and put her in demand there (13.1). They met at the Hi Hat late in 1953 when Twardzik was playing in the house band accompanying Sonny Stitt and Crystal Joy was the intermission act. It was her first-ever nightclub engagement. Twardzik was only a few weeks removed from his self-pitying visit to Miami Beach where he had come to the conclusion that "everyone must travel alone (most of the time)." Along came Crystal Joy by way of refutation. It is hard to imagine a better tonic.

Crystal Joy was 19 when they met at the Hi Hat, and in her first semester at Boston University. Her full name was Crystal Joy Billouin, and she was born in Montreal to Trinidadian parents, in the same Burgundy neighborhood that gave birth a few years before to the redoubtable jazz pianists Oscar Peterson and Oliver Jones. But her family moved, as she says, "back and forth between Montreal and Trinidad and New York." Everywhere they went, they seemed to find extended family members, and most of them were musical. Crystal Joy's father's cousin ran a children's orchestra in New York, and Crystal played cello in it and her younger brother, at the age of 3, played violin. She sang, as far as she can recall, from birth. "My mother was always taking me to concerts, and entering me in contests," she says. "I used to do my little-girl act. I did Ella Fitzgerald songs, and Judy Garland songs. When Judy Garland came along with *Over the Rainbow*, I was set then."

Her formative years were spent in Maine, where her father found wartime work in the shipyards around Portland. She went to grammar school and high school in South Portland. With her Trinidadian ancestry, she had little experience of African-American culture until she came face to face with the black diaspora in Maine. "A lot of black people came from the south for the work there," she told me. "They stuck us all in one section of the village. It was good. I loved it. I had good friends. I learned all about life in the south. Yeah, I was a northerner. I was a fresh kid. They considered me rude. Well, I wasn't going to do all that 'yes, ma'm, no ma'm,' like the southern kids. They were *too* polite for me. But we got along just fine. We became close friends."

[Illustration 13.1.] Crystal Joy, ca. 1959. Photograph courtesy of Crystal-Joy Albert.

She also developed her show business aptitudes there. "Every time there was some function," she said, "the B'nai B'rith or the NAACP or whoever would hire me to sing." She credits a man named Sidney Lerner for shaping her natural skills. Lerner was the kind of teacher who spawns legends in the memories of the people he worked with. Crystal Joy remembers him transcribing Errol Garner solos right off the records. He also staged musical productions in Portland, importing New York talent for the leads but finding roles for talented locals as well. He cast Crystal Joy and her little brother in *Finian's Rainbow*, and they stopped the show every night. Much later, when she moved from Boston to New York to further her career, those New York actors she worked with in Lerner's company took her in and helped her on her way.

She learned to accompany herself on piano, she says, on visits to New York. Her uncle Frank used to take her with him when he visited Hazel Scott, the Trinidad-American singer and pianist. "I would go down the basement and play her piano," Crystal Joy says. She was in élite company, though she could hardly know it at the time. Her uncle was Frank E. M. Hercules (1911–1996), who would gain recognition a few years after Crystal's childhood for his novels with Trinidad settings, and later for the 1972 political tract *American Society and Black Revolution*. Hazel Scott (1920–1981) was already a celebrity when Crystal was noodling on her grand piano, renowned for attending Juilliard School of Music at the age of eight and for having her own radio show at 16. When Crystal Joy visited her, she was a glamorous entertainer at Café Society in midtown Manhattan. As the wife of Congressman Adam Clayton Powell, the "mayor of Harlem," she would become a decorative fixture on social pages.

"I discovered I could play piano for myself at her place," Crystal Joy remembers. "All the time, my mother would get piano players for me who would just play the sheet music and it was never in my key. So I would sing in their key, and I never won the contests because I was singing in their key. Then I discovered I could accompany myself, and I would play in my own key, and that solved it." She credits that with the upturn in her fortunes, including her winning the Horace Heidt contest for Maine.

When the War ended, her father took a job in Boston, and the family moved into "a real nice, big house" in the Jamaica Plain borough.

Crystal Joy enrolled at Boston University as a scholarship student, but it seemed perfectly natural for her to keep on singing. She auditioned for the owner of the Hi Hat and was offered the intermission gig. It did not take long for her to find out that her success as a singer cut into her study time. She tried doing her homework between sets. That's what she was doing when she met Richard Twardzik. She was fretting over a Trigonometry assignment —"a dreadful course," she says, "I had no idea what the teacher was doing in that course"—when Richard leaned over her shoulder to see what she was doing.

By the second semester, she knew that she could not keep up her studies while she was working so many late nights. She tried switching her major to music. Crystal Joy says, "When I went to the professor, we went to a practice room, and I started playing, and the professor says, 'What are you doing here? Get out of here.' There wasn't much they could teach me. 'You've got to spread your wings.'" She took his advice and began concentrating on her singing career.

She had already noticed Twardzik before he spoke to her. "The first time I saw him, I thought, what a zombie," she says. "You know, he was walking on to the stage. He sauntered slowly onto the stage, his head up in the air. He walked around looking like someone who ran a funeral parlor. But then, if someone said something he appreciated, he would break into this maniacal laugh."

Symphony Sid was a familiar figure at the Hi Hat even on nights when he was not broadcasting from there. When he noticed Twardzik's interest in the 19-year-old college student, he took Crystal Joy aside. "Don't you dare get involved," he said. "He's a junkie. I'm like, 'What's a junkie?' I didn't know anything. But from then on Dick and I were practically inseparable."

To get home from the Hi Hat at the end of the night, Crystal Joy had to take the streetcar up Huntington Avenue, and Twardzik asked if he could walk her to the stop. They started talking about music walking up the street, and when they got to the streetcar stop, they sat on a bench and kept talking. "And I missed that train," she said, "and the next train." She remembers that at some point they traded Dizzy Gillespie and Charlie Parker licks, singing phrases and working out variations. "We spent the whole night doing that," she says, "and it was the most wonderful experience of my life, of my musical life. Because up until then, I pretty much did my music on my own. It was my own experience. And now I was sharing it with someone. It was just a great experience musically for me. And he too was pleased about it. It meant as much to him to share that music with someone. So we spent the whole night there in the Huntington Avenue station."

By the time Richard met Crystal Joy, Reba Stewart had split completely from him, working on her own artistic pursuits and staying away from the complications that seemed to crop up with him. Crystal Joy never met Reba Stewart but she heard about her. "Dick was crazy about her," she said. "She was so arty. He used to say to me, 'Why can't you be more arty?' Like Reba. Here I was in my Boston Public Library get-up." When I asked what that meant, she said, "You know, avocado green and black."

Twardzik and Crystal Joy were different in all kinds of ways. They made an odd couple. Twardzik's angularity contrasted with Crystal Joy's soft features, and the narrow oval of his face looked all the more austere beside her sensuous lips and bright eyes. His night-life pallor seemed all the more ghostly next to her cocoa complexion. He wore stovepipe pants and tight jackets, in the Ivy League fashion of the day, and she wore blowsy, colorful robes. On stage and sometimes off, he projected a moody, self-absorbed attitude, while she was chatty and outgoing, with a smile that could light up a room.

She adored him, and when he was clean and clear-thinking he adored her. "Dick was my first and real love," she told me soon after I told her why I had sought her, some 47 years after she had seen Dick Twardzik for the last time. In a later conversation, when I mentioned that Dick's parents had treated him like a genius from the day he was born, she latched onto the topic as if she was hoping to out-point Henryk and Clare. "He *was* a genius!" she said. "He was absolutely brilliant in everything he did. He put things together in such clever ways. In his music and in the way he talked, and the things he said, and the way he looked. Even the way he dressed."

When they met, he was, as always, in need of a place to live. She took him home to her parents' house in Jamaica Plain. She says it was not an unusual thing for her to do even in the 1950s. The Billouins had an open-door policy. Besides Crystal Joy and her five younger brothers, there were always other people living with them. Most of them were Trinidadians who had come to Boston as students or as visitors looking for better prospects. Some were immigrants, sponsored by the Billouin family. But even before Twardzik moved in, there were household members without Trinidad connections. "Even kids who lived in Boston would stay with us," Crystal Joy said. "Our parents were wonderful to our friends."

Twardzik wore out his welcome when Crystal Joy's parents found out he was using drugs. One night, he collapsed in his car from an overdose right in front of her house. "He had this small car and it had a stick shift," she said, "and I couldn't drive a stick shift, and it was a matter of life and death so I got in the car and drove him down to the Stable and went in and got Serge. And Serge came out and walked him out of it."

After that, Twardzik moved into the musicians' commune at 905 Boylston. For a while, Crystal Joy lived there too. "When they found out Dick was on drugs, that changed things for me with my parents," she says. "My parents were mad at me because of Dick, and I had to see him, so I moved out." For a while, she worked at a small bar right next door. (What was the name of the bar? I asked her, decades later. "Honey, do I know?" says she.) "All I remember," she says, "it was a narrow room with a piano at one end, and me and another girl worked the place. We took turns singing and playing piano there."

Richard and Crystal Joy visited Fowler House in Danvers several times. "Dick's parents had this mansion," she says, "it was like a showplace." Crystal Joy remembers that they behaved like gentry, not at all like custodians. She felt a distinct chill, especially from Clare. As a result, they usually visited the place on weekdays when they knew Clare and Henryk would be away at work.

On one occasion, they made a deliberate attempt at impressing his parents by showing off Crystal Joy's domestic skills. But it went up in smoke. "I remember I burnt the pork chops," Crystal Joy said. "You know, I was trying so hard to make a good impression. I wanted them to know that I wanted him to be as straight as they did. And I burnt the pork chops."

In her second year as a professional singer, Crystal Joy's career trajectory took her out of Richard's workspace. She played less at the Hi Hat and other jazz clubs and more often in the Jewel Room and other supper clubs, where she was expected to wear elegant gowns and sing sophisticated ballads (*You and the Night and the Music, On Green Dolphin Street*). She learned to field requests from well-heeled patrons, and gratified them especially by framing their songs in her own hip style, with the jazz beat that came to her instinctively and sometimes with a half-chorus of ad-lib piano.

Her success brought new demands. She signed with a New York manager, and he started getting her some bookings there. He told her that she would have to move to New York if she expected him to upgrade her bookings, but Richard objected on the grounds that they had to stay together. She could travel to New York from Boston when she had work there, he said, but her manager insisted that her work in the city would only increase when she was on the scene. To Crystal Joy, it seemed compelling, but when she told Richard of her decision he threw a tantrum. She was only thinking of herself, he screamed, not of *him*, not of *them*. The next day, he was calmer, though still upset. In the end, she made the move. Early in 1955, when Richard was working regularly at the Stable, she took up residence in New York and visited Boston whenever she had time off.

Richard's work at the Stable put him at the hub of an invigorating jazz climate. Herb Pomeroy assembled a crack sextet with Joe Gordon on first trumpet and himself on second, Varty Haroutunian on saxophones, Ray Santisi on piano, John Neves on bass and Jimmy Zitano on drums.

It is a measure of Pomeroy's resolve to attract a knowledgeable jazz audience that he hired Gordon, another trumpeter, rather than a trombonist or another saxophone player, the more usual instrumentation for a jazz sextet. Gordon was probably the most gifted improviser in the city and Pomeroy wanted him in the band. It wasn't only the instrumental imbalance that Pomeroy was willing to contend with by having Gordon in his band. "He had the same problem as Dick and Serge with narcotics," Pomeroy said (Gross 1998). Gordon's tenure ended abruptly when he showed up at the club one night in 1958 and said, "I've got to leave town or they're going to kill me." Gordon had large debts with his connections, and he may have informed on them to save himself from arrest. He left for California immediately. (A few years later, in 1963, he smothered in a fire in his Santa Monica bedroom, officially deemed an accident. He was 34.)

Pomeroy took on the leader's role at a time when, according to a contemporary comment, "local business was at its nadir" (Sylvester 1957).
With Storyville and the Hi Hat regularly booking big-name jazz musicians, the Stable, which relied on local talent, must have looked like a
risky business. It found its own niche by naming the performing area
the Jazz Workshop and projecting the image of youthful zest and ambition. Pomeroy began staging open rehearsals for a big band on Monday
nights, effectively taking on the role that Nat Pierce had played in
Boston jazz circles for years before that. The rehearsals proved so successful that Pomeroy eventually added a second night. He wrote and
arranged several charts for the band to get it started and then, as the
personnel stabilized, encouraged the regular members to contribute
arrangements of their own.

It was a golden era. Pomeroy says, "We had some wonderful experiences at the Jazz Workshop with musicians coming across the street
from Storyville. Anytime there was a big band like Dizzy or Basie or
Ellington, on our breaks we would go over and see them play. On their
breaks they would come and dig us. I was leading my band with my
back to the audience and I would not have to turn around to see if
some of the musicians from Storyville would stop by because my band
would crank it up a notch" (Gross 1998: 8). Word spread, not only in
Boston but beyond, abetted by the happy accident that the New York
office of *Down Beat* magazine at that very moment happened to be run
by two transplanted Bostonians, Nat Hentoff and Dom Cerulli.

Twardzik contributed a chart to the Pomeroy big band book called
Black Erich, named for his parents' prize stud. The chart has been lost,
but by Bob Zieff's recollection, it was an ambitious composition, with
unconventional harmonies. "The band was a bit dumbfounded," Zieff
recalls. "It had many humorous touches. They usually expected Dizzy
[Gillespie] Big Band or [Count] Basie from everyone." The band rehearsed *Black Erich*, and probably played it occasionally at the Stable
under the watchful eye of its composer, and maybe under his direction,
but it was never recorded.

The Boston jazz generation in which Twardzik grew up attained a
kind of apogee a couple of years after his death, when Pomeroy and his
16-piece orchestra accepted an invitation to play a two-week engagement at Birdland in New York in May 1957 and make a recording for
Roulette Records. By that time, Pomeroy's rehearsal band had become,

as Cerulli said in his *Down Beat* review of the LP, "a Boston institution."
The book included charts by front-line soloists Boots Mussulli, Ray
Santisi, Jaki Byard (who played tenor saxophone in the orchestra but
went on to become an internationally known jazz pianist) and Pomeroy. Other soloists included Gordon, Haroutunian, Neves and Zitano,
the original members of the sextet. Dedicated part-timers filled out
the sections, including a saxophone player who worked in a bank, a
trombonist who sold women's shoes, and a trumpeter who worked as a
maintenance man in a men's home (Sylvester 1957). The Roulette LP,
lugubriously titled *Life is a Many Splendored Gig* (Roulette R-52001),
a pun on the already lugubriously titled 1955 movie *Love is a Many
Splendored Thing*, caused ripples in the jazz world when the *Down Beat*
review awarded it five stars, its highest rating. At the time, five stars
were rare in *Down Beat*; in 1958, the year Pomeroy's big band recording
was reviewed, fewer than 5 percent—22 out of 442 LPs— got five stars
and the average rating was 3.3. The accolade is only slightly sullied by
the fact that the reviewer was Dom Cerulli, who was well known, as
Leonard Feather said in a thumbnail biography for *The New Yearbook
of Jazz*, as an "active advocate of Johnny Richards and Herb Pomeroy
bands" (1959: 86).

Cerulli disclosed in his review that the record company had brought in
Zoot Sims to solo on six tracks. "It obviously wasn't for his name value,"
he wryly noted, since Sims's presence was not acknowledged anywhere
in the package. Bringing him in stands as an obvious slight by the producers to Mussulli, Varoutunian and the other regular saxophone soloists. Nothwithstanding the high-handed treatment by Roulette, the
band made a distinguished showing, with well-drilled ensembles in the
style of the emergent Count Basie band in its second coming, including outstanding high-note lead trumpet by Lennie Johnson, the erst-
while maintenance man, and challenging, occasionally unpredictable
arrangements. Cerulli took some pains to vindicate his high ranking in
the *Down Beat* review by pointing out that "this band can hold its own
in any setting. It stood Birdland on its ear last summer, once an initial
nervousness wore off." But he got to the heart of the matter when he
lauded the LP for, as he said, "what can [be] (and was) done with some
competent musicians who needed a band."

The Birdland sojourn and its Roulette spin-off were something of a
communal triumph for the Boston jazz community, though they came

too late for Richard Twardzik. Still, he had been there at the start, and his unique talent added the aura of homegrown genius to the Jazz Workshop. If Pomeroy's bands were the main attractions, Twardzik's piano ruminations not only provided the sideshow but brought in their own audience. Maybe they were too quiet for some of the listeners, especially on big-band nights. But there were always people who sat up close, intent on Twardzik's ruminations. One of them was Steve Kuhn. "He would play relief piano at the Stable, and he was supposed to be on for about twenty minutes," Kuhn said (Williams 1970: 238). "But he would get so involved that he might play on and on, usually working on the same piece."

Night after night, as Twardzik's entr'acte went into overtime, the lis-teners huddled around the piano were swelled by the musicians from Pomeroy's band. Twardzik's devout fans hoped he would go on all night, but the musicians shifted their weight from foot to foot, impatient for him to finish. Eventually, they insisted that Pomeroy tell Twardzik that he had to stop cutting into the band's time. So from that night forward, Twardzik's warm-up ritual started with him setting a wind-up alarm clock on the piano—in Kuhn's version, Pomeroy gave him the clock. "And when it rang," Zieff said, "he would immediately stop!" "Dick would stop exactly where he was, pick up the clock and leave the stand," Kuhn said (Williams 1970: 238).

Serge Chaloff missed the first months of the boom at the Stable. He showed up in the middle of February 1955. His absence this time had a positive note. He had spent more than three months in rehabilitation, first as an out-patient at a Brookline clinic and then as a private patient in a withdrawal program at Bridgewater State Hospital 30 miles south of Boston.

He emerged drug free for the first time in nine years, and he could hardly wait to let the world know it. The *Boston Sunday Herald* carried a feature on 1 May headed "Musician Who Took Drug Cure Wants to Tell Addicts His Story" (Hanley 1955). "My gold-plated saxophone was in hock," he was quoted in the article. "But even if I had had it, nobody would have given me work. It was deeper than just being unreliable. Dope had ruined my music, too. My physical wreckage was growing into mental ruin."

By the time the feature appeared, some two and a half months after his release, Chaloff had already recorded a new album for Capitol. His agent Bob Martin, perhaps thinking that Chaloff's clean bill of health was too good to last, was working fast. He got Chaloff a contract for a record in the Capitol series called "Kenton presents," a series intended to spotlight overlooked talent by using the veteran bandleader Stan Kenton as a kind of sponsor. Boots Mussulli was a Kenton alumnus, "probably the most popular altoist that Kenton ever had," according to the liner note for Chaloff's record (MacFarland 1955). He had already recorded his own LP in the Kenton series, and he was prominently featured on Chaloff's record, which would be released in August as *Boston Blow-Up!* (Capitol T6510; now Toshiba-EMI TOCJ-9354 [Japan 2001]).

With the recording sessions coming so soon after Chaloff returned from rehab, Chaloff needed a band, and he solved the problem simply by inserting himself into Pomeroy's well-drilled sextet from the Stable, in effect taking Joe Gordon's place in the recording studio. (A bassist named Everett Evans had replaced John Neves.) Ray Santisi, not Twardzik, was the piano player. It worked well. The band supplied cohesive support, and Chaloff fronted them with his usual pizzazz. The high point was a rendition of *Body and Soul*, which Chaloff had been using as his showcase ever since he left Woody Herman. "Standing there next to him in the studio as he played it," Pomeroy said (Simosko 1998: 86), "we knew this was an important performance, you could feel it, we all felt it." Sunenblick (1994: 4) calls *Boston Blow-Up!* "a creative triumph that has been judged to be his best recorded work," but, of course, both *The Fable of Mabel* the year before and *Blue Serge* the year after would also be so judged. Chaloff, clearly, was riding a creative plateau both before and after he took the cure.

Twardzik's absence on the record date may have come about simply because Santisi was Pomeroy's regular piano player, but it was more likely the result of his temporary absence from performing. Sometime in the spring 1955, Twardzik himself went through a rehab program. Chet Baker would later say that when Twardzik joined his band in September that year he "had recently been discharged from the federal hospital in Lexington" (1997: 69), but Crystal Joy and Herb Pomeroy confirm that he followed Chaloff's lead and went into Bridgewater

State Hospital. Pomeroy says that Twardzik had submitted himself to the tough regimen at Bridgewater once before as well.

Twardzik hated Bridgewater, so much so that he would tell Pomeroy he would rather die than go back there (Gross 1998). He apparently tried to avoid it by curing himself before he gave in. Sometime in early 1955, he moved in with his friend Nick Dean and his wife in the West End apartment on Russell Place near Massachusetts General Hospital. Twardzik had lived with the Deans for short spells both there and at their earlier apartment on Charles Street at the bottom of Beacon Hill. Dean's memory of it is vague, but he says, "It was in the West End that he tried to go cold turkey and, as I recall, succeeded," and he puts the time around the spring 1955. When prodded for details about an incident that must have provided the supreme test of friendship, Dean responded with classic New England diffidence. "He certainly went through hell with us holding his hand and, in my case, occasionally his shoulders," he says, and leaves it at that.

Twardzik had lots of motivation. With Crystal Joy in New York, he had over-indulged in drugs even by his standards, to the point where procuring and using were occupying most of his time. His former running mate, Serge Chaloff, was now badgering his young follower with a convert's zeal. Chaloff found the trump card when Bob Martin lined up a summer tour for him with a sextet to promote *Boston Blow-Up!* Chaloff issued an ultimatum. He told Twardzik he could not play in his band unless he cleaned up.

This turnabout in their relations is undoubtedly what Bob Zieff had in mind when he told me, "I would guess that Serge may have gotten him started—and later tried to get him off—possibly."

Though Chaloff's tough edict gave Twardzik the heart to face the difficulties of withdrawal, he probably gained extra resolve from the news of the sudden death of Charlie Parker. On 10 March, Parker was about to board the train to Boston for an engagement at Storyville. Twardzik may have been slated to work as his piano player for the two-week gig. But Parker felt ill on his way to Grand Central Station, and he stopped at the hotel apartment of his friend, Baroness Pannonica De Koenigswarter. Two days later, after languishing on her sofa and resisting all but minimal medical help, Parker collapsed and died. Official causes were cirrhosis of the liver, perforated ulcer, pneumonia and heart attack. The coroner who signed the death certificate estimated Parker's age at 65; he was actually 35.

Parker's death came so suddenly that it sent shock waves far and wide. It became an iconic event for the jazz generation that Parker fostered. The New York subway system sported the graffito "Bird lives!" at every station on its uptown line, the famous 'A' train, and from there the graffiti spread, almost overnight, across the country and as far away as Paris. But once people got over the initial shock, they had to admit that Parker's death was not really unexpected. Twardzik, of course, knew that better than most. He mourned with all the other musicians, and then he shut himself in a bedroom at Nick Dean's place to ride it out. He spent his 24th birthday in the cold sweat and nausea of withdrawal, as he had spent his 22nd birthday en route to his first rehab in Mexico.

Twardzik's home-spun cure, aided only by the good instincts of the Deans, soon failed. Chaloff told him all along that it would. He came out of Bridgewater convinced that medical help was absolutely necessary for anyone who wanted to kick a habit permanently. "You can't make the trip alone," was his by-word (Hanley 1955). Twardzik, whose by-words included the sentiment "everyone must travel alone (most of the time)," had tried doing it on his own. In the end, he gave in and went to Bridgewater.

When Twardzik emerged in the early summer, no Sunday tabloid haled his return to the straight world. He simply reclaimed his old place in Chaloff's band. Their friendship resumed too, but with a fresh twist. Chaloff tried to get Twardzik interested in healthier diversions. One of them, improbable as it sounds, was baseball. To Twardzik, Chaloff (1956) recalled, it was an alien environment:

He was so consistent in his desires to learn that he spent very little time with anything else outside of the arts. I remember one day last summer [i.e., 1955] talking him into going to the Red Sox-Detroit ball game at Fenway Park. He arrived at the ball park armed with his usual books but I managed to keep his mind on the game by explaining every move on the field to him and he actually did enjoy it and even joined in with the excitement when Ted Williams hit one of his usual home runs.

That summer, Chaloff was again put in charge of the modern jazz contingent at the Boston Arts Festival. The inclusion of jazz the year before had made a strong impression, and this year the Festival sponsored an

expanded Jazz Night in the Public Gardens on 13 June 1955. The evening began with a panel discussion on "The Anatomy of Jazz," and one
of the participants was Bill Coss, editor of *Metronome* magazine.

The panel was followed by performances in the same format as the
year before, with Chaloff's modern jazz group first and then a traditional group, led this year by the trumpeter Ruby Braff, a Boston neo-
classicist who found the roots of his style not in Dizzy Gillespie but in
Louis Armstrong. Again this year the musical climax was supposed to
be a jam session with both bands on stage, but Chaloff turned it into
a kind of musical pillow fight. When Braff started the jam on *Indiana*,
Chaloff sidled up beside him playing *The Goof and I* (Coss 1955).

Bill Coss's presence at the Festival resulted in a *Metronome* review of the
modern half of the concert under the heading "In Person: Serge Chaloff" (Coss 1955). Chaloff's band was made up of Pomeroy's Stable sextet that had made the *Boston Blow-Up!* recording except that Twardzik
replaced Santisi on piano. Coss wrote, "Serge played an impressive set,
marred by his own lack of dynamics, but just as considerably aided
by the fresher tone and lighter feeling that is now his." The reviewer
in the *Boston Herald* the next day (quoted by Simosko 1998: 87) said,
"As a whole the harmonies of the group are tense and the melodies
resourceful and they play with a kind of controlled abandon."

Coss listed the repertoire in his review: a Chaloff original, *Sharp Six*,
"was an up-tempo romp;" *Kip*, from *Boston Blow-Up!* by Mussulli,
"named after his boy, had, reasonably enough, fine Mussulli;" Jimmy
Giuffre's *Four Brothers*, the source of Chaloff's celebrity in the jazz world
from his days with Herman, "demonstrated the group's precision and
swing;" *Round Robin*, presumably Chaloff's *Bob the Robin* from *Boston
Blow-Up!*, dedicated to Bob Martin, "gave everyone a chance to show
off a bit;" and Twardzik's *Fable of Mabel*, which, according to Coss, "was
a considerable improvement over the recorded version, Serge in complete control even when a low-flying plane drowned out the piano and
left him up the baritone without a paddle."

Twardzik, by all accounts, was dazzling. Coss concluded, "It's a fine
group with Twardzik and Chaloff the most glowing lights in the night."
Chaloff, in his eulogy for Twardzik that would be published in *Metronome* just seven months later, wrote, "His performance at the Arts Fes-

tival in Boston last summer was probably the greatest and most inspired he ever played."

The attention Twardzik was getting was not lost on a young student at the New England Conservatory. Cecil Taylor, two years younger than Twardzik, called him "the white pianist power up there" (Spellman 1966:59). A few years later Taylor would establish a unique space in the world of improvised piano music, not exactly jazz but more like jazz than any other genre. He was nearing the end of his student days when he watched Twardzik perform at the Arts Festival. Taylor, throughout his long career, has had very little to say about other musicians, almost nothing positive, and he gets defensive at any hint of outside influence on his music. But in an unguarded moment in his youth he made it clear that Twardzik had made a lasting impression on him. "He was a leading white exponent of Bud Powell, but I understand his bag included Tristano and Errol Garner and some others," Taylor said, and then he talked about the new developments he witnessed in Twardzik at the Arts Festival. "When I went back in 1955, he had destroyed some Kenton people by playing like Bud Powell first and getting them all excited and then going into his, at that time, Schoenbergian bag while they were playing Errol Garner chords."

"By 1954 my style of playing was developed," Taylor always claimed (Gioia 1997: 347), but Twardzik's influence on him that year and the next, 1955, is clearly audible to the few listeners who were paying attention to him that long ago. Twardzik happened to be close by when Taylor was seeking his own escape route from the bebop esthetic, and Twardzik discovered that route before him, as Michael Ullman, jazz writer for the *Boston Globe*, noted. "Taylor drew on his conservatory experience," Ullman (1989) wrote, "and on the piano playing of Duke Ellington, and, I believe, of the little-known Boston pianist Richard Twardzik." More specifically, Simosko (1998: 81) hears in the 1954 recording of *The Fable of Mabel* "an intriguing piano solo by Twardzik that seemed to anticipate the early Cecil Taylor (who was a student in Boston at the time)."

Twardzik's influence on Taylor resounds in the bold harmonies and the time inversions. It may go even deeper, in the example that Twardzik provided for Taylor by going against the main currents of the day, though in that respect the refractory Taylor probably needed no role models. Three or four years after admiring Twardzik's work at the Boston Arts Festival, Taylor pushed the limits of piano improvisation more radically, by abandoning chordal structures altogether. In Twardzik's lifetime, only Lennie Tristano had done that, notably in two short, spontaneously improvised pieces called "Intuition" and "Digression" (recorded in 1949 but not released until 1952), and, of course, closer to home there was a momentary stab at it from Chaloff in *The Fable of Mabel*, with Twardzik's collusion. It was definitely a direction that Twardzik's predilections pointed to, but he did not get the chance to push further in that direction.

In July and August, following the Arts Festival triumph, Twardzik toured with the Serge Chaloff sextet, with an itinerary similar to their 1951 excursions into the American heartland. This time the tour promised to be better organized with Bob Martin behind it and with Chaloff less erratic. The band was the one that had dazzled the Arts Festival audience, with one notable difference.

Jimmy Zitano decided to stay in Boston and work with Ray Santisi at the Stable for the summer. As Zitano's replacement, Chaloff recruited Gus Johnson, a masterful swing drummer. "Serge had gotten to know Gus when he was with Basie in 1950 and they became real good friends," Pomeroy said (Simosko 1998: 88). "It really made a difference to the feel of the group because Gus was out of the Kansas City style, not the bop style of drumming at all, but it worked."

At 42, Johnson (1913–2000) was older than the others, and his Kansas City reputation came not only from his work with Basie but, before that, with the Jay McShann big band, where he had played beside the neophyte Charlie Parker. In years to come, numerous jazz players would discover what Pomeroy noticed, that Johnson's rare combination of power and taste worked for bands of all sizes and styles. Johnson went on to contribute distinctively to Ella Fitzgerald's back-up trio (for which he was also musical director), Gerry Mulligan's concert band, and the moldy figs who called themselves the World's Greatest Jazz Band, among many others.

"The sextet had a character of its own," Pomeroy said, and Johnson, one of the great drummers of the day, must have made the difference. Pomeroy recalls working "two weeks at a time in clubs all that summer." The itinerary, judging by Pomeroy's recollection and the pay stubs that Twardzik saved from the trip, appears to have been the Giovanni Club in Baltimore (4–16 July), Rouge Lounge in River Rouge, Michigan (18–24 July), a Detroit club, possibly in the Hotel Wolverine, where they stayed (1–13 August), and an unnamed club in Washington (15–26 August). Chaloff and Mussulli roomed together, and Pomeroy roomed with Twardzik. Pomeroy later wrote a big band chart called *No One Will Room with Me* (recorded on *Life Is a Many-Splendored Gig* for Roulette in 1957, and one of the indisputable gems on that recording), presumably an oblique memorial to his late roommate.

Where Twardzik's first road trip with Chaloff had resulted in a string of letters home about his adventures, he was relatively silent on this one as a result of the cool relations with his mother. He sent a telegram to Henryk from the Hotel Schuyler on West 45th Street in New York that suggests that he was trying to arrange a recording session with Prestige Records. The telegram, sent collect to Henryk at C.J. Connick Associates, carries a familiar refrain: JUST ARRIVED IMPERATIVE SEE PRESTIGE PLEASE WIRE ELEVEN DOLLARS ONLY. It is dated 3 July, a Sunday, and Richard was presumably on his way from Boston to Baltimore for the Giovanni Club gig. The telegram implies he was intending to meet someone at the Prestige offices about a recording deal, perhaps on Monday morning before proceeding to Baltimore, but if so, there was no follow-up. Most likely, he stopped en route to spend some time in New York with Crystal Joy. "We tried to get together as often as we could after I left," she says.

Later that week, on Saturday the 9th, Twardzik sent a postcard, again addressed to Henryk only, with the simple message, "Boston is like Alaska in comparison to Baltimore. Be of good cheer. Love Dick."

Curiously, Twardzik saved three of his weekly pay memos from this tour. They are written in a bold hand, probably Bob Martin's, on hotel stationery. A memorandum from the River Rouge engagement, written on the back of Hotel Wolverine stationery, includes a carefully itemized accounting of Twardzik's credits and deductions. In the lower left-hand corner it carries the order, "HOLD THIS DATA DICK!" Both the itemization and the managerial imperative suggest that Twardzik was having trouble keeping his finances straight (13.2).

They were complicated, it must be admitted. Twardzik's gross pay on the road trip was $130 per week. In Maryland, he received the gross, but in Michigan there were deductions for taxes, union dues and unemployment insurance amounting to \$16.20, making his net salary \$113.80. From this amount, Twardzik had to pay \$49 to the Wolverine Hotel for room and board, which was tax-free. These figures seem straightforward, but every pay-day there were additional charges for draws Twardzik had made against his salary during the week. In Baltimore the first week, Twardzik's draws were added to a personal loan from Chaloff and actually exceeded his salary. The paymaster deducted \$75 for his draws and gave him \$55 but noted that he still owed Chaloff \$70. In Rouge River, his draw was \$42, and in Detroit it was \$72 with an additional deduction of \$12 for "liquor." Every week he was left with take-home pay that was miniscule.

The advances were not for drugs, and so there is some mystery about them. His debt to Chaloff may have been incurred for the stay at Bridgewater State Hospital. Medical costs were pricey, and Chaloff told everyone who would listen how crucial his mother's support had been, financial as well as moral. Twardzik by now had exhausted his parental support, or at least Clare's, and it seems that Chaloff paid part of Twardzik's bill as a kind of advance on his summer salary. Ironically, the other advances might have been sent home. Clare and Henryk were in

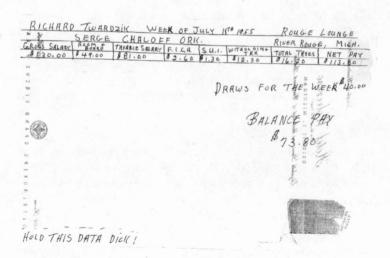

[illustration 13.2] Pay memorandum for Richard Twardzik for the week of 11 July 1955 at River Rouge, Michigan. From the Twardzik-Thompson Archive, courtesy of Rosamond Thompson and Jane Sumner. All rights reserved.

the midst of moving out of Fowler House to a house of their own in West Newbury, and Richard's aunt Roz says that Richard had promised to contribute financially to the move after he gained steady work. That might also account for his pay slips ending up in the Twardzik family effects.

Members of the drug underground showed up wherever the band played. "Once you're a known addict, the grapevine pushes the word ahead of you," Chaloff said (Hanley 1955). "Wherever you tour, you'll find pushers there waiting for you." Chaloff knew the signs intimately, and took a tough line against them. Somehow, Twardzik managed to stay clean throughout the tour. Chaloff's example was his best defence. Gus Johnson also seems to have played a role in keeping Twardzik straight. He took him aside and offered him advice about surviving on the road. He liked Twardzik, and his advice was avuncular, not threatening. Twardzik was impressed by him, so much so that he saw fit to tell Crystal Joy about their conversations.

Twardzik had good reason to feel insecure. After going through the rehabilitation ordeal in Mexico, he had slipped back into drugs soon after his release. If Pomeroy is right, he had already gone through the Bridgewater regimen once before and become addicted again. This time, he appeared more determined to resist the temptations around him, at least as long as Chaloff and Johnson were watching out for him. Slipping up obviously weighed on his mind. Pomeroy said, "We were rooming together on that tour and he would tell me that if he was to go back on [heroin], that he didn't want to go back to the hospital" (Gross 1998). "Many nights back in the hotel room after the gig he'd say to me, 'I'll never go back into treatment,'" Pomeroy said (Turner 1999: 172). "He told me if he went back on, he'd take his life."

Twardzik seemed jumpy. After the second week in Baltimore, around 18 July, he sent Crystal Joy a letter, with a progress report. The letter is written in pencil on both sides of two sheets of stationery from the Mount Royal Hotel in Baltimore, though by the time he wrote it the band had already moved to the Hotel Wolverine in Detroit:

> Do you remember what I said about wanting to sorta prove myself before we got married? Well, here's the way things stand. I got thro' the first week very well. I played as well as the good Lord would

let me, went straight home every night, had no eyes for anything or anybody and I miss you.

He lets her know he has had a change of heart about her career move to New York:

Honey please never lose faith in me. I love you.

For the first time I'm thinking in terms of people other than myself......YOU

How could I have been so self-centered and selfish? You have your own life, and I want to do my best to make it a rich and full one.

Can you forgive me for my cruelties and thoughtlessness?

You're the only girl ever in my whole life and I love and miss and need you terribly.

Do you love me?

Will you marry me?

Please say yes because I adore you and I want you to be mine. All mine.

He closes on an ecstatic note:

Let's get MARRIED!!!

(I'm sober, honey)

MARRIED!!! MARRIED!!!

MARRIED!!! let's do it.

We can make a go of it

I am certain, how about you?

Good night for now, my

darling. I love you above all

    Love

        Dick

P.S. If there was more to say I'd try and say it.

His agitation apparently did not affect on his nightly playing. Musically, Chaloff's band left a good impression. In Detroit, the crowds they attracted included some of the young jazz musicians who were plentiful in the city and would soon move onto the national stage in considerable numbers. Pomeroy remembers Pepper Adams, an up-and-coming baritone saxophone player, sitting near the bandstand every night, where he could study Chaloff's fingering. Pomeroy also remembers some blistering performances by Chaloff (Simosko 1998: 86): "We were playing the Rouge Lounge or someplace, and during the cadenza ending of *Body and Soul* Serge was playing with such intensity that the neck of the saxophone snapped off clean. ...Boots and I had to finish that night as just the two of us."

Like most jazz throughout history, this band's music evaporated in the smoke-choked rooms as soon as it was played. There is no permanent record of what they sounded like with the masterful Gus Johnson providing lift, or with the born-again Chaloff flexing new muscles. Or with the emboldened Dick Twardzik, fresh from winning raves at the Boston Arts Festival and prepping now for his move into the international big-time with Chet Baker, musing on harmonies that, perhaps, no one had heard before.

After the band closed in Washington on 22 August 1955, the musicians went their separate ways. Pomeroy would move onto the faculty of the Berklee School that fall, to teach a course in jazz history, and he continued his work at the Stable with the rehearsal band that would eventually earn him the Birdland booking.

Serge Chaloff went home to Boston and played in Pomeroy's rehearsal band for a while, but his revitalized career soon carried him further afield. He continued to lead pick-up bands on club tours, and as his reputation grew, his geographic range grew with it. Jazz fans were discovering in *Boston Blow-Up!* and in club dates that his career had righted itself. His personal life took on a new stability too. He married Susan Black, a socialite. "She was the most beautiful person," said Crystal Joy, who spent many hours in their company immediately after Twardzik's death. Chaloff continued to speak out against drug abuse and tried to soften the stigma attached to it. "Narcotics is a symbol of a troubled make-up," he told people whenever he got a chance (Simosko 1998: 84). "It's like a man having cancer. It's a sickness."

But Chaloff's new lease on life turned out to be tragically brief. He was playing an extended gig in California when he made his consummate recording, *Blue Serge* (Capitol CDP 7243 [1998]), in March 1956. A few days later, while he was golfing, his legs became paralyzed. Doctors discovered a tumor pressing against his spine. He returned to Boston for surgery and radiation therapy. People rallied around the one-time bad boy of the Four Brothers. Crystal Joy said, "We tried to make the end of his life more enjoyable." He continued playing from a wheelchair when he could, and he recorded from his wheelchair with Al Cohn, Zoot Sims and Herbie Steward, the other Brothers, at a New York studio reunion. He played the solos but a studio musician had to play his parts in the ensembles because he was too weak. He died of cancer in July 1957. He was only 33.

On 19 July 1955, the day before Crystal Joy received Richard Twardzik's hysterical marriage proposal in the mail, she wrote him a letter that was delivered to him at the Hotel Wolverine in Detroit the next day. Their letters crossed in the mails, and in their purposes too. Where Richard's letter is full of exclamations and anxiety, Crystal Joy's is playful and witty. Her tone is set at the start, where she indicates that she has recently recovered from some kind of ailment:

Hi Honey!

I have once again joined the ranks of healthy human beings.

Feel simply wonderful

Her recovery obviously left her in high spirits. The letter mixes girlish enthusiasm and musicianly irony, all of it suffused with genuine affection. When I showed the letter to her 47 years later, she seemed embarrassed by the Doppelganger who wrote it. She found her younger self, as she put it, "much too chatty, catty and youthfully arrogant," and asked me not to use any of the private jokes that were "meant for Dick's eyes only."

For jazz buffs, the letter takes on special interest because Crystal Joy talks about her impressions of the first-ever Newport Jazz Festival, which she attended for the Saturday performances, on 16 July. Her letter is a reminder of how novel it seemed in 1955 to listen to jazz in an upper-crust setting like Newport. "We had a simply mahvelous time deah!" she writes. Her letter is also a reminder that jazz festivals were in this first instance very much an outcropping of the Boston jazz community. She mentions casually running into George Wein and Wein's right-hand man, Charlie Bourgeois, who would both become, in the wake of their Newport triumph, front-rank international impresarios. She also ran into Symphony Sid Torin, who was there to introduce some of the acts, and who would leave Boston soon after to return to New York as the base for his radio remotes.

Crystal Joy clearly saw the Newport festival as a landmark occasion, and tried to convey its atmosphere to Richard, stuck as he was in lunch-bucket Detroit:

> We wore Bermuda shorts [*inserted lengthwise in left margin* You would have loved my hair Kinks — Kinks — Kinks] and raincoats (as it was raining) and wandered all about talking to all of our wonderful sick neurotic musician friends.

She passes along some "juicy news" about Wein, a rumor that he had recorded an album called *Wein, Women and Song* on which he sings. Her gossip about Wein apparently reminds her of some gossip (unspecified and now forgotten) that she suspects Richard might have passed on to a mutual friend about her, and she digresses from her Newport account to chide him about it. "You always have loved to talk huh darling?" she says. That in turn reminds her of the advice Richard was getting from Gus Johnson about being discreet, which he had obviously told her about. "What was that lesson that Gus J. taught you?" she asks rhetorically. "Please tell me."

She then goes back to recounting her day in Newport and starts to pass along greetings for Twardzik that various people had conveyed to her, but the only one she considers worth repeating is from the piano player in the Clifford Brown–Max Roach Quintet, whom they had met when the band played at Storyville about a year earlier: "Richie Powell says to tell you 'Hi — good luck —and stay straight'." In hindsight, Crystal Joy's mention of Powell provides another grim reminder of the toll exacted on this jazz generation. Less than a year later, Powell, then 24, would be killed along with the brilliant trumpeter Clifford Brown, 25, in a car crash on the Pennsylvania Turnpike.

Crystal Joy ends her letter affectionately, cramming her sentiments into a few lines at the bottom of the sheet: "I sho do miss you pretty boy, I could let life get dull around heare here if I'm not careful...— I love you alone—nobody else—I'm yours — Crystal"

The letter is written on both sides of a single sheet of lined paper in green ink. Twardzik's final recorded composition, *The Girl from Greenland*, was recorded in Paris three months after he had received Crystal Joy's letter. Chet Baker (1997: 71) attempted to explain Twardzik's title by saying, "It seemed that he cared a lot for an Eskimo girl from Greenland, for I noticed he wrote to her often." But the 'Eskimo girl' turns out, in all likelihood, to be Crystal Joy Billouin from Jamaica Plain, Mass., who wrote letters in green ink and sometimes dressed in green, wore a green ribbon in her hair, and carried a green umbrella. She was, in Twardzik's eyes, the girl from green-land, and among her souvenirs of the youthful love affair she had with Twardzik is *The Girl from Greenland*, one of the neatest musical portraits in jazz.

When I told her years later that she was Twardzik's girl from green-land, she admitted that she had never made the connection. She had heard the recording of *The Girl from Greenland* a year or two later, when she was still in shock over the suddenness of his death. She recognized the melody as a derivative of *Albuquerque Social Swim*, but as for its title, she never really thought about what it might mean. "Dick loved alliteration, you know," she said. And puns too, I said.

In the years immediately following Twardzik's death, Crystal Joy pursued her career with determination. She began working in clubs in Miami as well as Boston and New York. On her frequent visits to her family in Boston, she took informal piano lessons from Margaret Chaloff and some lessons with a vocal coach she recommended. In 1959, she came to the attention of Steve Allen, the late-night television host whose *Tonight Show* became the prototype of the whole talk-show genre. Much more than a television interviewer, Allen was comedian, songwriter, author, novelist and jazz piano player whose promotion of name jazz stars on his national network show became part of the spiral that broadened the jazz audience. After Crystal Joy appeared on Allen's television show, Allen invited her to record an album of his songs. The result was *The Fabulous Crystal Joy* (Hanover S 8002). The album included Allen's best-known song, *This Could Be the Start of Something Big*, but it became Steve Lawrence's hit, and none of the other songs made an impression. Over the years, Crystal Joy has recorded infrequently, but she loves the immediacy of live audiences and she has never stopped playing and singing. She is now affiliated with the Pensacola Jazz Society near her north Florida home.

Her talents led her naturally out of jazz and into supper clubs. Her best jazz credit came about almost accidentally, and because of some name confusion it brought her less attention than it should have. In 1964, she lived in a New York apartment next door to Roland Kirk, the woodwind genius (later known as Rahsaan Roland Kirk). The walls were thin, and Kirk and Crystal Joy had to schedule their practising alternately to avoid clashes. One day, Crystal recalls (Tesser 1998), Kirk invited her over and said, " 'Sing this with me.' I said, 'You mean in harmony?' and he said, 'No, just sing along with me.' " The tune, then untitled, was Kirk's *Serenade to a Cuckoo*. "I just never realized he was listening to me in terms of his own music," she said. She recorded *Serenade to a Cuckoo* with him on *I Talk With the Spirits* (Limelight, now a Verve CD), perhaps the greatest flute recording in jazz. She also sang background harmonies on the title track. The billing she requested on the record was "Miss C. J. Albert." It was a name that disconnected her from her past, probably intentionally, and also, unluckily, from her future. Nowadays, she goes by Crystal-Joy Albert.

The name changes after her Boston days when she was simply Crystal Joy were intended as a kind of protective coloration. Move on, she says. Leave the bygones where they lay. But it does not take much to raise the past. "I love love love you," Richard wrote in his marriage plea to Crystal Joy. "When I think how good and wonderfully kind you are I get such an ache in my heart that I want to cry." Almost half a century later, Crystal Joy said, "Dick was my first and real love."

Crystal Joy never got a chance to answer Dick's letter, at least not directly. Some years later she wrote a song called *Why Can't I*, her personal favorite of her own songs. Her lyric asks, "Why can't I give my love and never lose?" In spite of that note of despair, it is an upbeat song, as she is an upbeat person. Its theme is stated in two lines of the bridge, and they conveys optimism, though slightly tainted:

> Fleeting moments when dreams seem to come true
> Are inspiration for all the other things we do.

Make the most of it, she seems to say, when things are going good. Bank the good moments, and let them light up the gloom as you press onward.

Richard Twardzik also seemed to believe that, though he did not express it so neatly. He knew there had been a turnaround in his music and his life. He said so in a letter to Bill Coss (Twardzik 1956), and although he did not name Crystal Joy, it is surely about her.

"I'm glad that the music I play has reached someone," he wrote to Coss after Coss had singled him out for praise at the Boston Arts Festival. "I am trying hard to produce honest music like the [Roger] Session's [*sic*] Symphony which I'm listening to right now. I'm blessed that in the last four years I've swung from hate to love—of necessity one must play with love."

14 Sad Walk

Richard Twardzik's transition from Serge Chaloff's band to Chet Baker's was so smooth it seemed as if fate had greased the pole. Twardzik finished the gig with Chaloff in Washington on Sunday, 21 August. The next day the Chet Baker All Stars arrived for a week at the same club, the Patio Lounge. Twardzik was Baker's new piano player, hand-picked by Russ Freeman, and this Washington gig was the warm-up for an extended tour of Europe. Twardzik paid $3 for a blood test with one Dr. Cajigas on Eye Street on 24 August, and his passport was issued by the Washington office the next day.

The prospect of touring Europe was heady stuff, and going as a member of Baker's band made it better. Baker drew crowds wherever he went, but, more important for the men in his band, he had gained a measure of respect from the jazz musicians on the east coast. Playing with him now counted among musicians as well as fans.

Baker had taken bold steps to try to erase the skepticism that greeted his rapid rise to the front ranks. Among jazz critics and some musicians, at least in New York and Chicago, there was a taint associated with Baker and with West Coast jazz in general, which had gained middle-class acceptability in colleges and concert halls while the rest of the jazz world struggled to get a hearing in smoky cellars. West Coast jazz was cool jazz, whose pedigree came respectably from some music made at the end of the forties by Miles Davis and a cadre of like-minded youngsters that included J.J. Johnson, Gerry Mulligan, John Lewis and Max Roach. In its transliteration in balmy California, according to one widely-held view, the music had become cooler than cool, to the point of being effete, affected and downright effeminate. No one suffered more in the whisper campaign than Chet Baker, who looked like a pop star, played with facile lyricism, and caught the imagination of fans young and old, but mostly young. After less than two years as a full-blown professional, he won the *Down Beat* poll as best trumpeter over tougher players like Davis, Clifford Brown and Dizzy Gillespie. It was a stroke of crazy luck that embarrassed Baker at the time and probably steeled his resolve to show the skeptics, especially other musicians, that he had earned it.

At the start of 1954, Baker had decided to leave his comfort zone on the Pacific coast and face the music, literally, on the other side of the continent. Russ Freeman, his regular pianist since the summer of 1953 and an established player in his own right, gave up his day-job in the Hollywood studios to travel with Baker. Freeman benefited critically from the move too, almost as much as Baker. Reviewers and fans got a first-hand look at their technical facility and easy spontaneity. They also noticed that Baker and Freeman could play with an edge, especially in later sets in the night, best of all when someone came on the stand to play a tune or two with them. Gradually they were shedding the stereotype that clung to them from California.

Baker was known among jazzmen as the right kind of boss—laid-back, unflappable, in his life as in his music totally cool. "Chet was somebody you got along with easily," Freeman said. "He was an easy-going person. He was open to every suggestion. He made few demands. If there were problems, it was usually because of money or a girl" (de Valk 2000: 57). So if a young, untried piano player like Twardzik told Baker he wouldn't join his band if it meant he had to play *My Funny Valentine* every set, Baker would just shrug and say, 'Fine. Bring some new music.' And if Twardzik and some other easterners imagined that Baker might falter trying to play unfamiliar music like Bob Zieff's, Baker would just yawn and then play the music better than anyone else ever would—or perhaps could.

Twardzik's hiring seemed at the moment to be heaven-sent. Not only was Chet Baker on top of the world, but Russ Freeman, as everyone knew, had thrived in Baker's company. There was every reason to believe that Twardzik, coming into the position with better tools than Freeman, would come out of the experience as a leader in his own right and maybe as a mover in the forward thrust of the music. As Baker's right-hand man, Freeman had composed memorable tunes, framed them in ingenious arrangements, and played sensitive, facile piano, sometimes in striking counterpoint with Baker. His exposure put him on a creative peak scarcely predictable from his work around Los Angeles before joining Baker and, indeed, never equaled in the competent work he would do after leaving him. His years with Baker were his consummation. Freeman later said so himself. About Baker, he said, "He's the only one who could play my songs the way I heard them. He had such an innate feeling for them" (Tynan 1963: 20). For Twardzik, five years younger than Freeman, it was reasonable to expect a seminal experience with Baker that would raise his music to a new plateau.

Freeman's job was available because Baker decided to make an extended tour of Europe in the fall of 1955, and none of the regulars in his band was interested in going with him. They had been traveling for a year already, and they were sick of it. But there was more to it than that. Baker was mainly going because he was following his girlfriend. "In New York," he said (1997: 85), "I met a Parisian girl named Liliane. She…was like a breath of fresh air. She was quick, beautiful, and played chess well." But Liliane Cukier had to leave New York because her visa expired. She decided to return home to Paris, and for Baker there was no question what he would do. He was going to join her in Paris, he said, and he was taking the band along.

Nowadays, when the lowliest teenage phenoms get their careers hyper-managed, it is astounding to think that Baker could make his decision about Europe so casually, without wiser heads intervening. As a career move, the timing was all wrong. In the United States, he was one of the two or three top draws in jazz, and all signs indicated there was more to come. Pacific Jazz had just released his first vocal album, and its sales crossed over into pop. He had made a movie—*Hell's Horizon* (1955), in which he played a bashful but heroic American airman in the Korean War—which was expected to launch him as the next James Dean. Now, on an impulse, he was going to remove himself from the mainstream publicity outlets for six months or more.

Baker's obsession with Liliane had already caused problems in the band in New York. "She pulled us to pieces," Freeman said (de Valk 2000: 57). She drew Baker away from the jazz haunts and into her own circle. It appears to have been a drug cult, although Baker always denied it. "At that point I was very naïve about being strung out on stuff, although Liliane had shown some interest in stuff," he admitted (1997: 69–70). "She had merely chipped around, never getting really strung out." If so, it was only a matter of time. Even Baker could see that in hindsight. "Paris was full of people using in '56," he said, and Paris would be his headquarters with Twardzik and the other young musicians on the European tour. As Freeman and the other musicians in the original quartet saw it, Baker had already isolated himself from them in New York.

It wasn't only Liliane that made Freeman stay home. He had some
health worries too. He had started suffering from migraine headaches,
and partly because of them he first quit the band in late 1954, when
they were playing at Birdland, and went back to California. His loyalty
to Baker brought him back in the spring, but he discovered that in
his absence many things had changed. Baker was, as Freeman put it,
"now truly addicted." The cooperative feeling in their music had vanished too. Freeman had always been consulted on musical matters, but
no more. "Bob Neel [the drummer] had disappeared and Chet in the
meantime had hired a drummer who was also a junkie, Peter Littman,"
Freeman said (de Valk 2000: 58–59). He could not hide his contempt.
"The boy was exactly twenty years old. An impossible kid. The working relationship was anything but agreeable... Chet was addicted, his
drummer was addicted, and there is always a division between musicians who are clean and those who are using. Addicts hang with other
addicts. Our old friendship no longer existed."

Baker's version of the story was that he became addicted in 1956, after
returning to the States from Europe. He always maintained that he was
clean in New York and throughout the European tour. It was a story
he was called upon to re-tell many times, for the simple reason that no
one believed him. By the time he left for Europe, he had spent all his
professional life working with known users like Charlie Parker, Gerry
Mulligan and Art Pepper. Freeman and everyone else who worked for
him said he was using. Twardzik's friends all knew about Baker's habit
too. Nick Dean told me, "When Dick decided to go to Europe with
Chet Baker it worried the daylights out of us because, while Baker
was brilliant, he was also a thoroughly evil person." "Chet Baker was
the demon," Crystal Joy said, and when I told her Baker professed to
be innocent of drugs at the time, she said, "Are you kidding? He was
outrageous."

Baker's unwavering claim, against all kinds of contrary evidence, may
have darker motives. As de Valk (2000: 67) says, "He may have devised
the story that he was clean at the time to avoid any suggestion of in-
volvement in [Twardzik's] death." But he may not have been simply
lying. It may go even deeper. Baker always seemed utterly convinced
about his story, and he may have truly deluded himself about being
clean at the time as a way of absolving himself of any possible blame.

Once Freeman made up his mind to quit the band, Twardzik's appointment as Freeman's replacement had a tragic inevitability. Surprisingly, Twardzik may not have been Baker's first choice, or at least not the first piano player he offered the job to. While Twardzik was on the road with Chaloff, Baker was fretting in New York about replacing Freeman. In his later years, Baker was notorious for hiring musicians on impulse. As he circulated around Europe playing with pick-up bands in jazz clubs, he would invite musicians he took a liking to to join him for an upcoming recording session. A bass player from Italy would travel to the studio in, say, Frankfurt only to find bass players from Amsterdam and Munich already there warming up. That kind of impulsive recruiting may have begun the instant Freeman gave Baker his notice. Freeman had provided much of the stability in Baker's first years as a leader. By the time Baker gained enough credibility in Gerry Mulligan's band to qualify as a leader, Freeman was waiting to join him not only as piano player but also straw boss, arranger and buddy. Suddenly that old stability was gone.

By chance, while Baker was worrying about replacing Freeman, he ran into an old acquaintance from his Los Angeles days, probably at Charlie's Tavern, the jazz musicians hangout in New York. He was John Williams, whom Baker had got to know when Williams was Stan Getz's piano player at the Tiffany Club in May 1953 while Baker was playing with Mulligan at the Haig. "We went back and forth to the Haig every intermission, or nearly so, and Chet and Gerry did the reverse a few times," Williams told Steve Voce (2002: 8), recalling the events almost half a century later, as a 73-year-old retired municipal worker in Florida. Williams was raised in Vermont but worked his way to Los Angeles with Charlie Barnet's band in the 1950s. There he found himself in the middle of the burgeoning West Coast jazz movement. He was not out of place by any yardstick. His piano style was rooted in Bud Powell, as was Freeman's and nearly all the other California piano players. In a classic concert recording Williams made with Getz's band (*Stan Getz at the Shrine*, on Verve), he sounds like a ringer for Russ Freeman. "In those days people were making flattering (for me!) comparisons between us," he told Voce. "We had somewhat similar styles, except he was West Coast and I was East Coast!"

In summer 1955, Williams was living in New York and playing weekends at a place called the Lamplighter Lounge on Long Island. Some of

Williams's friends would drive out from the city and sit in with him for the evening when they had nothing better to do. He remembers Getz and Zoot Sims sitting in at different times. Baker came once, he says, and at the end of the evening surprised him by inviting him to join his band for the European tour. "I can only pay you $450 a week, what I've been paying Russ Freeman, but maybe I can do better later on," Baker said. Williams, who had been making $175 a week with Getz and less on his own, was flattered. But he had some reservations too.

Williams had gone to Birdland a week or two earlier to hear Baker's quartet with Peter Littman on drums. "Littman was *terrible*," Williams says. "And since everybody in Charlie's [Tavern] knew everything about everybody in those days, I knew he was a lost-cause junkie. I had assumed, as did most of the guys, that the junk was the reason Chet had him on the band. It certainly couldn't have been for his playing."

Williams told Baker he couldn't play with Littman, and Baker shrugged and said fine, he could choose whoever he wanted on bass and drums. Williams was excited by the prospect, but then a month went by with no follow-up, and Williams had pretty well given up on the idea when Baker phoned and asked him to come to a rehearsal in Yonkers. Williams arrived to find Littman setting up his drum kit. "As you would expect and as junkies always were, Chet was all apologies," Williams says. "He knew what he had promised me, but Peter had begged him to keep him on. Whine. Whine." Williams left. "I took the dream with me," he said, "and took the train back down to Manhattan."

Williams thinks that Baker may have asked him at that meeting what he thought about Twardzik's playing. If he did, Williams reckoned that he probably complained that Twardzik was too individualistic in the rhythm section. "But then, I never cared for Salvador Dali, either," he told Voce.

Williams's opinion, if he did get a chance to air it, could not have carried much weight. Russ Freeman says that he and Baker decided that Twardzik had to be the new piano player. He made no mention of Williams or anyone else. Baker says that Littman recommended Twardzik. De Valk (2000: 60) says that Twardzik sat in with the band one night and "Chet hired him on the spot." Probably all of the above were true. Twardzik had been in their orbit for some time.

Carson Smith also quit around the same time as Freeman, and Baker replaced him with Bob Carter, a veteran bebop bassist, but Carter was formally studying composition and had no intention of going to Europe. So the fourth member of the quartet, hired at the last minute, was Jimmy Bond from Philadelphia, a recent Juilliard graduate.

Baker flew to Paris on Trans World Airlines, arriving on 5 September 1955. The three sidemen boarded the Ile de France in New York Harbor a day or two later and arrived in France on the 14th or 15th. Baker had been stationed in Berlin as a teenaged private in the U.S. Army in 1947, but for the others it was the first time any of them had traveled outside North America. Twardzik was 24, Bond was 22 (b. 1933), Littman only 20 (b. 1935)—and Baker, for all his honors, was just 25 and, at that moment in his life, looked younger. They could hardly know that they were beginning what Bond would call "a really hairy trip" (Turner 1999: 172). This first European tour would be the last for three of them. Only Baker would ever return.

Crystal Joy went to New York harbor to see them off. She was surprised to find a party already underway in Littman and Twardzik's stateroom. "The room was supposed to be theirs but it was full of these groupie girls," she says. She went away a bit dazed, convinced that Twardzik was taking one of the groupies with him. "If you're a musician, I guess you get a free pass on a girl," she told me. There is no hint that Twardzik actually took a female companion with him, but for Crystal Joy that tinge of jealousy compounded her despair. "They were all so out-of-it that I had a feeling it was over for him," she said.

On the crossing, Jimmy Bond seldom saw Littman and Twardzik. One time when he ran into Twardzik on the deck he found him "totally reserved" (Turner 1999: 172). The uncharacteristic diffidence that Bond saw seems to have engulfed Twardzik on the voyage. There are no letters to his parents or to Crystal Joy about the crossing. It seems odd, even ominous, knowing his pattern when he was on the road, that he made no attempt to share his adventures on the ocean liner that was carrying him to the birthplace of Ravel and Debussy. Baker said, "I think now that Dick started getting high from that first night, but I was not to find out about this fact for some months" (1997: 69). The high he was on when Crystal Joy saw him may have lasted for the whole crossing.

The pace quickened when they docked at Le Havre. Baker, an indefatigable driver and a fearless one, met them and zoomed back to Paris
with them. The arrangements for Baker's tour were chaotic. They were
already too late for some bookings that had been arranged by Baker's
manager, Joe Napoli. To make matters worse, the September issue of
Jazz Hot, which arrived on French newsstands around the same time
Baker arrived at Orly airport, carried an announcement saying that
Baker's tour had been cancelled (Tercinet 1988). Baker had to get to
Paris in a hurry and make his presence known to the press if Napoli
had any chance of salvaging the missed dates and making new ones.

The full itinerary may never be recovered, but the first five weeks,
the part that Twardzik participated in, as far as I have been able to reconstruct it (with help from the Swedish scholar Olle Lind and Chet
Baker's ghostwritten liner notes [1956]), appears to have been fairly
open in September and busier in October, as news spread that Baker
had really arrived. If the sidemen arrived in France on 15 September,
Richard Twardzik would spend a total of 36 days in Europe up to the
day he died, on 21 October. In those 36 days, Twardzik and the others
played at least 18 concerts or club dates and two recording sessions at
18 different venues in 15 cities in six countries.

The band used Paris as home base, playing or recording there four
different times at three venues. From Paris, they set out in various directions for engagements in the Netherlands, West Germany (as it was
then), Switzerland, Belgium and England, scrambling for trains and
taxis, digging out passports for immigration officers at international
checkpoints (and keeping the drug paraphernalia safely stowed), shouting instructions at puzzled stage crews on strange stages and in small
clubs, and testing the good will of small-time promoters, some of them
just fans who took it on themselves to find a venue where the famous
Chet Baker could play in their city.

Over the years, details have gradually emerged about the band's adventures, and some of the music they played has come to light. There
will be more music made public eventually. For more than fifty years,
European jazz enthusiasts have found ways of preserving the jazz music
played in concerts and clubs by American visitors. National radio net-
works often contracted with them for concert broadcasts, and enterprising fans made private tapes, often from the audience but sometimes
through the sound system. It began as a way of compensating for the

infrequency of personal appearances. Parisians in 1948, for instance, under reconstruction after the War and lining up for rations, understandably thought they might be seeing Dizzy Gillespie for the one and only time. As time went by and touring musicians became fairly common, eventually with a coterie of expatriates supplementing local talent, recording practices, authorized or surreptitious, were so much a part of the European jazz tradition that fans simply carried on with them, unabated.

Taking the performances as datelines, the news at each stop along the way, starting in the Netherlands, is fraught with evidence of good music and some harrowing portents of the tragedy that lay ahead.

• 17 September: Chet Baker Quartet at Concertgebouw, Amsterdam, Netherlands

• 18 September: Chet Baker Quartet at Kurhaus, Scheveningen (The Hague), Netherlands

The tour began in style, in the opulent concert halls of Amsterdam and the Hague, Concertgebouw and Kurhaus, on successive Saturday and Sunday nights. The Quartet was preceded by the Tony Crombie orchestra from England—"almost an hour of loud swing," according to a reviewer at the Amsterdam concert (Sweens 1955), "which had a very limited success with this crowd." The concerts had been arranged before Baker left New York. Programs at both venues listed Russ Freeman, Bob Carter and Peter Littman in the band (Openneer 1993: 28), and Baker started both concerts by correcting the listings and introducing Twardzik and Bond to the audience. The opening half-hour of both concerts is preserved at the Netherlands Jazz Archive in Amsterdam, and the Kurhaus concert was edited and broadcast a few days later on AVRO radio Hilversum. Concert programs listed 16 song titles from which the repertoire would supposedly be selected, but only a couple of those titles were actually called. None of Zieff's charts is listed, and it appears that none was played before the sessions when they were recorded.

The list does not include *Tommyhawk*, the Johnny Mandel tune recorded by Baker for Pacific Jazz with a sextet a year before, which was used prominently as the opener at both concerts. A photograph from the Kurhaus concert by Hans Buter shows Twardzik with a large score spread out before him on the piano (14.1). It is probably *Tommyhawk*, on which Mandel's arrangement requires him to play the lively unison line with the trumpet and negotiate rapid changes that Freeman had carried out with such panache.

The repertoire overlaps at both concerts (as detailed in the discography), but Baker changed his ballad feature from *I'm Glad There is You* at Concertgebouw to *Someone to Watch Over Me* at Kurhaus. They fill the same stylistic niche in the program, as glacial ballads replete with romantic longing. Baker was obviously confident that these audiences would sit still not only for his wistful singing but also for Twardzik's ruminative accompaniment, and, in that, he was certainly right. A review in the Dutch daily *de Volkskrant* (translated for me by Bert Vuijsje,

[illustration 14.1] Chet Baker Quartet at Kurhaus, The Hague, on 18 September 1955. Photograph by Hans Buter in *Jazz Journaal* (October 1955). Netherlands Jazz Archive. All rights reserved.

as are the following) noted that Twardzik's "unabashedly romantic approach fits Baker's intimate playing wonderfully." *Jazz Journaal* credited
Twardzik with "a pleasant abundance of musicality," and *Rhythme*, another jazz magazine, praised Twardzik as "a highly original soloist who
journeys into melody à la Dave Brubeck and possesses a lively swing."
Melody Maker struck the same note in its review, identifying Twardzik as
"a young man who played terrifically," and adding: "He does not have
the usual West Coast style, but features a vividly swinging, Brubeck-
like playing."

Both concerts were adroitly photographed. At the Concertgebouw re-
cital, the prize-winning photojournalist Ed van der Elsken made his

[illustration 14.2] Richard Twardzik with Chet Baker at Concertgebouw, Amsterdam,
on 17 September 1955. Photograph by Ed van der Elsken (1991: 28). Netherlands
Jazz Archive. All rights reserved.

first foray into jazz photography. (He would photograph jazz only from 1955 to 1959, collected in Van der Elsken 1991.) We know that Liliane, the Helen of Troy who launched Baker's European conquest, was with Baker in the Netherlands because Van der Elsken photographed them there. Van der Elsken's most stunning image catches Twardzik in rapt concentration at the piano with Baker beside him, the glint of the spotlight on Baker's trumpet making a symbolic fusion of the minds of the two musicians (14.2).

Van der Elsken was mainly interested in Baker, of course, but another of his images caught Twardzik almost accidentally, at the bottom of the frame, and the detail, though grainy when blown up, shows him well groomed and natty at his first European performance, and on his first week on the continent (14.3). It would be hard to guess from his appearance that he was about to suffer the first of several crises.

[illustration 14.3] Richard Twardzik at Concertgebouw, Amsterdam, on 17 September 1955. Detail from photograph by Ed van der Elsken (1991: 29). Netherlands Jazz Archive. All rights reserved.

At some point on this Netherlands trip, Jimmy Bond found Twardzik teetering on the edge of consciousness from a heroin overdose. According to Turner (1999: 173), "Bond had to scrub Twardzik's naked back with a brush to bring him back from the edge." The incident probably took place after the Kurhaus concert on Sunday. A young jazz enthusiast, Arie van Breda, could not attend the concert that night because of family commitments, but he managed to skip out later to the Flying Dutchman, a jazz club, and he was delighted to find, as he suspected, that some of Baker's men had turned up there. He settled in to listen, and after a few hours one of his friends, Paul Acket (later the founder and producer of the Northsea Jazz Festival) paused at his table to tell him that Baker's piano player was sitting on a chair behind the piano, nodding, with drool running from his mouth. With the activity in the club and all the excitement, van Breda did not see how the incident ended—whether Jimmy Bond or anyone else went to Twardzik's rescue, or Twardzik snapped out of his stupor on his own. It was not until the next day, the proverbial morning after, that van Breda thought about the potential disaster that might have befallen the young piano player. The image of Twardzik nodding in the shadows stuck with him long after the music of the night was forgotten.

• 21 September: Chet Baker Quartet plus Rolfe Schnoebiegel, trumpet, at Mainz, West Germany (*Chet Baker in Europe 1955*, Philology CD W 42-2 in discography).

Three days later, the band was in Mainz, a comfortable trip south-southeast from Amsterdam. Twenty-five minutes of their one-night stand in Mainz survives in an amateur recording (14.4, also page 52). The source tape runs fast, which gives the piano a honky-tonk edge, causes the tempos to wobble, and makes Baker sound like a chipmunk in his spoken introductions. But beneath the echoes and wows of the homemade tape, the quartet can be heard playing bright, inventive, enthusiastic jazz.

The three recorded tunes were standard night-club fare, though unfamiliar in Baker's repertoire until now. *Walkin'*, Miles Davis's opener, was the kind of earthy blues that could stir the blood. It is an odd context for Twardzik, but he responds with a feisty, locked-hands solo that rouses the crowd and pleases Baker. "Yeah!" Baker shouts as Twardzik makes his two-fisted wrap-up. *Indian Summer*, a sentimental old Victor Herbert song (written in 1919) that the band had played at both

Dutch concerts as well, gets a clean, respectful reading from Baker. *All the Things You Are* is played fast, as a romp for the band's guest, German trumpeter Rolfe Schnoebiegel, whose straight, bold tone bolstered Kurt Edelhagen's trumpet section. It makes for undistinguished jamming except for Twardzik's mind-boggling eight-bar double-time introduction, a kind of fugue that nearly reels out of control before settling into the fast rhythm of the piece. For the few seconds it lasts, Twardzik communicates a frantic kind of glee.

• 27 September: Chet Baker Quartet in Geneva, Switzerland

It was probably after this Geneva concert that Twardzik suffered another spell. Baker later wrote (1997: 70): "We had just finished a concert somewhere in Switzerland and I was standing backstage speaking with people when there was a loud bang. Moving quickly toward the noise, as did everyone else, I saw Dick lying on the floor. He had passed out cold, and several people were trying to figure out what was wrong with him. We located a doctor and cleared the stage area."

[illustration14.4] cover of *Chet Baker in Europe, 1955*

In another account, Baker placed this incident in Zurich, though vaguely, which would make it some three weeks later. But other details suggest that it took place earlier, probably on this first visit to Geneva. In the later account, Baker said, "He played so well, and I didn't even know that he was using anything until a concert in Switzerland some-where, in Zurich I think. He passed out backstage one night and a doctor who was in the audience came in, and that was how I found out what was going on" (Weber 1988).

Twardzik's problems here and elsewhere on the trip stemmed from the purity of the heroin he and Littman were scoring. The difference in street-quality drugs between Europe and America is common knowl-edge now but was probably little understood in 1955. The quality was purer, the rush was more intense, the high was higher, and the palpita-tions—well, sometimes junkies woke up on the floor. And it was easier to get than in the States, even for jazz musicians, who expected to find dealers in the places where they worked. Teddy Blume, Charlie Parker's manager, had experienced it firsthand. "In Europe, it was even worse," he said (Reisner 1962: 57). "The pushers were everywhere. I tried to shoo them away, tried to get them to leave [Parker] alone… The min-ute he walked out of the theatre, they would spot him."

Purity and accessibility combined with Twardzik's fabled low threshold made a potentially lethal mix. But he was not alone. The European heroin hit Littman the same way. Jimmy Bond said, "On separate occa-sions both Littman and Twardzik passed out on stage from overdoses" (Turner 1999: 172–73). And so, it came to seem like a general prob-lem, not just Twardzik's. It was just something that happened once in a while, a minor miscalculation they expected to adjust to in a day or two.

At some point on their travels, probably after Twardzik's black-out in Geneva, Jimmy Bond took on the task of shepherding Twardzik to their gigs. He would call on Twardzik at his hotel room on working nights and accompany him to the club or concert hall. The reasons be-hind this arrangement are not certain. Punctuality was never a problem for Twardzik, and neither were binge-like disappearances. All his Bos-ton confreres said so, and there was no change in his days with Baker no matter what toll the drugs were taking. Baker himself said, "Dick had always taken care of business; always at work on time and always playing exceptionally" (1997: 70). So Bond seems to have taken on the role that Teddy Blume had played with Bird, shooing away pushers who might try to distract Twardzik on his way to work.

• 4 October: Chet Baker Quartet at Salle Pleyel, Paris, France

The initial round of concerts in the Netherlands, West Germany and Switzerland orbited Paris, and served as warm-ups for the Quartet's high-pressure Paris debut. It took place at Salle Pleyel, the capital's most prestigious concert hall. To this point, the young band members had, in effect, been getting used to one another, accommodating their styles and sorting out the repertoire for this highly publicized concert, which was broadcast across the nation by French radio.

For the advocates of modern jazz in the country, the Chet Baker Quartet at Salle Pleyel was a watershed. Opening for Baker that night were the cream of homegrown jazz modernists, the Bobby Jaspar All Stars and the pianist Martial Solal. Sidney Bechet, the American expatriate who had become as big a celebrity in France as Piaf, sat conspicuously in the audience (Tercinet 1988). Bechet's fame, with hit records (*Les Oignons*, *Petite Fleur*) and front-page love affairs, brought luster to the moldy figs. He was the darling of the French intellectuals, Fanon's *sauvage noble* incarnate. The constant attention he was getting seemed to the modernists like implied criticism of the new values they were trying to get across. Now here was Bechet at Salle Pleyel checking out the opposition.

The hipsters were understandably nervous. A lot was riding on Baker's shoulders, and the reputation that preceded him, especially his minimalist singing, gave them cause to worry. But as soon as he played his first notes on that famous stage, they relaxed. Tercinet (1988) said, "People expected a musician murmuring in the mist, and here stood an incisive, powerful trumpeter with a clear tone. Which detracted not at all from the poetic side of his playing." The concert was a triumph for Baker and everything he represented to the young audience (14.5).

Ironically, only the people gathered in the audience that evening have proof of Baker's prowess on the occasion. No keepsakes of the concert have turned up, notwithstanding the tradition of recording jazz concerts that actually had its origins at Salle Pleyel with Dizzy Gillespie's big band. Broadcast tapes for French radio normally find their way to the Vogue Record vaults, and from there onto records. Failing that, numerous enthusiasts make private recordings either from the radio or from the audience. But so far there have been no releases of this auspicious concert by the Chet Baker Quartet, either publicly or privately, which suggests, after all these years, that the radio transcriptions have been lost and the tapes made by fans on that night were tossed in the trash by their widows and children along with old Maigret pocketbooks. It is a scenario that is hard to believe. Dozens of lesser concerts have been preserved, and so there must be hope for a concert that was a symbolic event in the French cultural calendar for 1955.

• probably 8 October afternoon: Chet Baker Quartet in Brussels, Belgium

• evening of same day: Chet Baker Quartet in Antwerp, Belgium

[illustration 14.5] Chet Baker and Richard Twardzik backstage at Salle Pleyel, Paris, on 4 October 1955. Photograph by Jean-Pierre Leloir, *Jazzman* 89 (2003: 14). All rights reserved.

A few days later, the band was back on the road, playing an afternoon concert in Brussels and an evening concert 30 miles north in Antwerp. The Brussels concert was reportedly recorded for Belgian radio.

The date is inferred from postcards that Twardzik wrote to Clare and to Henryk from Brussels on the day of the performance, postmarked on 9 October but presumably written the day before, which was a Saturday.

To Henryk, Richard sent a picture postcard of the stately Belgian Congress building, with this message: "Hi Tatus! We play this afternoon in Brussels this evening in Antwerp with Tony Vos a Dutch outfit. The calibar [sic] of Dutch musicians is surprisingly high. Wish you were here to see Brussels. Take care   Love Dick."

To Clare, he sent a postcard of Brussels' landmark fountain featuring Manneken Pis, the cupid-like figure that urinates a continuous stream of clear Belgian water. Like thousands of American tourists before and since, Richard scribbled in the margin, "This little fellow never rests!" His scribbled note on the back begins, "Hello Mother dear," and is then taken up with this decidedly unsentimental message: "Send Henry's size to me in Paris c/o Am. Express. Brussels is very lovely a miniature Paris. Brussels this afternoon Antwerp tonight. Love Dick."

He sent the postcards to his parents' workplaces, to Clare at "Accoustic [sic] Lab, Mass Institute of Technology," and to Henryk "c/o C.J. Connick Ass."

• 9 October: Chet Baker Quartet at Börensaal in Cologne, Germany

This concert finally got a public airing in 2005, some 50 years after the fact (on RLR Records from Barcelona). It adds about 70 minutes of music to Twardzik's discography, counting the final 20 minutes in which the Quartet is augmented by Austrian saxophonists Hans Koller and Willi Sanner, from Koller's quintet who were also on the bill. Twardzik is sharp. His playing on *My Funny Valentine*, Baker's signature ballad, plumbs harmonic depths hardly imagined in other versions. Best of all, Baker generously allots him almost nine minutes for a trio feature on *Yellow Tango* that rolls along merrily in an expansive version that preserves some of the delicacy of the original but still moves it into much riskier territory.

Richard sent postcards again the next day, postmarked 10 October, with scenes of Strasbourg, almost 200 miles southeast of Brussels and Antwerp. His messages are full of enthusiasm, very much like his letters home a few years before.

To Henryk, the stained-glass master, Richard sends a picture of "Strasbourg La Cathedrale (côté Sud)," with this message:

> Hi Dad! Today was a real thrill for me. This is the most beautiful church I have ever seen! The windows absolutely take your breath away! The greatest symphony in color. I can't begin to describe it. Truly one of the world's masterpieces When I came in, many priests were singing so you see it was perfect. Love Dick

To Clare, on the back of a pastoral scene of storks in Alsace, he writes:

> Dear Mother, A wonderful town (Strasbourg) more German in character than any other of the French towns so far. The French tour is successful so far and next week I go to dear old England. The castles on the Rhine are breath taking. I am in good health. xxxx Love Dick

Twardzik's reassurances about the state of his health, so conventional in his writings to his mother, may be more than an automatic reflex. His resumption of his correspondence after the long silence suggests a kind of equanimity, even well-being. It undoubtedly indicates that Twardzik was working at imposing some controls on his drug use, probably because of the scare in Geneva. His boyish tone, evocative as it is of the tone he took when his relationship with his parents was less complicated, suggests that he might have been making some headway. The postcards leave little doubt that he was feeling good about himself.

• 10 October: Chet Baker Quartet in Lyons, France

The Strasbourg postcards were postmarked "Grenoble *gare*," the railway station at Grenoble, on the direct rail line south from Strasbourg. There, the musicians would have transferred to another line to get to Lyons, where they played that night. Following the concert, they left either on the night train or very early in the morning for Paris, where they had a studio date the next afternoon.

This "French tour," as Twardzik calls it in his postcard to Clare, is like a scale model of the rigors of the road. From Salle Pleyel, the band members had traveled to Belgium for a matinee in Brussels and evening performance in Antwerp (on the 8th), and then on successive days to Cologne (9th) and Lyons (10th), and back to Paris. That amounted to four concerts in three days. The round trip from Paris and back again covered about 980 miles as the crow flies, well over a thousand miles by rail, plus untold transfers to different lines with either a few minutes to catch the next train or hours to sit waiting for it. All this took place, of course, on unfamiliar terrain in an unknown language, though Liliane might have helped out on both counts, if she and Baker traveled in the same car as the others.

Twardzik was lucky in one respect. He did not have to carry his instrument along with his suitcase, as all the others did—Baker with his trumpet, probably a Martin Committee model at the time, Jimmy Bond with his ungainly bass, and Peter Littman with a crate of cymbals and drums. When the stresses of getting where they were going ended at their destination, they then faced a new set of hassles in getting to the performance venue and setting up. After all that there were the nerves involved in performing in front of expectant audiences.

The spirit-sucking fatigue that this kind of regimen must have induced is nowhere evident in Twardzik's genial postcards home. In fact, for jazz musicians of Twardzik's generation, as indeed for the three generations that came before him, any mention of occupational stresses and strains was decidedly square. Musicians who complained were considered burnouts, and they were soon gone, drummed out of the fraternity. Serge Chaloff eventually talked openly about the stresses of the road, but only years later, when he was in his confessional phase after cleaning up. One of his darkest memories was a debilitating tour he made as a 21-year-old in 1945, with the Boyd Raeburn orchestra. He had already been playing professionally for five years, but this tour was like no other. By Chaloff's reckoning, the band played 60 consecutive one-night stands with up to 500-mile bus rides in between. "I was tense and worn," he said (Hanley 1955: 16). "I had talent, but I was trying to keep up with musicians that had talent and 15 to 20 years of experience. I was insecure deep inside. I was worried. This fellow who was trying to be a friend gave me a shot [of heroin]. I began walking on clouds." For the next nine years, as long as he was a junkie, it was no problem for him to keep the cool code of the road.

Richard Twardzik would keep it too. In the eleven days that remained of his life as the musicians steamed toward Paris from Lyons, the pace would quicken. Border crossings would come more frequently, each one accompanied by passport inspections and luggage searches by uniformed men. The language of the inspectors, porters, and other travelers would sometimes be German and sometimes French, equally opaque for a kid with one year of each language in high school. For one of those eleven days, the language around him would be English, the common language, as Bernard Shaw said, that separates Americans and Britons. And this was just the beginning. The succession of concerts would accelerate (seven in six days after Paris), and the round-trip distance would quadruple to more than four thousand miles (Paris–London–Paris–Stuttgart–Lucerne–Zurich–Basel, and back to Paris).

Motion would be constant. Disgorged onto the platform half asleep after a long haul, Twardzik and the others could still sense the rocking

[14.6] cover of *Chet Baker Quartet* (Barclay Records, France, 1956)

of the train in their bones and hear the clacking of steel wheels on steel rails. The autumn air was chilly, and the days were shorter than at home. Of course, it was all just an illusion if you were walking on clouds. In Richard's postcards, he sounds like a tourist. It was harder to keep up the façade in more personal communications. "I had phone calls from him in Europe," Crystal Joy told me. "I knew he was high. He sounded like he was underwater." And sinking, we now know.

• 11 October: Chet Baker Quartet in Studio Pathé-Magellan, Paris, for Barclay Records

The quartet returned to Paris for the first of what should have been several recording sessions for Nicole Barclay, the owner of a record company with labels called Barclay and Blue Star. At some point on the tour, Baker signed a contract with Barclay to make seven albums (according to de Valk 2000: 66), but in the end he would record only three. His Barclay recordings would be his only studio sessions for fifteen months, from his last Los Angeles date with the previous quartet in March 1955 until June 1956, a couple of months after his return to the United States. Except for the records with Twardzik, Baker's Barclay recordings are distinguished almost solely by the fact that Baker himself was at something close to the pinnacle of his technical abilities, but he surrounded himself with a shifting cast of European musicians, none of whom, good as they were, could rise to his level in the impromptu studio sessions. For Baker, this European sojourn is like an interlude that splits his career symbolically into two phases. Leading up to it was his efficient rise into the top ranks of jazz, and following it was his tedious descent into something very close to living hell. For the rest of his days, Baker would learn to live with missed engagements, lost weekends, irate promoters, run-ins with the law, imprisonments, debilitation, deportations, incessant travel, and much more. The weeks leading up to the Paris recordings, eventful as they must have seemed at the time, were really the calm before a life-long storm.

For Twardzik, this moment must have been one of the most fulfilling of his musical life. Alain Tercinet (1988), who shadowed Baker and the others in Paris, said, "In his bags, Twardzik had brought the compositions of Bob Zieff." Now, at long last, it was time to unpack them. Zieff's compositions, eight of them, and one more of Twardzik's own would make up the first LP under the new contract. Baker, typically, got it wrong when he looked back at it. He said they recorded them "all in one afternoon" (1997: 71). It took two. At the first session, they recorded five Zieff charts: *Rondette, Mid-Forte, Sad Walk, Re-Search* and *Just Duo.* That in itself made an extraordinarily productive afternoon, especially considering the difficulty of the music and the quality of the performances. They would record the others as soon as they could, but that would be three days later, after a quick trip across the English Channel.

• 13 October: Chet Baker Quartet at the Flamingo Club, London, England

Twardzik, in his postcard to his mother, said, "next week I go to dear old England." His anticipation was rewarded when they got there. Baker, in the diary notes for the American release (1956) of his French Barclay recordings, recalls an exhilarating reception: "Not only are the British fans wild about modern jazz from the States, but they have their own fine jazzmen too." He extols the atmosphere in the Flamingo Club in Leicester Square, which has, he says, "been putting on the best in jazz here since the war," and mentions interviews on a BBC program called *Tonight in Town* and by a bevy of print journalists. There is no mention on this occasion of the stultifying conditions that would restrict his musical activities when he returned to London ten days later, for a second concert. Protectionist legislation by the British Musicians Union decreed that foreign instrumentalists could play in Britain only if British instrumentalists played in the visitors' country on an exchange basis. Only vocalists were exempt, along with their accompanists. But on this visit, the whole band seems to have been given dispensation to perform at the Flamingo Club.

• 14 October: Chet Baker Quartet in Studio Pathé-Magellan, Paris, for Barclay Records (*Chet Baker in Paris,* Vol. 1. EmArcy 837 474-2 [France 1988] in discography).

The next afternoon, they were back in Paris for the second recording session. The quartet recorded four more compositions at this sitting: Zieff's *Piece Caprice, Pomp* and *Brash,* and Twardzik's *The Girl from Greenland.* The latter would be Twardzik's last composition, but it is not entirely new. It is actually the second theme of *Albuquerque Social Swim.* (I originally identified it as "the bridge" and Zieff replied, "Well, it's where the bridge would be if there was one.") It is not a straight restatement. For *The Girl from Greenland,* the theme is slowed down

and re-worked from ten bars to eight, and, of course, arranged for
trumpet–piano counterpoint in the melody statement. For attentive
listeners, Twardzik leaves a clue. He ends his piano solo on *The Girl from
Greenland* (at 4:01) by playing *Albuquerque Social Swim.*

All this music—these four masters, with the five from the previous session—was a triumph of ambition and discipline, the pay-off for what
would seem, under normal circumstances, to have taken long hours
of careful rehearsal. The great mystery is that there is no evidence of
rehearsals, either on the road or in the studio. The schedule was too
tight and too wearying on the October leg to afford any work on fresh
material. Zieff's charts were apparently not worked out by performing
them in concerts leading up to the recording sessions, practical though
that might have been. That leaves the Barclay recording studios as the
site for rehearsing the tunes as well as recording them, but under those

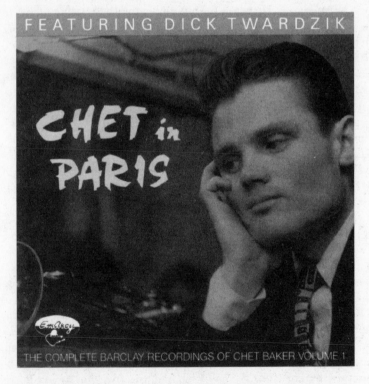

[14.7] cover of *Chet in Paris,* Vol. 1, featuring Dick Twardzik

circumstances there should have been a tape trail of breakdowns and alternate takes. So far, no alternate takes have come to light. That almost certainly means that there were none. The alternate takes from Baker's subsequent Barclay dates are compiled as a separate CD (*Chet Baker in Paris*, vol. 4), but none of them come from the sessions with Twardzik in the band.

The studio output on both days constitutes, in any case, a full day's work by ordinary standards, so there was hardly time for complete alternate takes. The only hint of musical development comes from the fact that the pieces played at the second session are slightly more expansive and less tightly controlled, though still played with solid discipline. The difference is that they are slightly longer, averaging just over five minutes, where the tunes recorded at the first session averaged slightly less than four.

For the Barclay producers, hearing the first fruits of what they expected to be a long association, the recording sessions must have exceeded their wildest dreams. In two afternoons of recording, they had garnered a full LP, nine tracks of intricate, memorable, impeccably realized chamber jazz (14.6, also page 52).

The extraordinary musicianship cries out for an explanation. Twardzik, of course, knew this music inside out; he understood every nuance, numerous as they were. He was finally getting the chance to record the Zieff compositions that fate had stolen from him back home.

But what about Baker? He comes to the music cold, but he carries off his lead role with utmost assurance and considerable warmth. Maybe Baker felt the need to concentrate a little harder with these kids from the New England Conservatory and the Juilliard School in his band. He was, we know in hindsight, at the peak of his powers. Baker had discovered, when he was first starting out, that he could invent spontaneous counter-melodies as readily as most musicians could play written lines. It was his gift, and it came so naturally to him that until he saw the looks of admiration and sometimes incredulity from other musicians he had assumed everyone could do it. From 1952 to 1955, he reveled in his gift. He pretended not to notice, of course, but out of the corner of his eye he caught the looks on the faces of Russ Freeman or Dick Bock or the New York cognoscenti when he hit the notes in just the right sequence and made something beautiful that no one had ever heard before. He had even caught snooty Gerry Mulligan admiring it when he thought no one was watching. Later on, Baker would take the gift for granted. He always made it seem effortless, and there would eventually be nights—lots of nights—when it was literally effortless, when the lines he played hardly carried beyond the chair he sat on at the edge of the stage. Those nights were a long way off when he went into the Barclay studios with Richard Twardzik and the other young musicians.

Baker was largely self-taught, and now he found himself surrounded by schooled players. This unfamiliar music that Richard Twardzik pulled out of his bags must have put his senses on the alert. Twardzik himself was more than a little intimidating to Baker, though he was way too cool to show it. Twardzik listened to Bartók; he wrote letters to a girl from Greenland; he visited cathedrals; he spoke a little French to the chambermaids. "He was a brilliant guy, really well read," Baker said (1997: 70). At this very minute, he was reading *The State of Music* by Virgil Thompson, for chrissake. Maybe Baker, though he would never let it enter his mind, feared the raised eyebrow if he screwed up on this music he had invited Twardzik to bring with him. Maybe he was leery about the look that might pass between the guys, the little barbs that might be tossed his way, jokingly or seeming so, if he didn't cut it.

So he cut it. There is tension in all the tracks, and it is creative tension. Baker and the others play Zieff's melodies as written, precisely as Dick Wetmore had played them but with more cohesion. And then they improvise on those melodies, logically and thoughtfully and lyrically, like jewelers examining their facets for reflections and colors and nuances, with each member of the quartet supplying his own light. The music has a delicacy uncommon in jazz, but at the same time there is the grit of the blues. There are caprices, as one title says, but there is also brashness, as another title says, and fortitude (if middling) and several kinds of sad walks.

• 15 October: Chet Baker Quartet with Lars Gullin, baritone saxophone, and Caterina Valente, vocal, at Villa Berg in Stuttgart, West Germany (Lars Gullin, *1955/56*, Vol. 1. *With Chet Baker*. Dragon DRCD 224 [Sweden 1992] in discography).

Immediately after the second recording session, the band was back on the road. They traveled to Stuttgart, 320 miles away, where they would participate in a couple of events at the start of a festival called *Woche der leichten Musik* (Popular Music Week). The Stuttgart events brought together a stunningly diverse mix of talents, including as a special feature a series of "third-stream" concerts in which composers auditioned symphonic pieces that imported jazz devices as integral compositional elements. The confluence of jazz and symphonic streams into the so-called third stream, a term coined by the American composer and teacher Gunther Schuller, was just beginning to make some headway in the United States. The Stuttgart organizers planted themselves squarely in the avant-garde by commissioning third-stream works by several young European composers and also by Bill Russo and Eddie Sauter, sometime arrangers for Stan Kenton and Benny Goodman now conscripted into the conservatory.

Within a few years, the third-stream movement would fizzle out, but at its inception it was buoyed up by pioneer spirit, with the promise of

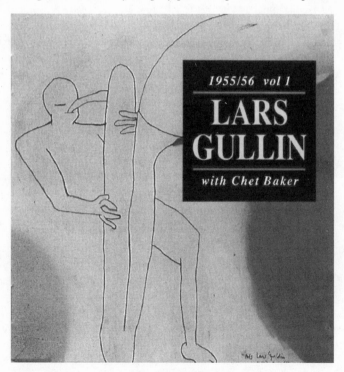

[Illustration14.8] cover of *Lars Gullin 1955/56*, Vol. 1

excursions into terra incognita or, as some saw it, leaps into the dark. For Richard Twardzik, with his proclivities for both streams, the prospects should have been doubly exciting. His overnight stay in Stuttgart must have afforded him some exposure to the inner workings of the movement, but it could only be a glimpse at best, because he was preoccupied with other things.

The Chet Baker Quartet was booked to play the opening concert, an auspicious billing in such a star-studded week. The sense of occasion was magnified when someone came up with the brilliant idea of teaming them with Lars Gullin, the Swedish baritone saxophonist, who was, by all accounts, the most authentic European jazz musician of the day. Gullin was already booked at the festival as featured soloist on Werner Heider's *Concerto for Trumpet, Baritone Saxophone and Large Orchestra* with the South German Symphony Orchestra. Putting him on stage beside Chet Baker at the kick-off concert was an inspiration. Baker's reputation had sprung from his work alongside another baritone saxophone player, Gerry Mulligan, and even though that partnership was now dead for two-and-a-half years, with Baker and Mulligan splitting up vituperatively in May 1953, their recordings continued to have great currency. Adding Gullin to Baker's quartet looked like an ingenious way of reviving the Mulligan–Baker glory days with a European twist.

As baritone stylists, Gullin and Mulligan, in fact, shared little common ground: Gullin had a deeper, fuller sound, and he sported bebop dexterity that rivaled Serge Chaloff. If the promoters thought that pairing him with Baker would resuscitate the Mulligan–Baker sound, they were dead wrong, but what Gullin could and would do was provide a deep and enveloping foil for Baker's pencil-thin middle-register lyricism. It was an inspired pairing in its own right.

Along with the imported American quartet and Gullin at the opening concert, there was also Caterina Valente, the beautiful Italian pop singer, who had a top-ten single, *The Breeze and I*, in England and America in 1953. Though her fame in much of the world never went beyond the hit parade, Valente was known in upper-class Europe for singing Gershwin and Weill as well as pop songs. She was worldly as well as beautiful. Born in France to Italian circus performers, she began singing professionally as a child with her accordion-playing father. She was the same age as Richard Twardzik, and by the time they met on the Stuttgart stage she had established her reputation not only for *The Breeze and I* but also for her cabaret act that included songs and repartee in English, French, Italian Spanish, German and Swedish.

The Stuttgart performance, at least in the 20 minutes that have survived, is heterogeneous, as might be expected (14.8, also page 52). The quartet begins by playing *Brash*, the Zieff composition they had ended their recording session with the previous day. Gullin then joins them for *Cool Blues*, the Charlie Parker line, and for the standard ballad *Lover Man*, and then Valente comes on to sing *I'll Remember April* with all five musicians backing her.

Brash is note-perfect in its intricate arrangement, and its presence in Baker's concert repertoire makes a significant and welcome innovation. Otherwise, the concert presents spontaneous bebop in a jam atmosphere. Baker and Gullin chase one another in *Cool Blues*, playing the kind of counterpoint that had been second nature for Baker with Mulligan. Gullin is featured on *Lover Man*, with Twardzik prominent in accompaniment. Valente scats *I'll Remember April*. She starts off flat, searching for tonality, and finds it by the time she gives way to solos by Baker and Gullin.

Baker's concert was reviewed in the Swedish jazz magazine *Estrad* by Lars Resberg, then 35, an enthusiast who had been writing about jazz since he was 16 and who would ultimately be influential in spreading the word about modern jazz in his country not only through his reviews but also by translating jazz books into Swedish and hosting record shows on Swedish Radio. He arrived at the Stuttgart festival in high spirits, but in the end he had to concede that his close-up view of the Baker Quartet left him with mixed emotions.

In the November *Estrad*, in a report filed soon after the concert, Resberg complained about the brevity of Baker's set, lamenting that the three numbers by the quartet and quintet were too few for him "to really form an opinion." (Resberg's columns were translated for me by Lars Westin.) Those three numbers were sufficient, however, for him to note that "Chet has changed his style considerably since he made his first records with Gerry Mulligan," especially showing the influence of Miles Davis, Clifford Brown and Dizzy Gillespie. It was an astute observation, inferring from Baker's style the changes that had come about from his year-long sojourn on the American east coast, which had gone largely unnoticed by reviewers in the States. "Chet plays with greater melodic simplicity than before," Resberg said, "but, beyond a doubt, with much more swing."

Of the other players, only Twardzik left a favorable impression on Resberg. He was "the only one to display much personality," Resberg said. "The bass player was competent. So was the drummer, but much too hard-hitting considering the style of the band." Apart from the music they played, he took a critical view of the way the band members conducted themselves on and off the stage too, but he held off reporting his complaints for a month, in the December issue of *Estrad*, after disaster had struck.

At the concert, Caterina Valente's choice of *I'll Remember April* as the set closer takes on a special poignancy because of the space it occupies in Richard Twardzik's works. *I'll Remember April* was the song that had been the vehicle for Twardzik's semi-audible solo with Charlie Parker three years earlier at the after-hours club when he was little more than a novice. Two years after that, he mulled over *I'll Remember April* for almost eight minutes on his practice tapes, and then he played it more compactly on his trio recording for Pacific Jazz, where it stands prominent in the music that is the best testament to his talent we will ever have. Now, in Stuttgart, this performance of *I'll Remember April* with Valente is, as I write this, the very last recorded title in the short list of his complete works. (It is last accidentally, and we hope momentarily; tapes exist of some subsequent performances of the Baker Quartet with Lars Gullin, and they will eventually be made public.) *I'll Remember April* is thus the most common title in Twardzik's recorded works, recurring in 1952, twice in 1954, and in 1955. Its title, though Valente could hardly know it, commemorates Twardzik's birth-month.

There should have been another recording of *I'll Remember April* by Twardzik. Eric van Aro, Valente's manager, told me (in September 2000), "After the concert, the record company proposed to record in the studio *I Remember April* and *Every Time We Say Good-Bye* but the musicians refused to be part of it." It is not hard to imagine Twardzik and the others taking a supercilious view of recording with the singer of *The Breeze and I*. Twardzik scoffed at the suggestion, apparently, and walked away. Baker, ever more malleable, did record these two songs with Valente, as a duet, with Valente playing guitar and singing and Baker playing trumpet. (According to discographies, the recording took place in Baden-Baden in March 1956, but van Aro believes that it followed the Stuttgart concert.) The songs were released as a single and attained some currency in Europe in 1956 (and were belatedly issued on the compilation CD, Chet Baker, *The Jazz Essentials*. Verve 840 632 [1989]).

In Stuttgart, there were unmistakable signs of dissolution in the Chet Baker Quartet for anyone watching with a critical eye. In his November review, Lars Resberg could not help but single out Peter Littman's deportment, though he could not bring himself to name him. "Chet is said to be an exceptionally kind person," he wrote, "but it is a mystery to me that he could tolerate the laissez-faire attitude of the group and the shabby behavior of the drummer." Resberg withheld further criticism for the time being, and made a more overarching complaint. "It is high time that certain American musicians find out that Europe is no romantic fairy-land where you can walk around and break ginger cookies off the corners of the houses, dressed up in only barely adequate human behavior."

It would take a discerning reader to realize that Resberg was complaining about drug abuse in the guise of ginger cookies, and about nodding-out disguised as shabby clothing.

By the time the next issue of *Estrad* appeared in December, Twardzik's death had sent shock waves through the European jazz community. Resberg took a more forthright stance on what he had seen in Stuttgart. He must have realized, in the month between, that Twardzik had gulled him at their meeting, telling him that he went by the nickname "Rudy" and that his greatest influence was the Swedish piano player Bengt Hallberg. Resberg had dutifully reported those two details as facts the month before. But his encounter obviously hurt him, and his December column, with a delicate balance of anger and remorse, is a sort of outcry. It is the only contemporary account by an eyewitness of the self-destruction as it was taking place.

Resberg began, "Have you ever had that subtle, slightly aching, overwhelming feeling of discomfort that appears when you find yourself in the company of a really intoxicated alcoholic who is on the verge of disgracing himself in public?" And then he continued:

> This feeling spread like an evil mist around Chet Baker's quartet, though not from the effects of liquor but of narcotics. The colored

bassist, whose name is Jimmy Bond, was doing no wrong. He was the only one in the band who neither injected, smoked nor drank. Chet himself wasn't in too bad a state either.

But the other two. The pianist Dick Twardzik, smiling and courteous when we first met, told some amusing anecdotes… Later, at a restaurant: "Just a sip of wine and some light food for me, thank you." Our conversation didn't proceed very well. He moved uneasily in his chair. Then a visit to the toilet, a long visit. When he eventually returned, he seemed overwhelmingly cordial until I noticed that some of his spirited transmissions were dysfunctional. A few days later: a dead pianist in a narrow hotel room in Paris, from a heroin overdose…

And the drummer trying out sticks during a rehearsal: a hundred-odd musicians in the hall, most of them pretty important. The expression on his face was macabre. It was the same celestial affliction you see on pictures of Jesus Christ in crucifixion. Then he dropped a stick. He noticed this after a while and bent down slowly to pick it up. He remained in this position for so long that you expected him to fall down on his drums at any moment. But with immense effort he managed to rise to an upright position again, and started to play—a bit hard, but with a rhythmic spark, swinging and driving. And in a completely different world from us 'common' people…

The problem, he says, is not merely local:

I can't understand how Chet could produce a single reasonable note with these two in his quartet. These hard-injecting youngsters are insidious in more ways than one. Not only do they spread a disease that is 'worse than death'. They also destroy Europe as a potential market for well-behaved and ambitious colleagues in the U.S.A…

What these fools don't consider is that they are objects of increasingly critical scrutiny. When Mr. Blow makes his entrance at the club, moving his knees as if he's up in the clouds, with dilated pupils staring out from smoke-colored glasses, the news reaches our little corner of the world in a short time. And Mr. Blow shouldn't take it for granted that he will find somebody in Europe who is willing to make such an unsafe investment as he seems to be.

Resberg's sense of decency remains intact, in spite of his outrage. He is willing to name Jimmy Bond, the innocent one, and Twardzik, but he still holds back on naming Littman, culpable though he is in Resberg's eyes, the survivor who still has a living to make.

• 15–16 October: Chet Baker Quartet with Lars Gullin, baritone saxophone, at Club Frascati in Stuttgart, West Germany

Lars Gullin seemed to have no qualms about the spacey antics of his American colleagues, at least not at first. He had let it be known beforehand that he was eager to meet Baker and play with him. After the festival opening, he stayed with the Chet Baker Quartet for a nightclub engagement in Stuttgart, and then he traveled with the band for a series of one-nighters in three cities in Switzerland, as shown in the datelines below, and then went back to Paris with them.

• 17 October: Chet Baker Quartet with Lars Gullin, in Lucerne, Switzerland

• 18 October: Chet Baker Quartet with Lars Gullin, in Zurich, Switzerland

• 19 October: Chet Baker Quartet with Lars Gullin, in Basel, Switzerland

Performances from these engagements, when they finally come to light, should reveal whether Zieff's compositions continued to be integrated into the quartet's repertoire as *Brash* had been in Stuttgart. They should also reveal the growing symbiosis between Gullin and Twardzik in the six days they spent together. Gullin (1928–1976) was a composer as well as an instrumentalist, and he wrote choral music and classical forms as well as jazz. Olle Lind told me that on this road trip "Gullin and Twardzik used to play classical music and Gullin's compositions on piano when they had the opportunity." The two young men shared both the breadth of their musical tastes and the intensity of their musical ambitions. It is easy to imagine the bonds between them strengthening in the jazz they played on those six successive nights.

Gullin's jazz reputation peaked internationally in the 1950s, when he appeared on American recordings with Stan Getz and Zoot Sims (on Roost, Prestige and Verve). In 1954, the year before he made this short tour with Baker, he was named the New Star on his instrument in *Down Beat*, the first European musician to win an American jazz poll.

In the two decades of his life after his time with Baker, Gullin's health declined, and his career petered out. He remains a venerated figure in European jazz circles, especially in Sweden, where there is a Lars Gullin Society, dedicated to keeping his works in public view through study programs and archival recordings of his performances. Independently, Stockholm's Dragon Records is issuing Gullin's recorded output from his peak years, produced by Lars Westin, the first volume of which is the source of the Stuttgart material with Baker and Twardzik.

Several Swedish scholars are engaged in searching out Gullin performance tapes. One of them wrote to tell me he had found the Cologne concert by the Chet Baker Quartet "on one of the dozens of old reels we have discovered in Germany in search of Lars Gullin recordings." When I asked for discographical details, he replied, "Yes, we have a tape with Twardzik and Chet, but no, Lars is not present." He eventually recognized the value of the rediscovered concert recording for Baker and especially for Twardzik, who was inventive all night, and released it on CD. But he could not disguise his bitter disappointment on his first hearing when he discovered that Gullin was not on the tape.

I inadvertently discovered the depth of the veneration for Gullin when I published the statement that Gullin "was the most authentic jazz musician of the day before ill health and heroin addiction distracted him and finally cost him his life at 48 in 1976" (Chambers 1997). True though that statement is, I soon discovered that it had offended Swedish sensibilities. Olle Lind, in the course of sending me some helpful notes he had made about Baker's European tour, scolded me. "During all my years of corresponding with jazz collectors," he said, "I have never before heard anyone talking about narcotics and Lars Gullin. They all loved him as a fantastic musician and a nice person." I hastened to reply that I too loved him as a fantastic musician. Soon after, one of Gullin's biographers, Keith Knox, alerted by Lind to my indiscretion, told me, "I'll have you know that Lars Gullin died of asthma at home." Knox then had the grace to concede that "he was addicted to heroin and morphine, this is true and he never denied it." He had suffered heart disease, and had stopped playing for several years in the 1970s when, Knox said, "his teeth fell out, were operated, and fell out again." In fact, according to Lars Westin, Gullin became "the first publicly identified addict in Sweden" around the time of his tour with Baker, and he suffered many indignities from the publicity that went with it. In his last years, Gullin was using methadone, according to Knox, and "would improvise on the piano at home through most of the night," in almost "trancelike" sessions. The asthma that killed him at the age of 48 was previously undiagnosed.

All of these tribulations were still to come when Gullin traveled through Switzerland with Twardzik and the other members of the Chet Baker Quartet. In those days, he was, in Knox's memorable phrase, "fluent and a demon for harmony."

• 20 October: Chet Baker Quartet with Lars Gullin, baritone saxophone, at Club Tabu in Paris, France

The musical bond between Gullin and the members of the quartet apparently crystallized at their performance on returning to Paris, where they played at Club Tabu. "According to Chet Baker this was one of the best gigs of his life," Olle Lind told me. "Gullin was fantastic. Chet said that he had only played with Gerry Mulligan before and that he did not know that anyone could play a baritone like Lars did."

Club Tabu was one of a handful of Paris clubs supplying the modernist alternative to the dominant traditionalist tastes in the city's jazz subculture. Baker and his young crew, including the redoubtable Gullin, roused the hipsters and became a second landmark occasion for them, a kind of underground version of the concert at Salle Pleyel 16 days earlier. Musicians flocked to the club, and the music flowed all night long.

Dawn had broken by the time Twardzik and his band-mates, exhausted from one-nighters and train rides but exhilarated by their reception in the capital, made their way to the Hôtel de la Madeleine on rue de Surène. They were mindful of the fact that they had a recording session that afternoon.

That day, 21 October 1955, was a Friday. Baker was set to record his next Barclay project at the Pathé-Magellan Studio at 4 p.m., and he had the brainwave of adding Gullin to the quartet. Their week together on the road, capped by the all-nighter at the Tabu, provided unbeatable rehearsal time.

Soon after 4 p.m., the musicians began wandering into the studio. Gullin and Bond arrived, and Baker came not long after. Littman arrived and set up his drums. They sat around smoking and waiting for

Twardzik for about an hour. Then they decided that someone should go and get him. Tercinet says it was Gullin who volunteered to go back to his room at the hotel. Baker says it was Littman. The official account, as we shall see, says that it was a hotel employee who actually went into the room and found him. For certain, it was not Bond, whose unofficial duty of shepherding the piano player to gigs was presumably suspended because this was an afternoon appointment.

Baker said, "We waited an hour, then Peter volunteered to go to his hotel room and see what was happening. About an hour later Peter rushed into the studio completely hysterical, screaming that Dick was dead. He said that he and the hotel manager had broken the door open and found Dick bright blue, the spike still in his arm" (1997: 71).

Twenty-three years later, Baker told an interviewer, "We really don't know if it was an intended thing or not. He was alone and the door was locked" (Rusch 1978: 33). Baker's emphasis on Twardzik's deliber-ate isolation implies that he thought it was suicide; this time he did not want to be rescued. Herb Pomeroy also suspected suicide, knowing how Twardzik dreaded the prospect of facing another rehabilitation program. But Russ Freeman doubted it. "You know, you don't find people who are really strung out dying from overdoses—which leads me to believe that he probably hadn't been deeply into it," he told Ted Gioia (1992: 184–85). "He probably hadn't built up a tolerance to it." Freeman's remarks seem naïve, given Twardzik's four-year history of heroin use. What was missing, surely, was not the tolerance, low as that always was, but the prudence against its purity. In that, Twardzik was not alone.

Littman—the "impossible kid," the "lost-cause junkie," the pal who seven weeks earlier had taken Twardzik into a stateroom on an ocean liner and revived his craving for euphoria— he too had passed out from overdoses. He passed out at least once on stage, according to Jimmy Bond, and another time at rehearsal, according to Resberg. So it was easy to miscalculate. Littman did it at least twice, maybe more, and laughed about it afterwards. Twardzik did it three times, and the third time he died.

Littman had no suicidal impulses. There is no reason to suspect that Twardzik did either apart from his melodramatic declaration to Herb Pomeroy. There was no depression beforehand, and there were no disappointments or failures, at least musically. Quite the contrary. He had guided his bandmates through scintillating performances of Zieff's compositions, and he was lionized wherever they went, by superb musicians like Gullin and Bobby Jaspar as well as by fans. Besides, there was no suicide note, and Twardzik would never have passed up the opportunity of dramatizing his plight if his death was intentional. The Parisian coroner found no evidence of suicide.

The technical term is death by misadventure.

Two days after Twardzik's death, Baker took Raymond Fol, the French bebop piano player, to Stoll Theatre in Kingsway, London, where he was scheduled to sing but not allowed to play his trumpet, as stipulated by the union rules. His performance there was the last act of an evening billed as the "International Jazz Festival," which, in the advertisement in *Melody Maker* on 15 October listed the Tony Kinsey Quartet and the Tony Crombie Orchestra with vocalist Annie Ross from England, Lars Gullin from Sweden, and "from U.S.A. CHET BAKER and pianist DICK TWARDZIK."

The tragedy obviously heightened the audience's anticipation. Twardzik's obituary was front-page news in *Melody Maker* in the same issue that carried the review of the festival. The obituary began, "Chet Baker walked on stage at London's Stoll theatre on Sunday night and told the audience that his 24-year-old pianist Dick Twardzik was dead." Two pages later, a reporter, Mike Navard, picked up the theme in his review. Navard obviously spent the evening watching Baker intently for signs of grief. "He walks confidently across the stage, skirts the music stands, makes a little bow, and faces the audience," he wrote (1955: 3). "His first words were a shock. White-faced, he clenched the microphone and announced that his pianist was dead." But Navard's next observation was also a shock. "For any normal jazz show, this would have put a blanket on the rest of the evening. For Chet Baker, it did not."

Baker, accompanied by Fol with two Englishmen from Tony Crombie's orchestra, Lennie Bush on bass and Crombie himself on drums (who had also accompanied Gullin in his 20-minute set), sang four songs: *This Is Always, My Funny Valentine, Someone to Watch Over Me,* and *But Not For Me.* Navard found Baker totally dispassionate even under microscopic scrutiny. "At one point, he stood watching Raymond Fol's hands caressing the keys," Navard said. "His mouth tightened and he swallowed. He bit his lip, flexed his shoulders and went on singing."

If you want grief, Navard seems to say, you should look at the audience instead of Chet Baker. "An air of compassion aided rather than hindered the mood," he noted. For the onlookers, Baker's "dark grey suit with black lapels heightened the air of tragedy. I suppose the structure of the human mind provides us all with a ghoulish streak; perhaps this is what gave his singing a strange fascination."

Navard makes it clear that Baker's truncated set had nothing to do with his personal feelings. "When he announced that the four numbers completed his programme, the audience respectfully restrained from comment. There were no yells for more; no shouts of encore," he said. "But this was because of [the audience's] realization of his personal difficulties. He had only worked out four numbers with his new pianist; there had not been time to rehearse more."

The *Melody Maker* obituary, the first for Twardzik and one of very few (Anonymous 1955), noted that Baker, Fol and Gullin had spent the Saturday night before the concert at the Flamingo Club in Leicester Square, where he had performed with Twardzik in the band ten days before.

The day after the London festival, 24 October, and the next day too, Baker was back in Paris at the Pathé-Magellan Studio working on the contract obligations that Twardzik's death had interrupted. Jimmy Bond, though absent in London, was there, but the other musicians were Europeans. The first day, with a quartet, they recorded eight standards, more than a full LP, using the kind of repertoire that seasoned jazz players can reel off even if they hardly know one another. The last tune of the day was *I'll Remember April*, but there is no way of knowing whether Baker or the others were aware of the association of that tune with Twardzik.

The next day, with a couple of horns added, they managed four titles including three originals. The last one on this day was entitled *In Memory of Dick*, in a minor mood but more eulogy than dirge, composed and arranged by Bobby Jaspar, the Belgian tenor saxophone player who had opened for the Baker Quartet at Salle Pleyel. Two months later, Jaspar himself would record a more polished version of the same eulogy with his own quintet in the same Paris studio (reissued on Bobby Jaspar

au club St-Germain, Gitanes 941 [2000]). The year after this, 1956, Jaspar
would venture out and make a name for himself in New York (and he
would die of misadventure at 37 in 1963).

Lars Gullin never did record with Baker in the Pathé-Magellan Studio
as he was waiting to do when Twardzik's body was found. Immediately
after, he had to stay nearby because of his booking two days later at the
Stoll Theatre in London, where he played with an English rhythm section before Baker. The *Melody Maker* reviewer had no way of knowing
how intimately Lars Gullin had been associated with Twardzik in the
week leading up to his death. Of Gullin's performance in London, he
wrote, "He was not playing as well as usual, but nevertheless worked
cleanly through his repertoire" (Navard 1955: 3). That innocuous cri-
tique may speak volumes about the depth of Gullin's grief. He seems
to have returned to Sweden immediately after. He never talked about
Twardzik's death, as far as I have been able to discover.

Jimmy Bond returned to the United States a month later, in November. Peter Littman was reportedly on his way back to America, according to the *Melody Maker* obituary, two days after Twardzik's death. That
information presumably came from Baker, and it appears to be wishful
thinking on his part. Although Littman was neither at the London
concert nor in the recording studio that following week, he stayed in
Europe and played with Baker for a month after that. "I fired Peter
during a concert at an Army base outside Paris," Baker (1997: 72) said.
"He was acting too strange."

Crystal Joy ran into Littman soon after he returned to the States. She
was in Boston visiting her parents, and she went around to the Stable.
"Peter Littman got out of a car, and we were just so glad to see one
another, we fell into one another's arms and we hugged," she said. You
had good feelings about him? I asked. "It was a link to Dick," she said.
"I remembered how much Dick loved him."

Baker roamed around Europe as an itinerant trumpet player for more
than five months afterwards, performing in France, Italy, Iceland, Sweden, Denmark, West Germany and Belgium. He finally returned to the
States at the beginning of April 1956, after breaking up with Liliane
Cukier. He had been away eight months. Jimmy Bond and Peter Littman rejoined his working band when he got back. His first recording
for Pacific Jazz after his return, in July 1956, had some unintended

tailings of the scant time that Twardzik had spent in the band. *Chet Baker and Crew* (Pacific Jazz CD 81205 [1993]) not only had the three survivors from that Quartet but it also added a pair of new Zieff compositions, *Slightly Above Moderate* and *Medium Rock*.

Neither Bond nor Littman stayed long with Baker. Both settled in Los Angeles, but they went their separate ways. Bond became a successful realtor and played his bass sporadically; he showed up occasionally in pick-up bands, sometimes surprisingly (as, for instance, at the Monterey Jazz Festival in 1963 playing with Jack Teagarden and his family). Littman disappeared. Baker's biographer, Jeroen de Valk, heard that he was serving gas in Los Angeles in the 1990s, but could not track him down.

Baker carried on unperturbed in the immediate aftermath of Twardzik's death. "I was trying to keep busy," he said (1997: 72). Many people took his outward calm for lack of feeling. Almost thirty years later, he said, "Dick's overdose totally destroyed me. Destroyed me. Dick's parents felt it was my fault, even though I was completely unaware of the situation" (Reece 1984: 136). But it had to be admitted, in his everyday demeanor he hid his hurt very well.

For the rest of his days, he wandered around like a person possessed. That first European tour, to an outsider's eyes fretted with uncertainties, discomfort, squalor and tragedy, seemed to cast a spell over him. He developed a taste for speedballs, injectable cocktails of cocaine and heroin. He was arrested in California, Italy, France, and several other places. Phil Urso, who played saxophone in Baker's bands off and on, thought some of his problems with the police could be traced back to Twardzik's death. "Plainclothesmen...were always asking Chet to step outside and have a talk with him," Urso said, in a rambling memoir. "I call it blatant harassment, he hadn't done anything wrong and it wasn't his fault that Richard Twardzik had o.d.'d and killed himself in Paris. Chet was very upset & called Twardzik's Mom & Dad how sorry he was" (Sjøgren 1993: 65).

Baker lost his matinée-idol looks. In 1969 his teeth rotted—Baker said five thugs knocked them out—and when he returned to playing a few years later it was as if his face had started caving in. He became prematurely wrinkled, and the lines on his face looked like a road map of a bad trip. His dentures clicked when he sang. One reviewer said, "He looked like he was dying from a cumulative overdose" (Davis 1990: 223). A documentary about him in the last year of his life, *Let's Get Lost* (Weber 1988), owes most of its dramatic power to juxtaposing the worn-out husk of his present self and the beautiful boy he used to be.

Somehow, through it all, he kept his cool. He remained insouciant, laconic, imperturbable. Admirers—mainly European men and American women— lined up to take care of him. His music never entirely abandoned him. He could always find the right notes, though by the end he had fewer to choose from. He left behind hundreds of hours of recordings, often bartering them for his next speedball. It is surprising how good many of them are. His trumpet playing became clichéd, but they were clichés he had invented, and his singing became monotonal, but the sight of him leaning into the microphone, eyes clenched shut, concentrating on hitting the note, carried its own eccentric thrill. He was still playing until the day before he jumped or fell to his death from the window of his hotel room in Amsterdam in May 1988. He was 58.

For Richard Twardzik, dead at 24, the legacy is miniscule. The recordings he left behind are little known but they have never been exactly neglected. Everyone who ever hears *A Crutch for the Crab* admires it. Hundreds of listeners find it indelible, tattooed on their minds. Much more of his music is available now than ever before. Besides *A Crutch for the Crab*, we can count *The Girl from Greenland*, *Albuquerque Social Swim*, *Yellow Tango* and *The Fable of Mabel* in his short list of masterworks. Herb Pomeroy chooses *Bess You Is My Woman Now* from the trio album when he wants to introduce people to Twardzik's music. Every lick he plays with Chet Baker on Bob Zieff's tunes rings with the joy of invention. Now we know there is even more. We can exalt in the richly contrasting versions of *Bess You Is My Woman Now* with the *Boston All Stars* and on his own piano record, and his filigree brilliance on Mariano's *Erosong* with the *Boston All Stars*, and his tempo-doubling extravaganza on *Don't Blame Me* with Mingus walking stodgily behind him, and his crazy eight-bar fugue on *All the Things You Are* at Mainz. His music has aged well. If it is too much to hope it might be played by new hands, invested with fresh sensibilities and spun into new silk, at least the originals will always be with us.

Some 50 years after he died, I have finally heard nearly all that Dick Twardzik left behind. There are a few more performances still to come, amounting to a couple of hours of music. When they come, I will happily strain my ears to catch what Twardzik plays through the tape hiss and audience noise and other impediments that go along with homemade recordings. But the sense of urgency is gone.

We have the best of what he left now. And it amounts to much more music than I ever dreamed there would be when I heard that first two-minute excerpt of *A Crutch for the Crab* with his obituary superimposed on it. Hearing it all makes it clearer than ever that it is still not enough.

15 "Regarding Disposition Remains"

Clare was alone in the kitchen on Saturday morning, 22 October 1955, when the phone rang. The house was still unfamiliar to her in many ways. She and Henryk had moved to West Newbury in September, less than two months before. There was a lot to get used to. It was a rambling Early American structure that Clare's sister Roz remembered as "a typically tall dark house surrounded by meadows and rolling hills with a pond beyond."

They had moved in just before their son Richard had left for Europe. In fact, Richard had never set foot in it, busy as he was on the tour with Serge Chaloff before he left. But he knew the address. He had sent Clare a postcard from Strasbourg about a week before addressed to her at "Middle St./ W. Newbury Mass./U.S.A." His other postcard to her, the one he sent her the day before that one, he had addressed to her work address at MIT, and the two he sent to Henryk at the same time both went to Henryk's work address, so until her second postcard arrived she had wondered if he even *knew* the new address.

Of course, they had discussed the move with him, especially because he loved Fowler House, the old mansion they had lived in and taken care of for more than eight years in Danvers. And he had been really positive about the move. In fact, as Roz remembered, he had promised to pay some of the expenses. It was the least he could do after all they had been through, he said, now that he was working steady for good money. West Newbury, Massachusetts, was 15 miles north of Danvers, and that much further from Boston, but still on Interstate 95, so only 15 minutes longer in commuting time.

Richard had been, at the time he made that promise, clean and feeling good about himself, preparing for a two-month tour with his old friends, and looking forward to a big-league venture into Europe with Chet Baker. His trio LP on Pacific Jazz would be released soon, and Baker promised they would makes lots of new recordings. Things were definitely looking up.

When the telephone rang, Clare might have wondered who would be calling when she knew so few people in town. The voice on the other end was serious, not unfriendly but businesslike. It was long distance. It was a telegram from the Department of State addressed to Mr. Henryk Twardzik. Henryk was in Buffalo, visiting relatives, Clare said. The telegram could not be delivered until Monday but the voice on the other end was authorized to read it to Mrs. Twardzik, if she wished. This is what it said, verbatim:

"Department regrets to inform you according message from American Embassy in Paris death your son Richard Henryk Twardzik Paris October 21. Department requires immediate information your wishes regarding disposition remains.

"Estimated cost local interment $250 if cremated $300. Shipment remains New York embalmed $1,300 cremated $350. Deposit funds payable Department of State."

It was signed "Francis E. Flaherty, Assistant Director, Office of Special Consular Services." A date-stamp shows the telegram had been received in the consulate office at 10:39 a. m. The telephone call came to Clare around noon.

Clare remembered nothing else that afternoon, according to both her sisters, until a pot on the stove boiled dry. Her younger sister Roz wrote, "Her familiar Revere saucepan rocked dry of soup on the kitchen electric stove and sizzled to a cinder." It was early evening when Clare phoned the Brehauts in Danvers. Elaine was alone in the house when the call came, on a short visit before going back to Texas and her new husband. Dick had had a "heart attack" in Paris and was dead, Clare said. She wondered if Bree would be kind enough to meet Henryk at the station in Boston and drive him to West Newbury. The minute her parents got home, her father drove directly to Clare's house and let off Elaine and her mother, and he carried on to Boston.

Several days later, a letter arrived from the American Embassy, on Avenue Gabriel in Paris, over the signature of John R. Wood, the American Consul. It was written on 24 October but received some days later, perhaps as late as 4 November, the date stamped on the copy that went to the Department of State. It offered some details about the circumstances surrounding Richard's death. It noted that on his passport, he had not filled in the contingency details— "the name and address of the person to be notified in case of accident or death"—and so the embassy had had to track down Henryk through their Washington channels before it could send the telegram.

Clare was angry at the time it took for the Embassy to follow up, but Henryk just frowned and said that with the recent change of address and all, it was a wonder the delay wasn't longer.

The Consul's letter made numerous official queries about possible kin (spouse, children, mother, brothers, sisters), and it included one paragraph with the official account of the death:

> From information obtained from the local police and the hotel proprietor, Mr. Twardzik had taken a room at the Hôtel de la Madeleine at about 2:30 p.m., Friday, October 21st, at about 2:30 p.m. [*sic*]. He had gone up to his room stating that he was going to have a rest. A friend with whom he had an appointment at 4 p.m. later called up to inquire why he had not appeared. An employee of the hotel went to Mr. Twardzik's room and found him dead, his body lying on the floor. A doctor was called but could only certify that your son was dead.

The letter went on to say that, "at the request of the French authorities, the remains were taken on Saturday afternoon to the Medico-Legal Institute ('Morgue') for an autopsy in order to ascertain the cause of death." The Twardziks would be informed of the exact cause when it was known, and they were assured that the Embassy was holding Richard's effects for safekeeping.

No one has ever explained how Richard spent the hours after leaving the jam session at Club Tabu as the sun was rising and checking into his hotel at 2:30 p.m. It was not a question the Twardziks would think to ask, because they had no way of knowing about Richard's movements on the day of his death.

They did ask other questions. By the time they received the Consul's letter, both Clare and Henryk had already responded to the telegram. Clare sent a letter on 28 October that crossed with the Embassy letter, demanding further details about her son's death. In a letter dated 9 November, the Consul replied: "According to a certificate issued by Dr. Georges Dhers, 113 Boulevard St-Germain, Paris, who was called upon to examine the body and who had access to the autopsy findings, your son died following an intra-veinous [*sic*] injection (probably heroin). His death appears to have been instantaneous."

The rest of this letter was taken up mainly with inquiries about Richard's possessions—whether there was a will, and, if not, the two legal procedures that the parents could follow to claim his possessions. It then added, "In view, however, of the small intrinsic value of your son's estate, if it is not possible for you to furnish the above mentioned documents, an affidavit corroborated by the sworn statements of two attesting witnesses familiar with the facts of this case, may be substituted." It also asks the Twardziks to make arrangements with a shipping company like American Express for the return of the possessions if they choose to claim them, or to authorize the Embassy to turn them over to a charitable organization like the American Aid Society of Paris if they were not going to claim them. Attached was an "Inventory of the Personal Effects of Richard Henryk Twardzik, Deceased."

The Twardziks instructed the Embassy to turn them over to charity.

Around the same time, Clare must have sent a letter to Chet Baker. Her mind fastened on the Consul's mention of "a friend," Richard's unnamed friend with whom he had a four-o-clock appointment that fateful afternoon. "Where was 'his friend' in the long waning hours before they discovered Dick Twardzik?" Clare asked over and over, Roz remembered, and then "Clare pursed her lips and shook her fist as helplessly as she had done years earlier when one shot of penicillin would have prolonged his life." Her unanswerable question must have been directed first of all at Henryk, and perhaps Henryk suggested that she should put it to Chet Baker himself in hopes of purging it from her mind once and for all.

So she wrote to Baker, and he was spooked by her letter—"Dick's parents felt it was my fault," he said—but he did not have the mother-wit to reply, even though he might have been able to salve his conscience by telling Clare that it was Jimmy Bond, not he, who failed to give him the wake-up call, or that it was Peter Littman who forgot to do it and had to go back, or that it was not his fault, above all, because he was so hopelessly ignorant about drugs. "If I had only been a little hipper, I might have been able to prevent what was soon to happen," he said later (1997: 70). Maybe if he had declared his innocence to Clare it would have helped both of them to come to terms with Dick's death, but perhaps it only occurred to him a few years later, when he had to try to convince himself. Maybe he should have been honest and admitted his helplessness. Dumb silence did no one any good.

Admitting he was helpless worked for Herb Pomeroy, though it took a few years. Pomeroy had left Twardzik in Washington in August, at the end of the Chaloff tour. They shook hands, and Pomeroy wished his friend and roommate well on the European trip. He envied him, he said. Two months later, Twardzik was dead. "As a younger person you think 'what could I have said or done to help?'" Pomeroy said (Gross 1998: 9). "As I have grown up I realize there was nothing I could have done about it. When he left Serge's group he was clean to the best of my knowledge." Pomeroy has visited Twardzik's grave once or twice a year ever since.

Henryk sent a telegram to the Embassy on 30 October answering their queries regarding the disposition of Richard's remains. His delay was not negligent, far from it. His first thought, when he started to think straight, was that he did not want the body or the ashes shipped back like freight. Richard's cousin, John Jones, June's son, was in the Army serving his draft. He had deferred his service until after he graduated from Boston College in June, and that fall he was in boot camp at Fort Dix, New Jersey. Henryk made a humanitarian request to John's superior officers, asking them to detail him to go to France and accompany his cousin's remains back to Boston. Their refusal took a few days to get back to him and it deepened his despair, but at least he could go ahead and make other arrangements.

Henryk then turned the matter over to a firm of funeral directors in Amesbury, the nearest big town to West Newbury with its own mortuary services. Richard's ashes, as the Consul's letter said, "were shipped from Orly Airport (Paris) to Boston, Massachusetts, on November 8th, via the Trans World Airlines, Flight 921," and consigned to the funeral directors "Messrs. Dean and Pillsbury, Amesbury Massachusetts."

With the urgent decisions out of the way, Henryk gave in to his grief. His doodling, as he sat around in the quiet recesses of the big house, turned to graves and epitaphs. It was what was on his mind. His pencil sketches found the form and content he wanted for his boy so quickly that he did not bother going to get his sketchpad. He made sketches on whatever scrap of paper was nearby. One of the best, a gravestone with graceful lines, is drawn on an MIT telephone message pad (15.1). At the top of the gravestone, Henryk drew a treble clef and a few notes as a kind of motif. Under that, "Richard Henryk Twardzik," and then the heartbreaking numbers, "1931–1955." And then, so there would be, as Dickie once said about Mabel, not too sad an ending, the mollifying refrain of the 33rd Psalm: "Sing unto him a new song/ Play skillfully with a loud noise."

Designing the gravestone helped, but it was not enough. Sometime in the grieving period, probably in the days immediately following the death but certainly carrying on for many months beyond, Henryk decided he would make a bronze bust of his son. He would immortalize him with the kind of solid, indestructible monument usually reserved for kings and heroes. He began with pencil sketches, detailing the physiognomy he had drawn countless times in numerous guises for 24 years

[illustration 15.1] Pencil sketch of gravestone and epitaph by Henryk Twardzik on MIT telephone message pad, late October–early November 1955. From the Twardzik-Thompson Archive, courtesy of Rosamond Thompson and Jane Sumner. All rights reserved.

(15.2). This time there was a new challenge posed by the new medium, for he had not worked in sculpture since his student days, and he knew he had three dimensions to capture this time.

When he was satisfied with the sketches, he started the tedious build-up of clay, working into the night, laying damp cloths on each day's work to keep it from drying out, savoring in the end the telling details, scooping out a thumbprint of clay from the cheekbones, building up the high forehead, adjusting the chin ever so slightly, the unassertive chin. When he finished the clay model, he had it bronzed, and when he saw it he was immensely proud of it (15.3). He photographed it from several angles, adjusting the light and shadow on it. He took the film to a good developing company and had multiple prints made.

The hard labor of making the bust seemed to serve Henryk's needs. The sweat in the humid room, the grit of the clay drying under his fingernails, the slow emergence of his son's likeness from the clammy earthen substance— all these things kept the heartbreak in check. Like

[illustration 15.2] Pencil sketch for bust of Richard Twardzik by Henryk Twardzik. From the Twardzik-Thompson Archive, courtesy of Rosamond Thompson and Jane Sumner. All rights reserved.

Henryk's oil paintings, the bust was never put on public display. When Henryk died, it was in a corner of his living room, visible amid some clutter but not prominent, and the glossy photographs he had taken of it were stashed in a drawer.

Here's your baby. Don't ask for any more.

On 14 November 1955, Clare and Henryk buried their son's ashes in the West Newbury cemetery on a knoll protected by large old trees. It happened to be the day after Clare's birthday. This year, as Clare turned 49, there would be no birthday party, and no masking the sense of mortality that birthdays inevitably bring closer. Roz remembers mainly the silence in the cemetery on the gray morning, and Clare and Henryk stepping out of the small gathering of onlookers to toss a handful of dirt into the hollow where the urn of ashes was deposited. In time, though not very soon (24 years later for Clare, 34 for Henryk), their own graves would flank their only child.

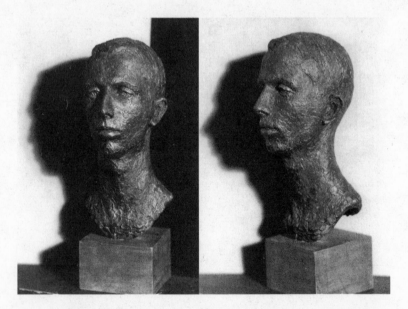

[illustration 15.3] Bust of Richard Twardzik in two views, by Henryk Twardzik. From the Twardzik-Thompson Archive, courtesy of Rosamond Thompson and Jane Sumner. All rights reserved.

Afterwards, back at the house, Clare wondered about a young woman they had seen on the edge of the crowd at the grave. She had not returned with the other mourners to the house. "Had she been left out only to disappear, the girl from Greenland wearing boots and a parka of grey skin with a hood widely banded in fox at the face and the knees?" Roz wondered. "We never saw her again." When I cross-examined Roz about who it was she had seen, she became defensive. "The Girl from Greenland was *not* an apparition," she said. "Clare saw her and mentioned it later on when people were gathering at the house. She should have been invited to join in but Clare was too distraught while at the same time affirming what a good idea it is to have a gathering of friends because you feel so terrible."

Perhaps it was Reba Stewart. It was not Crystal Joy.

Crystal Joy got a phone call in New York from Serge Chaloff *after* the funeral service. Until then, she knew nothing about Richard's death. She had heard nothing. "Serge called," Crystal Joy told me. "He said, 'He died. It's all over.' And I said why didn't they let me know. Serge said they thought I'd be too upset."

She was upset, of course, the more so for being excluded. She longed to know more, to be involved somehow in the end. She got her uncle Frank to take her to the French Embassy in New York and together they pored over the French newspapers searching for an obituary or a news story. Anything. "We looked through all the papers they had," she said. "Of course, we didn't really know what we were looking for. We kept looking until they kicked us out of there" at closing time.

"It was very hard for me to believe, just having heard from him a few days before, or maybe a week," she says. "But I knew something, I had a premonition that something was wrong then."

She assumed that Serge Chaloff was acting on Clare's orders in holding the news back from her until after the funeral. But she did not blame Chaloff. She was not a person who held grudges anyway. On her trips back to Boston to visit her parents, she took to dropping in at Serge's apartment. That was how she came to take a few piano lessons from his mother. When the cancer took hold of him, she visited him regularly. She fixed up a room for his wife Susie Black in her parents' capacious house, and she accompanied Serge in his wheelchair when he went to New York for his final recording session with the old Four Brothers.

She did not blame Peter Littman either. The only time they met after Dick's death, she embraced him and wept on his shoulder.

Her sympathy does not extend to Clare Twardzik, and not only for withholding the news of Dick's death from her. "She was cold to him," she says. "He was a warm person, and he needed warmth from other people. She was cold to me too. If she'd been warmer to me, then maybe, together, we might have been able to get him away from the course he was on. He was a loving person. He was very affectionate. And I think his father knew that he needed that, and tried to make up for it."

Perhaps because she missed out on the grieving, Dick's death remains an open spiritual wound for her. Forty-eight years later, after a rich life and a long sustained career, Crystal Joy reacts to a question that I intend as an innocuous request for facts by saying, "Please don't make me suffer through this relationship again."

There is no closure, apparently, not when the life that ends is so obviously incomplete. If Clare Twardzik succeeded in showing the world a mask after Dick's death, it was probably because she had had a few years of practice in the last years of his life.

You had to get closer to see that it was only a mask. But of course it was. Dickie was, after all, *her* genius first—"the son," she said in her memento mori, "the sun—the bird—the lark the fallen lark the doomed one."

Henryk presumably saw the depth of her hurt, but he was not a man for words. Clare's youngest sister, across a gulf of age and miles, caught glimpses. Roz wrote about Clare: "Hours of sleepless nights were filled with planning rooms of dark oaken furniture, cupboards with tankards of pewter, faded Persian rugs in front of a massive door with iron latch opening out onto a shaded trellis. She traveled the antique circuit and trotted awkwardly with a German Shepherd at the Westminster Dog Show."

"Not a day goes by that I don't think of him," Clare confided, though Roz says she "continued to travel the good life between dips in fortune. Sometimes with Henryk, or sometimes accompanied by Jane [Roz's daughter] to France, they traveled to out-of-the-way cathedrals, sitting quietly in wooden French pews where Dick had sat so many years before."

One of the items Clare listed in her memoir as a reminder of Dickie's childhood things is "Ducky lucky bowl." After his death, Clare used the bowl nightly, until the end. Roz says, "As her weakened life began fading, she forgave us all, one at a time, forgetting now and then to eat cornflakes at bedtime from his little pewter saucer with the triangular filigree handle."

Clare died in 1979. Henryk survived her by a decade. He joined the Newburyport Art Association and exhibited a few paintings, Roz says, "but when his loneliness and fortune both tailspinned, he sold the dark house on the hill for a song."

Richard Twardzik's ashes were in the ground almost four months when the American Consulate filed its last official document on the case, "Report on the Death of an American Citizen" (15.4). It contained nothing that his parents did not already know, but there was a sense of finality about it, the closing of the file, that must have seemed welcome.

Attached to the report as a kind of appendix was the "Inventory of Personal Effects." It listed all of Dick's earthly possessions at the moment of his death. Most of us do not meet death so publicly that we have the sum total of our belongings itemized and evaluated by strangers. Richard Twardzik's inventory is, for the most part, a mundane list, as it would be for anyone. There were no music manuscripts on the list. And no drugs or paraphernalia. Whatever he might have had in his possession along those lines was removed, either by his friends or by the consulate staff.

The other obvious gaps in the inventory were purposeful. Richard Twardzik carried a wardrobe befitting an itinerant musician who has to make concessions to portability. No bathrobe or slippers. Not even pajamas. Three pairs of undershorts, one torn, three handkerchiefs, but nine pairs of socks, all valued by the Embassy's appraisers at nil. A minimal toilet kit (toothbrush, razor, hair brush, face cloth), with no special vanities, also valued at nil. There were three shirts, one a maroon sport shirt and the others a blue and a white dress shirt, and three ties, also valued at nil. It was the outerwear that carried some value, in the appraiser's reckoning: a navy blue summer suit ($10), grey lightweight

suit jacket ($3), and black topcoat ($2). Oddly, there was no other pair
of pants on the list, such as might be worn with a grey lightweight
suit jacket, which probably means that the evaluators did not itemize
the clothes that Twardzik died in and was transported to the Morgue
in. So there were no shoes at all on the list. The brown suitcase in
which he carried these things from Paris to Amsterdam to Geneva
and back again had damaged handles and was valued at nil. Twardzik
had a silver money clip and a leather billfold containing various cards,
nil value. There were 4,000 francs among his effects, the only money

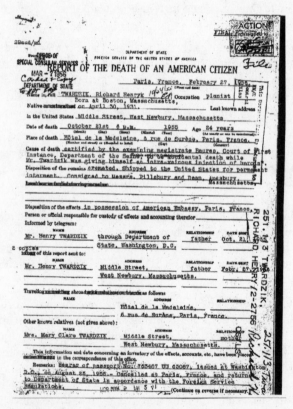

[illustration 15.4] Report of the Death of an American Citizen (2 pages), the last
official government document on Richard Twardzik's death, February–March 1956.
From the Twardzik-Thompson Archive, courtesy of Rosamond Thompson and Jane
Sumner. All rights reserved.

he had, with an exchange value in 1955 of $11.43. The total value of Twardzik's possessions, including his cash, amounted to $34.43.

Ultimately, the list includes some items that lend personality to Richard Twardzik. One pair of sunglasses, that could be worn onstage under bright lights when the eyeballs were dilated, one of the side-effects of analgesics made from poppies, but of course they were worn indoors and out for reasons of style too, a bebop affectation, so cats would *think* you had smack in your veins. There was a black umbrella ($3) and a plaid vest ($3) and a wool beret ($1), egghead trappings every bit as unambiguous as were the books jutting out of his overcoat pocket or spread open on his chest as he dozed on the train.

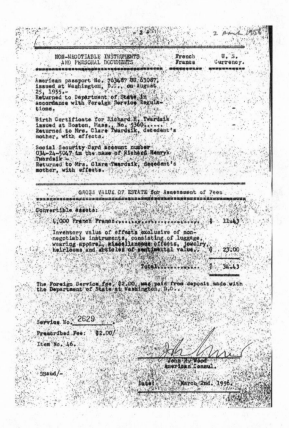

On the day he died, Richard had two books in his possession: *The State of Music* by Virgil Thompson and *Our New Music* by Aaron Copland (value of both, $1). Heavy reading. Deep thinking. Here, finally, is hint of something deeper than skin-deep. Everything else is mere surface.

Where is the real Richard Henryk Twardzik in all this? Where is Dick Twardzik? Where is Dickie?

Did he have a moment to think after he sank the fatal spike in the crook of his arm? A momentary thought. A moment, we hope with all our hearts, like eternity. The world, the universe in that final eye-blink.

What thought?

My best I gave/did not give. There is so much more/no more. The music I heard deep inside since the day I was born, nice music, why did it lurk so deep? I dredged it up, all I could. Released it into the air. Sent it out on waves. Swimming. Crab-like.

Give us more, they said. There must be more where that came from, they said. Give us the rest, they said. And there was more, much more. If only I could get to it down deep.

Help me get down deep, I pray. I am lame. If I must travel alone (most of the time), give me a crutch. Give me a divine crutch.

Aaah, there, now I hear it. Do I hear it? I hear it. How does it go? Aaah gone.

Silence.

Nice music.

Afterword
"Not Too Sad an Ending"

Do not make echoes of forgotten time,
Do not strike music from old broken keys,
Do not make ghosts
With faded tinklings on the yellowed board;
But play us a tune on an unbroken spinet,
Play lively music

Thomas Wolfe, "Play Us a Tune," *A Stone, A Leaf, A Door* (1945)

In 1997, I thought there was no more for me to learn about Richard Twardzik, and I set out to make a final accounting of what I knew. I had spent some fifteen years after 1956 listening to the same pieces of his music, and then in the 1970s I may have gone ten years or so without listening at all because I knew every note by heart. Then in the 1990s there was more music, as the obscure Boston-based LPs came out in digital versions.

So in 1997 I gathered together all the information on the music that was finally available—the hard-to-find LPs now in CD (*New Sounds from Boston, Boston All Stars, The Fable of Mabel*), the performance CDs (Charlie Parker in Boston, Chet Baker in Mainz), and Peter Morris's astonishing *1954 Improvisations*—and I wrote what I hoped would be a balanced appraisal in a bio-discography, and sent it off to *Coda* magazine.

I had been writing for *Coda*, off and on, since 1972, and Bill Smith was editor or co-editor all those years. (He retired in 2001.) Besides editing the magazine, Bill is a photographer, filmmaker, writer, free-form musician, and free spirit. As well as I know him, I have never flattered myself into thinking that I can guess how he will respond to anything, but I have to admit I was surprised when he sent a curt reply that the article was too long and anyway he wasn't interested in an article about someone for whom there was only one known photograph. Bill often chided us writers for filling the pages of the magazine with articles about "dead guys," and my guess is that the long-deadness of Richard Twardzik may have figured in his reaction.

At the very moment that I got his reply, I was working with a research assistant updating the linguistics side of my website, and in my slightly stunned reaction to Bill's reply I decided on an impulse to post the Twardzik stuff on the jazz side of the website. I thought of it as a kind of temporary holding place until I could get back to it.

To my surprise, I immediately started to receive e-mail about it. Most of the letters were fan notes, and they were very gratifying. Dr. Joseph Roberts wrote, "I ran into Richard Twardzik unexpectedly when in college I purchased a Russ Freeman recording and he was on the reverse side. This wonderful recording stayed in my mind forever." Some others made corrections and additions. They came from all over the world. One of them I called the "Amsterdam Blitzkrieg" because the correspondent was so relentless.

My main goal in writing the article, as for the book, was to get serious listeners interested in discovering the wonders of Richard Twardzik's music. Some of the e-mail I was getting made it clear that I was succeeding. But what I discovered was that I was also providing a focal point for an international fellowship of people who already knew those wonders and had never found a public occasion for celebrating them. Clarke Harris wrote, "Until I saw your website, I thought Richard Twardzik was a figment of my imagination."

The most gratifying moment came when I opened an e-mail message and read this:"Hello Jack! I am a second cousin of Dick; my Dad, John Jones, was his first cousin. What a joy it was to review your complete/ incomplete works page!" It was from Steve Jones, and after offering a bit of information about his family, he wrote, "I'll close with a 'Thank You' for getting all this info out there. I'm anxious to share this info with my Mom and others."

I wrote back immediately. I told Steve Jones that he had finally solved an old mystery for me. I now understood why all my efforts at tracking down the family had failed. I was searching for Twardziks when all the time I should have going after Joneses. I was only half-joking.

Almost 25 years earlier, when all of Richard Twardzik's records were out of print and there was absolutely nothing by him available for the new generation to hear, I had taken some steps to try and get his recordings back in print. One of the things I did was look up Twardziks in Massachusetts telephone directories. This was long before the worldwide web, and the best resource I could find was the fairly haphazard collection of phone books in the University of Toronto reference room. I found two listings, one for a Joseph Twardzik in Aldenville and another for Mitzie S. Twardzik in Chicopee Falls. I sent each of them a personal letter on 22 January 1975 that said this:

> I am trying to locate the immediate family of Richard Twardzik, the pianist from Boston who died in Paris in 1955 at the age of twenty-four.

> You are one of only two listings that I have been able to find in Massachusetts phone directories with the surname Twardzik. I am hoping that you will be able to supply me with some information about the family, if you are not yourself a member of it.

> My purpose is pure and simple. I remember the recordings of Richard Twardzik, and the considerable promise he showed before his early death. Most people have forgotten him entirely or never knew about him at all. I would like to try to restore his reputation as a jazz musician, at least to the point where his recordings might be reissued again.

> If I can get the approval and cooperation of the immediate family, I will begin research on a biography. Whether it will be a full-scale book-length biography or something less ambitious will depend on several factors, especially the attitude of the family.

> I am a jazz writer by avocation, contributing regularly to the magazine *Coda* and irregularly to the Toronto *Globe and Mail*. By profession, I am a linguist at the University of Toronto. (I will make a fuller identification of myself to the family when my contact is certain.)

> This letter may, of course, be meaningless to you, but at least your surname is somewhat less common than, say, Smith, and I feel that there is at least a 50-50 chance that you are related to, or know of,

the Twardziks I am trying to locate. I would appreciate it if you would let me know one way or the other.

I sent the letters on University letterhead hoping the folks would know I was not a nutcase or a necromancer. I guess it didn't work. Neither of them replied.

Around the same time, I sent a letter to Charlie Lourie at United Artists proposing a double LP reissue in his new "twofer" series with the Charlie Mariano Prestige tracks as well as the Pacific Jazz music. After some time, Lourie sent a vague reply addressed not to me but, egregiously, to one of my *Coda* editors.

I gave up on the whole venture.

Steve Jones's e-mail message in 1999 gave me the hope that there was indeed more for me to learn about Richard Twardzik. Through Steve, I met Richard's aunt Rosamond Thompson and her daughter Jane Sumner, Richard's first cousin. We started talking via e-mail, feeling one another out. I tried to find out how receptive they might be to someone digging up family skeletons. It gradually became clear that we were all more concerned about getting Richard's music into print than in any kind of personal interests.

It did not take long to realize that the living memories about Richard Twardzik were sketchy, 45 years after his death and even longer since the dispersal of the three families that made up his immediate family. But memory, luckily, was not all we had to depend on. Cousin Jane and Aunt Roz told me that, as executors of Henryk Twardzik's estate, they had rescued four cartons of personal effects from Henryk's house when he died in 1989, including some belongings of Richard. There were a lot of things, they said, all kinds—letters, drawings, clippings, music, photographs, and more.

I offered to catalogue it, or help them do it, and after a lot of four-way negotiation we converged on Jane's bungalow in backwoods New England in August 2000. Someone dubbed it the First International Richard Twardzik Conference, and the delegates included Roz and Jane, their dog Calli and their neighbor Jim, Steve and his wife Linda, their young son Austin and their one-week-old daughter Cassandra, Steve's mother, and my wife Sue and me. Steve's grandmother June,

Roz's sister (and Richard's aunt), was not well enough to travel, but she wished she could have, and she phoned every evening.

"I hope you aren't going to be too critical," Rosamond Thompson said to me on the morning of the second day of my visit. At the moment, my head was immersed in the artifacts that had survived more than four decades after Dick Twardzik's death. So she caught me off guard. Dick's Aunt Roz was 84, rheumy-eyed and slow afoot, but still the creative woman she had always been. That very spring she had finished writing and illustrating a book using an obsolete Macintosh toaster with a drawing program called MacPaint.

"Well," I said, afraid of setting off alarm bells that might lead her to show me the door, "at the very least I'm going to have to say that he squandered his talent, that he wasted it. "

"Why can't you say he made some wonderful music, and let it go at that?"

"I'll say that. That's what brought me here, the music he made, that's what it's all about," I said, and then I added, sotto voce, "But I can't let it go at that."

"Well, you don't need to be too critical," she said. "Dick had a wonderful sense of fun. That's how I remember him."

It occurred to me that Roz views her nephew with an artist's eye as well as an aunt's. Not a biographer's. In the family setting, Steve Jones understood and, I think, shared my sense of the job that lay ahead. Some feelings might get hurt, some lace-curtain-Irish proprieties might get smudged. Steve worked with me classifying documents, transcribing some of the letters on Jane's Macintosh computer, trying to fit them into sequence. (He has also been good at tracking down people who figure in Richard's story.) Jane has clerical skills too, and she also inherited the artistic sensibility that came to the fore in two generations of Grants, starting with her mother and her aunts. Jane combines art with craft. She retired early from classroom teaching, as a French teacher, in order to take up desktop publishing, designing and producing documents. She also works indefatigably at any number of crafts, doing magical things with flowers, clay, vegetables, paper, stones, or whatever else the season yields.

Bloodlines are capricious. There is no hope of understanding how this artistic sensibility gained ascendancy in two generations. There was no trace of it, according to Roz, in her parents, Dick's maternal grandparents. Neither showed the slightest aptitude for art or music, hardly even as spectators. But then it took root in two of their offspring, Clare and Roz, and might have in June, their other child, had June not bent her creative energies toward commerce. For Clare and Roz, their artistic interests as young women led them into a certain social milieu, and both ended up marrying artists. So in their offspring the bloodlines became more concentrated. And in Richard Twardzik it flowered into a creative bent that, in the moment of its bloom, few people in the world could rival, and into a creative output that, however miniscule, remains fresh and inspiring to this day.

For myself, I sometimes dare to think that being there among all Richard Twardzik's remaining blood relatives gave me a biographer's edge. I don't mean just the documents we catalogued, whose value for this book is huge but, I think, calculable. I mean being there, doing country things—singeing my arm hair with Steve at the barbeque, cajoling Roz to take another glass of wine at lunch, trying to keep up with Jane on the path to neighbor Jim's horse pasture, admiring the stars as we all walked down the lane on a pitch-black night. Those things humanize the documents. Only two of the people there, Roz and Jane, had actually known Dick—three counting June, who was there via telephone. Surrounded as I was by Richard Twardzik's surviving alleles at the same time that I was reading his letters from camp and postcards from Brussels surely contributed to what Herder called *Einfühlen*, my empathy for the long-dead boy and his long-gone days.

There were more living memories. Bob Zieff's memory I had been tapping off and on for years. With Steve's help, I eventually found the coterie of old Boston jazz musicians, and Nick Dean, one of Dick's best friends, and Crystal Joy, the love of his life. Elaine Marney, née Brehaut, whose parents were Clare and Henryk's best friends, found me accidentally in 2004 because she happened to extol Henryk's artistic talents, which led her daughter Cathy Dionne to google him on the internet.

Memories, after so many years, are piecemeal, but for the love of Dick, these people sat still while I prodded them for details, questioned their chronologies, and pleaded for more.

It was not always about the past. I got fresh news about Richard Twardzik soon after my visit to Jane's bungalow. I received in the mail a CD from the Netherlands called *A Crutch for the Crab*, by the Frank van Bommel Quartet (BCHaast 10235). The liner note by Jaap de Rijke acknowledged my Twardzik website, and I dare to hope that van Bommel's ambitious music took wing partly on the good karma that seems to have gone Twardzik's way ever since I posted my rejected typescript on that website.

Good karma is definitely a factor. It turned out that van Bommel's *A Crutch for the Crab* is an authentic gem, a delicate balance of harmonically astute arranging and passionate playing that is definitely worthy of Richard Twardzik. Van Bommel's interpretations of Twardzik not only preserve the subtleties of the originals but bring fresh insights to them. Van Bommel is a piano player trained at the Amsterdam Royal Sweelink Conservatory. He also studied privately with Misha Mengelberg, the venerable leader of the highly independent Dutch jazz movement. Although *A Crutch for the Crab* is van Bommel's first professional recording, he is now in his early forties, and his talent is mature.

On first listening to the CD, I found it hard to fathom that so much music could emanate from a quartet, but van Bommel works with solid rhythm partners in bassist Arjen Gorter and drummer Martin van Duynhoven, and they are fronted by tenor saxophonist Tobias Delius. Although I knew next to nothing about van Bommel when his CD arrived, I knew something about Delius from a tour he made of summer jazz festivals the year before, notably in Vancouver, where he stood out among a numbing parade of visiting players, many of them jazz stars. Delius has a vocalized sound on the tenor saxophone, assertive with a burr at the edges, almost cocky, and he is technically flawless, negotiating complex turns with precise intonation and unflagging confidence.

As it happened, Delius needed all his considerable gifts as the lead voice in this music. Seven of the 12 tracks on the CD are Van Bommel's original compositions, and he uses advanced harmonies and subtle counter-melodies in a way that, even if you were not clued in by his calling the CD *A Crutch for the Crab*, you could guess that he is an admirer of Twardzik's music.

The other five tracks on van Bommel's CD are the five extant compositions of Richard Twardzik. It is clear that van Bommel has learned from Twardzik's music, but it is equally clear that his own deep understanding enriches Twardzik's music and brings it brilliantly back to life. He does not re-create Twardzik but re-invents him, much the way that Gil Evans re-invented Gershwin's *Porgy and Bess* for Miles Davis. Parts originally played on Twardzik's recordings by the likes of Chet Baker and Serge Chaloff sound completely fresh, almost unfamiliar but congruous even played free, outside the changes, a concept that Twardzik was inching toward but never got to try because of his untimely death.

In jazz, as in all musical genres, the music only survives if new musicians breathe life into it—inspire it in the root sense (*in-spire*), literally respirate it. And it helps immeasurably when the new versions plumb its depths and seek new truths, as van Bommel's do. If enough people hear van Bommel's music, Twardzik may have a future after all. Better yet, if people listen to Twardzik's music with anything like the perspicacity van Bommel brought to it, his future is guaranteed.

It deserves that discerning audience. Herb Pomeroy, as educator and leader, saw that repeatedly. "After Dick died, there were a number of musicians I would come in contact with who had never heard of him, or had heard of him but had never heard his playing," Pomeroy said (Gross 1998). "I would play the trio recording and they would have a look of disbelief on their faces. I mean, it moves you to tears. It's art that just gets you churned up inside. You think, it's good to be alive."

We are dust, on the way to dust. Dust to dust. It is a home truth, the classic carpe diem, the old blues verity—

   You only live but once
   And when you're dead
   You're done.

Maybe not for Richard Twardzik. Maybe not, if your life is touched by genius. He may yet have a life.

That one's for you, Roz.

Discography: Recordings and Recorded Performances

Jazz discographers know, better than anyone, that there is no such thing as closure. More recorded performances might show up at any time.

Charlie Mariano, *The New Sounds from Boston*
Boston. December 1951
Sonny Truitt, tb; Charlie Mariano, as; Jim Clark, ts; Richard Twardzik, p; Jack Lawlor, b; Carl Goodwin, d.
•*Mariners* 3:34
Supervised by Ira Gitler. Prestige OJCCD-1745-2 [USA 1990]. Originally Prestige 130 (10″). On all other tracks, the piano player is Roy Frazee.

Serge Chaloff Quintet
Albany, New York. Spring 1952, WOKO Studio, Hotel Wellington
Possibly Sonny Truitt, tb (only on *Gabardine and Serge* and unidentified tune); Serge Chaloff, bs; Richard Twardzik, p; Jack Lawlor, b; Jimmy Weiner, d.
•*Love Is Just Around the Corner* unissued
•*Listen to Les*
•*Gabardine and Serge*
•unidentified tune
Details from Robert E. Sunenblick. Produced by Les Deuel, who used *Listen to Les*, a Chaloff original, as his theme on WOKO.

Charlie Parker, *The Happy Bird*
possibly Christy's Restaurant, Framingham, MA. possibly 8–14 December 1952
possibly Joe Gordon, tp; Charlie Parker, as; possibly Bill Wellington, ts; Richard Twardzik, p; Charles Mingus, b; Roy Haynes, d.
I'll Remember April 10:45
Collectables COL-5787 [1997]. Originally
Charlie Parker Records PLP404. Song title has invariably been listed as *I Remember April*.
Usually dated 12 or 17 April 1951 with Max Roach on drums, but that date is impossible; revised date and personnel from Robert Sunenblick's notes in Uptown UPCD 27.42 (1996; see next entry). It is equally possible, with so many unknowns, that the session took place in 3–9 March 1952, when Parker and Twardzik first met.

Charlie Parker, *Boston 1952*
Hi Hat, Boston. 14 December 1952
live broadcast, The Symphony Sid Show, WCOP
Joe Gordon, tp; Charlie Parker, as; Dick Twardzik, p; Charlie Mingus, b; Roy Haynes, d.
•Introduction by Symphony Sid Torin 0:54
•*Ornithology* 4:19
•*Cool Blues* 5:26
•*Groovin' High* 5:38
•Introduction of musicians by Torin 0:51
•*Don't Blame Me* 9:07
•*Scrapple from the Apple* 6:01
•*Cheryl* 5:27
•*Jumpin' with Symphony Sid* (theme with announcement by Ken Malden) 2:21
Produced by Robert E. Sunenblick, Uptown UPCD 27.42 [1996].

Charlie Mariano, *Boston All Stars*
Boston. 27 January 1953
Herb Pomeroy, tp; Charlie Mariano, as; Richard Twardzik, p; Bernie Griggs, b; Jimmy Weiner, d.
•*Bye Bye Blues* 4:42
•*I'm Old Fashioned* 3:00
•*Erosong* 3:42
•*Bess, You Is My Woman Now* 3:48
•*Barsac* 4:16
•*Stella by Starlight* 3:40
Supervised by Ira Gitler. Prestige OJCCD-1745-2 [USA 1990]. Originally Prestige 153 (10″). Gitler plays bells on *Barsac*.

Allen Eager Quartet
Hi Hat, Boston. 1 February 1953
live broadcast, The Symphony Sid Show, WBMS
Allen Eager, ts; Richard Twardzik, p; Bernie Griggs, b; Gene Glennon, d.
•*Jumpin' with Symphony Sid* 1:36
•*This Time the Dream's On Me* 4:59
•*Out of Nowhere* 5:03
•*Zootcase* (announced as *Oy Vey*) 4:43
•*Jumpin' with Symphony Sid* 1:46
Produced by Robert E. Sunenblick, on Allen Eager *In the Land of Oo-Bla-Dee 1947-1953*. Uptown UPCD 27.49 [2003]

Sam Margolis Quintet
Melody Lounge. Lynn, Mass. 11 October 1953, live broadcast, *The Symphony Sid Show*, WBMS
Dick Wetmore, tp; Sam Margolis, ts; Richard Twardzik, p; Whitney Cronin, b; Jimmy Zitano, d.
•Theme (unidentified)   unissued
•*Jumpin' at the Woodside*
•*Mean to Me*
•*Stompin' at the Savoy*
•Ballad medley: *Laura* (Twardzik with rhythm)/*Body and Soul*

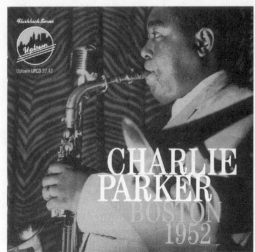

Uptown UPCD 27.42 [1996]

•*Caravan*
•*Round Midnight*
•*One O' Clock Jump*
•Theme
Details from Robert E. Sunenblick.

Serge Chaloff, *The Fable of Mabel*
Boston. 3 September 1954
Herb Pomeroy, Nick Capazutto, tp; Gene DiStachio, tb; Charlie Mariano, as; Varty
Haritounian, ts; Chaloff, bs; Richard Twardzik, p; Ray Oliveri, b; Jimmy Zitano, d.
•*The Fable of Mabel* (master take) 4:15
•*The Fable of Mabel* (take 2 previously unissued) 4:28
•*The Fable of Mabel* (take 3 previously unissued) 4:22
•*Sherry* 2:06
•*Slam [Slan]* 5:49
•*A Salute to Tiny* (take 1 previously unissued) 3:11
•*A Salute to Tiny* (master take [2]) 3:09
•*Eenie Meenie Minor Mode* (take 1 previously unissued) 3:39
•*Eenie Meenie Minor Mode* (master take [2]) 3:39
•*Let's Jump* (take 1 previously unissued) 6:51
•*Let's Jump* (master take [2]) 6:03

Black Lion BLCD 760923 [UK 1990]. Same on 1201 Music 9003 (USA). Produced
by George Wein. Master takes originally Storyville EP 426. Twardzik composed
The Fable of Mabel. Slam by Mariano was later recorded as *Slan* by Mariano with
Shelley Manne and His Men (January 1956).

Dick Twardzik, *1954 Improvisations*
Boston. Probably October 1954
Richard Twardzik, p
•*Warming Up* 4:16
•*Nice Work If You Can Get It* 1:29
•*'Round Midnight* 3:32
•*Get Happy* 3:05
•*It Could Happen to You* 2:29
•*All the Things You Are* 2:49
Recorded by Peter Morris. *Warming Up* includes snatches from *Yesterdays, 'Round Midnight*, and *A Crutch For the Crab.* These six tracks, played on an instrument described by Morris as "an upright piano untuned," appear to be a continuous rehearsal.

Dick Twardzik, *1954 Improvisations*
Boston. Probably October 1954
Richard Twardzik, p; Jack Lawlor, b (on *I Get a Kick Out of You*); Peter Littman, d.
•*Yesterdays* 2:22
•*Original* 2:49
•*Our Love Is Here to Stay* 4:47
•*I Get a Kick Out of You* 1:49
•*Bess, You Is My Woman* 3:36
Recorded by Peter Morris. According to Bob Zieff, *Original* is based on chord changes of *I Got Rhythm* with substitute chords at end of A sections. Zieff reports (via drummer Joe Hunt) that *I Get a Kick Out of You* is *Tootsie Roll* by Stan Getz, with the A section of *I Get a Kick Out of You* as the bridge. (Brian Priestly (1990) said *I Get a Kick Out of You* is an improvisation on *Lullaby in Rhythm* by Edgar Sampson with quotation from *I Get a Kick Out of You*.) The coda on *Bess, You Is My Woman* is from *A Crutch For the Crab.*

Dick Twardzik, *1954 Improvisations*
Boston. Probably October 1954
Richard Twardzik, p; Peter Littman, drum pad and/or table top
•*I'll Remember April* 7:53
New Artists 1006CD [USA 1990]
Recorded by Peter Morris. All 12 titles of *1954 Improvisations* are reissued with improved sound on Dick Twardzik Trio, *Complete Recordings*, LoneHill Jazz 10120 [Barcelona, 2004].

Richard Twardzik *Trio*
Van Gelder Studio, Hackensack, NJ.
27 October 1954
Richard Twardzik, p; Carson Smith, b; Peter Littman, d.
•*Albuquerque Social Swim* 3:03
•*Bess, You Is My Woman* 3:24
•*Yellow Tango* 4:18
•*'Round Midnight* 3:44
•*I'll Remember April* 4:04
•*A Crutch for the Crab* 3:25
•*Just One of Those Things* 3:06
Produced by Russ Freeman. Twardzik composed *Albuquerque Social Swim, Yellow*

Uptown UPCD 27.49 [2003]

Tango, and *A Crutch for the Crab.* Pacific Jazz CDP 7 46861 2 [USA 1989]. Originally issued on Russ Freeman/Richard Twardzik, *Trio.* Pacific Jazz 1212 (side 1 [1956]). *Just One of Those Things* and 'alternate take' of *A Crutch for the Crab* first issued on Richard Twardzik, *The Last Set,* Pacific Jazz PJ-37 [1962], along with the other trio titles and *The Girl from Greenland* from the second Paris recording session (below). The alternate take of *A Crutch for the Crab* is actually the same take with a truncated beginning, according to spectrographic analysis by James Harrod. Because of damage to the master tape in 1962, the only complete take (3:25) is the original on PJ 1212 (remastered 24 bit on Toshiba-EMI Limited Edition facsimile 2001). Also on Dick Twardzik Trio, *Complete Recordings,* LoneHill Jazz 10120 [Barcelona, 2004] along with *1954 Improvisations* above.

Chet Baker Quartet in Amsterdam
Concertgebouw. 17 September 1955
Chet Baker, tp, voc*; Richard Twardzik, p; Jimmy Bond, b; Peter Littman, d.
•Introduction by Baker 1:23 (unissued)
•*Tommyhawk* 6:02
•*Indian Summer* 7:51
•*I'm Glad There Is You* 5:30
•*But Not For Me** 7:00
•*My Funny Valentine** (inc.)
•*Ray's Idea* (not broadcast)
Details courtesy Bert Vuijsje. First five titles (as shown) were edited for half-hour radio broadcast. The broadcast tape is stored at the Dutch Jazz Archive. *Ray's Idea* was identified in a contemporary review of the concert by Pieter Sweens; another review by Michiel de Ruyter says that the opener (presumably *Tommyhawk*) was followed by *You Don't Know What Love Is.*

Storyville EP 426 [1955]

Chet Baker Quartet in The Hague
Kurhaus. 18 September 1955
Chet Baker, tp, voc★; Richard Twardzik, p; Jimmy Bond, b; Peter Littman, d.
•Introduction by Lou van Rees and Baker 1:27   unissued
•*Tommyhawk* 6:16
•*Indian Summer* 8:52
•*Someone to Watch Over Me*★ 6:04
•*Imagination* 3:30
•*CTA* (inc.) 5:54
Details courtesy Bert Vuijsje. This is the first half-hour of the concert, edited for radio broadcast. The broadcast tape is stored at the Dutch Jazz Archive.

Chet Baker Quartet *In Mainz*
Mainz, Germany. 21 September 1955
Chet Baker, tp; Rolfe Schnoebiegel, tp (on *All the Things You Are*); Richard Twardzik, p; Jimmy Bond, b; Peter Littman, d.
•*Walkin'* 7:25
•*Indian Summer* 7:54
•*All the Things You Are* 8:58
Produced by Paolo Piangiarelli. Philology W 42-2 [Italy 1991]

Chet Baker Quartet featuring Richard Twardzik, Köln Concert
Börensaal, 9 October 1955
Chet Baker, tp, voc; Richard Twardzik, p; Jimmy Bond, b; Peter Littman, d.
opening announcement (Chet Baker, Gigi Campi) 2:49
•*Exitus* 7:26
•*Tommyhawk* 7:10
•*Imagination* 3:26
Baker introduces Twardzik 0:52

New Artists 1006 [USA 1990]

•*Yellow Tango* 8:40
•*Someone to Watch Over Me* 5:28
•*CTA* 9:27
•*My Funny Valentine* 6:06
Add Hans Koller, ts, and Willy Sanner, bs
•*Cool Blues* 10:00
•*I'll Remember April* 15:13
closing theme and announcement (Baker) 0:57

RLR Records 88618 [2005]. Concert produced by Gigi Campi. Baker incorrectly dates this concert 26 September in his notes to Chet Baker in Europe (1956). *Yellow Tango* is played by Twardzik, Bond and Littman.

Chet Baker Quartet, *In Paris*
Studio Pathé-Magellan, Paris. 11 October 1955
Chet Baker, tp; Richard Twardzik, p; Jimmy
Bond, b; Peter Littman, d.
•*Rondette* 2:09
•*Mid-Forte* 3:06
•*Sad Walk* 4:13
•*Re-Search* 4:57
•*Just Duo* 4:10

Same. 14 October 1955
•*Piece Caprice* 5:08
•*Pomp* 4:39
•*The Girl From Greenland* 5:13
•*Brash* 5:53
EmArcy 837 474-2 [France 1988]. Originally Barclay Records [France]. First
released in the United States on *Chet Baker in Europe,* World-Pacific 1218 [1956].
Twardzik composed *The Girl From Greenland.* Robert L. (Bob) Zieff composed all
other titles.

Lars Gullin and the Chet Baker Quartet
Stuttgart. 15 October 1955
Chet Baker, tp; Lars Gullin, bs (except *Brash*); Richard Twardzik, p; Jimmy Bond, b;
Peter Littman, d; Caterina Valente, voc (on *I'll Remember April*).
•*Cool Blues* 3:21
•*Brash* 4:36
•*Lover Man* 5:24
•*I'll Remember April* 6:37
Produced by Lars Westin. *Lars Gullin,* Vol. 2. Dragon DRCD 224 [Sweden 1992].

*Richard Twardzik died of a heroin overdose in a Paris hotel on 21 October
1955.*

References

Anonymous [unsigned news item]. 1955. "Eve-of-concert death of Dick Twardzik." *Melody Maker* (29 October): 1, 20.

Anonymous. 1956-57. "Understanding the jazz musician: the artist and his problems" *Jazz Today* 1 (December 1956); *Jazz Today* 2 (January, March 1957).

Baker, Chet. 1956. Liner note for *Chet Baker in Europe: A Jazz Tour of the NATO Countries*. Pacific Jazz 1218.

Baker, Chet. 1997. *As Though I Had Wings: The Lost Memoir*. New York: St. Martin's Press.

Balliett, Whitney. 1972. "Jeru." *New Yorker*. In *Collected Works: A Journal of Jazz 1954-2001*. New York: St. Martin's Griffin. 2002. 378-83.

Barnett, Anthony. 1998. "Rediscovering Dick Wetmore." *Fable Bulletin: Violin Improvisation Studies* 3 (No. 10): 4-28.

Berger, Morroe. 1947. "Jazz: resistance to the diffusion of a culture pattern." *Journal of Negro History* 32: 461-94.

Brown, George F. 1954. "Lionel Hampton Electrifies NY with Dynamic New Orchestra." Pittsburgh *Courier*, 27 February. P. 29.

Brubeck, Dave. 1956. Liner note for *Dave Brubeck Octet*. Reissued on Fantasy OJCCD-101-2 [USA 1991].

Cameron, William Bruce. 1954. "Sociological notes on the jam session." *Social Forces* 33: 177-82.

Cerulli, Dom. 1958. Review of Herb Pomeroy, *Life Is a Many-Splendored Gig*. Reprinted in *Down Beat Jazz Record Reviews*, Vol. III, ed. Don Gold. Chicago: Maher Publications. 1959. 164-65.

Chaloff, Serge. 1955. Liner note for *Boston Blow-Up!* Capitol T6510. Facsimile reissue on Toshiba-EMI TOCJ-9354 [Japan 2001].

Chaloff, Serge. 1956. "Eulogy for Twardzik." *Metronome* (January).

Chambers, Jack. 1983. *Milestones 1: The Music and Times of Miles Davis to 1960*. Toronto: University of Toronto Press. Reprinted with *Milestones 2* as *Milestones: The Music and Times of Miles Davis*. New York: Da Capo. 1998.

Chambers, Jack. 1985. *Milestones 2: The Music and Times of Miles Davis since 1960.* Toronto: University of Toronto Press. Reprinted as above. 1998.

Chambers, Jack. 1997. Bio-discography of Richard Twardzik (including draft versions of "The incomplete works of Richard Twardzik" and "The complete works on CD"). www.chass.utoronto.ca/~chambers.

Chambers, Jack. 1999. "Bravo, Brubeck!" *Coda* 285 (May/June): 30-32.

Chambers, Jack. 2003a. "Walking on Clouds: Richard Twardzik with Chet Baker in Europe 1955." Posted on Jazzitude (www.jazzitude.com) 30 April 2003.

Chambers, Jack. 2003b. "Spåren efter Dick Twardzik" [Traces of DT]. Trans. Lars Westin. *Orkester Journalen* July/August (Part 1): 18-25, and September (Part 2): 2-6.

Chambers, Jack. 2004a. "Walking on Clouds: Richard Twardzik with Chet Baker in Europe 1955." Coda 316 (July/August): 10-15.

Chambers, Jack. 2004b. "Revenge of the underground jazz composer." Sirena 2: 130-40.

Claxton, William. 1993. *Young Chet.* Schirmer Art Books. Munich: Mosel Verlag.

Cohen, Noal, and Michael Fitzgerald. 2002. *Rat Race Blues: The Musical Life of Gigi Gryce.* Berkeley, CA: Berkeley Hills Books.

Condon, Eddie, with Thomas Sugrue. 1947. *We Called It Music: A Generation of Jazz.* Introduction by Gary Giddins. New York: Da Capo. 1992.

Coss, Bill. 1955. "In Person: Serge Chaloff." *Metronome* (August). 11.

Cuscuna, Michael. 1989. Liner note for Russ Freeman/Richard Twardzik, *Trio.* Pacific Jazz CDP 7 46861.

Davis, Francis. 1986. *In the Moment: Jazz in the 1980s.* New York: Oxford University Press.

Davis, Francis. 1990. *Outcats: Jazz Composers, Instrumentalists and Singers.* New York: Oxford University Press.

Davis, Francis. 2001. *Like Young: Jazz, Pop. Youth and Middle Age.* New York: DaCapo.

Davis, Miles. 1957. "Self-portrait of the artist." Columbia Records Biographical Service (26 November). Reprinted in *Down Beat* (6 March 1958).

Dean, Nick. 1956. Letter to editor. Quoted in "Eulogy for Twardzik." *Metronome* (January).

de Ruyter, Michiel. 1955. "Jazz." *Disco Discussies* (October). Monthly magazine of Phonogram Records. Amsterdam. P. 235.

de Valk, J. [Jeroen]. 2000. *Chet Baker: His Life and Music.* Berkeley, CA: Berkeley Hills Books.

Ellington, Duke. 1965. "The most essential instrument." *Jazz Journal* 18 (December): 14-15. Reprinted in *The Duke Ellington Reader*, ed. Mark Tucker. New York: Oxford University Press. 1993. 368-71.

Esman, Aaron H. 1951. "Jazz—a study in social conflict." *The American Imago: A Psychoanalytic Journal for the Arts and Sciences* 8: 219-26.

Feather, Leonard. 1959. *The New Yearbook of Jazz.* London: Arthur Barker Ltd.

Feather, Leonard. 1960. *The Encyclopedia of Jazz: Completely Revised, Enlarged and Brought Up To Date.* New York: Bonanza Books.

Feather, Leonard. 1987. "Goffin, *Esquire* and the moldy figs." *The Jazz Years: Earwitness to an Era.* New York: DaCapo. 76-94.

Feather, Leonard, and Ira Gitler. 1999. *The Biographical Encyclopedia of Jazz.* New York: Oxford University Press.

Freeman, Russ. 1956. "Richard Twardzik." Liner note for *Trio*. Pacific Jazz 1212.

Gilliespie, Dizzy, with Al Fraser. 1971. *To Be or Not to Bop.* New York: Doubleday.

Ginsberg, Allen. 1956. *Howl and Other Poems.* The Pocket Poet Series, Number Four. San Francisco: City Lights Books.

Gioia, Ted. 1992. *West Coast Jazz.* Berkeley, California: University of California Press.

Gioia, Ted. 1997. *The History of Jazz.* New York: Oxford University Press.

Gitler, Ira. 1952. Liner note for *The New Sounds from Boston*. Prestige 130. Reissued Prestige OJCCD-1745-2 [USA 1990].

Gitler, Ira. 1953. Liner note for *Boston All Stars*. Prestige 153. Reissued Prestige OJCCD-1745-2 [USA 1990].

Gitler, Ira. 1985. *Swing to Bop: An Oral History of the Transition in Jazz in the 1940s*. New York: Oxford University Press.

Gold, Herbert. 1960. "The Beat mystique." In *The Beats*, ed. Seymour Krim. Greenwich, Conn.: Fawcett Publications. 154–64.

Gross, Walter. 1998. "A many-spendored life: a conversation with Herb Pomeroy." *Interlude: Official Journal of the Boston Musicians' Association*. July–August–September. 7–12.

Hammond, John, with Irving Townsend. 1977. *John Hammond on Record: An Autobiography*. Harmondsworth, UK: Penguin.

Hampton, Lionel, with James Haskins. 1989. *Hamp: An Autobiography*. New York: Warner Books.

Hanley, Wayne. 1955. "Musician Who Took Drug Cure Wants to Tell Addicts His Story." *Boston Sunday Herald* (1 May): 1, 16.

Hardy, John William. 1962. Liner note for Richard Twardzik, *The Last Set*. Pacific Jazz PJ-37.

Harrison, Max. 1963. "Serge Chaloff." *Jazz Monthly* (May). Reprinted in *A Jazz Retrospect*. Boston: Crescendo. 1976. 161–65.

Harrod, James A. 2000–2001. Liner notes for *Chet Baker Quartet Live*, Vols. 1–3. Pacific Jazz 25248, 27693, 31573.

Hentoff, Nat. 1951. "Serge seeks action again after two years in Boston." *Down Beat* (14 December): 3, 5.

Hercules, Frank E.M. 1972. *American Society and Black Revolution*. New York: Harcourt Brace Jovanovich.

Kerouac, Jack. 1957. *On the Road*. New York and London: Penguin Putnam. Reprinted 1976.

Kerouac, Jack. 1958. "Aftermath: the philosophy of the Beat Generation." *Esquire*. Published in complete original version as "About the Beat Generation" in *The Portable Jack Kerouac*, ed. Ann Charters. New York: Viking Penguin. 1995. 559–62.

Kyes, John F. 1954. "Hampton Band Gives Exciting Concert Here." Unidentified newspaper. 14 January.

Lees, Gene. 1995. *Leader of the Band: The Life of Woody Herman*. New York: Oxford University Press.

Lyons, Len. 1983. *The Great Jazz Pianists: Speaking of Their Lives and Music*. New York: Quill.

MacFarland, Will. 1955. Liner note for *Boston Blow-Up!* Capitol T6510. Facsimile reissue on Toshiba-EMI TOCJ-9354 [Japan 2001].

Margolis, Norman M. 1954. "A theory on the psychology of jazz." *The American Imago: A Psychoanalytic Journal for the Arts and Sciences* 11: 263-91.

McMillan, Geneviève [collection]. 2002. Reba Stewart. Coordinator: Michèle Oshima. http://web.mit.edu/womens-studies/www/arts/reba.

Merriam, Alan P., and Raymond W. Mack. 1960. "The jazz community." *Social Forces* 38: 211-22.

Morgan, Alun. 1963. "Dick Twardzik" [discography]. *Jazz Monthly* 9 (November): 27.

Morgan, Alun. 1990. Liner note for Serge Chaloff, *The Fable of Mabel*. Black Lion CD 760923.

Nevard, Mike. 1955. "Young man without a horn…"[Chet Baker at Stoll Theatre, London.] *Melody Maker* (29 October): 3.

Nicholson, Stuart. 2000. *Portrait of Duke Ellington: Reminiscing in Tempo*. London: Pan Books.

Openneer, Herman. 1993. "Chet Baker's debuut in Nederland 1955." *Jazz Archief Bulletin* 9 (September): 27-38.

Parker, Chan. 1993. *My Life in E-Flat*. Columbia, SC: University of South Carolina Press.

Priestly, Brian. 1990. Review of Richard Twardzik, *1954 Improvisations*. *The Wire*. Reprinted www. newartistsrecords. com.

Reece, Jerome. 1984. "Chet Baker." *Musician* magazine. Reprinted in *The Jazz Musician*, ed. Mark Rowland and Tony Scherman. New York: St, Martin's Press. 1994. 129-45.

Reisner, Robert George. 1962. *Bird: The Legend of Charlie Parker*. New York: Bonanza Books.

Rusch, Robert. 1978. "Chet Baker: Interview." *Cadence* (August): 33.

Schuller, Gunther. 1989. *The Swing Era: The Development of Jazz 1930-1945*. New York: Oxford University Press.

Simosko, Vladimir. 1998. *Serge Chaloff: A Musical Biography and Discography*. Studies in Jazz No. 27. Lanham, Maryland, and London: The Scarecrow Press and Institute of Jazz Studies, Rutgers, the State University of New Jersey.

Sjøgren, Thorbjørn. 1993. *Chet: The Music of Chesney Henry Baker*. Copenhagen: JazzMedia

Spellman, A.B. 1966. *Black Music: Four Lives*. [Orig. *Four Lives in the Bebop Business*.] New York: Schocken Books.

Stewart, Tom. 1955. Liner note for *Dick Wetmore*. Bethlehem BCP 1035. Facsimile 10" LP by Toshiba-EMI TOJJ-1035 [2000].

Sunenblick, Robert. 1994. Liner note for Serge Chaloff, *Boston 1950*. Uptown UPCD 2738.

Sunenblick, Robert. 1996. Liner note for Charlie Parker, *Boston 1952*. Uptown UPCD 2742.

Sweens, Pieter. 1955. "Chet Baker: triomf van de triestheid." [Triumph of tristesse: review of concert at Concertgebouw, Amsterdam]. *Disco Discussies* (October). Monthly magazine of Phonogram Records. Amsterdam. P. 227.

Sylvester, Robert. ca. 1957. Liner note for Herb Pomeroy, *Life is a Many Splendored Gig*. Roulette R-52001. Fresh Sound Records CD84 [1989].

Tesser, Neil. 1998. "Reissuing *I Talk With the Spirits*." Liner note for Roland Kirk, *I Talk With the Spirits*. Verve 314 558076-2.

Tercinet. Alain. 1988. Liner note for *Chet Baker in Paris*, Vol. 1. Trans. Martin Deo. EmArcy 837 474-2 [France].

Turner, Frederick. 1999. "Too fast to live." *Boston Magazine* (March): 170, 172-3.

Twardzik, Richard. 1956. Excerpt of letter to Bill Coss. Quoted in "Eulogy for Twardzik." *Metronome* (August).

Tynan, John. 1963. "Straight talk from Russ Freeman." *Down Beat* (14 March): 20-21.

Ullmann, Michael. 1980. Jazz Lives. Washington: New Republic Books.

Ullmann, Michael. 1989. "Evans and Taylor: two differing piano greats." *Boston Globe* (28 July).

Vail, Ken. 1996. *Bird's Diary: The Life of Charlie Parker 1945-1955.* Chessington, UK: Castle Communications.

Van der Elsken, Ed. 1991. *Jazz.* Amsterdam: Fragment Uitgeverij.

Voce, Steve. 2002. "Comment by John Williams on *Deep in a Dream* [Chet Baker biography by James Gavin]." *Jazz Journal International* (December): 8-9.

Weber, Bruce dir. 1988. *Let's Get Lost: A Film Journal* [on Chet Baker]. Little Bear Films.

Williams, Martin. 1970. *Jazz Masters in Transition, 1957-1969.* New York: Da Capo.

Wills, Geoffrey I. 2003. "Forty lives in the bebop business: a study of mental health in a group of eminent jazz musicians." *British Journal of Psychiatry* 183: 255-59.

Winick, Charles. 1959-60. "The use of drugs by jazz musicians." *Social Problems* 7: 240-53.

Wolfe, Thomas. 1945. *A Stone, A Leaf, A Door.* Poems Selected and Arranged in Verse by John S. Barnes. New York: Charles Scribner's Sons.

Zieff, Robert L. 1955. Annotations for *Dick Wetmore.* Bethlehem BCP 1035. Facsimile 10" LP by Toshiba-EMI TOJJ-1035 [2000].

INDEX

Acapulco 146, 147
Acket, Paul 251
Adams, Pepper 232
Adamson, Steve 78, 189
Aeolian-Skinner Organs 139
Africa 147, 173
African-American 114, 157, 170, 177, 213
Akiyoshi, Toshiko 71, 72
Akron, Ohio 82
Albany, NY 95, 303
Albert, Crystal-Joy. *See* Crystal Joy
Albright Art School (Buffalo) 20
Albright-Knox Art Gallery 20
Albuquerque, NM 145, 150, 161, 162, 163, 164, 165, 167, 168, 169
Albuquerque Social Swim (Twardzik) 6, 7, 13, 63, 145, 165, 235, 261, 262, 279, 306
Allen, Bob 149
Allen, Gene 122
Allen, Steve 235
All the Things You Are 204, 252, 279, 306, 308
Alvin Hotel, New York 144
American Aid Society of Paris 284
American Art Post Card Co. 53
American Church of Paris, the 20
American Consulate, Paris 282, 292
American British Cowdray Hospital, Mexico City 149, 152, 153
American Embassy, Paris 282
American Express 284
American Revolution 54
American Society and Black Revolution 214
Amesbury, Mass. 285
Ammons, Gene 126, 154

Amsterdam 243, 247, 249, 250, 251, 279, 293, 307
Amsterdam Blitzkrieg, the 296
Anderson, Leroy 212
Anonymous 156, 276
Antwerp 255-257, 258
Araki, James 180, 184
Armstrong, Louis 6, 99, 158, 176, 225
Assorted Flavors of Pacific Jazz (Pacific Jazz LP) 1, 2, 51
Auld, Georgie 75, 80
Auntie. *See* Longwell, Hannah Marie

Bach, Johann Sebastian 69, 118
Baden-Baden 269
Baker, Chet 1, 8, 10-13, 14, 57, 58, 118, 122-25, 126, 138, 142, 143, 144, 153, 154, 157, 185, 188, 189, 196, 199, 200, 202, 206, 208, 222, 232, 235, 239-58, 261-71, 273-79, 281, 284, 296, 302, 307, 309, 308, 310
Balliett, Whitney 78
Baltimore, Md. 64, 228-29, 230
Barclay, Nicole 260
Barclay Records 10, 11, 52, 259, 260-61, 262-63, 264, 273, 310
Barnet, Charlie 9, 243
Barnett, Anthony 102, 137, 139
Barsac (Mariano) 128, 304
Bartok (Nichols) 131
Bartók, Béla 53, 59, 61, 62, 63, 64, 87, 92, 100-01, 110, 131, 165, 193, 195, 264
Bartók Records 92
Basel 259. 271
Basie, Count 36, 73, 74, 116, 180, 219, 220, 227
Bates, Alan 191

BCHaast Records 301

Beacon Hill, Boston 27, 117, 223

Beat Generation 154-55, 163, 169

bebop 59. 65, 68, 76, 92, 103, 106, 107, 113, 127, 129, 136, 137, 154, 158, 161, 176, 179, 194, 196, 226, 245, 226, 267, 275, 293

Bechet, Sidney 6, 64-65, 66, 67, 188, 194, 254

Beethoven, Ludwig van 59

Beiderbecke, Bix 158

Belgian Congo Records 87, 92

Belgium 133, 246, 255, 256, 258, 276, 277

Bellvue Sanitarium, NY 152

Belmondo, Jean-Paul 57

Benford, Tommy 136

Berg, Alban 92

Berger, Monroe 156

Berklee School of Music 71, 72, 73, 79, 92, 99, 133, 232

Berlin, Germany 245

Berlin, Buddy 150, 161, 163-65

Berlin, Wuzza (Mary Ann) 163, 164, 165

Berman, Sonny 76, 153-54, 189

Bernstein, Leonard 71

Bess You Is My Woman Now 6, 128, 132, 204, 279, 304, 306

Bethlehem, Pa. 95, 96

Bethlehem Records 51, 126, 137, 139-40, 142

Billouin, Crystal Joy. See Crystal Joy

Birdland 94, 104, 106, 200, 219, 220, 232, 242, 244

Bishop, Walter, Jr. 104-05

Black Eagle Jazz Band 113

Black, Linda (Joann Mary) 83, 86-87

Black, Susan 232, 289

Blacksburg, Virginia 39, 40, 41

Black Erich, German Shepherd 56, 148

Black Erich (Twardzik) 56, 219

Black Lion Records 191, 192, 305

Blakey, Art 105, 154

Bley, Paul 158

Bloch, Ernest 86, 92

Blue Note Records 42, 141, 200

Blue Serge (Capitol LP) 191, 222, 233

Blue Star Records 260

Blue Tango (Anderson) 211

Blumberg, Jerry 64

Blume, Teddy 100, 253, 254

B'nai B'rith 214

Bob the Robin (Chaloff) 225

Bock, Richard 263

Body and Soul 108, 188, 189, 222, 232, 304

Bolden, Buddy 65

Bolshevik 21, 22

Bond, Jimmy 245, 247, 251, 253, 258, 270, 271, 273, 274, 275, 276, 277, 278, 284, 307, 308, 309, 310

boogie-woogie 36, 39, 42, 59, 64, 175, 179

Boston, Mass. 1, 5, 9, 12, 16, 17, 18, 19, 20, 22, 24, 26, 32, 33, 35, 42, 53, 64, 65, 67, 68, 71, 73, 74, 75, 76, 78, 79, 80, 82, 83, 85, 92, 94, 95, 96, 97, 99, 100, 102, 105, 107, 108, 109, 111, 113, 114, 116, 118, 125, 127, 131, 132, 133, 135, 136, 137, 140, 149, 150, 151, 161, 163, 166, 167, 168, 169, 172, 173, 176, 181, 185, 187, 189, 191, 196, 197, 200, 201, 202, 203, 211, 214, 216, 217, 218, 219, 220, 221, 227, 228, 233, 234, 235, 236, 253, 277, 281, 282, 285, 289

Boston All-Stars (Prestige LP) 127, 128, 131, 145, 149, 279, 295

Boston & Maine Railroad 16

Boston Arts Festival   172, 190, 195, 196, 224, 232, 237

Boston Blow-Up (Capitol LP)   76, 191, 222, 223, 225, 232

Boston College   285

Boston Daily Record   79

Boston Globe   226

Boston Herald   225

Boston 1950 (Charlie Parker CD)   79, 106, 295

Boston Red Sox   57, 224

Boston Sunday Herald   221

Boston University   71, 108, 188, 212, 215

Boylston Street, 905 (Boston)   133, 135, 136, 138, 143, 157, 217

Bouncin' with Bartok (Twardzik)   53, 60-64, 195

Bourbon Street, Toronto jazz club   123

Boy Scouts   41

Braff, Ruby   225

Brash (Zieff)   13, 138, 143, 261, 267, 271, 310

Brauer, Ricky   180

Breeze and I, The   266, 267, 268

Brehaut, Elaine   26, 31, 34, 37, 149-50, 161, 162, 163, 164, 170, 282, 300

Brehaut, Ellerton (Bree)   26, 31, 35, 282

Brehaut, Kay   26, 33, 34, 35, 282

Bridgewater State Hospital, Ma.   153, 221, 222-23, 224, 229, 230

British Musicians Union   261, 275

Brookline, Mass.   53, 84, 221

Brookmeyer, Bob   102

Brown, Clifford   179, 182, 234, 239, 267

Brown, Ray   101, 184

Brubeck, Dave   113, 131, 132, 188, 249

Brussels   255, 256, 257, 258, 300

Budwig, Monty   125

Buffalo, New York   9, 19, 20, 282

Burke, Vinnie   137

Burns, Ralph   71, 77

Burrell, Kenny   125

Bush, Lennie   275

But Not For Me   275, 307

Buter, Hans   247, 248

Byard, Jaki   136, 220

Bye Bye Blues   129, 304

Café Society   214

California   4, 5, 123, 131, 133, 152, 155, 163, 218, 233, 239, 240, 242, 243, 278

Calli   298

Camarillo State Hospital, Ca.   152

Cameron, William Bruce   156, 157

Cambridge, Mass.   38, 41, 42, 55, 58, 59, 173

Cambridge High and Latin School   56, 58

Cape Cod   85, 92, 111, 136

Capitol Records   141, 191, 209, 210, 222, 233

Carnegie Hall   104, 105

Carney, Harry   76

Carreno, Larry   85, 86, 88

Carter, Betty   180-81

Carter, Bob   245, 247

Carter, Jack   166

Casher, Ted   133, 135

Catherine, Philip   124

Catholicism, Roman   16, 17, 19, 21, 23, 28, 30, 39, 40, 41

Caulfield, Holden   57

Cerulli, Dom   211, 219, 220

Chaloff, Julius L.   71

Chaloff, Linda Jeanne (Serge's daughter) 83
Chaloff, Margaret Stedman 71–73, 190, 235
Chaloff, Richard 71, 72
Chaloff School of Music 71
Chaloff, Serge 9, 10, 57, 59, 67, 68, 71, 73–79. 80–83, 85–92, 94–95, 96–97, 99, 122, 126, 127, 135, 145, 152–53, 154, 185, 187–89, 190, 191–94, 199, 221–23, 224, 225, 227, 228, 229, 230, 232–33, 239, 243, 258, 266, 281, 285, 289, 302, 303, 305
Charles J. Connick Stained Glass Studio 20, 22, 31, 165, 228, 256
Charles Street, Boston 5, 117, 223
Charlie's Tavern, New York 243
Chet Baker and Crew (Pacific Jazz LP) 123, 278
Chet Baker in Europe (Pacific Jazz LP) 8, 10, 11, 13, 251, 252, 310
Chet Baker in Paris, vol. 4 (EmArcy CD) 261, 262, 263, 309
Chet Baker Quartet Live (Pacific Jazz 3-CD) 208
Chicago 16, 66, 94, 95, 97, 239
Christy's Restaurant, Framingham 102, 103, 110, 303
Clayton Powell, Adam 214
Claxton, William 2, 3, 4, 5, 8, 11, 51, 52
Clef Records 184
Cleveland, Jimmy 179
Clifford Brown–Max Roach Quintet 234
Clift, Montgomery 57
Coastal Studios, New York 139
Coda magazine 295–96, 297, 298
Cohn, Al 77, 190, 233
Cold War 21, 57
Cologne. See Köln, West Germany

Coltrane, John 99, 109
Columbia Records 131, 132, 141
Communism 21, 57
Community Development Corporation 181
Compulsion (1959 film) 125
Concerto for Trumpet, Baritone Saxophone and Large Orchestra (Heider) 266
Condon, Eddie 16, 58
Connecticut 139, 166
Connick Stained Glass. See Charles J. Connick Stained Glass Studio
Contoocook Lake 41, 45, 49
Cook and Brown, comedy duo 177
Cool Blues (Parker) 107, 267, 304, 309, 310
Cooper, Buster 179, 180
Copland, Aaron 294
Copley Square, Boston 134
Coppertone 1, 13
Corea, Chick 71
Coss, Bill 118, 225, 237
Crane, Hart 156
Crawford, Joan 23
Creeden, Dick 83–84
Creeley, Robert 163
Crest Lounge, Detroit 94
Crombie, Tony 247, 275
Crown, Jackie 180, 181, 182, 185
Crutch for the Crab, A (Twardzik) 1, 6, 7, 13, 14, 52, 55, 113, 121, 155, 158, 196, 207–10, 279, 280, 301, 307
Crystal Joy 62, 73, 98, 111, 116, 133, 135, 157, 191, 203, 212–18, 222–23, 228, 230–31, 232–34, 235–37, 242, 245, 260, 277, 289–90, 300
CTI Records 141
Cuscuna, Michael 200
Cukier, Liliane 241–42, 250, 258, 277

Dali, Salvador 244
Dameron, Tadd 60, 119, 153
Danvers, Mass. 42, 45-47, 48-49, 50, 51, 52, 58, 60, 61, 71, 83, 84, 119, 120, 157, 196, 217, 281, 282
Darrow, Clarence 125
Davenport, Wallace 180, 182
Davis, Francis 72, 158, 279
Davis, Miles 6, 58, 99, 102, 109, 113, 123, 132, 135-36, 239, 251, 267, 302
Davis, Ron 53-56
Dawson, Alan 179
Dean and Pillsbury, funeral directors 284
Dean, James 49, 156, 241
Dean, Nick 4, 5, 83, 96, 113, 114, 116-18, 204, 205, 223, 242, 300
Dean, Zibette 116, 117
Debussy, Claude 56, 196, 244
De Franco, Buddy 184
De Koenigswarter, Baroness Pannonica 223
Delius, Tobias 301
Denmark 276
Dennis, Jerome (Jay) 180
Denver Cathedral 20
de Rijke, Jaap 301
Desmond, Paul 131
Detroit, Mich. 9, 94, 224, 228, 229, 230, 232, 233, 234
Deuel, Les 95, 303
de Valk, Jeroen 199, 240, 241, 242, 260, 278
Dhers, Dr. Georges 283
Dickenson, Vic 188
Dick Wetmore (Bethlehem LP) 51, 126, 139, 140, 141, 142
Dillman, Bradford 125
Dionne, Cathy 300

Dixieland 84, 129, 136, 188
Dixie Tour, the 178, 182-83, 185, 196
Dixon, Gus 79-80
Dr. Cajigas 239
Don't Blame Me 107, 279, 304
Dorsey, Jimmy 75
Down Beat 75, 77, 94, 97, 211, 219, 220, 239, 271
Dragon Records 264, 272, 310
Duke, The (Brubeck) 152

Eager, Allen 126-27, 304
Earl, Dean 167
East Brewster, Mass. 111
East St. Louis, Ill. 92, 94, 95, 97
Easy Street 189, 191
Ecker, Dave 180
Eckstine, Billy 99
Edelhagen, Kurt 252
Eenie Meenie Minor Mode (Mariano) 192, 305
Ellington, Duke 13, 55, 58, 74, 139, 158, 180, 219, 226
Ellington, Mercer 158
Emerson, Ralph Waldo 122
Encyclopedia of Jazz (Feather 1960) 122
England 9, 16, 71, 189, 246, 247, 257, 259, 261, 266, 275-77
Englewood Cliffs, NJ 200
Enja Records 124
Erosong (Mariano) 279, 304
Esman, Aaron H. 156, 157
Estell, Oscar 180
Estrad (Swedish magazine) 267-68, 269
Esquire magazine 154
Evans, Everett 222
Evans, Gil 6, 135, 302

Every Time We Say Good-Bye   268
Excalibur Jazz Band   136

Fable of Mabel, The (Twardzik)   9, 13, 60, 73, 76, 162, 191, 192-96, 197, 199, 222, 225, 227, 279, 286, 295, 305
Fabulous Crystal Joy, The (Hanover LP)   235
"Fallen Striker" (sketch by Henryk Twardzik)   21-22, 24
Farmer, Art   125, 179
Fantasy Records   131, 188
Fanon, Fritz   254
Feather, Leonard   58, 122, 130, 220
Federal Hospital, Lexington, Kentucky   153, 222
Fenway, the   3
Fêtes (Debussy)   64, 196
Fields, Shep   75
Finian's Rainbow   214
Fitzgerald, Ella   6, 212, 227
Flaherty, Francis E.   282
Flamingo Club, London   261, 276
Flying Dutchman   251
Flying Home (Hampton)   175, 185
Frishberg, Dave   65
Fogg Museum, Harvard   173
Fol, Raymond   275-76
Footloose (Prestige LP)   158
Four Brothers, the   74, 80, 190, 225, 233, 289
Fowler House, Danvers   53-55, 56, 69, 217, 230, 281
Fowler, Samuel   54
Frazee, Roy   92-93, 303
Freeman, Russ   3, 4-6, 8-9, 129-30, 135, 189, 196, 199-200, 201-02, 240-41, 242, 243, 244, 245, 247, 248, 263, 274, 296, 306, 307
French Embassy, New York   289

Garland, Judy   212
Garner, Errol   116, 188, 214, 226
Garcia Lorca, Federico   156
General Records   92
Geneva   252, 253, 257, 293
Geneviève McMillan-Reba Stewart Lecture series   173
Gershwin, George   6, 266, 302
Get Happy   204, 306
Getz, Stan   74, 77-78, 109, 154, 184, 188, 243, 244, 271, 306
Gibbs, Terry   77
Gillespie, Dizzy   66, 67, 76, 99, 101, 102, 106, 126, 138, 163, 194, 215, 219, 225, 239, 247, 254, 267
Ginsberg, Allen   154
Giovanni Club, Baltimore   227, 228
Girl from Greenland, The (Twardzik)   13, 60, 206, 235, 261-62, 279, 288, 307, 310
Gioia, Ted   65, 123, 130, 202, 226, 274
Gitler, Ira   77, 92, 127, 128-29, 155, 161, 303, 304
Giuffre, Jimmy   74, 225
Glennon, Gene   85, 86, 126, 304
Globe and Mail (Toronto)   297
Gloucester, Mass.   32, 68, 182
Goldblatt, Burt   51, 140
Golden Nugget. See Izzy Ort's Golden Nugget
Gonsales, Marty   166
Goodman, Benny   176, 177, 184, 265
Goodspeed, Mert   85, 86
Goof and I, The (Cohn)   190, 225
Gordon, Dexter   154
Gordon, Joe   105, 110, 154, 218, 220, 222, 303, 304
Gorter, Arjen   301
Graettinger, Bob   154

Graham, Martha   190

Grant, Julie, née Maloney (Richard's maternal grandmother)   16, 17, 19, 22, 23, 25-26, 27, 28, 40, 42-43, 82, 300

Grant, Robert Charles (Richard's maternal grandfather)   16-17, 19, 21, 23, 33, 42-43, 300

Grant, Robert Charles, Jr. (Richard's uncle)   17

Granz, Norman   141, 184, 185

Gray, Wardell   73, 154

Greenstein, Arnold   180

Griggs, Bernie   126, 129, 304

Gross, Norman   84-85

Gryce, Gigi   179

Guernica (Picasso)   3

Gullin, Lars   264, 265, 266, 267, 268, 271, 272-73, 274, 275, 276, 277, 310

Hackensack, NJ   5, 199, 200, 201, 202, 306

Hackett, Bobby   102, 188

Hagerstown, Md   95

Hague, the   247, 248, 308

Haig, the (LA jazz club)   1, 243

Hallberg, Bengt   269

Hammond, John   188

Hamner, Curley   177, 178

Hamp, Jr.   178

Hampton, Gladys   178, 179, 181

Hampton, Lionel   9, 105, 175-77, 178, 179, 180, 181-82, 183-85, 187, 199

Hancock, Herbie   71, 109

Hanley, Wayne   221, 224, 230, 258

Happy "Bird," The (Parker LP)   101, 103, 104, 107, 303

Harcourt Street, Boston   20

Harbor Kennels, Danvers   55

Hardy, John William   206-07

Haroutunian, Varty   134, 193, 194, 196, 218, 220, 305

Harris, Bill   102, 122, 125, 132-33

Harris, Clarke   8, 52, 296

Harrison, Max   189

Harrod, James A.   51, 208-10, 307

Harvard University   21, 38, 99, 114, 163, 165, 173

Hawes, Hampton   154

Hawkins, Coleman   99

Haynes, Roy   92, 102, 105, 108, 303, 304

Hayse, Al   180

Heath, Percy   138

Heider, Werner   266

Heidt, Horace   214

Hell's Horizon (film)   241

Henderson, Fletcher   99

Henri Quatre restaurant, Cambridge   172-73

Henry, Ernie   154

Hentoff, Nat   94, 95, 219

Herbert, Victor   251

Hercules, Frank E. M.   214, 289

Herder, Johann Gottfried von   300

Herman, Woody   73, 74-75, 76, 77, 78, 79, 80, 133, 185, 190, 191, 222, 225

Hermosa Beach, California   123

hi-fi   74, 142

Hi Hat, the   79, 100, 101, 104, 105, 107, 110, 113, 126, 127, 129, 133, 146, 167, 187, 212, 215, 217, 219, 304

Hit Parade   212

Holiday, Billie   154

Holten High School, Danvers   56, 58, 71

Hopper, Edward   30

Hôtel de la Madeleine   273, 283

How High the Moon 190
Howl (Ginsberg) 154
Huntington Avenue, Boston 203, 215, 216
Hutton, Ina Ray 75
Hyannis 85, 126
Hyannisport 85, 86

Iceland 277
I Got Rhythm 159, 204, 306
Ile de France 144, 245
I'll Remember April 6, 101, 102, 103, 104, 205, 211, 267, 268-69, 276, 303, 306, 309, 310
I'm Glad There is You 248, 307
I'm Hip (Frishberg) 65
I'm Old-Fashioned 128, 304
India 60, 133
Indiana 225
Indian Summer 251, 307, 308
In Memory of Dick (Jaspar) 276-77
In the Land of Oo-Bla-Dee (Uptown CD) 127, 304
Interracial Jazz Society 64
Inventory of Personal Effects 284, 292
In Your Own Sweet Way (Brubeck) 152
Isaacs, Reginald 173
It Could Happen to You 204, 306
I Talk With the Spirits (Limelight LP) 236
Italy 52, 125, 243, 277, 278, 308
Ivy League fashion 216
Izzy Ort's Golden Nugget, Boston 113

Jackson, Chubby 132
Jamaica Plain, Boston 133, 214, 216, 235
Jamal, Ahmad 6

Japan 50, 72, 114, 115, 133, 139, 172, 184, 191, 201, 210, 222
Jarrett, Keith 71
Jaspar, Bobby 254, 275, 276-77
Jazz at the Philharmonic 184
Jazz for Young Moderns (Bethlehem LP) 126
Jazz Hot 246
Jazz Journaal 248, 249
Jazz Monthly 9
Jazz Night in the Public Gardens 235
Jazz Workshop at The Stable, Boston 133, 134, 219, 221
J.C. Penney Department Stores 19
Jesu Joy of Man's Desiring (Bach) 69
Johnson, Dick 137
Johnson, Gus 227, 230, 232, 234, 240
Johnson, J.J. 76, 126, 154
Johnson, Lennie 220
Jones, Austin 298
Jones, Cassandra 298
Jones, Helen 158
Jones, John (Richard's cousin) 18, 42, 43, 84, 285, 296
Jones, June (Richard's aunt) 17-18, 84, 157, 285, 298-99, 296
Jones, Lillie Mae. See Carter, Betty
Jones, Linda 298
Jones, Oliver 212
Jones, Steve (Richard's second cousin) 296, 298-99, 300
Jones, Ted (Richard's uncle) 18, 43
Jones, Quincy 179, 182
Joy, Ron 52, 207
Juilliard School of Music 214, 245, 263
Jumpin' at the Woodside 136, 304
Jumpin' with Symphony Sid (Young) 106, 304

Just Duo (Zieff) 13, 138, 143, 261, 309
Just One of Those Things 206, 306, 307

Kahn, Tiny 154, 192
Kansas City 73, 100, 101, 156, 227
Keats, John 15
Kendall, Bob 68
Kenton, Stan 73, 102, 133, 196, 197, 211, 222, 226, 265
Kerouac, Jack 119, 154-55, 156
Kinsey, Tony 275
Kip (Mussulli) 225
Kirk, (Rahsaan) Roland 236
Knox, Keith 272-73
Kohn, Edmund 3, 4, 52
Koller, Hans 256, 309
Köln, West Germany 356, 272, 308
Konitz, Lee 126
Korean War 84, 241
Krupa, Gene 177
Kuhn, Steve 71, 72, 78, 190, 221
Ku Klux Klan 183
Kyes, John F. 178, 181

Lacy, Steve 122
Lamplighter Lounge, Long Island 243-44
LaRoca, Pete 158
Last Set, The (Pacific Jazz LP) 52, 206-07, 209, 307
Lawlor, Jack 95, 204, 205, 303, 306
Lee, Bill 58
Lees, Gene 77, 78
Le Havre 246
Lerner, Sidney 214
Les Oignons (Bechet) 254
Let's Get Lost (film documentary) 279

Let's Jump (Killian) 192, 305
Levin, Meyer 125
Lewis, John 135, 239
Liebestraum (Liebie) Dachshund 35, 36, 37, 162
Life is a Many Splendored Gig (Roulette LP) 220, 228
Lighthouse, the, jazz club 123
Lind, Olle 246, 271, 272, 273
"Lionel Hampton Houses" 181
Listen to Les (Chaloff) 95, 303
Littman, Peter 5, 134-35, 166, 190, 199, 200, 201, 202, 203, 204, 205, 206, 242, 244, 245, 247, 253, 258, 269, 271, 273-74, 277-78, 284, 290, 306, 307, 308, 309, 310
Log Cabin Inn, Appleton, Wis. 94
Lombardo, Carmen 132
Longwell, Hannah Marie (Auntie, Richard's great-aunt) 34, 39-41, 178
Longwell, Major W. F. M. (Uncle Bill, Richard's great-uncle) 34, 39-41
Lop-Pow 74
Los Angeles 5, 105, 122, 123, 124, 240, 243, 260, 278
Lourie, Charlie 298
Love is a Many Splendored Thing (film) 220
Lover Man 267, 310
Lowe, Mundell 6
Lucerne 259, 271
Lynn, Mass. 68, 79, 92, 94, 96, 118, 119, 120, 136, 161, 304
Lyons, France 257, 258, 259
Lyons, Len 72

Macintosh computer 18, 299
Mack Brown, Johnny 23
Mack, Raymond W. 160
Mackel, Billy 180

MacPaint 299
Mafia 156
Maigret 255
Maine 16, 18, 42, 118, 212-13, 214
Mainz, West Germany 251, 279, 296, 308
Maisel, Bob 92, 94, 95, 97
Malaysia 113
Malraux, André 172
Mandel, Johnny 77, 247-48
Manne, Shelley 133, 305
Manneken Pis 256
Margolis, Sam 136, 304
Margolis, Norman M. 156, 157
Mariano, Charlie 9, 10, 67, 92, 93, 94, 127, 128, 129, 132, 133, 135, 136, 145, 152, 165, 190, 191, 193, 194, 196, 197, 205, 279, 298, 303, 304, 305
Mariners (Mariano) 93, 303
Marney, Elaine. *See* Brehaut, Elaine
Marsh, Warne 203
Martin, Bob 187-88, 189, 222, 223, 225, 227, 228
Maryland College 172
Maryland Institute of Art 173
Marx, Groucho 165
Massachusetts Institute of Technology, See MIT
Mazman, Eddie 119
McFarland, Will 2, 51
McGhee, Howard 102
McKonky Artists Corp., Chicago 95
McLean, Jackie 154
McLellan, John 101, 133
McMaster, Ron 210
McMillan, Geneviève (Ginou) 50, 114-15, 145, 148, 171-72, 173
McShann, Jay 227
Medico-Legal Institute (Morgue) 283, 293

Medium Rock (Zieff) 122, 123, 278
Meldonian, Dick 122
Melody Lounge, Lynn 68, 96, 118, 136, 304
Melody Maker 249, 275, 276, 277
Mengelberg, Misha 301
Merriam, Alan P. 160
Metro-Goldwyn-Mayer 23
Metronome 59, 75, 77, 116, 118, 187, 225
Mexico City 122, 145, 146, 148, 149
Miami 114, 169, 170, 180, 183, 212, 235
Migliori, Jay 134, 187, 188, 212
Mikrokosmos (Bartók) 59, 61
Mid-Forte (Zieff) 12, 138, 143, 261, 309
Miles Davis at the Lighthouse (Prestige LP) 123
Milhaud, Darius 132
Miller, Mulgrew 71, 72
Mills College, Oakland 132
Mingus, Charles 103, 105, 107-08, 109, 110, 122, 152, 156, 279, 303, 304
Minor Benign, A (Zieff) 124
MIT, Cambridge 20, 26, 173, 281, 286
Miss Port of Boston 83
Modern Jazz Quartet 116, 138
Modigliani, Amadeo 156
moldy figs 65-67, 106, 137, 194, 227, 254
Monk, Thelonious 6, 68, 130, 152, 154
Monterey Jazz Festival 278
Montgomery, Monk 179
Monticello College, Alton, Il. 172
Moriarty, Dean 57, 155
Morgan, Alun 9, 191, 200, 202
Morris, Newbold 203

Morris, Peter Van Cortland 157, 203-04, 205, 295. 306
Morton, Jelly Roll 136
Mount Royal Hotel, Baltimore 230
Mozart, Amadeus 36
Mullens, Eddie 180
Mulligan, Gerry 1, 5, 12, 122, 135, 137, 154, 227, 239, 242, 243, 264, 266, 267, 273
Munich 243
Münster, Germany 124
Murdoch, George 138-39
Museum of Fine Arts, Boston 21, 27, 114, 173
Music for Stringed Instruments, Percussion and Celeste (Bartok) 101
Mussulli, Boots 102, 220, 222, 225
My Funny Valentine 240, 256, 275, 307, 309

NAACP 175, 182, 185, 214
Napoli, Joe 125, 246
National Association for the Advancement of Colored People. See NAACP
Nature Boy 57
Navard, Mike 275, 276, 277
Navarro, Fats 154
Neel, Bob 242
Netherlands, the 133, 246, 247-251, 254, 301
Netherlands Jazz Archive 247
Neves, John 134, 218, 220, 222
New Artists Records 202, 203, 306, 309
Newburyport Art Association 22, 31, 291
New England Conservatory of Music 71, 133, 211, 226, 263
New England School of Art and Design 20

New Mexico Quarterly 164
Newport Jazz Festival 122, 188, 233-34
New Sounds from Boston, The (Prestige LP) 92-93, 94, 105, 127, 205, 295, 303
Newton Center, Mass. 17, 42, 77, 84
Newton, Race 163
Newton-Waltham Bank and Trust Co. 17
New Yearbook of Jazz (Feather 1959) 122, 220
New York 20, 68, 79, 82, 92, 94, 103-04, 105, 107, 115, 122, 123, 135, 136, 137, 139, 152, 149, 144, 149, 152, 155, 161, 173, 185, 199, 202, 212, 214, 218, 219, 223, 224, 228, 231, 233, 234, 235, 236, 239, 241, 242, 243, 245, 247, 263, 277, 282, 289
Nieske, Bob 83
Nice Work If You Can Get It 204, 306
Nichols, Herbie 130-31
Nicholson, Stuart 158
Nimitz, Jack 125
1954 Improvisations (New Artists CD) 202-03, 206, 295, 306-07
Nocturne (Chaloff) 189
No One Will Room With Me (Pomeroy) 228
Nordstrom, Bill 137, 139
Norgran Records 184
Northsea Jazz Festival 251
Not Too Sad an Ending (Twardzik) 193, 194, 286, 295
Nova Scotia 16

Oldham, England 13
Oliver, King 199
Olivieri, Ray 133-34, 305
One O'Clock Jump 136. 305
On Green Dolphin Street 218

On the Road (Kerouac) 154–55

Openneer, Herman 247

Orly Airport 246, 285

Ormandy, Eugene 95–96

Ortega, Tony 125, 126, 179

Our Dancing Daughters (1928 movie) 23

Our New Music (Copland book) 294

Over the Rainbow 212

Oxford, Miss. 183–84

Pacific Jazz Records 1, 2, 3, 4, 5, 6, 8, 10, 11, 13, 14, 51, 52, 123, 124, 165, 199, 202, 204, 206, 207, 208, 209, 210, 211, 241, 247, 268, 277, 278, 281, 298, 307

Pacific Jazz Years, The (Chet Baker CD) 124

Pacifica educational programming 123

Pan American Airlines 11

Paradise, Sal 155

Paris 1, 6, 10, 11, 13, 14, 15, 20, 123, 124, 138, 144, 164, 172, 179, 193, 206, 224, 235, 241, 245, 246, 247, 254, 255, 256, 257, 258, 259, 260, 261, 262, 263, 270, 271, 273, 275, 276, 277, 278, 282, 283, 284, 285, 293, 297, 302, 309, 310

Parker, Baird 111

Parker, Chan Richardson 111

Parker, Charlie (Bird) 9, 10, 51, 71, 76, 92, 99–105, 106, 107, 108, 110, 111–12, 113, 126, 152, 154, 156, 157, 158, 163, 166–67, 188, 196, 204, 215, 223–24, 227, 242, 253, 267, 268, 295, 303, 304

Parker, Sonny 177

Pathé-Magellan. *See* Studio Pathé-Magellan

Pennsylvania 81, 122, 182, 183, 234

Pensacola, Fla. 126, 182, 236

Peoria, Il. 126

Pepper, Art 152, 154, 158, 242

Peters, Helen 55

Peters, Jay 180

Peterson, Oscar 184, 212

Petite Fleur (Bechet) 254

Pettiford, Oscar 125

Petty Lounge, the 79

Philadelphia Orchestra, the 95

Phillips, Harvey 122

Philology Records 52, 251, 308

Piaf, Edith 254

Picadilly (nightclub), Green Bay 94

Picasso, Pablo 3

Piece Caprice 12, 138, 143, 261, 310

Pierce, Nat 80, 82, 85, 219

Pilot, The (Catholic weekly) 19

Pilsbury, Bob 84, 109, 113, 136

Pittsburgh Courier 177, 178, 182, 183

Pittsburgh, Penn. 20, 82, 182, 183

Plater, Bobby 180

"Play Us a Tune" (Wolfe) 295

Polaroid Research Laboratories 19, 116, 118

Pollock, Jackson 59

Pomeroy, Herb 56, 68, 80, 99, 107, 129, 166, 167, 175, 180, 181, 182, 185, 189–90, 191, 192, 194, 196, 197, 218–21, 222, 223, 225, 227, 228, 230, 232, 274, 279, 285, 302, 304, 305

Pomp (Zieff) 13, 138, 143, 261, 310

Ponder (Zieff) 124

Porgy and Bess 6, 302

Portland, Maine 212–13, 214

Potts, Bill 6

Powell, Bud 68, 119, 129–30, 154, 204, 226, 243

Powell, Richie 234

Practical Arts School, Boston 20

Prestige Records 51, 92, 93, 123,
   127, 128, 129, 133, 135, 141, 191,
   228, 271, 298, 303, 304
Preview (nightclub), Chicago 94
Price, Leontyne 6
Priestly, Brian 204, 306
Primo's (nightclub), Lynn 90, 94
Princeton University 20
Prokofiev, Sergei 100
Psychology of Music, The (Mursell
   book) 83
Puerto Rico 173

Quill, Gene 126

Radcliffe College 173
Raeburn, Boyd 75, 155, 258
Randall's Island Jazz Festival 122,
   139
Rassinfosse, Jean-Louis 124
Ravel, Maurice 100, 196, 245
RCA Victor Records 141
Red Fox Café 79, 80
Re-Search (Zieff) 12, 138, 143, 261,
   309
Reece, Jerome 278
Reisner, Robert 100, 105, 107, 108,
   111, 156, 253
Resberg, Lars 185, 267, 268, 269-71,
   274
Reynolds, Tommy 9, 74
rheumatic fever 33-34, 98, 169, 284
Rhythme 249
Rich, Buddy 184
Richards, Johnny 220
Rico, Joe 9
Rivers, Sam 79
River Rouge, Mi. 228, 231
Riverside Records 141
Roach, Max 239, 303

Roberts, Dr. Joseph 296
Rochester, NY 19
rock 'n' roll 74
Rockport, Mass. 32, 33, 34, 35, 169
Rodney, Red 154, 161
Rogers, Shorty 94
Rollins, Sonny 152, 156
Rondette (Zieff) 12, 13, 137, 141,
   143, 261, 309
Roost Records 271
Ross, Annie 179, 275
Ross, Curtis 180
Rouge Lounge, River Rouge, Mi.
   228, 229, 232
Roulette Records 219, 220, 228
'Round About Midnight 6, 201, 204,
   211, 305, 306
Round Robin (Chaloff) 225
Royal Roost (jazz club), NY 106
Royal Sweelink Conservatory,
   Amsterdam 301
Rudy Van Gelder Project, the 200-
   02
Rusch, Robert 274
Russell, George 135, 159
Russell, Pee Wee 188
Russia 21, 71, 119
Russian technique, the 72-73
Russo, Bill 265

Sacco, Nicola 21
Sad Walk (Zieff) 13, 124, 137-38,
   143, 261, 309
St. Botolph St., Boston 138
St. John the Divine, NY 20
St Patrick's Cathedral, NY 20
St. Vitus Dance 33
Salem, Mass. 53, 54
Salem Village Witchcraft Victims'
   Memorial 53

Salle Pleyel 254-55, 257, 273, 276
Salute to Tiny, A (Pomeroy) 192, 305
Samuel Fowler House. *See* Fowler House
San Angelo, Texas 150, 162
San Francisco 131
Sanner, Willi 256, 309
Santisi, Ray 134, 139, 211, 218, 220, 222, 224, 225, 227
Saturday Evening Post 17
Sauter, Eddie 265
Schenectady, NY 95, 96
Schillinger House, Boston 68, 79, 94, 99
Schnoebiegel, Rolfe 251, 252, 308
Schoenberg, Arnold 59, 226
Schuller, Gunther 175-76, 265
Schumann, Robert 59
Scrapple from the Apple (Parker) 107, 304
Scott, Hazel 214
Sean, Irish setter 34, 41
Second Herd 72, 76, 77, 187. Also see Herman, Woody
Serenade to a Cuckoo (Kirk) 236
Serly, Tibor 92
Sessions, Roger 237
Shahn, Ben 30
Shaw, Bernard 259
Shayne, Roy 81-82
Sharp Six (Chaloff) 225
Shearing, George 71, 188
Shelley Manne and His Men 133, 305
Shiftful (Zieff) 138, 142, 143
Silver, Horace 105
Silver Sea House, Hyannis 86
Sims, Zoot 74, 77, 126, 154, 220, 233, 244, 271

Simosko, Vladimir 72, 76, 78, 83, 85, 94, 99, 188, 190, 192, 193, 222, 225, 226, 227, 232
Sing Sing 152
Sjøgren, Thorbjørn 278
Skea, Dan 200, 201, 202
Skelton, Red 95
Sleigh Ride (Anderson) 211
Slightly Above Moderate (Zieff) 122, 123, 278
Smeterlin, Jan 7
Smith, Bessie 158
Smith, Bill 295
Smith, Carson 5, 199, 200, 201, 202, 205, 245, 306
Smith, Jabbo 158
Socolow, Frankie 155
Soda Fountain Rag (Ellington) 63
Solal, Martial 254
Someone to Watch Over Me 248, 275, 308, 309
SoundEdit 16 (software) 208
South German Symphony Orchestra 266
Southward Inn, Orleans, Mass. 136
Spellman, A.B. 226
Stable, The 116, 117, 133, 134, 138, 143, 189-90, 211, 217, 218, 219, 221, 222, 225, 227, 232, 277
Stan Getz at the Shrine (Roost LP) 243
Stardust 181
State of Music, The (Virgil Thompson) 264, 294
Steelworkers 96
Stella By Starlight 128, 129, 130, 131, 132, 304
Steward, Herbie 74, 233
Stewart, Reba 50, 113--15, 138, 145, 146, 147, 165, 168, 171-73, 216, 289

Stewart, Tom 122, 139-42

Stinky (Twardzik's lap dog) 83, 86-87, 168

Stitt, Sonny 10, 126, 154, 212

Stockwell, Dean 125

Stoll Theatre, London 275-76, 277

Stompin' at the Savoy 136, 304

Stone, A Leaf, A Door, A (Wolfe book) 295

Stoney Creek, Ont. 1

Storyville Jazz Club 64-65, 67, 84, 107, 114, 116, 131, 133, 187, 188, 189, 199, 201, 223, 202, 205, 219, 234

Storyville Records 9, 51, 188, 189, 190, 191, 192, 196, 305

Strasbourg 237, 281

Stratton, Don 85

Stravinsky, Igor 36, 58

Streets of Paris, LA club 124

Strollin' (Baker CD) 124

Studio Pathé-Magellan 260, 261, 273, 276-77, 309-10

Stuttgart 259, 264-65, 266, 267, 268, 269, 271, 272, 310

Suite for the Miraculous Mandarin (Bartók) 92, 193

Suite for Viola (Bloch) 86, 92

Suki, the Dachshund 162

Summertime 6

Sumner, Jane (Richard's cousin) 18, 20, 22, 24, 31, 32, 36, 37, 38, 39, 40, 41, 43, 45, 46, 47, 48, 49, 54, 60, 62-63, 67, 69, 70, 75, 81, 88-91, 117, 134, 153, 162, 194, 195, 205, 229, 286, 287, 288, 290, 291, 298, 299, 300, 301

Sunkel, Phil 122

Sunenblick, Robert E. 79, 94, 95, 96, 102, 104, 106, 107, 108, 109, 110, 111, 187, 188, 189, 196, 212, 222, 303, 304, 305

Sweden 52, 185, 246, 264, 266, 267, 272, 275, 277, 310

Sweens, Pieter 247, 307

Swing Era 12, 175

Switzerland 133, 246, 252-53, 254, 271, 273

Sylvester, Robert 219, 220

Symphony Sid. See Torin, Symphony Sid

Synanon, Santa Monica, Ca. 152

Syncopated Clock (Anderson) 211

Takas, Bill 122

Tatum, Art 68, 72, 184

Taylor, Al 177

Taylor, Cecil 226-27

Taylor, Creed 141

Teagarden, Jack 278

Tercinet, Alain 246, 254, 260, 274

Terrace (nightclub), E. St. Louis 94

Terry, Clark 73

Tesser, Neil 236

"third-stream" 265-66

33rd Psalm 286

This Could Be the Start of Something Big (Allen) 235

This Is Always 275

Thomas, Dylan 156

Thompson, Arthur (Richard's uncle) 18, 34, 39, 43, 59, 67, 300

Thompson, Rosamund (Roz) (Richard's aunt) 17, 18, 19, 20, 21, 22, 23, 24, 25, 26, 27, 31, 32, 33, 34, 35, 36, 37, 38, 39, 42, 43, 45, 46, 47, 48, 49, 54, 55, 59, 60, 62-63, 67, 69, 70, 75, 81, 88-91, 114, 117, 134, 153, 162, 194, 195, 205, 229, 230, 281, 282, 284, 286, 287, 288, 289, 290, 291, 298, 298, 299, 300, 302

Thompson, Virgil 264, 294

Three Bips and a Bop 42, 74

Thuston, Pearl 177
Tiffany Club, LA 243
Timmons, Bobby 122
Toluca, Mexico 148-49
Tommyhawk (Mandel) 247, 307, 308
Tonight in Town (BBC) 261
Tonight Show (CBS) 235
Tonooka, Sumi 72
Torin, Symphony Sid 105-07, 108,
  109, 111, 126, 127, 133, 136, 187,
  215, 234, 304
Toshiba-EMI Records 139, 191, 201,
  210, 122, 307
Trans World Airlines 245, 285
Trenton Hall and the Melody
  Ramblers 113
Trinidad 212, 213, 214, 217
Trio (Pacific Jazz 1212) 2-8, 61, 116,
  118, 206, 208, 209, 210, 306-07
Tristano, Lennie 113, 203, 204, 226,
  227
Truitt, Sonny 94, 137, 303
Turner, Frederick 58, 68, 230, 245,
  251, 253
Twardzik, Clare (mother) 15-24, 25-
  28, 30, 32-34, 36, 37, 38, 39, 40, 41,
  42, 43, 53, 55, 56, 57, 68-69, 70,
  82, 86-87, 95, 97, 145, 146-48, 152,
  161, 169-71, 178, 216, 217, 229-30,
  256-57, 281-83, 284, 288, 289, 290-
  91, 300
Twardzik, Henryk (father) 15-24, 25,
  26, 27, 28-32, 33, 34, 35, 37, 38, 40,
  42, 43, 45-49, 53, 55, 56, 57-58, 64,
  67, 68-69, 70, 80-81, 82, 86-87, 95,
  97, 145, 146-48, 149-52, 161, 165,
  167, 169-71, 216, 217, 228, 229-30,
  256-57, 281, 282, 284, 285-88, 290,
  291-92, 298, 300
Twardzik, Joseph 297
Twardzik, Maria (Richard's paternal
  grandmother) 19-20, 28
Twardzik, Mitzie S. 297

Twardzik, Richard Henryk (Richard's
  paternal grandfather) 19-20, 28
Twardzik, Richard Henryk (Dick,
  Dickie)
  birth and childhood 24, 25-26,
    27-28, 32, 39-42
  education 35, 36, 56, 59, 68, 71-
    72, 97, 122
  health 33-35, 42, 98, 169, 284
  adolescence 56-58, 67-69, 157
relations with parents 15-16, 147,
  161, 167-68, 169, 217, 281, 290-91
in paintings by Henryk 28-30, 37-
  38, 45-49, 57-58
  with Serge Chaloff's bands 79-
    80, 80-83, 85-92, 94-96, 189, 190,
    224-26, 227-32
  with Lionel Hampton orchestra
    178-79, 182-84, 187
  with Chet Baker quartet 1, 239,
    246-73
  and drugs 15, 101, 135, 139, 153-
    54, 162-63, 215, 217, 218, 222-24,
    230, 245, 252-53
  letters 82, 85, 86-87, 146, 146-48,
    148-49, 150-51, 151-52, 161-62,
    163-65, 166-67, 169-71, 228, 230-
    31, 256, 257
  studio recordings 1, 2-8, 10-13,
    92-93, 127-32, 191-97, 199-202,
    260-61, 261-64
  live recordings 9-10, 101-04,
    105-10, 202-06, 247-49, 251-52,
    266-67
  as leader 69-70, 197, 199-206
  as composer 6-8, 13, 56, 60-64,
    73, 113, 121, 158, 165, 168, 193-
    96, 211-12, 219, 261-62
  as musician 58, 59-60, 64, 100,
    108-09, 126-27, 129-32, 138-39,
    143-44, 197, 199, 211, 268, 279-80
  death 1, 14, 15, 111-12, 273-75,
    276, 282-84
Twenties Late (Zieff) 124

Tynan, John   240
Tyner, McCoy   109

Ullmann, Michael   159
Uncle Bill. See Longwell, Major W.
    F. M.
United Artists   298
United Nations Combo   175, 182,
    183
University of Pittsburgh   20
University of Toronto   297
Untamed (1929 movie)   23
Urso, Phil   278

Vachsteen, Charlie   145, 146, 147,
    148, 149
Vachsteen, Gene   145, 148, 149
Valente, Caterina   265, 266, 267,
    268-69
van Aro, Eric   268-69
van Bommel, Frank   301, 302
van Breda, Arie   251
van der Elsken, Ed   249-50
van Duynhoven, Martin   301
Vanelli, Rudy   138
Van Gelder, Rudy   5, 199-200, 202,
    206, 306
Van Gogh, Vincent   156
Vanzetti, Bartolomeo   21
Varese, Edgar   101
Vaughan, Sarah   102
Verve Records   141, 184, 236, 243,
    271
Vibraphone Blues (Hampton)   176
Vinnie Burke String Jazz Quartet
    137
Voce, Steve   109, 243, 244
Vogue Records   254
Volkskrant, de   248
Vos, Tony   256

Vuijsje, Bert   248

Walkin' (Carpenter)   251, 308
Wallington, George   179
Warren, Earl   180
Washington, D.C.   228, 232, 239,
    283, 285
Washington, Dinah   175
Washington, Jack   76
WCOP, Boston   133
Weber, Bruce   199, 253, 279
Webster, Ben   157
Webster, Freddie   153
Weill, Kurt   266
Wein, George   65, 71, 116, 188-89,
    190, 191, 234, 305
Wein, Women and Song (Storyville LP)
    234
Weiner, Jimmy   92, 94, 95, 96, 108-
    09, 129, 134, 303, 304
Welles, Orson   125
Wellington, Bill   137, 303
Welsh's Butcher Shop   1
West Coast jazz   1, 4, 125, 129-30,
    131, 239-40, 243, 249
West Germany   246, 251, 254, 264,
    271, 277
West Newbury, Mass.   230, 281, 282,
    285, 288
West Ringe, NH   41
West Yarmouth, Mass.   85, 86, 88, 96
Western Union   150, 152
Westin, Lars   267, 272, 310
Westminster Dog Show   290
Wetmore, Dick   102, 122, 126, 135,
    136-40, 141, 142, 143, 144, 264,
    304
WHDH, Boston   133
Wheaton, Jim   136
White, Walter   175, 182

Who the Hell is Bob Zieff? (Dutch song) 124
Why Can't I (Crystal-Joy Albert) 236
Wilbur, Bob 102
Williams, Floyd 180
Williams, John 109, 243-44
Williams, Martin 71, 190, 221
Williams, Ted 224
Williams, Walter 180
Wills, Geoffrey 159, 196
Wilson, Teddy 68, 177, 188
Winding, Kai 76
Winick, Charles 156, 159-61
WJZ, New York 106
WMEX, Boston 94
Woche der leichten Musik 265
WOKO, Albany 95, 303
Wolcott, Al 136
Wolfe, Thomas 295
Wolverine Hotel, Detroit 228, 229, 230, 233
Wood, John R. 282
Woode, Jimmy 137, 139, 190
Woodward, Woody 52, 207
World Pacific Records 52, 206, 207, 310

World's Greatest Jazz Band 227
Wozzeck (Alban Berg) 87, 92
Wyeth, Andrew 18

X (Zieff) 124

Yellow Tango (Twardzik) 6, 7-8, 211-12, 256, 279, 306-07, 309
Yesterdays 204, 211, 306
You and the Night and the Music 218
Young, Chester S. 161
Young Chet (Claxton book) 11
Young, Lester 106, 158
Youngstown, Ohio 81, 82

Zdot (Chaloff) 189
Zieff, Robert L. (Bob) 11-13, 14, 67-68, 108, 113, 114, 115, 118-26, 132, 133, 134, 135, 136, 137-38, 139-43, 144, 168, 196, 203, 204, 211, 219, 221, 223, 240, 247, 260-61, 262, 263, 264, 267, 271, 275, 278, 279, 300, 306, 310
Zitano, Jimmy 134, 139, 218, 220, 227, 304, 305
Zurich 253, 259, 271

Marquis Book Printing Inc.

Québec, Canada
2008